# VEGETABLES
*for the*
# GOURMET GARDENER

**Simon Akeroyd** is a garden writer and contributor to *Grow Your Own* magazine. He is the author of *Shrubs and Small Trees, Lawns and Ground Cover*, and the *Allotment Handbook*, and the coauthor of *Grow Your Own Fruit*. He lives in lives in Surrey.

The University of Chicago Press, Chicago 60637
The University of Chicago Press, Ltd., London
© 2014 Quid Publishing
All rights reserved. Published 2014.
Printed in China

22 21 20 19 18 17 16 15 14 13     1 2 3 4 5

ISBN-13: 978-0-226-15713-9 (cloth)

ISBN-13: 978-0-226-15727-6 (e-book)

DOI: 10.7208/chicago/9780226157276.001.0001

Library of Congress Cataloging-in-Publication Data

Akeroyd, Simon, author.
 Vegetables for the gourmet gardener : a practical resource from the garden to the table / Simon Akeroyd.
    pages : illustrations ; cm
  ISBN 978-0-226-15713-9 (cloth : alk. paper) — ISBN 978-0-226-15727-6 (e-book)
  1. Vegetable gardening. 2. Vegetable gardens. I. Title.
  SB320.9.A37 2014
  635—dc23
                    2014010715

# VEGETABLES
## *for the*
# GOURMET
# GARDENER

A Practical Resource from
the Garden to the Table

SIMON AKEROYD

The University of Chicago Press

Chicago and London

# CONTENTS

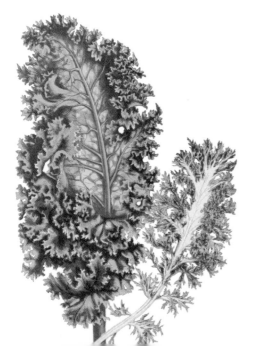

**LEFT:** One of the most common vegetables in medieval Europe, curly kale (*Brassica oleracea* Acephala Group) dropped out of fashion until it was repopularized during the "Dig for Victory" campaign in World War Two.

**ABOVE:** The under-appreciated radish (*Raphanus sativus*) is ideal for kitchen gardens: quick to grow and easy to store, it is packed with vitamin C.

# HOW TO USE THIS BOOK

## THE VEGETABLES

At the top of the page in large letters
are vegetables' common names, and
in smaller italics the Latin name(s).
Headings regarding plant type,
climatic requirements, origins and brief
cultural requirements are beneath in bold.

## TASTING NOTES

Look out for the boxes with the knife-and-
fork icon for culinary tips to identifying
different varieties or cultivars for flavor, as
well as simple gourmet recipes to try.

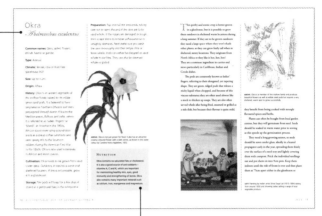

## NUTRITIONAL INFORMATION

Health benefits specific to a vegetable
are detailed in boxes.

## PRACTICAL GUIDANCE

Line illustrations show hands-on
explanations such as how best to
garden or prepare vegetables.

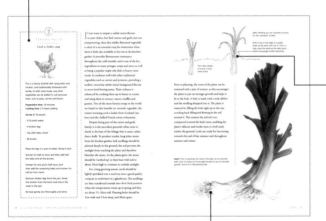

## BOTANICAL ILLUSTRATIONS

There are more to vegetables than
their green leaves. The beautiful
illustrations in this book also highlight
flowers, roots and seeds.

## FEATURE SPREADS

The roles culinary vegetables can play
in the garden or the kitchen are given
additional detail in pages dedicated to
traditional methods to put into practice.

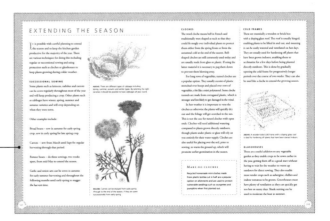

# Introduction

Growing your own gourmet vegetables is guaranteed to take you on a life-absorbing adventure where the action occurs just a few feet from your back door. You will discover a range of new skills touching on geology, botany, horticulture, and cookery, and you will learn to read the weather like a meteorologist and unearth incredible stories associated with historic and ancient varieties only found listed at the back of esoteric seed catalogs. Many such varieties have a long, exciting history that subsequently brought them to be common in our gardens and on our kitchen tables.

## HISTORY OF THE HUMAN DIET

Mankind has toiled in the soil for thousands of years to produce its food. Growing vegetables was one of the first building blocks to creating ancient civilizations and societies, prior to which humans had been hunter gatherers, traveling around as they foraged for plants and animals. The ability to grow crops enabled them to settle down near fertile soil, cultivate land, and build houses, villages, and towns in the area. Following on from the building of houses, the next obvious transition was to create gardens where vegetables could be grown close to where they were to be cooked and consumed.

Many of the ancient techniques such as digging, sowing, and weeding remain the same now as they did for our forefathers. In addition, the plants' requirements have not changed either—they still need the basic natural elements of sunlight, water, and nutrients in the soil. But the one thing that has changed is the huge rise in popularity of kitchen gardening and allotments as people clamber to grow their own food.

Vegetables are packed full of healthy nutrients and goodness including potassium, folic acid, and vitamins. Evidence shows they can reduce risks of heart disease, strokes, obesity, type 2 diabetes, and cancer, to name a few. Because vegetables are naturally low in fat and calories and they do not contain cholesterol, they provide nutritional food to improve people's health and well-being.

**LEFT:** 19th-century artwork for a series of adverts for a Parisian seed company, illustrating vegetables available at the time. The collection was finally published as *Album Vilmorin (Les Plantes Potageres)*. This image dates from 1891.

With simply thousands of different vegetables to choose from, it should not be too hard to find even just a handful of vegetables that you enjoy eating regularly as part of a healthy, balanced diet for life.

## BECOMING A GOURMET GARDENER

As you gain experience, you will develop practical arts ranging from crop rotation basics to how to create a seed drill with the edge of your draw hoe. You will do battle with slugs, snails, and tiny pests such as the carrot fly. Before too long you will start to treat your vegetable plot like a wine connoisseur treats his vineyard or cellar. You will find the subtle nuances of your plot, know which areas have the best soil or receive the most sun. You will recognize which crops to pick small and young to savor the best flavors, and which vegetables need time to mature like a fine wine. You will understand the best time to harvest and the optimum moment for storage to maximize the complex flavors.

In the kitchen, this book will show you how to transform these home-grown crops into delicious and sumptuous dishes. You will be able to hone your skills down to a fine art, and like a conjurer you will be able to magic up blue roast potatoes or purple carrots. Impress yourself by growing lettuce leaves in winter and Brussels sprouts that do not taste bitter.

A gourmet gardener always has half their eye on the weather, with a brow to match the crooked furrow made by the rake in the soil. They know that all their hard work will always be in the hands of mother nature. Armed with fleeces and cloches in

**ABOVE:** 1879 artwork from the series of illustrations called *Album Vilmorin* (*Les Plantes Potageres*) from a Parisian seed company, Vilmorin-Andrieux & Co. The volume only survives in a few libraries today.

the fall and spring, and watering cans and shade netting in summer, the gourmet gardener becomes a master at adapting to the outside environment.

Whether you want the perfect recipe for making a cake mix or a compost mix, this book has it all. Once you start growing your own gourmet vegetables in the garden, it will take you on a learning journey that will become a rewarding hobby that will last a lifetime. And this healthy exercise and eating can only contribute to a longer and more rewarding life. So what are you waiting for? Grab your gum boots and start sowing.

# WHY GROW YOUR OWN?

To the lover of gourmet vegetables nothing beats growing food from your own garden. Anyone who has grown their own food knows how much better it tastes than anything bought from a store. Nothing rivals tasting a tomato warmed in the summer sun and picked fresh from the vine. And once tasted, who can forget the tender succulent flavor of asparagus harvested from the vegetable plot in the early morning dew and lightly steamed with butter for a breakfast treat? This is the experience that only a gourmet gardener can enjoy and embrace.

**BELOW:** Vegetables, such as these onions, come in many shapes and sizes. Growing your own enables you to cook with a range of flavors and colors not found in the store.

## WIDER CHOICE

The vast range of vegetables available from seed companies cannot be matched on the shelves of the stores. Walk into a store and there is a choice of about two varieties of onions. Open up a seed catalog and there are often 15 or 20 varieties coming in all shapes, sizes, and colors.

Suddenly there is a whole new world of exciting new vegetables to try that are almost impossible to buy in the store. How often will you find blue potatoes or purple carrots, or be able to try the early spring hosta shoots as they unfurl from the ground or enjoy the subtle asparagus flavor from the asparagus pea? Only by growing these unique crops will a gourmet cook be able to embrace the full range of ingredients needed to make great food.

## MAGICAL EXPERIENCE—FROM PLOT TO PLATE

Feeling part of the rhythms of life and embracing the seasons can only be felt outdoors. Feeling the soil in your hands and the sun on your back as seeds are sown and crops are harvested becomes an intoxicating experience. Growing food with the distinct flavor of the minerals and nutrients from your own soil gives the gourmet gardener magical

"In a world where we are becoming increasingly alienated from what we eat, growing our own vegetables is a fundamental way to reassert the connection between ourselves and our food."

*RHS Grow Your Own Veg*, Carol Klein, (2007)

ingredients that make the food produced completely unique to that location. Like alchemy, once in the kitchen those exclusive gourmet crops are transformed into great-tasting dishes that cannot be replicated anywhere else in the world.

## HEALTHIER

For those with environmental concerns, there are of course no air miles involved with bringing your "plot to plate." As a gardener you have complete control over whether it is treated with chemicals or fertilizers or not. The physical exertion of growing gourmet vegetables is better than any gym workout, and will make your muscles ache in a good way.

It is considered by many that home-grown vegetables have a higher nutritional value, far better for you than the produce of commercial farming practices that have squeezed the health and nutritional benefits out of the plants in a quest for uniformity and long-term storage benefits.

## KEEPING OUR RICH HERITAGE ALIVE

If variety is the spice of life then growing your own gourmet crops is a must for anybody interested in growing and cooking food. Without that passion, all of those unique flavors, colors, and varieties—many of which have wonderful historic stories attached to them—will be lost. The lover of gourmet food will be foraging back in the grocery stores with a choice of just a handful of uniform and often bland-tasting vegetables.

**RIGHT:** Growing your own food promises crops of exciting vegetables to grow all year round.

## HISTORY FROM THE VEGETABLE PATCH

Some of the older and quirkier vegetables have unique flavors, colors, shapes, and textures that are no longer in existence in the modern commercial vegetable world. By growing these gourmet crops you will help to keep them and the stories behind them alive. Often referred to as heritage or Heirloom varieties, the French call them by the evocative name *les legumes oubliés*, the "forgotten vegetables."

There are some wonderful stories attached to some of these historic vegetables. For instance, the French bean "Cherokee Trail of Tears" commemorates the 1838 march of the displaced Native American Cherokee nation, who are said to have carried these seeds on the journey to their new homeland.

When Howard Carter excavated the tomb of the Egyptian boy king Tutankhamen in 1922, pea seeds were among the treasures he unearthed. Today the archeologically minded gardener can grow *Pisum sativum* "Tutankhamen," which originates from the English Highclere Castle estate of Carter's patron Lord Carnarvon.

# Okra
## *Abelmoschus esculentus*

**Common names:** Okra, ladies' fingers, bhindi, bamia, or gumbo

**Type:** Annual

**Climate:** Tender, cool, or frost-free glasshouse

**Size:** Up to 4ft (1.2m)

**Origin:** Africa

**History:** Okra is an ancient vegetable of the mallow family valued for its edible green seed pods. It is believed to have originated in southern Ethiopia and then propagated through North Africa to the Mediterranean, Balkans, and India, where it is referred to as "ladies' fingers" or "bhindi." In America in the 1800s, African slaves used ground okra seeds as a cheap coffee substitute and gave this to the Southern soldiers during the American Civil War in the 1860s. Okra is now used extensively in African and Asian cuisine.

**Cultivation:** Okra needs to be grown from seed under glass. Outdoors, it requires a warm and sheltered location. If this is not possible, grow it in a glasshouse.

**Storage:** The pods will keep for a few days if stored in a perforated bag in the refrigerator.

**Preparation:** Top and tail the seed pods, taking care not to open the pod if the okra are to be used whole. If the ridges are damaged or tough, then scrape them to remove unflavorsome or unsightly elements. Next make sure you wash the okra thoroughly and then simply slice or leave whole. Pods can either be chopped or used whole in stir-fries. They can also be steamed whole or broiled.

**ABOVE:** Okra is not just grown for food. It also has an attractive creamy-colored flower with a dark center, as shown in this watercolor by Caroline Maria Applebee, 1832.

## NUTRITION

Okra contains no saturated fats or cholesterol. It is also a good source of antioxidants—vitamins A, C, and K—which are important for maintaining healthy skin, eyes, good immunity, and strengthening of bones. Okra also contains many important minerals such as calcium, iron, manganese, and magnesium.

This quirky and exotic crop is better grown in a glasshouse, but it is possible to grow them outdoors in sheltered warm locations during a long summer. If they are to be grown outdoors they need a large space where they will not shade other plants, as they can grow fairly tall when in sheltered, sunny locations. They originate from North Africa so they like it hot, hot, hot! They are a common ingredient in curries and stews particularly in Caribbean, Indian, and Creole dishes.

The pods are commonly known as ladies' fingers, referring to their elongated, yet tapering shape. They are green, ridged pods that release a sticky liquid when chopped, and because of this viscous substance they are often used almost like a broth to thicken up soups. They are also often served whole after being fried, steamed, or broiled as a side dish, but because their flavor is quite mild,

**ABOVE:** Okra is a member of the mallow family and produces beautiful flowers as well as edible seed pods but requires a very sheltered, warm spot to grow successfully.

they benefit from being cooked with strongly flavored spices and herbs.

Plants can often be bought from local garden centers, but they will germinate from seed. Seeds should be soaked in warm water prior to sowing as this speeds up the germination process.

They need a long growing season, so seeds should be sown under glass, ideally in a heated propagator early in the year, spreading them thinly over the surface of a seed tray and lightly covering them with compost. Prick the individual seedlings out and pot them into 3½in pots. Keep them indoors until the risk of frosts is over and then plant them at 29½in apart either in the glasshouse

**LEFT:** Painting by Indian artist Shiva Dayal Lal (1815–1884) dating from around 1850 and showing ladies selling a range of local vegetable produce.

or outside in a very sunny, sheltered spot. If okra is to be grown outdoors, then it should be placed in a cold frame first for a few weeks prior to being planted in its final position. Tall plants will benefit from being staked as they start to grow. Tips can be pinched out to encourage a bushier plant.

Pods start to form in midsummer and should be harvested when they are about 4in apart. If they are left too long they lose their viscosity and become stringy.

**BELOW:** The pods of okra are commonly known as ladies' fingers because of their distinctive, tapering length. Pods can be chopped or used whole.

### Okra raita

Raita is a spiced yogurt dish with fried okra for added crunch and can be served as a side to accompany an Indian meal.

**Preparation time:** 15 minutes
**Cooking time:** 10 minutes
**Serves:** 2 people (as a side dish)

- 2 tbsp oil

- 8oz (250g) okra, washed and cut into chunks

- $\frac{1}{2}$ tsp salt

- 1 fresh green chilli, seeded and chopped

- 5oz (125g) thick set natural yogurt

- $\frac{1}{2}$ tsp mustard powder

- $\frac{1}{2}$ tsp black mustard seeds

- 1 tbsp curry leaves

Deep fry the okra in 1 tablespoon of oil in a frying pan until well browned and crisp.

Drain off the oil and allow to cool.

Add the salt to the chilli and crush to a pulp.

Beat the yogurt with a fork until smooth, add the mustard powder and chilli paste, and mix well. Add in the fried okra.

Heat 1 tablespoon of oil in a small pan and fry the mustard seeds until they crackle, then add the curry leaves and fry for 15–20 seconds.

Remove the pan from the heat and stir the flavored oil into the okra raita mix.

# Elephant garlic
## *Allium ampeloprasum*

**Common names:** Elephant garlic, Russian garlic, Levant garlic

**Type:** Bulb

**Climate:** Hardy, average to cold winter

**Size:** Up to 4ft (1.2m)

**Origin:** Europe (particularly the Mediterranean area)

**History:** It originates from Central Asia where it has been grown for thousands of years, making it one of the most ancient vegetables ever cultivated. Archeological and literary sources confirm its early usage by the Egyptians, Romans, and Greeks as far back as 2100 BC.

**Cultivation:** Elephant garlic copes better with damper conditions than standard garlic, but still requires a well-drained soil in full sun. They are fully hardy and benefit from their individual cloves being planted in the fall as the cold winter promotes bulb development.

**Storage:** After harvest, leave them to dry in the sunshine for a week or two before storing. Trim the stem up to within 2–2½in. They should last for a few months if kept in frost-free, dry conditions. One handy tip is to store them in a nylon stocking and hang them up out of the way until needed in the kitchen.

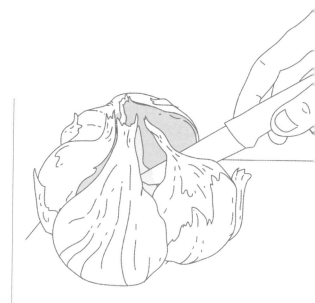

**ABOVE:** Elephant garlic bulbs are much larger than the usual garlic, and often a sharp knife is needed to prize the cloves apart.

**Preparation:** They can be cooked as a whole bulb or individual cloves. Due to its taste being milder than garlic, elephant garlic can be eaten raw in salads. Before eating in this way it is important firstly to peel away the papery skin, which can be removed easily. It is also possible to use cloves of elephant garlic as a vegetable—sliced and sautéed in butter or olive oil—as well as a flavoring agent. When cooking elephant garlic, be aware that it tends to brown even more quickly than other types of garlic, and this may give it a bitter taste. However, once cooked or broiled, elephant garlic takes on a gentle, sweet taste. It is good simply eaten on its own or spread on to a piece of crusty bread.

If you like cooking with garlic, but do not want to be overpowered by its pungent aroma, then give these closely related but milder cousins a try.

Elephant garlic is so called due to the size of its enormous cloves. They are probably about four or five times bigger than standard garlic cloves, but what they make up for in size certainly is not reflected in the pungency and strength of their flavor. They are much milder than standard garlic and have a sweeter more nutty aroma, making them popular with cooks wishing to impart a subtle garlic flavor to their dishes. The bulb itself is the size of a large clenched fist, and will break up into individual cloves. Occasionally the bulb instead just forms one swollen bulb. These are called "rounds" or "solos" in regular gardener's parlance, and can still be chopped up and either cooked or used raw to flavor dishes. Alternatively, solos can be replanted the following fall and will usually produce cloves.

Like other members of the onion family, it produces an attractive spherical flowerhead that can get as tall as 5ft, making it an additional feature of a flower border, just as much as the vegetable beds. However, if you want large bulbs then the flower bud should be pinched out as soon as it starts to form.

Elephant garlic is planted exactly like standard garlic, pushing the cloves so that the tips are just below the surface. Due to their size, they benefit from being planted at a wider spacing, at 8in between each clove in a row, and 12in between the row. They tend to cope with slightly damper conditions, although the soil should still be well drained. They require a long growing season, so ideally they should be planted in the fall. However, they can also be planted out in early spring, but this

## TASTING NOTES

### *Oven-baked elephant garlic*

The less intense flavor and larger size of the elephant garlic lends itself perfectly to being baked. Delicious spread warm on crusty bread.

**Preparation time:** 10 minutes
**Cooking time:** 30 minutes
**Serves:** 2 people

• 1 elephant garlic bulb

• 2–3 tbsp olive oil

• Salt and pepper, to taste


Preheat a conventional oven to 400°F (200°C / gas mark 6 / fan 180°C).

Slice off the top of the garlic head and trim the bottom of the bulb so that it lies flat. Puncture with a fork.

Discard any loose skins and place the garlic bulb on a flat piece of aluminum foil.

Drizzle oil in the head of the garlic until it is filled. Season with salt and pepper and wrap tightly with the surrounding aluminum foil.

Place on a baking tray (or muffin tray) for 30 minutes. Baste several times during baking.

Once cool, peel the outside skins off of the bulbs and gently squeeze each clove out.

can result in smaller cloves or producing "rounds." Keep the bulbs well watered as they start to grow and swell during spring. Harvest the swollen bulbs in summer when the foliage starts to turn brown and wilt, by carefully digging them up with a fork.

# Leek
## *Allium porrum*

**Common names:** Leek, poor man's asparagus

**Type:** Annual/biennial

**Climate:** Hardy, average to cold winter

**Size:** Up to 15¾in (40cm)

**Origin:** Mediterranean area, Asia

**History:** Popular in ancient society, it was the Roman Emperor Nero's favorite vegetable as he believed it improved his singing voice.

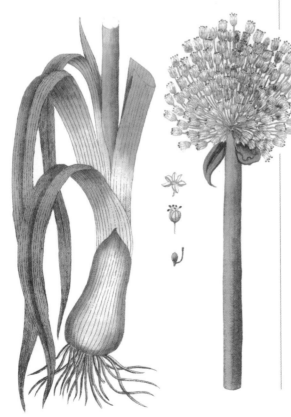

Leeks are one of the national emblems of Wales, possibly due to a Welsh legend of when King Cadwaladr of Gwynedd requested his soldiers should identify themselves in a battle against the Saxons by wearing leeks on their helmets. Welsh folklore has it that sleeping with a leek under the pillow will cause maidens to dream of their future husband.

**Cultivation:** Leeks prefer a well-drained soil, but reasonably rich and heavy. Add plenty of organic matter to light soil. Grow from seed in midwinter or buy seedlings in spring.

**Storage:** Leeks are best stored in nature's own larder—outside in the soil. They can be left growing in the ground throughout winter and best harvested before spring, as the center forms a hard core rendering them inedible. They will store in the fridge for a couple of weeks. Freezing them will make them mushy, but they can still be used in soups and purées.

**Preparation:** Chop the untidy foliage off the top of the plant, and remove the roots by chopping off the very base of the stem. Strip off the outer layer to reveal the succulent white stem. Clean thoroughly to remove the mud by slitting the leek lengthwise to the center of the stem and rinsing with running water. Slice the remaining vegetable into sections and boil, steam, or fry.

**LEFT:** Leeks are grown for their mild onion-flavored stems, but they also produce attractive allium-like flowers (and seedheads) if left in the ground.

*Cock-a-leekie soup*

This is a hearty Scottish dish using leeks and chicken, and traditionally thickened with barley. As with most soups, any other vegetables can be added to suit personal taste, such as peas, carrots, and beans.

**Preparation time:** 10 minutes
**Cooking time:** 2 ½ hours
**Serves:** 8–10 people

• 5 pints (3l) water

• 4 chicken legs

• 2lb (1kg) leeks, sliced

• 20 prunes

Place the legs in a pan of water. Bring to boil.

Simmer for half an hour and then add half the leeks and all the prunes.

Simmer for one and a half hours and then add the remaining leeks and simmer for half an hour more.

Remove chicken legs from the pan, shred the chicken from the bone, and return the meat to the pan.

Reheat gently but thoroughly and serve.

If you want to impart a subtle onion flavor to your dishes, but find onions and garlic just too overpowering, then this milder-flavored vegetable is ideal. It is an essential crop for wintertime when there is little else available to harvest in the kitchen garden. It provides flavorsome sustenance throughout the cold months, and is one of the key ingredients in many potages, soups, and stews as well as being a popular staple side dish to hearty roast meals. It combines well with other traditional vegetables such as carrots and potatoes, providing a mellow, sweet, but subtle onion background flavor to more hard-hitting tastes. Their richness is enhanced by cooking them in butter or cream, and using them in savory sauces, soufflés, and gratins. Two of the most famous soups in the world are based on this humble yet versatile vegetable: the winter-warming cock-a-leekie from Scotland (see box) and the chilled French crème vichyssoise.

Despite being part of the onion and garlic family, it is the succulent greenish-white stem or shank at the base of the foliage that is eaten, rather than a bulb. To produce tender, long white stems from the kitchen garden, leek seedlings should be planted deeply in the ground; the soil prevents the sunlight from reaching the plant and therefore blanches the stems. As the plants grow, the stems should be "earthed-up" at their base with soil to about 4in high to continue to exclude sunlight.

For a long growing season, seeds should be lightly sprinkled over a seed tray into a good-quality compost in midwinter in a glasshouse. The seedlings are then transferred outside into their final position when the temperatures warm up in spring and they are about 6–8in tall. Planting holes should be 2in wide and 6in deep, and 12in apart.

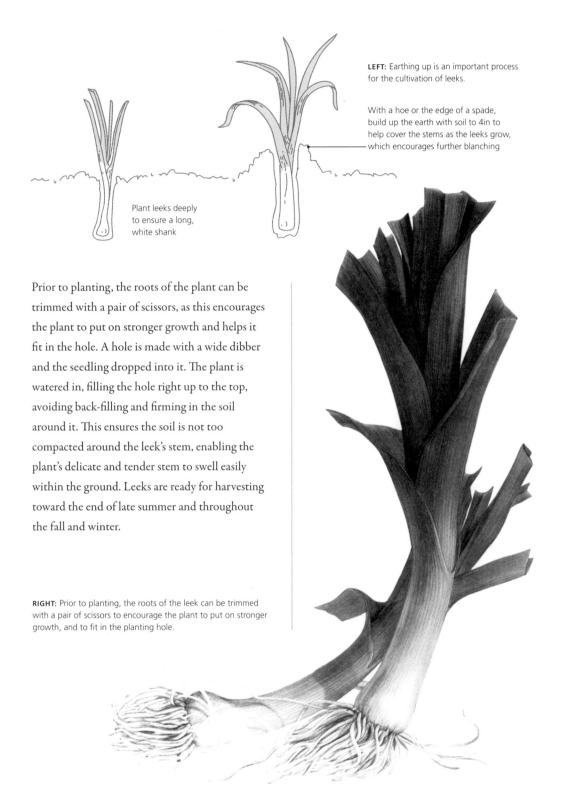

**LEFT:** Earthing up is an important process for the cultivation of leeks.

With a hoe or the edge of a spade, build up the earth with soil to 4in to help cover the stems as the leeks grow, which encourages further blanching

Plant leeks deeply to ensure a long, white shank

Prior to planting, the roots of the plant can be trimmed with a pair of scissors, as this encourages the plant to put on stronger growth and helps it fit in the hole. A hole is made with a wide dibber and the seedling dropped into it. The plant is watered in, filling the hole right up to the top, avoiding back-filling and firming in the soil around it. This ensures the soil is not too compacted around the leek's stem, enabling the plant's delicate and tender stem to swell easily within the ground. Leeks are ready for harvesting toward the end of late summer and throughout the fall and winter.

**RIGHT:** Prior to planting, the roots of the leek can be trimmed with a pair of scissors to encourage the plant to put on stronger growth, and to fit in the planting hole.

# Onion
## *Allium cepa*

**Common names:** Onion, bulb onion, or common onion

**Type:** Bulb

**Climate:** Half-hardy, mild winter

**Size:** 15¾in (40cm)

**Origin**: Middle East

**History:** The onion is possibly one of the earliest crops grown, with records of its cultivation dating back some 5,000 years. Its anatomy of circles within circles led the Egyptians to believe it held powers of eternal life and it became a source of worship. Drawings and paintings of onions were found in Egyptian tombs and they buried their Pharaohs with onions too. Onions were also believed by many cultures to sustain life and prevent thirst. The onion is very hardy and can be grown almost anywhere, and was therefore seen as an important food in early diets.

**Cultivation:** Onions should be grown in a sunny, well-drained soil. They are usually grown from sets, which are immature onions, but they can also be grown from seed.

**Storage:** Leave onions to dry out in the sun for a few days before bringing them inside. They can be platted together or placed in a nylon stocking and hung up in a cool dry place where they will keep for a few months.

**Preparation:** The best way to prepare an onion is first to cut a slice from the top and then peel off the skin. Cut the onion in half lengthwise and chop each half separately.

To prevent eyes from watering when cutting onions, simply prepare them under running water or place them in a freezer for about 8–10 minutes before preparing.

Onions are indispensable to anyone who enjoys cooking. They are used worldwide to flavor a huge range of savory dishes and can be eaten raw, but are more commonly fried. They can also be stored for years in jars of malt vinegar, and pickled onions are a popular healthy snack. Red onions tend to be milder and are more popular in dishes requiring a raw onion, whereas brown and white onions are more often fried. Onions can be caramelized with sugar for a sweeter flavor.

**LEFT:** The onion is one of the most popular vegetables in the culinary world as it is used in such a wide range of dishes. It is also very easy to grow.

**ABOVE:** An image by French-Polish painter Jean-Pierre Norblin de La Gourdaine (1745–1830) showing a character with a traditional "string" of onions around his neck.

Onions are usually grown from "sets," which are simply immature onion bulbs. Once planted in the ground they start to swell, and after a few months of growing in the ground are harvested. They can be grown from seed too, but sets are easier and give the gardener a head start during the season.

Onions require a sunny site with well-drained soil. Avoid damp conditions as the bulbs are prone to rotting.

Onion sets should be planted out at 2–4in apart in rows 12in apart. Japanese and over-wintering onions can be planted in fall for harvesting in midsummer, whereas onion sets should be planted in spring and harvested between midsummer and fall.

TASTING NOTES

*Onion bhajis*

Onions are a common ingredient in Asian and particularly Indian cuisine. These easy-to-make onion bhajis are a great accompaniment to many of these dishes or they can be enjoyed on their own as a tasty snack or served on a bed of salad or pilau rice.

**Preparation time:** 20 minutes
**Cooking time:** 10 minutes
**Serves:** 4 people

· 2 eggs

· 3 onions sliced

· 4oz (120g) all-purpose flour

· 1 tsp ground cilantro

· 1 tsp cumin seeds

· 3 tbsp vegetable oil

Beat the eggs together, then mix in the onions.

Add the flour, cilantro, and cumin seeds and stir well. Heat the oil in a deep pan over a medium heat.

Add a large spoonful of the bhaji mixture to the oil and fry on each side for 30 seconds until it is golden brown.

Allow the bhaji to drain on a paper towel.

Continue the process with the rest of the mixture.

Onions are ready for harvesting when the foliage starts to turn yellow and flop over. Gently lift out of the ground with a fork and leave to dry in the sun for a few days before taking them inside for storage.

Onions are relatively problem free, but there are a few pests and diseases to look out for. They can be prone to white rot, which produces a fluffy white appearance on the bottom of the bulb and causes the bulb to deteriorate rapidly. If this is seen, remove the bulbs immediately to prevent it spreading and avoid growing any other members of the onion family (garlic, shallots, and scallions) on the same ground for the next few years. Rotating your crops will help prevent this, and other infections in the soil. Growing carrots nearby should deter onion fly (see carrot fly on p.131), or covering them with a fine mesh should help prevent them. In damp, wet summers they can be prone to mildew. Regularly picking off the affected leaves should help contain the problem.

**LEFT:** This chromolithograph plate dating from 1876 by artist Ernst Benary shows a range of onion varieties taken from the *Album Benary*. It is one of 28 color plates showing lots of different vegetables in cultivation at that time.

# Scallion
## *Allium cepa*

**Common name:** Scallion, spring onion, salad onion, green onion

**Type:** Annual

**Climate:** Half-hardy, mild winter

**Size:** 10in (25cm)

**Origin:** Middle East

**History:** The word onion comes from the Latin word *Unio*, which means "large pearl." In Middle English, it became *unyon*. Eaten and cultivated since prehistoric times, onions were mentioned in the first dynasty of ancient Egypt as far back as 3200 BC. References to scallions also occur in Chinese literature dating back over 2,000 years and they have also been used extensively in Chinese traditional medicines.

**Cultivation:** Like all members of the onion family, they require a sunny, well-drained site. Seeds should be sown in spring.

**Storage:** Unlike onions and shallots, scallions do not store for long. They will last for a few weeks if kept in the refrigerator or can be chopped and stored in the freezer.

**Preparation:** Cut off the roots and trim the green leaves to about 1in above the white. Scallions are almost always eaten raw and can be used whole or sliced in salads or chopped and put into stir-fried dishes.

**ABOVE:** Scallions are a popular springtime vegetable and if left in the ground they will eventually produce clusters of eye-catching flowerheads.

These leafy, small bulb vegetables impart a mild onion flavor to savory dishes. They are often referred to as spring onions and are eaten or cooked fresh as they do not store for long. They are one of the first of the onion family to be harvested and they are picked from spring to early summer. They produce a thin stem of green foliage with a tiny white bulb at the base. Usually both the small bulb and the foliage are chopped up and added raw to flavor dishes, including salads and fish, and they taste particularly good in mashed potato.

**ABOVE:** Placing scallions under cloches in late winter means they can be harvested earlier in the season. Cloches are traditionally glass domed, but recycled plastic bottles work just as well.

Onions need to be grown in full sun in a well-drained soil. Manure should be added in the fall before sowing the seeds in early spring. Sow every three weeks throughout spring to early summer. They can also be sown in late winter and kept under a cloche for an early spring harvest.

Seeds should be sown thinly in shallow drills 6in apart. They shouldn't need thinning out as they are harvested when young and pencil thick. Avoid leaving them in the ground for too long as they tend to become tough quickly. They are usually ready for harvesting about 8 weeks after sowing. Remember to water them in dry weather and regularly remove weeds with a hoe to prevent the plants being deprived of nutrients and sunlight.

Scallion bulbs are also occasionally used for pickling—although, for the genuine article, the cocktail or pearl onions should be used, which have slightly larger bulbs and a sweeter taste. There are a few varieties of scallion worth trying. The most commonly grown variety is called "White Lisbon," which is an old favorite with great flavor but prone to disease, particularly downy mildew. It is suitable for spring sowing and probably has the sweetest flavor of all the scallion varieties. It is also one of the fastest growing. Another spring-sown variety worth trying is a hybrid called "Laser" which is a nonbulbing type with white stems and good flavor.

Varieties suitable for sowing in late summer or early fall, and that produce a crop the next spring, include "Guardsman," which has some resistance to mildew, and "Winter White Bunching" and "Winter Over" which are hardier versions of "White Lisbon."

### TASTING NOTES

*Spicy cheese dip*

This simple dip goes well with spicy sweet potato wedges. (See sweet potato on p.148 for recipe.)

**Preparation time:** 10 minutes
**Serves:** 10–15 people

- 1 scallion, finely chopped

- 9oz (250g) cottage cheese

- Pinch of chilli flakes

- $1/2$ tsp cilantro

Simply mix all the ingredients together and spoon into a dipping bowl.

# Shallot
## *Allium cepa* var. *aggregatum*

**Common name:** Shallot, kanda, gandana, or pyaaz (India)

**Type:** Bulb

**Climate:** Half-hardy, mild winter

**Size:** 15¾in (40cm)

**Origin:** Middle East

**History:** The shallot is a popular vegetable worldwide, particularly in French and Asian dishes. It is named for the ancient Palestine port of Ascalon, which is now modern Ashqueion.

**Cultivation:** Shallots grow in well-drained soil in full sun. They are usually planted as small bulbs or sets in early spring and harvested from mid to late summer.

**Storage:** Shallots will store for a few months after harvesting if kept in a dry, dark but cool place such as a cellar or garage.

**Preparation:** Shallots have a papery outer skin that should be removed first. Using a knife, cut off the root end and discard. They are often left whole in casseroles. Alternatively, they can be diced on a chopping board by making horizontal cuts into the shallot, almost to the root end. Then cut the shallot vertically into thin slices, holding it with fingers to keep its shape. Turn the shallot and cut it crosswise to the root end.

Shallots have just as rich a heritage as onions, have been cultivated for centuries, and used worldwide in dishes for their intense and aromatic flavors. Less eye-watering in the kitchen than their bigger cousins, their taste can sometimes be more intense yet sweeter; they are often used to impart a more subtle background flavor to culinary dishes. They can be enjoyed raw in salads or added whole to stews and casseroles. They are also delicious when roasted. They come in a range of colors including yellow and brown, and they can be banana or torpedo shaped, but most of them are round. The pink ones tend to have the strongest flavor, and the red Thai shallots are popular in Asian cuisine.

**RIGHT:** Shallots are easy to grow from sets and are basically mini-onions, although rather than form one bulb, they form a cluster. They are grown for their aromatic flavors.

The main obvious difference between onions and shallots is their size. The other difference is that as the onion grows in the ground, it swells as one large bulb, whereas a shallot divides and multiplies into small clusters of bulbs.

Shallots are traditionally planted on December 26 by gardeners in the Northern hemisphere, but for many this may be too early and it is better to wait until late winter or early spring. Like onions, shallots are best grown from sets, which are immature or smaller onions. They should be spaced at between 4 to 6in between each bulb in rows 12in apart. Push them into the soil with the tip just showing above ground level. Keep them weed-free as they grow and avoid watering them except in extremely dry periods, as the moisture can cause them to rot. Harvest shallots in summer by digging them up gently with a fork and leaving them to dry in the sun before bringing them inside to harvest.

A simple drying rack can be made to dry out shallots or onions immediately after harvesting. Stretch a piece of fine mesh between blocks of wood or bricks about 12in off the ground. This will help the air circulate around the harvested crop. If available, place a recycled window pane or sheet of rigid plastic suspended above the bulbs to keep them dry in case of rain.

**LEFT:** Some shallot bulbs are unusual shapes and colors, such as this one with a red skin and mild sweet flavor.

*Red wine and shallot sauce*

This sauce makes the perfect accompaniment to rump or sirloin steak.

**Preparation time:** 5 minutes
**Cooking time:** 30 minutes
**Serves:** 2 people

• 1oz (25g) butter

• 4 shallots, finely sliced

• 7floz (200ml) red wine

• 7floz (200ml) beef broth

Melt the butter in a large frying pan over a medium heat.

Add the shallots and cook for 2–3 minutes, to soften.

Add the red wine, increase the heat, and boil for a few minutes to reduce by half.

Make up the beef stock and pour in.

Boil until reduced by half again.

## NUTRITION

Shallots have more antioxidants, minerals, and vitamins than onions. They are rich in vitamins A, B, and E and essential minerals iron, calcium, potassium, and phosphorus. Regular consumption of shallots can contribute to lowering cholesterol levels, improving the blood circulation, and reducing the risk of cardiovascular disease.

# Bunching onion
## *Allium fistulosum*

**Common names:** Bunching onion, Japanese bunching onion, salad onion, perennial onion

**Type:** Perennial

**Climate:** Hardy, very cold winter

**Size:** 19½in (50cm)

**Origin:** Asia, China

**History:** Despite its name, this onion is neither indigenous to Wales nor that popular in Welsh cuisine. The word "welsh" hails from the old English word *welisc*, which simply means "foreign." The bunching onion is believed to have originated in Asia.

**Cultivation:** Bunching onions can cope with partial shade or full sun. They can generally tolerate slightly moister soil than most onions as there is no bulb to rot.

**Storage:** They will store in the fridge for a couple of weeks. Alternatively they can be chopped up, placed into plastic bags or containers, and frozen.

**Preparation:** Trim off both ends and chop in the same way as for a scallion.

Probably the least known of the onion family, bunching onions are a clump-forming perennial. The beauty of this plant is that it is fully hardy and can be harvested during winter and added to hearty warming soups and stews as a milder substitute for onions or shallots.

Bunching onions do not form a single large bulb but instead produce onion-flavored stems with clumps of small bulbs beneath the ground, a bit like chives. They also produce an attractive flowerhead, making them a useful plant in the herbaceous border as well as the vegetable garden. Some varieties reach the size of leeks or larger while others more closely resemble chives.

Bunching onions are popular in Russia, where they are used in green salads. They are also commonly used in Chinese, Japanese, and Korean dishes. It is the stem that is usually chopped up and eaten. They are usually eaten raw, but can be steamed or fried if they feel slightly tough.

**LEFT:** Bunching onions are a perennial type of allium and can be harvested at any time of the year. This makes them a useful ingredient during the winter months.

Bunching onions are generally evergreen, but in particularly cold winters they will die back and regenerate new shoots in spring.

When it comes to harvesting, the stems or foliage can simply be cut from the plant as required. Alternatively, the entire plant can be dug up and brought inside for cooking. Due to their tendency to produce clumps of bulbs, even when the entire plant is harvested there are usually plenty of bulbs left in the ground to regenerate.

In spring, seed should be sown indoors into seed trays and kept on a sunny windowsill. In April they can be hardened off for a few days in a cold frame before being planted outdoors. Seedlings should be planted 4in apart.

The other method of propagating them is by division. Simply use a spade to dig them out of the ground and pull apart their bulbs, replanting them in a fresh place in the vegetable patch. Bulbs should be planted so that their tips are just below the surface.

TASTING NOTES

*Cooking with bunching onions*

Bunching onions can be added to stews, casseroles, and fish dishes after they are cooked. They must be used fresh and not cooked or their flavor will be lost. They are also good in salads and are lovely with butter in baked potatoes.

They can be used as an additional flavor in many other dishes to impart their mild onion flavor, substituting chives in an egg and mayonnaise baguette, or a new potato salad, for example. Chop them up and add them to a sage and onion stuffing to accompany a roast chicken meal. Alternatively, use them as a milder substitute to an onion bhaji.

### WALKING ONIONS

Walking onions, also known as Egyptian onions or tree onions (*Allium cepa* Proliferum Group), are a hardy perennial member of the onion family that produce small onion bulbils above ground in the tips of the plants. They have a milder flavor than onions, but are a useful addition to the kitchen garden as they will appear year after year once planted. They are called walking onions because the weight of the bulbils makes the plant flop over onto the ground, where they will start to root, and the whole process repeats itself.

Prior to planting bunching onions, add plenty of organic matter, such as well-rotted horse manure or garden compost. This helps the soil to retain moisture, which will prevent the crop from drying out.

**RIGHT:** This is one of the lesser known onions, which is a popular ingredient in Asian cooking. It has a variety of common names including Japanese bunching onion and bunching onion.

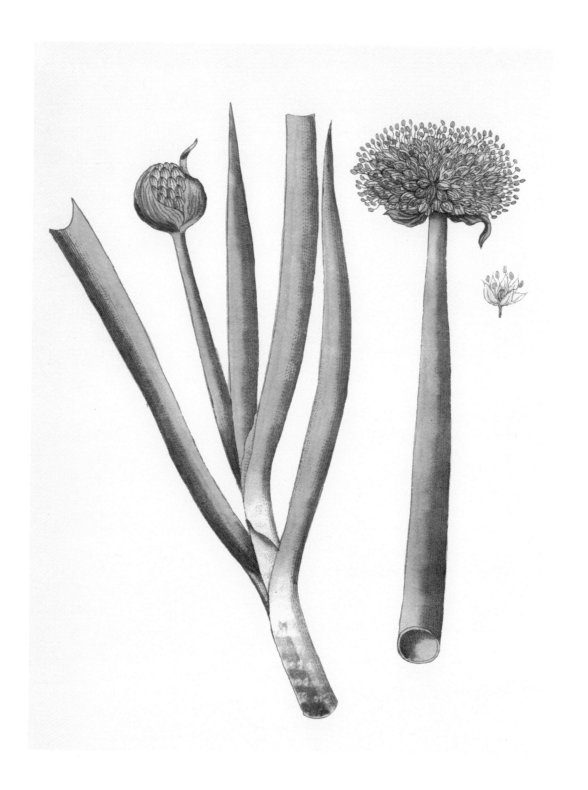

# COMPOSTING

The compost heap is the heart of the vegetable plot and the compost produced from it is often referred to by gardeners as "black gold", and for good reason: every kitchen garden should have one.

A compost heap provides a green method of recycling all the waste produced from the kitchen garden. Once the waste has broken down, it provides material to help improve the soil. This can be dug into the ground prior to sowing or planting and can be used to mulch around fruit trees too, which will suppress weeds and retain moisture. Doing this reduces evaporation rates and is particularly useful in dry or poor soil. Compost adds a certain amount of nutrients to the soil and it also helps to aerate the soil as the organic matter attracts worms and other soil wildlife.

## WHAT NOT TO ADD

- Avoid adding eggshells, meat, and fish as these will quickly attract vermin and cause unpleasant odors that may affect you and your neighbors.
- Potato tubers will quickly sprout in your compost pile. Boil them first if you want to add them to the heap.
- Perennial weeds will also quickly spread their pernicious roots through the heap. Instead, dry these plants out in the sun before adding fresh from the garden.

## RECIPE FOR PERFECT COMPOST

Making good compost is a bit like following a recipe. There are four essential ingredients: nitrogen, carbon, water, and air. Ideally there will be about a 60:40 ratio between nitrogen and carbon.

| | |
|---|---|
| Nitrogen | Herbaceous material such as grass clippings, stems, flowerheads, and shredded foliage are the main sources of nitrogen. If there is too much green waste in a compost heap it will become smelly and slimy. |
| Carbon | Shredded paper, cardboard, fall leaves, straw, and shredded prunings from shrubs and trees provide carbon. |
| Water | If there is too much carbon in a mix, water may need to be added as this willl provide the extra nitrogen. Compost heaps shouldn't dry out. |
| Air | Without air, the compost heap will not break down. Regularly turning the compost will speed up the process. |

**LEFT:** Harvest leaves from the ground in fall and winter and add them to the compost heap or make a devoted heap purely for leaf mold.

## LOOKING AFTER THE COMPOST HEAP

- Turn the compost as regularly as you can—every 3 or 4 months if possible. The more you do it, the quicker the waste will rot down. Turning involves digging it out and placing it back into the heap, allowing the air to circulate around the heap. Having more than one heap is useful as the compost can be emptied from one into the other.
- If the weather is dry, the heap will benefit from being watered to speed up the decomposition.
- Regularly check on the compost heap and pull out any weeds or plants that start growing from it as they will spread.

## TYPES OF COMPOST HEAPS

There are lots of different types of compost heaps that can be bought. These include drum types (dalek), rotating bins, and sectional types.

A compost facility can simply be made by nailing or screwing three old pallets together to form a back and two sides. Pallets have gaps enabling air to circulate around the material.

Ideally there should be at least two compost heaps at different stages of decomposition. One that is ready to use, and one in the process of decomposition. Three is optimum, as shown in the diagram below.

## METHODS OF RECYCLING

There are other useful ways of recycling plant waste. These include worm bins and bokashi. Weedy plants, such as comfrey or stinging nettles, can be used to make a natural liquid plant food. To do this, simply steep the leaves in a bucket of water and leave them to rot for a few weeks. The resulting liquid can then be diluted and fed to plants.

Another technique is to make leaf mold from deciduous leaves in fall. Collect up all the fallen leaves and either place them in a punctured black sack or make a pile of them in a corner of the garden. They will eventually rot down, making a beautifully crumbly, rich black soil improver.

**BELOW:** Ideally there should be at least two compost sections in use—one to keep adding material to, and one to be left to rot down. The system below shows an optional third section for the final rotting stage.

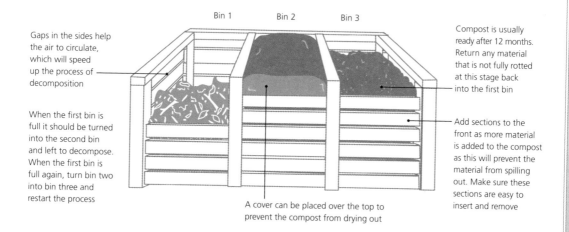

Bin 1    Bin 2    Bin 3

Gaps in the sides help the air to circulate, which will speed up the process of decomposition

When the first bin is full it should be turned into the second bin and left to decompose. When the first bin is full again, turn bin two into bin three and restart the process

A cover can be placed over the top to prevent the compost from drying out

Compost is usually ready after 12 months. Return any material that is not fully rotted at this stage back into the first bin

Add sections to the front as more material is added to the compost as this will prevent the material from spilling out. Make sure these sections are easy to insert and remove

# Garlic
## *Allium sativum*

**Common names:** Garlic, garlick, rocambole

**Type:** Bulb

**Climate:** Hardy, average winter

**Size:** Up to 12in (30cm)

**Origin:** Central Asia

**History:** The word "garlic" comes from the Anglo Saxon word *garleac* (*gar* meaning "spear" and *leac* meaning "leek." It has a similar history to the leek and onion and can be dated back over 7,000 years to Central Asia. The Egyptians worshipped garlic and placed models of garlic bulbs made out of clay in the tomb of Tutankhamen. The Romans believed that garlic held properties of strength and courage and fed it to their soldiers to give them the best start in battle.

**Cultivation:** Garlic requires a well-drained soil in full sun. It is fully hardy and its individual cloves are best planted in late fall as the cold winter promotes bulb development, although it can be planted anytime through winter until early spring.

**Storage:** Leave bulbs out in the sun for a few days if the weather is dry, before collecting them up and storing them in a frost-free, dry place. They will store for 6 months or more.

**Preparation:** When choosing garlic it is important to look for bulbs that are hard and firm. The less papery the skin, the more moist the cloves will be. The papery skin should be removed and the cloves prized apart. The smooth skin surrounding individual cloves comes off more easily if gently crushed.

Garlic is one of the more pungent ingredients in the vegetable world, and just a tiny crushed clove is enough to flavor an entire dish. Anyone who has cooked with it will know how hard the smell can be to eradicate from the skin; it remains with the cook for hours afterward. Popular in both Asian and Mediterranean cooking, garlic is a member of the onion family and is simply a bulb made up of usually between 8 and 12 individual cloves. The papery skin that

**LEFT AND ABOVE:** Garlic is a popular bulb vegetable, closely related to onions, and with a pungent, aromatic flavor. It is used in a range of culinary dishes from around the world.

## NUTRITION

Garlic contains high levels of potassium, iron, calcium, magnesium, manganese, zinc, and selenium, which are essential for optimum health. Garlic also contains health-promoting substances that that have proven benefits against coronary artery diseases, infections, and cancers.

**ABOVE:** A colored engraving of a peasant women c.1735 by Martin Engelbrecht illustrating a peasant lady with a variety of pink and white garlic bulbs attached around her waist.

surrounds the bulb is usually white but there are attractive pink- and purple-tinged varieties too.

Vampires might not be fond of this pungent bulb, but garlic is probably one of the most popular vegetables, with people from around the globe using it to impart exciting flavors to otherwise bland dishes.

Garlic cloves are usually crushed or sliced in cooking, but they can be cooked whole. To provide a real punch of the garlic flavor, they can be added raw to salads, but breath mints will be required for hours afterward if you do not want to upset your friends, family, and work colleagues. For a milder garlic flavor, the stem or scapes can be harvested and cooked in stir-fries.

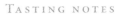

Garlic should be planted between late fall and midwinter, ideally before Christmas. It is fully hardy and in fact requires a cold period of between 32–43°F to encourage the bulb to develop.

Garlic requires a sheltered, sunny site with well-drained soil. They struggle to grow on damp ground and will require plenty of grit or sand to be added if this is the case. Remove the papery covering from around the bulb and gently prize apart the individual cloves. These segments should then be pushed into the ground at 6in apart ensuring that the basal plate (the flat section) is at the bottom. The tip of the clove should just be below the surface. Rows should be 12in apart. Choose only the fat, plump bulbs for planting and discard any withered or thin ones. A net or fleece may need to be placed over them if birds are attracted to the bulbs after planting. Avoid planting cloves bought from the grocery store as they may not be virus-free or suitable for the climate.

## HARDNECKS OR SOFTNECKS

Garlic is divided into two categories, hardnecks and softnecks, referring to the stem of the plant.

**Hardnecks**—the hardiest garlic, often producing a flower stem that can be cooked. They are usually planted out in the fall although they can also be planted in early spring. They generally have more complex flavors than the softnecks and a shorter shelf life, only lasting until midwinter time in storage. Varieties include "Chesnok Wight" and "Lautrec Wight."

**Softneck**—this garlic contains more cloves, which are more tightly packed. They will last until late winter or early spring if stored correctly.

Varieties include "Early Wight" and "Solent Wight."

The soft stem produced is useful for plaiting for storage

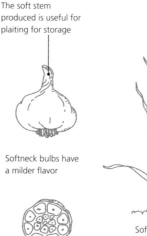

Softneck bulbs have a milder flavor

Softnecks do not produce scapes, hence their earlier bulb production

The bulb below ground stores for longer than hardnecks, which is why they are more common in grocery stores

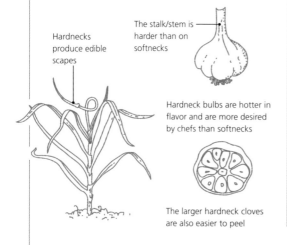

Hardnecks produce edible scapes

The stalk/stem is harder than on softnecks

Hardneck bulbs are hotter in flavor and are more desired by chefs than softnecks

The larger hardneck cloves are also easier to peel

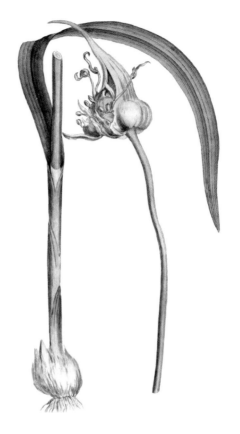

## Planting garlic in modules

When the soil is heavy and wet, garlic can benefit from being planted out in modules in late fall, left in a cold frame, and planted out in early spring. Fill the modules up with multipurpose compost and push a clove into each individual cell, ensuring the tip is just below the surface. Place them in a cold frame, but ensure that the vents are open as garlic needs a cold period, and keep them moist.

**ABOVE:** Garlic scapes are the "flower stalks" of hardneck garlic plants that are often removed as they divert energy from bulb production, but can be added to dishes as they taste delicious.

After planting, water the bulbs during dry periods only—if overwatered, the bulbs may begin to rot. Regularly weed between the rows during the growing season as they are very susceptible to competition from weeds, and weak foliage is a sign of this. Remove any flower stems that may emerge from the bulb. Once the foliage turns yellow about midsummer, the bulbs are ready for harvesting. Unlike onion bulbs, garlic forms below the surface of the soil. Dig them up gently with a fork before the foliage dies down—otherwise it is next to impossible to know where they are in the soil— and leave them to dry in the sun for a few days.

Garlic can be stored in various ways for use during fall and winter, including in net bags or by plaiting their stems together as you would a string of onions, leaving them to hang in a cool, dry place.

The simplest and by far the most effective method is to thread a stiff wire through the base of the dry stem, adding one on top of another. They can then be hung up until needed. Avoid storing them in the kitchen as temperatures are often too warm.

"I must tell you that I have had a whole field of garlic planted for your benefit, so that when you come, we may be able to have plenty of your favorite dishes."

Beatrice D'Este, letter to her sister Isabella, (1491)

# Love-lies-bleeding
## *Amaranthus caudatus*

**Common name:** Love-lies-bleeding, love-lies-a-bleeding, pendant amaranth, velvet flower, foxtail, amaranth

**Type:** Annual

**Climate:** Tender to half-hardy

**Size:** 3¼ft (1m)

**Origin:** South America

**History:** This plant was extremely popular in the decorative gardens of the Victorian era. Its genus name comes from the Greek word *amarantos*, which means "unfading" with reference to its long-lasting blooms; its species name *caudatus*

means "with a tail." This can clearly be seen from its wonderful long strings of cascading flowers. For many centuries amaranth was the principle grain crop of the Aztec people, who referred to it as "the golden grain of the gods." Its use was widespread on all continents. It has similar properties to corn and is classed as an ancient grain that was used long before wheat and corn became staple crops. In fact its seeds can be popped just like popcorn.

**Cultivation:** Requires a warm, sunny site outdoors but will tolerate fairly impoverished soil. It should be grown as an annual, sowing the seeds outdoors in spring, harvesting the leaves in summer, seeding in late summer, and then adding the plant to the compost heap when the first frosts arrive in the fall.

**Storage:** The leaves do not store for long and can be kept fresh in the refrigerator for about 10 days. The seeds should be collected in paper bags and stored in a dry, cool, and dark place such as a garage or cellar.

**Preparation:** Amaranth leaves can simply be washed in cold water and served as a salad vegetable. It can be cooked and served as a leafy vegetable similar to cabbage. Some gardeners prune larger plants for their tender leaves and tips. Others prefer to time plantings two weeks apart and pull up the young tender plants to eat.

**LEFT:** Love-lies-bleeding was a popular, decorative addition to the 19th-century garden but is equally popular in cuisine. Its name is derived from its impressive cascade of bright red flowers.

If you want to brighten up your vegetable garden, then this is the "must have" plant. Adding a touch of the exotic to the vegetable beds, it is commonly known as love-lies-bleeding as the flowerheads evoke a sense of blood being spilled from the plant. The attractiveness of its foliage and its brightly colored catkin-like flowers that cascade down to the ground make it an architectural feature in the ornamental garden as well as the vegetable beds. It is sometimes grown as part of a bedding display. There are many different types of amaranth species, but the easiest one to find in seed catalogs is *Amaranthus caudatus*. It is very closely related to the grain quinoa.

Most of the plant is edible but it is the foliage and the seeds that it is mainly grown for. Leaves can be picked and either eaten raw or cooked like spinach. The seeds can be collected in paper bags and stored in a cool, dark but dry location like other grains until needed for cooking.

It requires a warm, sunny aspect in well-drained soil. The soil should be enriched with organic matter prior to planting or sowing although it will tolerate poorer soil than many vegetable plants. Seeds should be sown in spring under cover about

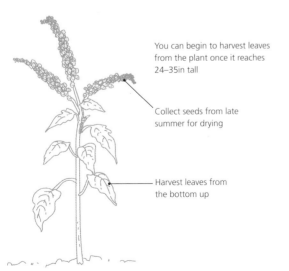

You can begin to harvest leaves from the plant once it reaches 24–35in tall

Collect seeds from late summer for drying

Harvest leaves from the bottom up

TASTING NOTES

*Amaranth leaf pasta*

Amaranth leaves are a healthy, flavorsome addition to a slightly spicy pasta dish.

**Preparation time:** 5 minutes
**Cooking time:** 15 minutes
**Serves**: 4 people

• ½lb (250g) whole wheat pasta shells

• 1 tbsp olive oil

• 5oz (150g) Amaranth leaves, chopped

• 3–4 cloves garlic, minced

• ½ tsp dried red pepper flakes

• Parmesan cheese, freshly grated, to taste

Cook the pasta, drain, and put to one side.

Heat oil in a large skillet over medium heat. Add leaves, garlic, and red pepper flakes; sautée for 5 minutes or until the garlic turns light gold. Add cooked pasta and mix well.

four to five weeks before the last frost is predicted. Plant them out in late spring about 19in apart. Alternatively they can be directly sown in the soil, scattering the tiny seed in the vegetable bed. As the seedlings emerge they can be spread to their final spacing of 19in. The thinnings can be eaten like microgreens. Keep the plants well watered as they grow, and stake them with canes to prevent them flopping over. The seeds ripen toward the end of summer and can be harvested then. There can be as many as 100,000 seeds from one plant.

# Celery

## *Apium graveolens* var. *dulce*

**Common name:** Celery

**Type:** Annual

**Climate:** Hardy, mild to average winter

**Size:** 18in (45cm)

**Origin:** Mediterranean

**History:** The name celery is believed to be derived from the French word *celeri*, which in turn comes from the Greek version of the word. Celery is believed to have originated in the Mediterranean although other countries lay claim to this. Originally used for medicinal purposes as a flavoring herb, it was not until the 1600s in France that celery was seen to be actually edible and began to be used in cooking. The Greeks believed that celery was a holy plant and archeologists have found drawings of celery in ancient Egyptian tombs.

**Cultivation:** Celery requires a moist soil but will tolerate some moderate shade. Seeds are sown in spring and the crop is usually harvested in fall. Stems are traditionally blanched to sweeten them by covering them up with soil, but there are modern self-blanching varieties available.

**Storage:** Celery can be stored in a perforated bag in the fridge for around 10 days. If blanched for three minutes in boiling water, it can be frozen for later use, but it will have lost its crispness and is only suitable for cooking.

**Preparation:** Stems can be broken off when ready to use. The outer stems are tougher and are better for cooking, whereas the inner ones are more tender and suitable for eating raw. The leafy tops can also be used in salads. Wash thoroughly to remove the soil from the base of the stems.

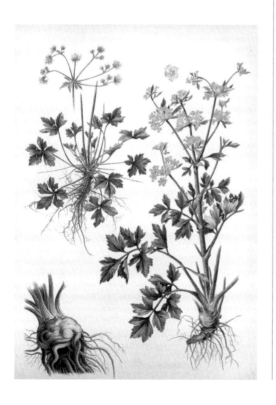

**LEFT:** Celery was originally used as a flavoring herb to make medicines more palatable, but it is now an important addition to the cook's list of ingredients.

Celery has been putting the crunch into salad for the last few centuries. It consists of a cluster of long juicy stems grown around a central heart. Stems vary from green to white, the lighter stems being sweeter and less bitter. The flavor is unmistakable and reminiscent of very mild onions. The stems are crisp and popular with dieters as it is claimed more calories are burned eating this succulent vegetable than are consumed. The best way to eat celery is simply to chop off a stem and eat it whole, some people preferring to shake salt over it. However, stems can be sliced diagonally and mixed into stir-fries, or chopped into ½in lengths and added to soups and stews. The leafy tops are often used to add flavoring to dishes.

Growing celery has fallen out of favor in recent years as it has a reputation for being difficult to grow. It requires constant moisture to thrive and can be considered hard work to dig out of the garden trenches. This is a shame, as home-grown celery is far superior to most of the bland varieties for sale in the store. There are green, red, and pink-stemmed varieties available.

Celery always tastes better when the sunlight has been excluded from the stem. This is called blanching and there are two methods of doing this.

To blanch celery the traditional way, a trench should be dug 18in wide and 12in deep in the fall. Add well-rotted manure to the bottom of the trench so the trench is left at 4in deep. Seeds should be sown under glass in spring in a heated propagator. Once they have been hardened off in a cold frame for a few days, they should be planted in the trench at a spacing of 12in apart. Rows should be at 24in apart. As they start to grow, the stems should be loosely tied together just below the leaves, and the soil earthed up around the stem with a draw hoe. This should be repeated every few weeks during the growing season until the soil has reached up to the lower leaves.

The other method of blanching is less labor intensive. Rather than digging out a trench, the celery is simply planted out at 12in apart, and cardboard collars or waterproof papers are wrapped around the stems every three or so weeks, as the stems grow.

Nowadays, there are self-blanching celery varieties available, although some claim that they do not taste as good. They should be planted in blocks rather than rows as their dense foliage prevents the sunlight from reaching the neighboring plants, which is how the stems are blanched.

It is essential that celery is kept well watered throughout the growing season. Regularly weed between the rows to prevent them competing for moisture with the plants.

Celery is ready for harvesting in the fall. The plants can remain in their trench until ready to use in the kitchen, but should all be harvested before the weather becomes too cold.

**RIGHT:** Celery is easier to grow than you think, and modern varieties do not need blanching to create white stems.

# Celeriac

## *Apium graveolens* var. *rapaceum*

**Common name:** Celeriac, knob celery, celery root, turnip-rooted celery

**Type:** Annual

**Climate:** Hardy, average winter

**Size:** 14in (35cm)

**Origin:** Mediterranean

**History:** Celeriac is derived from wild celery, which has a small, edible root and has been cultivated as an edible plant for thousands of years. In the Middle Ages, it spread from the Mediterranean, finding its way into northern European cuisine.

**Cultivation:** Liking a sheltered position in the sun, celeriac will tolerate moderate shade. It requires a long growing season to fully mature and, like celery, needs a moist soil to thrive.

**Storage:** The best way to store celeriac is in the ground until it is needed. It can be stored in a cool dark place for a few weeks, but once it is chopped up it needs to be used as it discolors rapidly.

**Preparation:** Cut off the top and base of the celeriac then remove the coarse, tough skin with a knife or sharp potato peeler. Sections of it can then be chopped as required.

**LEFT:** This ugly-looking vegetable, to the right of the celery, is often called turnip-rooted celery as the base of the plant looks like a turnip, yet the flavor of the swollen stem is reminiscent of celery.

This knobbly vegetable would not win a beauty contest, but what it lacks in looks it makes up for with its versatility in the kitchen. It is not just the name that is similar to celery; the flavor is reminiscent too with slightly nutty overtones. It makes a great celery-flavored substitute for winter dishes, when fresh celery will not be available in the vegetable garden, and it can be grated and fried to add to salads. Alternatively, it can be treated like a potato and chopped into large chunks and boiled for 20 minutes or baked or roasted in the oven for 40 minutes. Celeriac mash with garlic and cream is a delicious winter-warming treat.

**LEFT:** It is possible to harvest the swollen stems when young, once they reach anything from 4in across.

**RIGHT:** "Giant Prague" celeriac is a heritage variety first cultivated about 1871, grown for its large, white roots.

Celeriac is much easier to grow
than celery but it does need a
long growing season in order to
develop its swollen stem. They are
quite hungry plants so the soil should
be enriched with plenty of organic matter
and left to settle for several weeks prior to
planting. Seeds should be sown under glass in
modules or small plastic pots in late winter or
in early spring. Place them in a propagator at
59°F to encourage germination. When the
plants reach 4in tall they can be hardened off
in a cold frame and planted out at 12in apart in
rows 12in apart. The base of the stem should be
level with the surface of the soil.

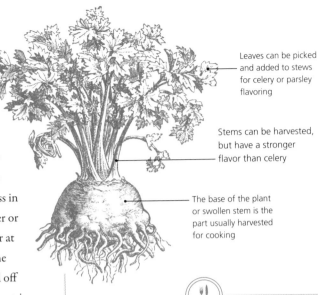

Leaves can be picked
and added to stews
for celery or parsley
flavoring

Stems can be harvested,
but have a stronger
flavor than celery

The base of the plant
or swollen stem is the
part usually harvested
for cooking

As the plant grows and the stem swells it is
important that the soil is kept moist during dry
conditions. Remove side shoots as soon as they
appear as these will compete for nutrients. Also
remove some of the lower leaves in late summer
and earth up around the stem. In cold areas, as
fall approaches the plants will benefit from being
mulched around their base with straw.

Harvest the swollen stems during fall and
winter as required using a fork to gently lift them
out of the ground. Celeriac should be left in the
ground for as long as possible to allow the stem to
swell. However, they can be harvested and eaten
when they are about 4in across.

In cold areas where there is a risk of the ground
freezing over and becoming difficult to dig, the
celeriac can be lifted and stored in trays covered in
moist sand and kept in a dark, frost-free place such
as a cool garage or cellar. Regularly check the crops
and throw out any that spoil.

## TASTING NOTES

### Celeriac remoulade

The texture of celeriac is ideal for making a
simple remoulade, which is a classic French
dish of grated celeriac in a mustard-flavored
mayonnaise. It is great for accompanying fish
dishes or can be served with toast.

**Preparation time:** 10 minutes, plus 2 hours
for chilling
**Serves:** 4 people

· ¹/₂ small celeriac, cut into thin strips

· 2 tbsp crème fraîche

· 3 tbsp mayonnaise

· 2 tsp Dijon mustard

· Lemon juice, to taste

· Salt and pepper, to taste

Mix the ingredients together and place in the
fridge for a couple of hours before serving.

# Asparagus
## *Asparagus officinalis*

**Common names:** Asparagus, speargrass, spargel

**Type:** Perennial

**Climate:** Hardy, average to cold winter

**Size:** Up to 5ft (1.5m)

**Origin:** Europe and particularly the eastern Mediterranean area

**History:** There are references of asparagus dating back to the ancient Egyptians, Greeks, and Romans. Popular throughout history, not just as a vegetable but also for its medicinal properties and use as a diuretic. Probably due to its shape and high phosphorous content, it has also had a reputation as an aphrodisiac throughout history.

**Cultivation:** Asparagus plants require a well-drained soil. On heavy soils with poor drainage, they will benefit from being grown in raised beds where excess moisture will drain away.

**Storage:** Stand them on their base in a glass of water and keep in the fridge for a few days. Trim and briefly blanch them with boiling water prior to freezing, either as whole spears or chopped.

**Preparation:** Remove the base of the stem with a knife, or simply snap it off. Older thicker stems can be peeled. Asparagus is usually briefly steamed or boiled for a few minutes. It can also be roasted or eaten raw by using a vegetable peeler to strip off thin lengths from spears and added to salads. It can be broiled over hot charcoal and is often stir-fried in Asian cuisine.

**LEFT:** Asparagus is an early springtime treat. The emerging shoots are harvested when they are between 4¾ and 8in tall. Shoots can vary in thickness depending on growing conditions and variety.

## NUTRITION

Asparagus contains asparanin, high levels of vitamins C and E, together with the minerals zinc, manganese, and selenium, which all help to provide anti-inflammatory and antioxidant health benefits.

The season is short but the memory of these gourmet treats will linger for much longer. Often considered a luxury crop and backed up by luxury prices in quality food stores, growing them is surprisingly easy and will reward a gardener with succulent, tender spears for many years after planting.

The emerging spring shoots of this herbaceous perennial are often referred to as spears. In fact the word *asparag* is derived from an ancient Persian word meaning "spear." They are usually green but occasionally white when the emerging shoots have been covered to exclude light. It is also possible to grow purple varieties.

The spears have a refreshingly delicate yet herbaceous flavor and epitomize spring dishes. They are the perfect accompaniment to pork, chicken, and fish, particularly salmon. To maximize their fresh, spring flavors, simply steam them for a couple of minutes, and add melted butter, a splash of lemon juice, and season with cracked black pepper. The skill in steaming asparagus is all in the timing. Too quickly and the spears are al dente and too hard. Too long and the spears turn to mush. Yet the difference between the two extremes can be a matter of seconds in the steamer.

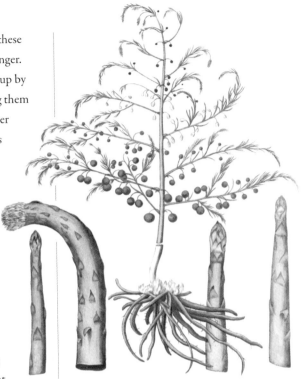

**ABOVE:** Harvest shoots regularly as they will quickly turn thick and unpalatable. Asparagus also produces attractive ferny foliage and berries in late summer and early fall.

The ferny foliage and berries make an attractive late-summer and fall feature in the kitchen garden, but may require staking with strings to prevent them flopping over. Give careful consideration to where you want to grow these plants, as they are a long-term crop and could remain in the same bed for 15 to 20 years.

Patience is a virtue and this is certainly the case with this delicious spring delicacy. You should wait two or three years before harvesting the first

**LEFT:** Asparagus spears are more commonly green, but the stems can be covered with soil to blanch them and cause them to go white.

delicate spears after planting, which will allow the plants to get properly established.

Harvest the spears when they are between 5in and 8in tall. They grow quickly, so the beds will need checking for ready spears every two or three days to avoid any wastage. Cut the spears just below the surface of the ground using either an old knife or a special asparagus knife. Ignore any thin spears that appear and let them grow.

Asparagus is usually planted as small one-year-old crowns in early spring. Dig out a trench 12in wide and 8in deep. Add lots of well-rotted manure into the base and then create a 4in-high ridge along the trench. The crowns should be planted along the ridge 12in apart and the roots should be spread downward on either side. Partially backfill the trench, gradually refill as the spears begin to emerge, and then completely refill when the spears are above the top of the trench. Rows should be 18in apart and the crowns should be staggered with the rows on either side. Cut back the foliage to near-ground level in the fall when it starts to turn yellow and die back.

**BELOW:** The common method of planting asparagus is to create a mound in a trench and place the plant on top of it, spreading the roots around it.

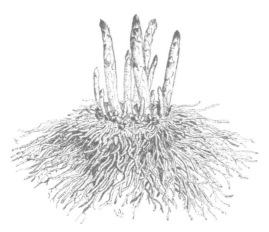

TASTING NOTES

*Asparagus soup*

A simple way to capture the delicate flavors of asparagus is to create a smooth creamy soup from freshly harvested spears.

**Preparation time:** 10 minutes
**Cooking time:** 20 minutes
**Serves:** 4–6 people

- 1 tbsp olive oil

- 1 onion, finely chopped

- 13oz (400g) fresh asparagus spears

- Knob of butter

- 16floz (500ml) vegetable broth

- Salt and pepper, to taste

- 4 tbsp crème fraîche

Heat up the oil in a pan. Add the onion and fry for about 5 minutes until soft.

Add the asparagus spears with the butter, cover, and sautée for 10 minutes.

Make and pour in the vegetable broth. Bring to the boil. Season and then simmer for 5 minutes.

Drizzle in the crème fraîche and use a hand blender to mix together to a smooth soup.

# SOWING TECHNIQUES

Most vegetables can be bought as plants from local garden centers. However, seeds are much cheaper to buy and there is a far greater range of varieties available. Furthermore, it is far more satisfying to grow something from seed, nurture it, and finally harvest the vegetables. With many plants you can also harvest the seed and use it next year.

There are no hard and fast rules for seed sowing. Essentially, seeds simply need soil, water, and sunlight. However, learning a few basic seed-sowing techniques should ensure the vegetables get off to the best possible start.

### DIRECT SOWING

Many seeds can be sown directly into the soil. The packets of seed will provide information on the distance between each plant, between each row, and the depth it should be planted at. Some seeds, such as fava beans and parsnips, are hardy and can be planted out in colder weather; other plants, such as string beans, should not be sown until the soil has warmed up in early summer.

### DIRECT SOWING OF SMALLER SEEDS

Some of the smaller seeds such as carrots, radishes, parsnips, and lettuce, require a shallow drill to be made into which the seeds are evenly sprinkled. Sand can be mixed with small seeds to make them simpler to spread. Once these seeds have germinated they will need to be thinned out to their final spacing as recommended on the seed packet. If they are not thinned out, then the vegetables will remain small, which some chefs prefer.

### DIRECT SOWING OF LARGER SEEDS

Larger seeds, such as beans and peas are often individually placed into the soil using a dibber. After the seed is dropped into the hole, it is backfilled with soil. Occasionally larger seeds are planted in clusters and once germination has occurred the weaker ones are removed, allowing the stronger ones to grow.

**LEFT:** Parsnips should be sown directly into the ground in light soil, as their long tap root makes them difficult to transplant from pots.

"We plough the fields, and scatter the good seed on the land
But it is fed and watered by God's almighty hand."

Matthias Claudius, *Garland of Songs*, (1782, published 1861)

## SOWING INDOORS

Some seeds, such as tomatoes and chillies, need to be sown indoors as they need a long season to grow, yet need warmth to provide germination. Usually one or two seeds are sown into individual plastic pots or in modules. They should be left to germinate in a sunny, dry place such as a window ledge or glasshouse. After germination, the seeds can usually be thinned out to the strongest seedling. Large seeds such as pumpkins, squashes, and zucchinis are often sown on their side to avoid the water sitting on the surface, causing the seed to rot.

## HARDENING OFF

Seeds that have been grown indoors benefit from being hardened off before being planted outdoors. This involves placing the seedlings in the porch or cold frame to toughen them up, preventing them from going into shock when being planted outside.

## SOWING INTO SEED TRAYS

Seeds such as leeks are often sown indoors in seed trays full of compost. Seeds are lightly sprinkled over the surface, before being lightly covered over with more compost and watered.

**STEP 1:** Fill a container with a good quality sowing compost until it is just below the top of the rim. Gently firm it down using fingertips, or a piece of wood, or the base of another tray.

**STEP 2:** Sprinkle the seeds lightly in one direction and then turn the tray 90 degrees and sow the remaining seeds evenly across the surface.

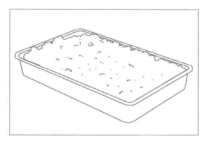

**STEP 3:** Cover the seeds very lightly with more of the potting compost so that they are just covered over.

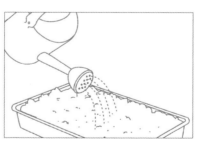

**STEP 4:** Water the plants well using a watering can with a fine rose. Alternatively, stand the container in a tray of water for 15 minutes and allow to drain.

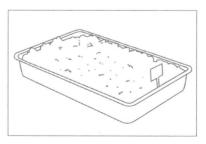

**STEP 5:** Remember to label the seeds with their full name and date of sowing. Place the tray on a sunny window ledge and keep the compost evenly moist but not wet.

# Swiss chard

*Beta vulgaris* subsp. *cicla* var. *flavescens*

**Common name:** Spinach beet, sea kale beet, chard, perpetual spinach, silverbeet; red-stemmed types are called rhubarb, red or ruby chard; mixed colors are known as rainbow chard

**Type:** Annual

**Climate:** Half-hardy, mild winter

**Size:** 14in (35cm)

**Origin:** Sicily

**History:** Swiss chard does not, as its name suggests, originate in Switzerland but was named by the Swiss botanist Koch in the 19th century to distinguish chard from French spinach varieties. Its actual origins lie farther south in the Mediterranean in Sicily. The ancient Greeks, and later the Romans, honored chard for its medicinal properties rather than its culinary ones.

**Cultivation:** Sow in spring in a sunny and sheltered site in fertile soil. Leaves and stems should be ready for harvesting during summer and fall. Alternatively, late summer sowings will provide harvests the following spring.

**Storage:** Like most leaf crops, they do not last long after being picked, so harvest as needed from the vegetable plot. The stems can be chopped and frozen but will be mushy when defrosted so can only be useful for flavoring spinach-type dishes.

**RIGHT:** Swiss chard is a popular leafy vegetable with edible stems and foliage, and is a useful substitute for spinach, hence its common name, spinach beet.

### NUTRITION

Swiss chard is an excellent source of vitamins K, A, and C, as well as a good source of magnesium, potassium, iron, and dietary fiber. It also contains phytonutrients (shown in the vibrant colors of chard) which are known to provide antioxidant, anti-inflammatory, and detoxification support.

**Preparation:** Stems should be separated from the leaves. Young leaves simply need washing and can be added whole or chopped to brighten up salads. Do not soak leaves as this will result in loss of water-soluble nutrients to the water. Remove any brown or slimy parts of the leaves and any damage. The stalks should then be trimmed. If they are too fibrous then simply make incisions, as you would with celery, near the base of the stalk and peel away the fibers. Mature chard is tougher and should be typically cooked or sautéed.

Chard is a popular leaf salad crop that comes in a range of bright colors that can brighten up the dullest of days on the allotment or vegetable plot. Both the stems and the leaves can be eaten and are popular either raw or steamed. The young leaves are particularly suitable for using in salads, whereas the more mature leaves and stems are steamed or sautéed to reduce their bitterness. Their flavor is reminiscent of cooked spinach. Leaves should be boiled or steamed for two or three minutes, stems a couple of minutes longer. Stems can also be stir-fried or even roasted. There are generally three different types of Swiss chard.

**RIGHT:** Chard comes in a range of stunning bright colors that look great in the garden, and brighten up many salad dishes. The mixed colors are known as rainbow chard.

### Cheesy chard gratin

This side dish is a quick and tasty recipe using chard leaves and stems. It can be garnished with colorful stems of rainbow or red-stemmed chard.

**Preparation time:** 10 minutes
**Cooking time:** 30 minutes
**Serves:** 6 people (as side dish)

- 11oz (340g) chard

- ¼ pint (150ml) crème fraîche

- 1 tbsp wholegrain mustard

- 5oz (140g) strong flavored cheese such as mature cheddar or Gruyère, coarsely grated

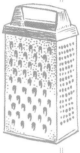

- 2 tbsp Parmesan, finely grated

Preheat a conventional oven to 400°F (200°C/ gas mark 6 / fan 180°C).

Remove the leaves from the stalks and chop the stems into matchstick-thick strips.

Mix the crème fraîche, cheddar or Gruyère, and mustard with the chard in a gratin dish.

Grate Parmesan into the dish and place in the oven for 30 minutes.

First, there are the popular brightly colored stems known as rainbow chard, which is not a single variety but a mix of colored types, and second there are the red-stemmed varieties known as ruby, red, and rhubarb chard. Finally, there are the standard green glossy-leaved chards held aloft on attractive white stems. All of them add a wonderful splash of color to the kitchen garden. Just to complicate things further, there is perpetual spinach, which is very similar to Swiss chard but has slightly thinner stems and is an excellent alternative to standard spinach. All of them are grown in exactly the same way, though chard is often preferred by gardeners as, unlike true spinach, it does not run to seed at the first hint of drought.

Chard likes a warm, sunny, and sheltered site. Dig in lots of organic material in the fall before planting and sow the seeds directly into the soil in spring. Use the edge of a draw hoe to create a shallow drill about ½in deep and sow every 15½in. Rows should also be 15½in apart. Keep the plants well watered and regularly weed between them. A late summer sowing can also be made for a spring crop, but this will need protection in cold areas with a fleece during the colder period, although in milder areas it is tough enough to survive without.

Harvest as and when required during summer and fall. Chard is a bit like large cut-and-come-again plants, whereby stems and leaves can be harvested when needed and yet they will keep producing stems. Use a sharp knife to cut the stems at the base of the plant. They are fairly fast growing and are usually ready for picking about 10 weeks after sowing, although the sweet-flavored baby leaves can be picked after 4 to 6 weeks.

**BELOW:** This historic, colorful illustration, dated pre-1400 from the *Tacuinum Sanitatis*, a medieval health handbook, depicts a woman harvesting chard from a kitchen garden.

# Beet
## *Beta vulgaris*

**Common name:** Beet, table beet, garden beet, red beet, golden beet, or beet

**Type:** Annual

**Climate:** Half-hardy, mild winter

**Size:** 14in (35cm)

**Origin:** Mediterranean

**History:** The beet evolved from wild sea beet, which is native along the coastlines from India to Britain. This would explain why at first it was only the leaves that were used for cooking purposes. Generally used for medicinal rather than culinary purposes, it helped aid digestion and was used to cure ailments of the blood. Around 800 BC beet was mentioned in an Assyrian text as growing in the Hanging Gardens of Babylon and was even presented to the sun god Apollo at his temple in Delphi. The beet also began to appear in Roman recipes, being cooked with honey and wine, but it was not until the 18th century that the beet actually became widely used in central and eastern Europe, where most of the recipes used today come from.

**Cultivation:** Sow beet from early spring and harvest during summer and fall. It prefers fertile, well-drained soil. Sow every two or three weeks if you want to harvest a continual supply of mini beets for their tender, succulent flavor.

**ABOVE:** Beet has a rich and historic horticultural past and is even thought to have been one of the vegetables growing in the legendary Hanging Gardens of Babylon.

**Storage:** Beet can be left in the ground until needed, except in very cold areas where it should be lifted and placed in trays of moist sand. Small beets can be pickled in jars of malt vinegar after boiling and peeling them.

**Preparation:** Twist off the stalks about an inch above the roots and wash the beet. Take care not to pierce the skin or juices will bleed into your cooking water. Beet can be boiled in salted water until soft, which can take up to 1½ hours for a large beet, or alternatively baked in the oven at 355°F for 2–3 hours. It can be peeled and sliced and served hot in melted butter or cold in salads. If adding to salads, it is important to add it at the last minute or the juice can bleed into the other ingredients.

For the gourmet cook there are two treats in store from just the one plant. First, there are the deliciously flavored beet leaves, which are brightly colored and can be picked when very small, and then there are the juicy and succulent roots, which have a unique earthy flavor. The roots can either be picked when young and tender or left to mature and be cooked then used in a huge array of dishes. One unfortunate side effect is that not only does it stain your clothes, skin, and can make you look like you are wearing lipstick, but it can also even turn your toilet waste red or purple. The beet-red coloration comes from its sap. Growing your own enables you to enjoy beets that you rarely see in stores, including white and gold varieties.

There are also impressive varieties containing concentric rings or white within the red flesh. "Albinia Vereduna," for example, is sweet with white roots and sap that does not stain clothes and "Burpee's Golden" has orange skin and yellow flesh, so it keeps its color when cooked and does not bleed. The "Babieto di Chioggia" variety has white internal rings when the flesh is sliced.

For a regular harvest of the roots and leaves, sowings should be made every couple of weeks from spring through to late summer. Some varieties have been bred for their winter storage qualities, meaning that it is almost possible for the vegetable garden to supply beet all year round.

Large beets are often sliced into salads and smaller ones eaten whole, but their versatile flavor can be used in so many dishes. They can be roasted as a flavorsome side dish or even used as a garnish slice in burgers. Their rich flavor is also used in sweet dishes such as chocolate brownies (see box).

Beets should be grown in fertile well-drained soil in full sun. They can be sown as early as February under cloches and outdoors without protection in March and April. Create a shallow 1in drill and sow three seeds every 4in in rows 12in apart. For early sowings it is best to use bolt-resistant varieties. When the seedlings are about 2in high they should be thinned to one beet per 4in. Do not throw away the thinnings but eat the immature

**LEFT:** Beet is a quick-growing vegetable that has a succulent edible rootball after cooking, but also has striking edible foliage with red veins down its center.

bulbs and leaves. Keep the plants well watered and weed-free during the growing season, and harvest the beets when they are the size of a golf ball, leaving the ones that remain to further develop to the size of a tennis ball.

If you want to grow something different, then try "Touchstone Gold" which has bright yellow roots, an earthy flavor, and is both tender and sweet. Alternatively, try a white beet called "Albina Vereduna." Not only does it have tasty white roots, but is also pointy and has leaves and stems that make a suitable substitute for chard. In fact, the plant was bred for its leaf beet qualities. The white root is a practical choice if you are worried about staining your kitchen surfaces with bright red beet juice—it is a far more discreet option.

BELOW: By the 18th century beet had become widely used in culinary dishes in central and eastern Europe, and this is where many of the recipes used today come from, including borscht.

TASTING NOTES

### Beet brownies

The deep red color and earthy, rich flavors of beet fuse well with the sweetness and texture of chocolate in this brownie recipe.

**Preparation time:** 20 minutes
**Cooking time:** 25 minutes
**Serves:** makes 24 squares

· 8oz (250g) beet

· 8oz (250g) salted butter, cubed

· 8oz (250g) dark chocolate

· 3 medium eggs

· 8oz (250g) superfine sugar

· 7oz (150g) self-rising flour

Preheat a conventional oven to 350°F (180°C / gas mark 4 / fan 160°C).

Boil the beet until tender, allow to cool, then grate.

Melt the butter and chocolate in a bowl over a pan of hot water.

Beat together the eggs and sugar, and mix in the melted butter and chocolate until smooth.

Sieve in the flour.

Add the beet and fold everything together with a large metal spoon.

Pour into a greased and lined shallow baking tin, about 8 x 10in, and level with a spatula. Bake for 20–25 minutes.

Cool on a wire rack, then cut into squares.

# Turnip

## *Brassica rapa* Rapifera Group

**Common name:** Turnip, rutabaga, yellow turnip, or neep

**Type:** Annual

**Climate:** Half-hardy, mild winter

**Size:** 10in (25cm)

**Origin:** Europe

**History:** Used as a vegetable in Europe since prehistoric times, there is evidence of the turnip's domestication over 4,000 years ago. A well-established crop in Roman times, the turnip was considered a food for the poorer country folk that could be grown easily and cheaply. It is now widely grown around the world.

**Cultivation:** Turnips prefer an open, sunny but fertile soil improved with plenty of well-rotted organic matter to prevent plants drying out. Seeds should be sown in late winter for early spring harvests with regular sowings from early spring until midsummer for a continual supply as late as early winter.

**Storage:** Turnip greens should be eaten soon after harvesting and will only keep in the fridge for a few days. Small spring and summer turnips will keep for a couple of weeks in the fridge, whereas the larger fall and winter turnips can be left in the ground over winter until required but in areas with mild winters only.

**ABOVE:** Turnips are a member of the cabbage or brassica family. They are grown for their tasty swollen roots. Their flavorsome leaves are also edible and suitable for salad.

**Preparation:** Cut off the greens from the top of the turnip, which can be steamed and eaten as spring greens. Young baby turnips shouldn't need to be peeled, but larger and older types should have their outer skin removed with a knife by carving down the sides just as you would cut a pineapple. Then slice, dice, or cut into chunks. Place in cold salted water and boil for 20 minutes or until tender. Drain and serve or mash lightly and serve hot with butter. Young turnips can be served raw, sliced thinly, and put into salads.

For centuries, turnips were considered a staple peasant food. How times have changed, as these flavorsome root vegetables are now highly sought after—particularly the young and tender spring turnips.

Turnips, like rutabaga, are a member of the cabbage family and grown for their large, swollen root. Confusingly, in Scotland rutabaga are also called "turnips," or "neeps" for short.

Most turnips are perfectly round but there are more flattened forms. The skins are usually creamy white and their tops are usually green, purple, white or yellow. The flesh is usually white or yellowish. The vegetable is mainly grown for the swollen root, which can be eaten when small and succulent in spring or summer. The winter types are larger, tougher, and often cooked in casseroles, stews, and soups. The young leaf tops are also a gourmet treat and have a slightly peppery flavor. They are cooked and eaten as spring greens.

As turnips are part of the cabbage family, they are best grown with other brassicas, such as kale, Brussels sprouts, and cauliflower. In this manner, all their needs can be met as if growing one crop.

Like most root crops, turnips do not transplant well, and so they should be sown directly where they are to be grown. Early varieties can be sown under cloches in late winter to produce the young succulent roots for spring. From early spring onward, they can be sown directly into the soil without the need for protection. Create a shallow drill and sow them in rows 8in apart. Seeds should be sown into ½in-deep drills, and the seedlings thinned out to 5in apart when they are about 2in tall.

For fall and winter harvesting, seeds should be sown in midsummer, but in rows that are 12in apart as these roots will get much bigger. The seedlings should be thinned out to 8in apart.

> "On rainy days he sat and talked for hours together with his mother about turnips ..."
> Mark Twain, *Roughing It*, (1886)

RIGHT: A watercolor on paper of a turnip from *Collection du Regne Vegetal, Fleurs, Plantes, Arbres, et Arbustes* possibly by Pierre Francois Ledoulx, a Belgian painter of flowers and insects.

Harvest the late winter, spring, and early summer sowings when they are about the size of golf balls for the best flavor. Sow every two or three weeks in short rows, for a continual supply of tender turnips. Keep the plants well watered to ensure they grow quickly and keep them weed-free as they grow.

Midsummer sowings should be harvested from fall onward. They can be left in the ground until required, but in very cold areas where the ground is likely to be frozen solid over winter, it is better to dig them up with a fork, remove the leaves, and store them in damp sand.

For the old Celtic festival of Samhain (Hallowe'en), candle lanterns were traditionally carved out of turnips and not pumpkins.

BELOW: *The Incorruptible Consul Curius Dentatus Preferring Turnips to Gold* (1656). Turnips have a long, colorful history of cultivation and were often the subject of stories and paintings.

### Mashed turnips with crispy bacon

Mashed turnip is just as smooth and creamy as mashed potato, but with a slightly stronger flavor. The added crunch of crispy bacon makes this a great side dish to meat dishes, particularly roast lamb, beef, or haggis.

**Preparation time:** 20 minutes
**Cooking time:** 30 minutes
**Serves:** 4 people

• 3–4 turnips

• 2oz (60g) butter

• Salt and pepper, to taste

• 4oz (120g) cooked bacon, chopped

• Handful of chives, chopped

• 2oz (50g) Parmesan, grated

Preheat a conventional oven to 400°F (200°C / gas mark 6 / fan 180°C).

Peel and cut up the turnips, then boil in salted water until tender.

Drain and mash with butter, then season.

Fold in the cooked bacon and chives.

Cover with Parmesan and cook in the oven for 30 minutes.

(For a stronger flavor, add goat's cheese, or blue cheese such as Stilton, Roquefort, Gorgonzola, Cambozola, or Danish Blue.)

# Rutabaga
## *Brassica napus* Napobrassica Group

**Common name:** Swede, yellow turnip, Swedish turnip, and Russian turnip and, in America, rutabaga. In Scotland, rutabagas are called neeps

**Type:** Annual

**Climate:** Hardy, average to cold winter

**Size:** 12in (30cm)

**Origin:** Central Europe

**History:** The rutabaga is thought to have originated in central Europe and has a relatively short culinary history compared with many vegetables. In 1620, a Swiss botanist called Gaspard Bauhin noted that rutabaga was growing wild in Sweden, which is where one of its common names comes from, and it was known in France and England during this century; it is recorded as being present in the Royal gardens of England as early as 1669. By the 18th century, it had become an important European crop.

**Cultivation:** Sow the seeds in fertile sunny sites, enriched with organic matter, in spring. Harvest in fall and late winter.

**Storage:** Leave rutabagas in the ground until required or dig them up and store in sand in a garage or cellar if there is a risk that they may become frozen in the ground.

**ABOVE:** Rutabaga is a popular root vegetable, belonging to the cabbage family. Its first recorded use as a vegetable is from the 17th century.

**Preparation:** Peel thickly to remove all the skin and roots before use. As the skin is quite thick and uneven, you may find it easier to quarter the rutabaga first and then cut off the skin with a knife. Cut into chunks or cubes, according to preference, and place in cold salted water and boil for 20 minutes or until tender. If roasting, place in the oven at 390°F for around 30 to 45 minutes. Rutabaga can also be used raw and is delicious finely grated and tossed into a salad.

Closely related to the turnip, the rutabaga is a welcome treat in the winter vegetable garden when there is little else to harvest. The flavor is milder and sweeter than the turnip and it tastes sensational when roasted or sautéed. Mashing it with garlic and cream is the perfect accompaniment to a pot roast, while it can also be added to bulk up casseroles and soups. Due to its mildness it benefits from plenty of seasoning, particularly pepper, to get the best from its subtle flavor. When cooked it turns a light orange color, which looks attractive on the plate, particularly when contrasted with other winter vegetables, such as leeks and kale.

Unlike its close cousin the turnip, which is sown throughout the year for frequent harvesting, rutabagas only have one season of interest in winter, so enjoy it while it lasts.

Like other members of the cabbage family, rutabaga requires a fertile soil that has been enriched with organic matter to help retain moisture. It prefers a sheltered site in full sun. On acid soil rutabagas can be prone to a disease called clubroot, which deforms the root system. To avoid this, it is beneficial to add a dressing of lime before planting to increase the alkalinity.

Like most root crops, rutabagas do not transplant well and should be directly sown in spring into shallow ½in drills, in rows 14in apart. The seedlings should be gradually thinned out until they are at a final spacing of 10in apart in the row. Keep the plants well watered during dry periods to avoid the roots splitting. It is also necessary to remove weeds regularly to prevent them competing for moisture and nutrients.

Rutabagas are ready to harvest from fall onward, but there is no need to harvest them immediately as they are very tough and can remain out in the winter cold until required in the kitchen. As with turnips, in really cold areas where the ground may freeze over, they can be dug up in late fall and stored in damp sand in a garage or cellar.

## GASPARD BAUHIN

A Swiss botanist and anatomist, Gaspard Bauhin was born in Basel, the son of a French physician, and studied medicine at Padua, Montpellier, and in Germany. He was also a pioneer in binomial nomenclature and organized the names and synonyms of 6,000 species in his illustrated exposition of plants, *Pinax theatri botanici*, which has become a landmark of botanical history.

This classification system was quite basic and used traditional groups such as trees, shrubs, and herbs. He did, however, correctly group legumes, grasses, and several others. His most important contribution is in the description of genera and species. He introduced many names of genera that were adopted by Carl Linnaeus, a Swedish botanist, and which remain in use today.

"This is the plant which the English Government thought of value enough to be procured at public expense from Sweden, cultivated and dispersed. It has such advantage over the common turnep that it is spreading rapidly over England and will become their chief turnep."

Thomas Jefferson, letter to a friend, (June 1795)

**BELOW:** The rutabaga is an invaluable vegetable during the colder winter months when there is not much else available to harvest from the kitchen garden. If left to go to seed, its yellow flowers are attractive.

### Spicy rutabaga wedges

This is a dish that puts the spice into one of the more traditional vegetables, the rutabaga. These wedges make a great appetizer—try them dipped in a curry sauce, or as a side dish to traditional meals such as a pot roast.

**Preparation time:** 5 minutes
**Cooking time:** 30–35 minutes
**Serves**: 4 people

· 1lb (750g) rutabaga, peeled

· 1 tbsp olive oil

· Pinch of paprika

· Salt and pepper, to taste

Preheat a conventional oven to 400°F (200°C / gas mark 6 / fan 180°C).

Slice the rutabaga into finger-width discs. Slice again across each disc to make thin wedges.

Tip the rutabaga, olive oil, and paprika into a shallow roasting tin. Season and toss well, arranging in one layer.

Roast for 30–35 minutes, turning halfway through cooking, until golden brown.

Drain on a paper towel and lightly salt to serve.

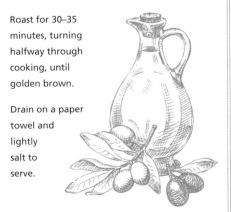

# Kale
## *Brassica oleracea* Acephala Group

**Common name:** Kale, borecole

**Type:** Annual or Biennial

**Climate:** Hardy, cold winter

**Size:** 14in (35cm)

**Origin:** Asia, Mediterranean

**History:** Kale has been cultivated for over 2,000 years and is a descendent of the wild cabbage, a plant thought to have been brought to Europe around 600 BC by groups of Celtic wanderers. In much of Europe it was the most widely eaten green vegetable until the Middle Ages when cabbages became more popular.

During World War Two, the cultivation of kale in the UK was encouraged by the 'Dig for Victory' campaign. The vegetable was easy to grow and so provided important nutrients to supplement those missing from a normal diet because of food rationing.

**Cultivation:** Kale should be sown directly outdoors into shallow drills. When they reach a height of 4in they can be transplanted to their final planting position, 18in apart. Leaves are ready for harvesting from fall until spring.

**Storage:** Kale is winter hardy so can remain in the ground until needed in the kitchen. Once picked, cook it within a day or two.

**ABOVE:** Kale is a member of the cabbage family grown for its healthy leaves. It makes an attractive addition to the garden during the winter months with its strong structure and texture.

Alternatively, cook it in dishes and freeze for eating later.

**Preparation:** Snap off the stalks; wash the kale thoroughly in cold salted water and drain. The leaves can be cooked whole or chopped up.

Kale leaves are enjoying something of a renaissance among chefs and gourmets, who admire the versatility of this leafy member of the cabbage family. It goes well with fish and meat, and is usually boiled or steamed but is equally good when used in stir-fries and casseroles. Some people may find the flavor slightly bitter, but when cooked well it provides a wonderful background flavor in soups and stews. Combine with cheese, onion, and eggs to make a delicious winter warming filo pastry pie.

Gardeners also appreciate this previously underrated vegetable for a number of reasons. First, it is fully winter hardy and fills a gap in the late

**ABOVE:** There are lots of different varieties of kale but they all have attractive foliage ranging from crinkly red-leaved varieties through to dark narrow-leaved types such as "Nero di Toscana."

winter and early spring culinary calendar when there is little else available on the plot. Second, it is more tolerant than most of the other brassica plants to poor soil and wet conditions. Kale is also valued for its fantastic-tasting and nutritionally packed leaves, and in the garden the different colors and forms can provide a beautiful tapestry of textures. In fact, they give a wonderful display when used to edge borders, which is unsurpassed by other ornamental plants in the depth of winter. Varieties such as "Red Russian" have attractive crinkly red leaves, while the dark narrow-leaved variety "Nero

di Toscana" (also called palm tree cabbage) provides an attractive visual depth to any vegetable bed.

Kale requires a fertile soil in full sun. Prior to sowing, the site should be thoroughly dug over and lots of organic matter added, such as garden compost or well-rotted manure. Seed should be sown in late spring either in pots or directly outside into shallow drills that are ½in deep. Rows should be 8in apart. When they reach a height of about 4in high they can be transplanted to their final planting position, at spacings of 18–24in, depending on the variety, in rows 24in apart. Keep the plants well watered during summer, and weed between the rows and around the plants each week to prevent any competition for nutrients and water from these hungry vegetable plants.

Kale is extremely hardy and the plants will remain resolutely outside in the freezing cold weather. When harvesting, it is best just to take a few leaves from each plant as required rather than stripping an entire plant at once as it may not recover. Harvest the lower leaves first, before using the leaves higher up later in the season.

BELOW: Kale is grown for its tasty foliage and there are many ornamental varieties to choose from. These can also be used to provide evergreen structure in herbaceous borders and flower beds.

## NUTRITION

Kale is high in iron which is essential for good health, since iron is used in the formation of hemoglobin to transport oxygen to various parts of the body, cell growth, and liver function. It is also high in vitamins A, C, and K, which help to maintain a healthy body and immune system. It is also recommended for detoxing as it is filled with fiber and sulfur.

# Cabbage
## *Brassica oleracea* Capitata Group

**Common name:** Cabbage, cabbage leaf, green cabbage

**Type:** Annual

**Climate:** Hardy, average to cold winter

**Size:** 16in (40cm)

**Origin:** Europe

**History:** The word "cabbage" is an Anglicized form of the French *caboche*, meaning "head," referring to its round bulbous shape. In addition the word *Brassica* comes from the Celtic word *bresic*, meaning "cabbage." Cabbage has been cultivated for more than 4,000 years and domesticated for over 2,500 years. Since cabbage grows well in cool climates, yields large harvests, and stores well during winter, it soon became a major crop in northern Europe.

**Cultivation:** Cabbages require a fertile soil with plenty of added organic matter in full sun. Sow in modules or in nursery beds to transplant into its final position later. Sowing times depend on when the cabbage is to be harvested during the year.

**Storage:** Most cabbages are hardy and can remain in place until required in the kitchen. On harvest, they can be stored in a cool place for several weeks or longer, depending on type.

**ABOVE:** The illustration above is a chromolithograph of cabbage varieties taken from the *Album Benary*, illustrated by Ernst Benary, and dates from 1876. The album contains 28 color plates of different vegetable varieties, named in English, German, French, and Russian.

**Preparation:** Remove the outer leaves first and cut the cabbage in half. Cut out and discard the center stalk, then wash and cut the leaves as required. Cabbage can be shredded for using raw in salads; for cooking it can be cut into thick wedges; alternatively the center can be stuffed. Shredded red cabbage is best braised.

Where would the culinary world be without cabbages? Much better off, might think many people who have had to eat overcooked, boiled cabbage. However, there are many fantastic reasons why cabbages are one of the most widely grown vegetables, as they have been for centuries. There are so many famous international dishes made from this staple vegetable, and possibly two of the best known are the fermented sauerkraut and the popular salad coleslaw, where it is thinly chopped up with other raw vegetables and mixed with mayonnaise. However, it is a wonderful hearty vegetable and has so many more uses in the kitchen. What can be more satisfying than a large bowl of mashed potatoes with steamed cabbage, garlic, onions, and Bramley apples in the depth of winter?

Cabbages look beautiful in the vegetable garden and create a wonderful tapestry of texture and color. They come in many shades including green, red, and purple, and in a range of different shapes from pointy to spherical or open. They can be smooth or crinkly and provide structure in the kitchen garden throughout the year if planted in blocks.

There are cabbages for every season and are so named after the period they are picked: summer, fall, winter, and spring. These are mainly hearting cabbages, but spring cabbages can also provide loose heads of green leaves. Savoy cabbages are a popular type of winter cabbage as are some of the white-, red-, or purple-tinted varieties, one of the most popular being "January King."

The cultivation of cabbages, whatever the season, is basically the same; the main difference is when they are harvested. Cabbages should be grown in full sun in fertile, well-drained soil. They are hungry plants so enrich the soil with plenty of organic matter prior to sowing. Most gardeners raise the seedlings in outdoor nursery beds before transplanting, but they can be grown in modules indoors or in situ if space allows.

TASTING NOTES

*Creamy coleslaw*

Coleslaw is a classic cabbage recipe and is now a popular side dish and garnish around the world. For a healthier alternative, use natural yogurt instead of mayonnaise to coat the delicious shredded vegetables.

**Preparation time:** 10 minutes
**Serves**: 10 people

• ¹/₂ white cabbage, finely shredded

• 2 large carrots, finely shredded

• 6–8 tbsp mayonnaise

• ¹/₂ red onion, thinly sliced

• 1 tsp lemon juice

• Salt and pepper, to taste

Combine the shredded cabbage and carrots in a large bowl.

Stir together the mayonnaise, onion, lemon juice, salt, and pepper in a medium bowl.

Add to the cabbage mixture. Mix well. Serve.

**RIGHT:** Cabbages provide a beautiful splash of color in the garden all year round particularly throughout the winter months. They have a variety of textures, shapes, and colors as can be seen with the facing illustration of Savoy, red, and white cabbages.

# WISE WATERING

Water is the giver of life. Without it, plants can't survive and in dry summers this can cause a real problem. However, it is important to get it right as plants can also die from being overwatered.

Water during the summer is becoming a rare commodity in certain areas and so it is important that plants are watered responsibly and with minimum wastage.

**LEFT:** Watering cans are the best way to moderate and control the amount of water to be used. Roses attached to the end of the nozzle distribute a fine spray.

### TIPS FOR RESPONSIBLE WATERING

Avoid using sprinklers as they tend to waste a lot of water and do not always provide plants directly with water at their roots. Seep hoses are more effective as they target the root area, slowly soaking water into the soil and reducing the amount of evaporation. Seep hoses can be bought from most garden retail outlets, but can simply be made by poking small holes in a standard hose with a sharp needle. Lay the hose down among the plants.

Using a watering can gives better directional control than using a hose, thereby avoiding wastage. Ideally it should be aimed at the area directly surrounding the root zone of the individual plant, avoiding the leaves. Allow the water to soak through thoroughly; placing a rose over the end of the nozzle slows down the water flow, giving it time to soak into the soil and avoid run-off. Roses are also the best way to water delicate seedlings. Creating a sump or hollow around individual plants also helps to direct water to where it is needed.

Watering is most effective in early morning or in the evening. Avoid watering during the middle of the day, particularly in warm weather, as much of the water will be lost to evaporation.

Use shade netting or shade paint in the glasshouse as this will reduce water loss and prevent the leaves from getting scorched.

Plants grown in containers and hanging baskets usually require more watering than those grown in the ground. However, their watering requirements can be reduced if they are moved into the shade during the hottest part of the day.

Set up water butts and any other water-tight collection units so that rainwater can be harvested. Attach them to the down pipes on glasshouses,

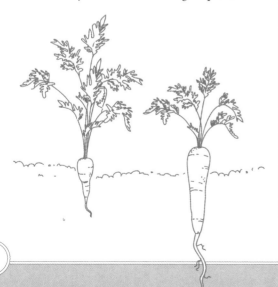

**LEFT:** Excessive watering and fertilizing can lead to lots of foliage (left) at the expense of root development. Regular but not excessive watering is better.

## When to water what

The general rule of thumb is that plants need regular watering during dry spells, but individual types of vegetables do have varying requirements.

| | |
|---|---|
| Potatoes | Regular watering is especially important during the flowering period as this is when the tubers start to form in the ground. Give them one good drenching every few days, rather than each day as little and often encourages shallow rooting. |
| Carrots | A free-draining soil is preferred, and therefore they should not be kept too moist. Overwatering will lead to an excess of leaves and a stunted root system, as it does not need to grow deeply to find moisture. |
| Onions | Avoid overwatering onions when the bulb is swollen as this will not help them cure and harden prior to harvesting. Excessive watering can also lead to fungal problems. Pulling back some of the moisture-retaining mulch will also expose the bulb to the sun and help keep it drier. |
| Cabbages | Give cabbages a thorough soaking when planting and they should only need regular watering every few days afterward. Once their heads start to form, generous amounts of watering will improve their size. |

**ABOVE:** Peas need plenty of moisture, particularly around flowering time to encourage pods to form.

garages, sheds, and the house to maximize the amount of water that can be collected.

Recycle water from baths, showers, and the kitchen sink—this is sometimes called gray water. Avoid reusing water that is contaminated with too much soap, detergents, and bleach.

Containers such as plastic cartons and bottles can have their bases removed and be buried mouth-downward next to individual plants. When topped up with water, they will slowly seep out water into the root zone, where it will be most needed.

Mulch vegetable beds with garden compost or well-rotted manure; this will help to keep moisture in the soil. Mulches also suppress weeds, which will compete with your vegetables for moisture and nutrients.

# Cauliflower
## *Brassica oleracea* Botrytis Group

**Common name:** Cauliflower

**Type:** Annual

**Climate:** Half-hardy to hardy; mild to cold winter

**Size:** 14in (35cm)

**Origin:** Mediterranean

**History:** Cauliflower can trace its ancestry to the wild cabbage and has been an important vegetable in Turkey and Italy since at least 600 BC. It became popular in France in the mid-16th century and was subsequently cultivated in northern Europe and the British Isles. The United States, France, Italy, India, and China are countries that produce significant amounts of cauliflower.

**Cultivation:** Cauliflowers prefer a fertile, well-drained soil in sun. Seeds can be started outdoors by sowing in shallow drills ½in deep in rows 8in apart and transplanted to their final position of 20in apart. Sowing times vary depending on variety and season of harvest.

**Storage:** Cauliflowers will keep better if they are stored upside down in a cool dark place. They can also be preserved as pickles and preserves, the most popular being piccalilli. Florets can be placed in containers and frozen.

**ABOVE:** The beautiful creamy white florets of the cauliflower plant makes this one of the most attractive members of the cabbage family but also one of the trickier ones to grow.

**Preparation:** Cut away the outer leaves and chop off the stem. Next cut a cross in the stump to aid in the cooking process. Wash and drain, then boil or steam. It can also be served raw in salads or dipped in batter and deep-fried.

Sometimes the simplest food is the best, and there is nothing simpler or better than the classic cauliflower cheese (see box).

Cauliflowers are probably one of the more difficult members of the cabbage family to grow, but as they are expensive in the stores and a wider range of attractive and flavorsome varieties are available from the seed companies, they are well worth the effort.

There are plenty of different varieties to choose from including orange-yellow ones, such as "Cheddar," and ones with deep purple heads, such as "Graffiti." However, even the usual white-headed dome varieties look attractive in the flower garden. Most cauliflowers produce large curds—the gardener's name for the dome-shaped flowerheads—which usually measure about 6in to 8in across. However, the modern hybrid mini cauliflowers producing curds just 4in across are becoming increasingly popular with chefs and gardeners alike.

**BELOW:** This still life painting called *Egg and Cauliflower* painted by George Washington Lambert in 1926 clearly illustrates the attractive and textural qualities of this commonly grown vegetable.

## TASTING NOTES

### *Cauliflower cheese*

Cauliflower cheese is easy to prepare and versatile. It is filling enough to be served as a main meal or as a side dish to a pot roast.

**Preparation time:** 5 minutes
**Cooking time:** 30 minutes
**Serves**: 6 people (as a side dish)

- 2½oz (75g) butter

- 2oz (50g) all-purpose flour

- 1¾ pints (1l) milk

- 4oz (100g) cheddar cheese, grated (plus 1oz/25g grated for topping)

- 1 medium cauliflower, cooked florets

- 4 slices white bread, breadcrumbs

- 2floz (75ml) crème fraîche

Melt three-quarters of the butter in a saucepan and stir in the flour. Cook for 1 minute.

Gradually add the milk, stirring to a smooth sauce. Simmer for 15–20 minutes until thick, then sprinkle in half of the cheese.

Melt most of the remaining butter in a pan and fry the cauliflower until slightly browned. Spoon into a baking dish.

Put the rest of the butter into the pan, add the breadcrumbs, and fry until golden.

Stir the remaining cheese into the sauce until it melts and add the crème fraîche.

Pour the sauce over cooked cauliflower florets.

Cauliflowers can be produced almost all year round by choosing the correct varieties and sowing them at the right time. However, winter types are technically not ready until springtime, and if you are short on growing areas in the vegetable patch then they are probably not worth it as they take up so much space.

The skill with growing a cauliflower is to get the curd to develop regularly and not be misshapen. This means regular watering throughout the growing season. Very hot summers can cause problems as cauliflowers prefer slightly cooler conditions than many other vegetables.

They prefer a fertile, well-drained soil. Well-rotted manure or garden compost should be dug into the soil prior to planting as this not only enriches the soil, but, more importantly, will also help to retain the moisture and prevent the plant from drying out; a common cause of misshapen cauliflowers. Avoid acidic soil as this can cause club root, a soil-borne fungus that causes a misshapen root system. A dressing of lime can be added to temporarily increase the alkalinity of the soil.

Get seeds started outdoors by sowing them in shallow drills ½in deep in rows 8in apart either in a prepared seedbed or in trays of potting compost. Seedlings should be thinned to 2in apart. Once they have produced about five or six leaves they should be transplanted to their final position and planted about 19½in apart. Sowing times vary depending on variety and season of harvest. Check the seed packet for details.

**ABOVE:** Historic cauliflower varieties from 1904. "Easter Winter," "Scilly Black," and "Chalon Early" by Vilmorin-Andrieux. None of these are now commerically available.

During the growing season the leaves should be folded over the curd to prevent it discoloring in the sun. Plants should be covered with a protective mesh or fleece to prevent attack from birds and insects.

The summer and fall varieties are usually ready about 16 weeks from sowing in spring. Winter varieties are ready about 40 weeks from sowing. Cut through the base of the stem with a sharp knife as and when they are needed in the kitchen. They will keep for about three weeks if stored in a dark, cool place.

**LEFT:** Cauliflowers are usually eaten for their attractive central florets but the luscious green rosettes of leaves are just as tasty as other cabbage varieties when boiled or steamed.

"Training is everything. A peach was once a bitter almond;
a cauliflower is nothing but a cabbage with a college education."

**Mark Twain,** *Pudd'nhead Wilson*, (1894)

# Pak choi
## *Brassica oleracea* Chinensis Group

**Common name**: Pak choi, bok choi, Chinese chard, Chinese mustard, celery mustard, Chinese cabbage, spoon cabbage

**Type:** Annual

**Climate:** Half-hardy, mild winter

**Size:** 12in (30cm)

**Origin:** South China

**History:** Records show that pak choi was first cultivated in south China as far back as the 5th century AD. By the 19th century, pak choi plantations were found in Japan and south Malaya. Pak choi was not introduced to Europe until the mid-18th century when in 1751, Pehr Osbeck (see p.74), a friend of the famed botanist Carl Linnaeus, brought seeds of the vegetable to Europe, making its cultivation very popular.

**Cultivation:** Seeds can be sown under glass in early spring or directly in the open in midspring in shallow drills. Make sowings every few weeks throughout summer to regularly harvest either the baby leaves, or the semimature or full-headed plants.

**Storage:** The leaves and mature heads should be used fresh from the garden. They will only keep for a few days in the fridge, although they will last for much longer if made into soups and other dishes and frozen.

**Preparation:** Wash thoroughly. The leaves can be cut from the stems, as they cook at different speeds—the leaves cook much quicker, so you could add for 2 minutes just toward the end of cooking. Alternatively, to put leaves and stems in the pan at the same time, cut the stems into thin strips. Very young pak choi can be left whole; larger plants can be halved or quartered.

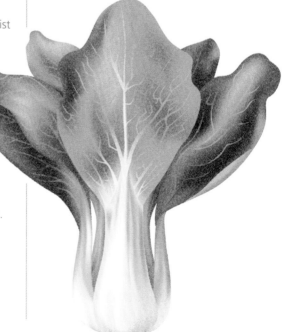

**RIGHT:** Pak choi is also known as bok choi and is a member of the cabbage family, grown for its tasty foliage. It is often used in Asian cuisine, particularly in Chinese and Japanese recipes.

Pak choi is also confusingly known as bok choi, but it is exactly the same vegetable. It is part of the ever-growing popularity among chefs and gardeners for a taste of the exotic—valued for its spicy, flavorsome leaves from the Far East. Seed catalogs and even grocery store shelves have a range of exciting Asia vegetables to try including Chinese lettuce, Japanese mustard spinach (also known as komatsuna), Japanese turnip, and chopsuey greens. All these vegetables have opened up a whole new culinary world not just as mature vegetables but also when grown as micro greens (baby leaf vegetables eaten young as seedlings).

Pak choi is one of the most popular vegetables in Asian cuisine. It is used in salads and stir-fries when grown for its micro leaves, but it is also used in a range of dishes when it is allowed more time to develop its fully grown head. Leaves can be eaten raw or can be lightly steamed.

For those of you impatient to harvest your first crop, the good news is that it takes merely 30 days from sowing to the picking of its first leaves. However, it takes approximately 45 to 80 days if the semimature or full-sized head is required, depending on the weather. As with most members of the cabbage family, pak choi requires a sunny position in fertile soil. For those with limited space, it can also be grown in a window box, making it easy to harvest the leaves for a salad whenever required. Seeds can be sown any time from midspring through to midsummer; sow them thinly at about ½in deep. Rows should be about 12in apart if the plants are being grown for their young, baby leaves, but slightly wider if they are going to develop into mature plants with full-sized heads. In mild areas it is possible to sow

TASTING NOTES

### Stir-fried pak choi

This recipe is healthy and can be made as spicy as you like by adding more chilli. It is an ideal accompaniment to a bed of rice or mixed in with egg noodles in a stir-fry.

**Preparation time:** 5 minutes
**Cooking time:** 5 minutes
**Serves**: 2 people (as an appetizer)

• 2 tbsp sunflower oil

• 1½in (4cm / thumb length) root ginger, peeled and finely chopped

• 1–2 red chillies, finely sliced

• 3 cloves of garlic, chopped finely

• 2 pak choi, stalks finely sliced, leaves roughly sliced

• Salt, to taste

• ½ tsp soy sauce

• ½ tsp sesame oil

Heat the sunflower oil in a large frying pan or wok until very hot. Add the ginger, followed by the chilli and garlic.

Then immediately add the pak choi stalks and quickly stir.

Cook for 1 minute then add the leaves and stir until just wilting; takes about 1 minute. Then remove from heat.

Add the salt, a shake of soy sauce, and a few drops of sesame oil and serve.

them under cloches or fleece for an early spring start, or to extend the season into the fall.

Seedlings should be thinned out to 24in apart if growing for baby leaves and about 12in apart for the full-sized heads. Instead of throwing the thinnings on the compost heap, they can be eaten as delicious microgreens.

**PEHR OSBECK**

Pehr Osbeck was a Swedish explorer and naturalist. He was born in 1723 and studied at Uppsala, Sweden, with botanist Carl Linnaeus. In 1750, he traveled to Asia and spent four months studying the flora, fauna, and people of Canton in China. His studies led him to

contribute more than 600 species of plant to Linnaeus's *Species Plantarum* (*The Species of Plants*) in 1753.

**ABOVE:** Pak Choi will need watering most days during dry periods as they are prone to bolting to seed. Fresh baby leaves can be picked just a few weeks after sowing or the plants can be left to develop a head. The baby plants can be removed and eaten, and the remaining plants left at 12in spacings to mature.

As the plants continue to grow it is important that they are watered every few days as in warm or dry weather they can be prone to bolting (quickly growing to seed, making the leaves taste bitter) in warm or dry weather. "Joy Choi" is a good variety to try as it does have some bolting resistance. Other popular varieties include the dark-leaved "Baraku," "Choko," "Glacier," "Ivory," "Red Choi," and "Summer Breeze."

The leaves can be picked at any stage three to four weeks after sowing. Pick them young as the older leaves can become tough. The mature heads can be harvested by cutting through the stem with a knife. Leave the stump in place, though, as it should resprout more baby leaves for harvesting a few weeks later. The flowerhead can also be harvested and cooked in stir-fries.

# Brussels sprout
## *Brassica oleracea* Gemmifera Group

**Common name:** Brussels sprout, cruciferous, sprout

**Type:** Annual

**Climate:** Hardy, average to cold winter

**Size:** 24in (60cm)

**Origin:** Belgium

**History:** Sprouts are believed to have been cultivated in Italy in Roman times, and possibly as early as the 1200s in Belgium. Records show that they were cultivated in large quantities in Belgium as early as 1587 (hence the name "Brussels" sprouts). They remained a local crop in this area until their use spread across Europe during World War One. Brussels sprouts are now cultivated throughout Europe and the United States. California is the center for Brussels sprout production in North America.

**ABOVE:** The humble Brussels sprout is a commonly used vegetable during the winter months due to its ability to withstand very cold conditions.

**Cultivation:** Sow seeds in drills in spring into fertile soil in full sun. Plants should eventually be about 20 to 30in apart and may need to be supported with a stake to prevent them blowing over in the wind. Pick from fall onward and throughout winter.

**Storage:** The best way to store sprouts is to keep them on the plant until they are needed in the kitchen. They are fully winter hardy and so will be fine even in the depth of winter. Once picked they will keep in the fridge for a couple of weeks.

**Preparation:** Remove any damaged and wilted leaves and cut off the stems. If the sprouts are large some people believe it is best to cut a cross in the base to allow the thick part to cook at the same time as the leaves. Wash the sprouts to remove any dirt and pests. Brussels sprouts may be boiled in salted water for 8–10 minutes or steamed for about 15 minutes until tender.

"Brussels sprouts are a winter vegetable of great worth, each stem a column of close-packed and firm buttons with a small loose cabbage or bunch of greens at the top."

Charles Boff, *How to Grow and Produce Your Own Food*, (1946)

Brussels sprouts must be the most maligned vegetable in the world, with many people associating them with hard, bitter bullets that have to be suffered just once a year at Christmas dinner. However, with a little imagination they can be cooked in many different ways, including steamed, stir-fried, or added to numerous dishes, meaning there should always be some way of enjoying this very healthy and nutritional stalwart of the vegetable kingdom. Depending on variety, they can be picked from as early as August, although their flavor is considered to be better if they have been sweetened by the fall frosts. Some sprouts will last well into late winter and early spring. At the end of the season their leafy "sprout tops" can be removed and cooked.

When in crop, Brussels sprout plants can be top heavy. Some gardeners recommend not digging over the ground immediately prior to planting as this loosens the soil, meaning that sprouts are more prone to toppling over in the wind. However, plenty of organic matter should be added to the soil in the fall before planting as Brussels sprouts, like other members of the cabbage family, are hungry plants requiring a fertile and moist but well-drained soil in full sun. Ideally the soil should not be too acidic, and if this is the case, a dressing of lime can be added to make the pH between 6.5 and 7.

**BELOW:** To cross or not to cross—in the sprout world chefs are divided as to whether or not cutting a cross through the base of the sprout is beneficial to the cooking process.

## TASTING NOTES

### Brussels sprout alternatives

If you do not like Brussels sprouts then blame Belgium as it is supposed to have originated from there, hence the name "Brussels."

There are now modern varieties that are sweeter than the traditional varieties such as "Trafalgar," which is said to have reduced some of the bitterness. Alternatively there are interesting crosses between kale and Brussels sprouts such as *Brassica* "Petit Posy Mix" that produce rosettes of loose frilly edged buttons in an attractive mix of purple and green colors. The flavor is closer to eating spring greens, but it is a good substitute for those who feel that there should be a sprout-related vegetable on the Thanksgiving or Christmas dinner plate. Finally, if you really cannot face a side dish of sprouts on their own, there are lots of delicious recipes (see p.77).

Sprouts can be sown indoors in modules in February and planted out in spring. Alternatively, they can be sown directly outdoors into a nursery or seed bed in March ready for planting in their final position later.

Sprouts are usually ready for transplanting into their final position about five weeks after sowing or when the seedlings have reached a height of 4in. Spacing should be between 20 and 28in depending on the size and height of the individual variety. Rows should be 29in apart and the plants should be firmed in after planting to prevent them being rocked in the wind. As the plants grow they will require staking to prevent them being blown over. Alternatively, some gardeners prefer to mound soil around the base to steady them. Weeds should be often removed from around the plants and watering should be carried out regularly to retain the moisture that they require to produce their good sprouts.

Remove any sprouts that have unfurled, called "blown" in the horticultural world. Leave the sprouts on the plant until required for cooking as they only keep for a couple of weeks after harvesting. Pick the lower sprouts first and work your way up the plant as the season continues into winter. They can be picked by hand by giving them a sharp, downward tug.

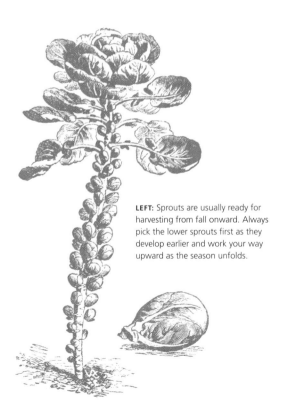

**LEFT:** Sprouts are usually ready for harvesting from fall onward. Always pick the lower sprouts first as they develop earlier and work your way upward as the season unfolds.

## TASTING NOTES

### *Pancetta and thyme Brussels sprouts*

The thyme and pancetta in this recipe balance out any bitterness of Brussels sprouts. Bacon can be substituted for pancetta if preferred.

**Preparation time:** 15 minutes
**Cooking time:** 25 minutes
**Serves**: 10 people (as a side dish)

· 2lb (1kg) Brussels sprouts

· 3 tbsp olive oil

· 4oz (100g) pancetta, diced

· 1 tbsp thyme, chopped

· Salt and pepper, to taste

Preheat a conventional oven to 400°F (200°C / gas mark 6 / fan 180°C).

Blanch the Brussels sprouts in a pan of boiling, salted water for 3 minutes.

Drain and tip into a bowl of iced water to cool quickly. Drain again, quarter, and set aside.

Heat the olive oil in a pan. Add the pancetta and cook until slightly crisp.

Slowly spoon in the Brussels sprouts and toss with the oil and pancetta to coat evenly.

Sprinkle over the freshly chopped thyme and season with salt and pepper.

Bake in the oven for about 10–15 minutes until nicely caramelized. Serve.

# Kohlrabi

## *Brassica oleracea* Gongylodes Group

**Common name:** Kohlrabi, stem turnip, turnip cabbage

**Type:** Annual

**Climate:** Half-hardy, mild winter

**Size:** 16in (40cm)

**Origin:** Europe

**History:** Kohlrabi is a German word meaning cabbage turnip, *kohl* meaning cabbage and *rabi* meaning "turnip." Charlemagne, who was crowned emperor of the Holy Roman Empire in AD 800, ordered kohlrabi to be grown in the lands under his reign. Charlemagne, although connected with the French empire, was actually from Aix-la-Chapelle, which is now called Aachen and located in Germany. This accounts for kohlrabi's German name. Marcus Gavious Apicius, who wrote the oldest known book on cooking and dining in imperial Rome, mentions kohlrabi in his recipes.

The first description of kohlrabi was, however, written by a European botanist in 1554. By the end of the 16<sup>th</sup> century it was known in Germany, England, Italy, Spain, Tripoli, and the eastern Mediterranean. It was not until 1734 in Ireland and 1837 in England that kohlrabi was grown on a large scale.

**ABOVE:** Kohlrabi resembles something more likely found in outer space than in the garden, but this member of the cabbage family has both an edible swollen stem and leaves.

**LEFT:** Charlemagne was the emperor of the Holy Roman Empire and in AD 800 he ordered that kohlrabi should be grown throughout his land. The name is German, meaning "cabbage turnip."

**Cultivation:** Sow seeds from early winter onward in a shallow ½in drill. Thin the plants out to 8in spacing once they have germinated. Alternatively, they can be sown indoors in modules and planted out in spring.

**Storage:** Kohlrabi will keep in the fridge for a couple of weeks, but the leaves should be removed as they leach out the moisture. Ideally, keep kohlrabi outside and harvest as needed.

**Preparation:** Remove the leaves and top and tail the swollen stem. Use a potato peeler to remove the skin. It can then be sliced or cut into wedges. To cook, simply boil it in salted water for 20–30 minutes, steam for 30–40 minutes, or fry it in butter. If served raw it can be grated to add sweetness to a winter salad.

This lesser known member of the cabbage family is a gourmet delight for food connoisseurs as it has a distinctive nutty flavor mildly reminiscent of celery. It is hard to find in stores and can be expensive to buy. The swollen stem can be roasted, steamed, or stir-fried, and the leaves can also be cooked in the same way as cabbage. It is often cooked in soups but can also be eaten raw in salads and is a good alternative to cabbage in coleslaw. It is a bit of a quirky curiosity with its strange-looking, swollen round stem. The leaves not only sprout from the top but also spiral out from the sides, making a great talking point among gardeners and cooks alike.

It is part of the cabbage family and its mild taste is not too dissimilar to another family member, the turnip, but with a crunchier texture. The skin is usually purple or green, the former usually being slightly hardier, and both have a white flesh.

Like all brassicas, it needs a really fertile, moist but well-drained soil to encourage it to fully develop. They should be grown in full sun and with

**LEFT:** Purple varieties of kohlrabi, such as "Purple Danube" can be grown as spring annuals in the flower garden—they are that colorful.

## NUTRITION

Kohlrabi is low in saturated fat and cholesterol, which makes for a healthier heart and circulatory system. It also contains high levels of vitamins B and C including B6 thiamin, riboflavin, niacin, pantothenic acid, and folate, helping to boost immunity, increase metabolic rate, and maintain healthy skin and hair.

The edible part of [...] hi is not a root but a sw[...] m that grows just abo[...] round. The aromatic le[...] be eaten raw or substit[...] kale leaves in recipes.

plenty of well-rotted organic matter d[...] well before planting.

Sowing can be st[...] ed under glass in late winter for an early cr[...] or they can be sown directly in open gr[...] a from spring onward. They usually take ab[...] 6–8 weeks to mature. Frequent sowings can [...] e made every few weeks so that there are regular crops from summer until early winter. Keep the area surrounding the kohlra[...] eed-free by hoeing between the rows every o[...] r two weeks. Watering is less important than for ot[...] members of the cabbage family, but it is impo[...] nt to keep moisture levels constant as otherwi[...] he plants have a tendency to split.

Vegetabl[...] usually harvested when they are about [...] ze of a baseball, but some varieties can [...] uge, as big as 60lb. Other varieties worth trying include "Adriana," "Erko," "Kolibri," "Korist," "Lanro," "Olivia," "Quickstar," and "Rapidstar," or the purple variety "Purple Danube" as it looks beautiful in the vegetable patch although it is slower growing and can be tougher. If kohlrabi is left for too long in the ground it becomes slightly woody and much less palatable. Kohlrabi should not need storing as it can be kept in the ground until required. However, like many other root crops it can be picked and buried in trays of damp sand.

# Calabrese and broccoli
## *Brassica oleracea* Italica Group

**Common name:** Calabrese: green broccoli and broccoli. Broccoli: purple sprouting, purple cauliflower, purple-hearting

**Type:** Annual or Biennial

**Climate:** Calabrese is more tender: half-hardy to tender, mild winter. Broccoli is hardier: Hardy, average to cold winter

**Size:** 18–40in (45–100cm)

**Origin:** Asia and the Mediterranean region, particularly Italy

**History:** Broccoli is a member of the cabbage family and it evolved from a wilder version in Europe. The history of the wild cabbage dates back over 2,000 years; it would have been a popular food in Roman times. The Italians developed broccoli in the 17th century, and from there it spread across the rest of Europe. Broccoli is still very popular in Italy and the name is derived from *broccolo*, referring to the "flowering top of a cabbage." It was Italian immigrants who brought the plants to America.

**Cultivation:** Sow calabrese and broccoli from early spring to early summer. They require a fertile, well-drained soil in full sun. Calabrese do not like to have their roots disturbed so should be grown directly in situ 12in apart. Broccoli can be sown indoors in pots or modules, or in nursery beds, and should eventually be planted out at 24in apart.

**RIGHT:** Often called broccoli in the grocery stores, this large-headed green vegetable is properly known as calabrese. It is grown for its delicious flowerheads, stems, and leaves.

**Storage:** They should be harvested before the flowers open and can remain in the fridge for a few days after harvesting. Florets can also be frozen for using later in the year.

**Preparation:** Remove florets from the plant as required, wash them under running water, and then eat either raw in salads, or more commonly boiled or steamed. They can also be added to stir-fries.

You would not be blamed for getting confused about broccoli and calabrese. Calabrese is the large-headed, greenish-blue vegetable with chunky stems that is commonly available in the grocery stores, but confusingly labeled as broccoli. Yet what most gardeners refer to when talking about broccoli is the much less commonly seen purple or white sprouting broccoli that has much smaller florets. As if that is not confusing enough, there is also the quirky looking, lime-green "Romanesco" variety (see p.84), sometimes referred to as a calabrese, sometimes a cauliflower, and sometimes a broccoli!

Despite the confusion, the good news is that they are all closely related, delicious, easy to grow, and are packed full of nutritional goodness, meaning that whichever type of broccoli you grow,

you will be rewarded with a vegetable that can be used in a wide range of exciting dishes. They can be added to pasta and coated with garlic and tomato sauces, mixed with chillies and Parmesan. They can also be puréed down into soups. The "Romanesco" variety has a deliciously rich and nutty flavor and can be made into a version of cauliflower cheese, with plenty of crème fraiche, Parmesan, and a topping of breadcrumbs. Finally, for a touch of indulgence and decadence, try cooking up the florets in batter and dipping them into a sweet-and-sour sauce.

### Sprouting broccoli

Many people consider the sprouting varieties to have a superior taste to the standard calabrese, which is why it is more commonly seen in public kitchen gardens with restaurants attached, enabling the chef to go out and harvest florets as and when required. The flavor has been compared by many to

**BELOW:** Purple sprouting broccoli has smaller florets than calabrese and is a useful crop for filling the spring gap in the harvesting calendar, being ready from late winter onward.

a mixture of asparagus and cauliflower, and it is stronger flavored than calabrese. It makes an attractive-looking plant, producing its small edible florets at the top of the plant, but also on side shoots. There are purple and creamy white types, with the former considered to be slightly hardier in the garden. If you are likely to forget to sow seeds each year, then you can try the perennial form called "Nine Star Perennial," which will keep cropping for five or so years, if it is harvested each season.

Sprouting broccoli is wonderfully versatile in the kitchen because the leaves and stalks can also be eaten and added to stir-fries. One of the many benefits of growing this plant is that it provides a crop in the gap between the last of the winter vegetables and before the new season starts.

They have a long growing season, meaning it is probably not an ideal plant if space is short. They take almost a year from when they are sown in midspring to harvesting from later winter. However, quick growing catch crops such as radishes and cut-and-come-again leaves can be sown in between rows if space is tight.

Seeds should be sown in spring, either outdoors in nursery beds or in modules in a glasshouse or sunny windowsill. If sowing in pots, place two seeds in each and thin them out to one after germination. In a nursery bed they should be sown thinly in shallow drills and thinned out to 6in after germination. When the seedlings are about 3in to 4in tall they can be planted out in rows at their final spacing of 24in between each plant, and 24in between each row. Plants that were raised indoors

**ABOVE:** Calabrese should be grown in fertile soil in full sun. It is not particularly hardy and so should be harvested before the first of the frosts arrive in fall.

will benefit from being hardened off for a few days in a cold frame or porch before being planted outside.

Purple sprouting broccoli requires a sheltered position in full sun. Like other members of the cabbage family, they are not ideal in acidic soil due to their susceptibility to the club root fungus. If this is a problem, then a dressing of lime should be applied to increase the pH to about 6.5 to 7. The plants will need to be kept weed-free to avoid competition for nutrients and moisture.

Harvesting begins in late winter. The tiny florets should simply be snapped off as they begin to swell, but before they open up as flowers. If the flowers do open, the plants at least look attractive with their rich yellow flowers against the dark green foliage early in the year. Regularly pick over the plant from late winter to midspring, because if the buds do open the plant will go over quickly and stop producing a crop. Excess amounts of florets can be frozen.

## "*Romanesco*"

The "Romanesco" is a bizarre-looking variety, with tightly whorled, pointed florets in an almost alien-type of florescent green. The texture looks like something you are more likely to see as coral at the bottom of an ocean bed, rather than in a vegetable bed. Among connoisseurs it is supposed to have the finest flavors of all the broccoli/cauliflower types, with a sweet herbaceous nuttyness. In many potagers and kitchen gardens it is used almost as much as a decorative feature as it is as an edible crop. It is hardier than calabrese and is usually harvested in the gap after calabrese has finished in the fall and before the sprouting types have started in late winter.

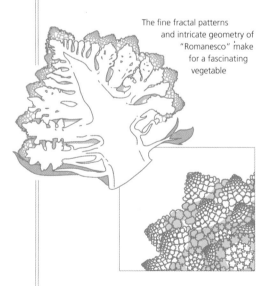

The fine fractal patterns and intricate geometry of "Romanesco" make for a fascinating vegetable

**ABOVE:** "Romanesco" a fantastic but quirky addition to the kitchen garden and is a useful "filler" as it is ready for harvesting after calabrese and before purple sprouting broccoli.

## HOW TO GROW CALABRESE

If you are short of space, yet want to grow a broccoli-type of vegetable, then grow this one rather than the purple/white sprouting type. It is much faster growing and can be harvested in time for the fall crops to be sown and planted, such as fava beans and garlic. However, it is not particularly hardy, and must be harvested before the fall. It is grown for its one large central head, although after harvesting some varieties will continue to produce side shoots with smaller florets. "Romanesco" types (see box) do not produce side shoots after being cut and should be dug up and added to the compost heap after harvesting.

Calabrese requires a fertile site in full sun with a well-drained soil. Add lots of organic matter to the soil well before planting as this will help to retain the moisture during summer. Unlike brocolli, calabrese do not like to have their root system disturbed and for that reason are sown directly in the place they are to grow for the season.

Use the corner of a draw hoe to create a shallow drill and then sow "stations" or "clusters" of three seeds every 12in. Rows should also be 12in apart. After germination, the seedlings should be thinned out to 1 per station. Calabrese should be kept weed-free and well watered during the summer.

The heads should be ready for harvesting about 12 weeks after sowing and be cut before the buds open. Keep an eye out for subsequent smaller heads from the side shoots that can also be harvested and eaten. The calabrese should be eaten soon after harvesting, but if there is a glut, the head can be chopped up into florets and frozen.

# Mizuna
## *Brassica rapa* var. *nipposinica*

**Common names**: Mizuna green, shui cai, kyona, Japanese mustard, potherb mustard, Japanese greens

**Type:** Annual

**Climate:** Half-hardy, mild winter

**Size:** 12in (30cm)

**Origin:** China

**History:** Mizuna is native to China, though it is considered a Japanese green as it has been cultivated there for several centuries. The name for this leafy green comes from the Japanese *mizu*, meaning "water," and *nu*, meaning "mustard plant."

**BELOW:** Mizuna hails from China and is popular in Asian cuisine. It has a slightly mustardy flavor and can be grown as a cut-and-come-again plant, harvesting leaves regularly as required.

**Cultivation:** Sow directly into the soil between March and August in shallow drills about ½in deep. Grow as cut-and-come-again leaves and thin seedlings to 2in apart, or grow as larger plants and thin to 8in apart.

**Storage:** Like any salad leaf, mizuna does not last long after being put in the fridge so are better being harvested as and when they are needed in the kitchen.

**Preparation:** Mizuna has a mild flavor that is almost sweet, with a faint hint of a mustardy tang. When fresh and in good condition, the plant is crisp with a bright, clear flavor and a hint of a crunch, adding texture as well as flavor to the dishes it is included in. It is an Asian green that can be eaten raw (in salads) or cooked.

Mizuna and mibuna are two types of "cut-and-come-again" Japanese leafy vegetables that are becoming increasingly popular with foodies who like to pep up their salads or stir-fries with peppery, mustard-flavored leaves. Very similar to mizuna, but with more of a punch, is the similarly named mibuna. Both are worth trying in raw in salads or side dishes, or adding to soups.

Mizuna and mibuna plants can either be grazed as cut-and-come-again every few weeks after sowing, or if left in the ground they form heads or rosettes with the dissected leaves. Looking very much like arugula, they can be harvested with a pair of scissors at the base of each plant when young, and allowed to resprout. Or they can be left to mature to form semimature or mature cabbage heads. The foliage is decorative with its serrated, dark leaves held aloft on white stalks, making them both a popular feature for edging flower borders and garnishing dinner plates. A variety called "Mizuna Purple" has particularly attractive purple stems. The young flower stems can also be cooked.

Whereas pak choi can be prone to bolting in dry weather, mizuna and mibuna tend to be less prone to this problem. Mizuna and mibuna are easy to grow and tolerate moderately cool and damp conditions, but they can struggle in very dry conditions and will need frequent watering every few days.

Seed should be sown directly into the soil any time between March and August in shallow drills about ½in deep. Rows should be 12in apart. It is best to make regular sowings throughout the season so that the salad leaves are ready to harvest at different stages throughout spring and summer. To do this, grow them in short rows every

### BOLTING

Bolting is often caused by the plant becoming stressed, often by a hot or cold spell. Usually it is caused by a dry spell just after sowing the seed. It causes the plant to panic, send out a flower shoot, and go to seed very quickly. Usually the few leaves that have been produced taste bitter and aren't worth eating. Sowing early when it is cooler can help to mitigate this problem. Alternatively there are bolt-resistant varieties that can be grown. Finally, regularly watering the plant after sowing should help to avoid the problem.

2–3 weeks, rather than just one sowing in a single long row. Remember to eat the thinnings as microgreens—see p.85 for how best to space the plant.

For a really early crop it is possible to grow them under glass in February in pots. Place them in a cold frame to harden them off for a few days before planting them outdoors.

Cut-and-come-again crops can usually be harvested up to fives times for baby leaves throughout the season, after which time they can be dug up and composted or left to grow large. Larger heads should be harvested just below the rosette, using a sharp knife.

# Canna lily
## *Canna indica*

**Common name:** Canna lily, Queensland arrowroot, Indian shot plant

**Type:** Rhizomatous perennial

**Climate:** Half-hardy, mild winter

**Size:** 5¼ft (1.6m)

**Origin:** North and South America

**History:** Canna lilies have been used as a food crop for thousands of years, but they were not well known to European botanists until the 1500s, and it was not until the late 1800s, the Victorian era, that they became widely popular as ornamental plants. Unfortunately these lilies were largely lost in gardens because European gardeners stopped growing cannas during the upheaval from World War One through World War Two. In addition, garden fashions changed. In the first half of the 20th century, garden designers, such as Gertrude Jekyll, replaced formal-looking Victorian gardens with informal, relaxed perennial borders. This led gardeners to abandon many plants used by the previous generation, including the canna.

**Cultivation:** Grow them in fertile, well-drained soil with lots of well-rotted organic matter. Grow them from rhizomes or as plants bought from a garden center.

**Storage:** Store the rhizomes in a dark place such as a paper bag in a cupboard for a few weeks until ready to use.

**Preparation:** Canna root does not store well so it is best left in the ground until ready for use. It can be eaten raw, but is often boiled. The best method of preparation is to bake it. Rinse the canna root in clean water, dry it using a paper towel, then cut it into small pieces. The root may be cubed, diced, or julienned. Fill a pot with water and bring to the boil, then place the root into boiling water for 10–15 minutes. Cooking time will vary based on how small the root is chopped.

**RIGHT:** The beautiful ornamental canna lily has deliciously tasty roots. Do not confuse it with other types of lilies that are not edible.

Cannas are more commonly seen in subtropical borders and bedding displays than in the kitchen garden. Their huge, lush, and glossy leaves hold aloft spikes of fiery colored flowers, yet underground, cannas offer a gourmet alternative for people who like to try something a bit different. This Amazonian root vegetable produces sweet rhizomes that can be cooked and treated like the potato or a Jerusalem artichoke. Whether you prefer mash or French fries, simply substitute the roots of this exotic-looking plant for the potato, although they usually need boiling for longer to break down the more fibrous structure. Canna chips make for an impressive recipe to serve to friends. In South America the leaves are wrapped around meat, fish, and poultry; they are also used in rice dishes and can be baked, steamed, or broiled.

**LEFT:** Canna lilies are beautiful, architectural plants with bright flowers. Their roots are commonly known as arrowroot.

Plant cannas in a sunny, sheltered site in well-drained soil. Several weeks before planting, dig in lots of organic matter, such as well-rotted manure into the ground, as the large glossy leaves need plenty of moisture and nourishment to keep them going.

For those on a lower budget, the plants can simply be grown from a packet of rhizomes rather than buying plants. In March, place individual

**ABOVE:** Harvesting the canna lilies' roots should be done toward the end of the growing season when the plants are tall and mature.

## PERPETUATING CANNAS

- Gently dig up canna rhizomes with a fork in the fall months, taking care not to damage the root system.

- Select some of the plumper rhizomes for cooking by carefully breaking them off—do not remove more than about a third.

- Leave the remaining rhizomes attached to the plant—these are needed for next year.

- Cut back the stems and foliage.

- Place the remaining rhizomes in compost or moist sand over winter in a cool, frost-free place. Do not let them get too wet as they will rot, but at the same time do not let them dry out.

- Plant the overwintered rhizomes out again in late spring.

In milder areas overwintering cannas do not have to be stored indoors but can simply be replanted after harvesting. For frost protection, cover them with a 6in-deep mulch to protect the base of the plant during winter. There may be some losses but it is much easier than having to store them over winter.

rhizomes into plastic pots full of general-purpose compost and keep them in a warm place in a heated glasshouse, conservatory, or windowsill, remembering to water them regularly. They can be planted out in late spring after the risk of frost has passed. However, if purchased from the garden center, avoid eating them for the first year as they may have been treated with chemicals. Wait until the following year, when the chemical should no longer be present. There are lots of different varieties to try and some will be better than others, so it is worth experimenting with a few different types.

Some of the taller plants will need to be staked to prevent the plants collapsing on each other. Keep them weed-free throughout the growing season and regularly watered.

# SMALL SPACES

Vegetable growing is possible in the tiniest of spaces. If space is restricted, then it makes sense to only grow the vegetables that you really love and cannot buy in the store. In many ways, growing in a small space is better as it helps concentrate your efforts on the vegetables you really want to grow, it avoids gluts, and, for people who are time-poor, maintenance and management is far easier. Vegetables can be grown anywhere including roof gardens, balconies, and small courtyard gardens.

**ABOVE:** Rhubarb will tolerate shade, making it ideal for growing at the base of north-facing walls and fences, or in the shade of a shed or house.

## GROWING IN SHADE

In many urban gardens, shade is a problem as there are lots of buildings casting their shadows over all or part of the garden. This can initially make it appear tricky for vegetable growing, but there are many crops that will tolerate shade. They generally tend to be the leafy crops, such as lettuces, spinach, Swiss chard, and cut-and-come-again crops, as they produce more leaves when light levels are lower. Plants that produce fruits, such as tomatoes, eggplants, squashes, and zucchinis should be avoided. The cabbage family, such as sprouts, broccoli, kohlrabi, and kale will only tolerate light shade. Most of the root family including carrots, beet, turnips, and potatoes require at least half a day of sun.

Rhubarb thrives in shady conditions, needs hardly any attention, and will smother out any weeds.

## VERTICAL WALLS

Structures can be attached to walls with irrigation systems, enabling vegetable plants to be grown on vertical structures. It is important to ensure that the vegetables are either shade tolerant or are not casting shade over each other. Careful monitoring of their watering requirements is also needed.

## CONTAINERS

Vegetables can be grown in almost any container, so long as there is enough space for the roots to develop and they have a drainage hole in the bottom. Vegetables grown in containers will require much more watering and feeding than if they were grown in the ground. In warm weather they may need watering as often

**LEFT:** Vegetables can be grown in almost any type of container. Even an old gardening boot with a drainage hole is suitable.

> "The possessor of an acre, or a smaller portion, may receive a real pleasure, from observing the progress of vegetation ... A very limited tract, properly attended to, will furnish ample employment for an individual."
>
> **Vicesimus Knox**, *Essays Moral and Literary*, (1778)

as once or twice a day and feeding once a week with a liquid fertilizer during the growing season. One of the benefits of growing in a container is that they can be moved into the shade if the heat gets too much. Containers may also benefit from being turned during the day so that all sides of the container receive the sun.

### RAISED BEDS

If your back or front garden is covered in concrete or patio slabs, then do not despair. Raised beds could be the answer. Growing vegetables in this manner is low maintenance, allows for easy weeding, and saves on all that back-bending work. Vegetables in raised beds usually have better drainage and ripen earlier as the soil within them warms up more quickly. The raised beds should be filled with the very best, loam-based compost, meaning the vegetables have the greatest possible growing conditions.

### USING RECYCLED MATERIALS

Potatoes can be grown in an old trash can or in a stack of old car tires, with more types and soil simply added to the stack as the foliage grows. They can also be grown in large builder's bags, simply unrolling the bag and topping up with more compost as they grow.

Plants such as zucchinis, pumpkins, and squashes can also be grown on the top of builder's bags filled with compost.

### PLANTS SUITABLE FOR WINDOW BOXES

A window box just outside the kitchen is ideal for growing leaves. They are easy to maintain and regular sowings can be made every few weeks to ensure there is always a plentiful supply.

Most vegetables can be grown in containers, but some are better than others for window boxes as they are more compact and require a shallow root area. Tall plants will block the view from your window.

Here are some of the best vegetables to grow in a window box:

Lettuce, radish, beet, arugula, mizuna, scallion, chives, spinach, carrot (such as globe types or dwarf chantenay types), watercress in damp soil, and trailing tomatoes.

**BELOW:** Pumpkins and squashes are hungry feeders and have traditionally been grown directly on compost heaps, an ideal space-saving solution.

# Pepper and chilli
## *Capsicum annuum* Longum and Grossum Groups

**Common name:** Pepper and chilli, chilli pepper, capsicum

**Type:** Annual

**Climate:** Tender, warm-temperate glasshouse

**Size:** Between 10in–3¼ft (25cm–1m)

**Origin:** South and Central America

**History:** Chilli peppers were perhaps one of the first plants to be domesticated in Central America, where there is evidence that they were consumed in 7500 BC. They were introduced to South Asia in the 1500s and have come to dominate the world spice trade. India is now the largest producer of chillies in the world.

**Cultivation:** They should be sown indoors in late winter or early spring and then grown under glass in cold areas. Growing tips should be pinched out when the plants reach about 8in to encourage a bushier plant. Outdoors they can be planted directly into fertile, free-draining soil or in grow bags or containers in a warm, sunny location in more favorable climates.

**LEFT:** Chillies require a long season for them to fully develop their spicy flavors, so seeds should be sown early on in the year under cover.

**RIGHT:** Peppers have a wonderful ornamental quality and develop into an array of different colors, including green, yellow, orange, red, and purple.

**Storage:** Peppers unfortunately go mushy if frozen, although chillies tend to fare better. Peppers will keep for a couple of weeks in the fridge. The best way to preserve chillies is to dry them in the sun on a wire mesh, such as chicken wire, or to hang them from strings and allow them to dry. Another alternative is to use them to infuse cooking oil.

**Preparation:** Chilli peppers contain oils that can burn your skin and especially your eyes, so it is important to be very careful when handling them. It is a good idea to wear gloves when preparing hot chillies and, whatever you do, do not rub your eyes. Slice chillies in half lengthwise and remove the seeds before chopping them finely. Cut out the core from peppers and slice or dice.

## Tasting notes

### Sticky chilli jam

This chilli jam is the perfect accompaniment to cheese and crackers or can simply be spread on crusty French bread.

**Preparation time:** 10 minutes
**Cooking time:** 1 hour
**Serves**: makes 1lb (3–4 ½l) jars

- 13oz (400g) cherry tomatoes

- 9 red peppers

- 10 red chillies

- 7 garlic cloves, peeled

- 1½in (4cm / thumb length) of root ginger, peeled and chopped

- 1½lb (750g sugar

- 8floz (250ml) red wine vinegar

Place the tomatoes, peppers, chillies, garlic, and ginger into a food processor and whizz until finely chopped.

In a pan, dissolve the sugar in the vinegar over a low heat.

Add the tomatoes, peppers, chillies, garlic, and ginger mix and simmer for about 40 minutes, or until the liquid has reduced and it has a thick, sticky consistency.

Once the jam is becoming sticky, cook for 10–15 mins more, stirring frequently.

Cool slightly, then transfer into sterilized jars.

Once reopened, it will keep for about 1 month in the fridge.

**ABOVE:** Peppers should be grown indoors in cooler climates. In a warm and sheltered spot they can be grown outside in full sun.

Some like them hot and spicy, others like them sweet and crunchy; whatever your taste there is a chilli or pepper for everyone. The two types are very closely related; peppers are milder and larger while chillies are usually hotter, although there are varieties that are gentler on the taste buds. The popularity of chillies has grown thanks to the increase in popularity of Indian, Thai, Chinese, and Mexican dishes over the last few decades. Mediterranean food is also often flavored with both peppers and chillies as well as the spicy paprika powder that is extracted from this plant once it has dried out. It is mainly the pith that provides the knockout fiery punch, so wash and remove the seeds if you want something milder.

Peppers and chillies require a warm, sunny position outdoors in mild areas. In cooler regions they may have to be grown in an unheated polythene tunnel, glasshouse, or conservatory.

They need a well-drained but moist soil, which should ideally be slightly acidic. Lots of organic matter should be added to the soil as this helps to retain the moisture. Most people however, do not grow these plants directly in the ground, but instead grow them in containers filled with general-purpose compost or growing bags. If using the latter, then no more than two plants should be planted per bag.

Sowing takes place indoors in pots in a heated propagator or a warm and sunny windowsill. Chillies need a longer growing season to achieve their heat so should be sown in late winter. Peppers can be sown a few weeks later. They should be transplanted into 3½in pots when they have produced their first two true leaves. Once the risk of frost is over, they should be hardened off in a cold frame for a few days before being planted out at 18in apart. When the growing tips reach about

---

### THE SCOVILLE HEAT SCALE

The Scoville heat scale measures the compound called capsaicin, which gives chillies their heat. The hotter the chilli, the higher it scores in the scale. It was developed by Wilbur Scoville in 1912. Prior to this scale, the heat of chillies was simply determined by taste.

The Guinness World Record holder for the hottest chilli is currently Smokin Ed's "Carolina Reaper," grown by The PuckerButt Pepper Company of South Carolina, which rates at an average of 1,569,300 Scoville Heat Units (SHU).

As an idea of scale, a Scotch Bonnet scores between 100,000 and 300,000; a Tabasco pepper between 30,00 and 50,000; a Hungarian wax pepper 3,500 to 8,000; a pimento between 100 and 900; and a bell pepper scores 0.

---

8in they should be pinched out to encourage a bushy plant, which in turn will produce a larger crop. Plants will require regular watering, although avoid overwatering chillies too close to harvest time as it can dilute the heat.

You can expect to get up to 5–10 peppers per plant, whereas chillies will produce a few dozen depending on variety and growing conditions. Fruits should be harvested when they are green to encourage the plant to produce more. They will change color if left on the plant, with peppers turning red, yellow, orange, and purple and becoming sweeter, while chillies will become hotter.

They are usually ready for harvesting outdoors from August and will continue to crop in a favorable location until the fall.

# Chop suey greens
## *Chrysanthemum coronarium*

**Common name:** Chop suey greens, chrysanthemum greens, garland chrysanthemum, crown daisy, kikuna, mirabeles, and shungiku

**Type:** Annual

**Climate:** Half-hardy, mild winter

**Size:** 10in (25cm)

**Origin:** Mediterranean, East Asia

**History:** In the 8th century, the chrysanthemum was introduced into Japan where it was quickly named as the national symbol by the Emperor and became the inspiration for the royal seal. Carolus Linnaeus named it by taking the Greek word *chrys*, which means "gold colored," and adding *anthemon*, meaning "flower."

**Cultivation:** Sow seeds directly in the soil in shallow drills in midspring. The site should be in full sun and the soil should be free-draining and fertile. Harvest leaves like a cut-and-come-again plant, and make regular sowings throughout the season so that there is plenty to harvest.

**Storage:** Leaves will only last for a day or two after picking so only harvest on days when they are going to be used in the kitchen.

**Preparation:** Simply wash and cut the leaves or eat them whole, raw, or cooked.

This is a fast-growing and attractive form of the garden chrysanthemum and is grown for its delicious, dissected young leaves, which can be added to salads. There is a double-whammy in that the flowers can also be eaten, but if you let them flower then the flavor in the leaves turns bitter and unpleasant. They have a mildly herbal and nutty flavor and are eaten raw or lightly cooked. The leaves are best picked young when they can be steamed or added to stir-fries. The leaves are

popular in Japanese soups but their attractive shape and color makes them a great visual feature in the salad bowl or as a garnish too. The flowers, both fresh and dried, and the unopened buds can also be used to make an aromatic herbal tea.

With deeply serrated leaves and attractive pale yellow and orange chrysanthemum flowers, this is an attractive plant for vegetable gardens and potagers, but is just as at home in the flowerbed. It is a low-growing plant and so is a good choice for separating out areas of the kitchen garden and for edging paths. It can be interplanted with other larger crops, such as sweetcorn, among other cut flowers, and also in brassica beds where it contrasts well with the textures of cabbages and kale. The light green foliage also looks good when grown next to red cabbages or red chicory. This must be one of the easiest vegetable plants to grow and the leaves can literally be harvested a mere six weeks after sowing.

If you cannot find the seeds in the vegetable seed catalogs, then try the ornamental and flowering sections as they are very often listed there. Sow them outdoors from midspring onward in fertile, well-drained soil in full sun, ½in apart in shallow drills, with 12in between the rows. Thin the seeds out to 8in apart when they are large enough to handle. Seeds should be sown regularly every couple of weeks to ensure a regular crop of chop suey greens, but avoid midsummer as the dry weather can cause the plants to bolt and prematurely flower.

**RIGHT:** Chop suey greens are a type of chrysanthemum and are just as likely to be found in an ornamental flowerbed as they are to be grown in the kitchen garden.

To get an early crop, seed can be scattered indoors in trays of seed compost at ¼in deep, before hardening them off in cold frame for a few days prior to planting them out at 8in apart outdoors.

A few weeks after sowing the chop suey leaves will be ready for harvesting. They can be harvested like a cut-and-come-again plant by cutting leaves with scissors above the base of the plant and allowing it to resprout for harvesting a few weeks later. If you have a number of plants, leave some uncut so that their flowers can be enjoyed later to add to salads or for making tea.

Golden flowerheads can be added to salads

Unopened flowerbuds can be used to make herbal tea

Leaves are best when eaten young

# Chicory

## *Cichorium endivia*

**Common name:** Chicory, endive

**Type:** Annual

**Climate:** Half-hardy, mild winter

**Size:** 12in (30cm)

**Origin:** Middle East

**History:** It is thought that chicory originated somewhere in the Near East and the ancient Egyptians were thought to have cultivated them. In ancient times, chicory and endive were classed as the same plant and they have always been eaten as a salad crop. They became a popular crop in southern Europe before spreading into northern Europe.

**Cultivation:** Chicory should be sown in spring, in shallow drills, although the broad-leaved types are more winter hardy and can be sown in late summer for a winter harvest. Cloches should be placed over the seedlings once the fall frosts arrive. The curly-leaved types are often blanched before harvest by placing a pot over the plant. This reduces some of the bitterness of the leaves (see p.100).

**Storage:** The leaves only last for a few days in the fridge once picked, so it is best to harvest little and often as required in the kitchen.

**Preparation:** Chop up the leaves and add raw to salads or leave whole and boil by plunging into salted boiling water for about 5 minutes.

Chicory is a popular leaf vegetable that can be eaten either raw, although it can taste slightly bitter, or sautéed, added to stir-fries, soups, and stews. There is often a huge amount of confusion between the two members of the daisy family, chicory and endive, but that is not really surprising. After all, in France and America endive is what the

**BELOW:** Believed to have originated somewhere in the Near East, the ancient Egyptians are known to have grown chicory. Their popularity spread to southern Europe, and then farther north.

## NUTRITION

Among all the green vegetables, chicory is one of the richest sources of vitamins A and C. It also contains calcium, chlorine, iron, phosphorus, potassium, and sulfur and is an excellent provider of fiber and carotene.

English call chicory and very often the name is used interchangeably in restaurants to describe bitter or blanched leaves. However, there is one important distinction to the gardener; chicory is an annual that needs to be sown each year, whereas endive is a perennial that will provide a crop year after year.

*Chicory and prawn omelette*

Chicory is low in calories and provides a great chance to include less-known vegetables in a healthy diet. Try combining with eggs to make an alternative to the traditional omelette.

**Preparation time:** 5 minutes
**Cooking time:** 10 minutes
**Serves**: 1 person

• 3 large eggs

• ½oz (15g) butter

• 2 chicory, chopped

• 4oz (100g) prawns, cooked and peeled

• Salt and pepper, to taste

Beat the eggs in a bowl. Add pepper and salt.

Melt the butter in a frying pan and fry the endives; season with pepper and salt.

Pour the beaten eggs on to the chicory and cook on low heat. Make sure not to overcook.

Sprinkle the prawns on top and serve.

**RIGHT:** Escarole or bativan chicory has broad, deep green leaves and are hardier than the frizzy types, making them suitable for growing during winter.

There are two distinct types of chicory available to the gardener. First there is the frizzy-leaved type, which has attractive frilly, tightly curled leaves. It is often called *frisée*, or the French call it *chicorée frisée*. It looks stunning when grown in a potager or even edging a flowerbed, with the foliage creating a wonderful textured effect. However, it is not winter hardy, so it is grown just as a summer crop. The other type is sometimes called Batavian chicory or escarole which has broader, deep green leaves that are slightly wavy. These are much hardier than the crinkly type and are suitable for growing during winter. Chicory is either grown as a cut-and-come-again plant, where two or three harvests can be made throughout the the year, or it is harvested when it has formed its rosette of leaves.

This popular leafy vegetable does have a slightly bitter taste and this is far more noticeable in a hot summer. It is not so commonly grown as lettuce, one of the main reasons being that it lacks the sweetness. However, the one benefit it has over lettuce is that it can be grown as a winter crop, whereas lettuce can sometimes struggle. Also, the slight bitterness does appeal to some people and provides a nice contrast to some of the other sweeter leaves in mixed salads. Chicory is also generally less prone to diseases or bolting.

Chicory should be grown in fertile, well-drained soil in full sun. The site should have good moisture retention, however, so that an abundance of leaves is produced. Dig over the soil prior to sowing seeds and add plenty of well-rotted organic matter. Both types of chicory, flat and frizzy, should be sown in spring, although for a winter crop the flat type can be sown in late summer. Seeds should be sown in shallow drills that are about ½in deep, with rows 16in apart. Once the seedlings appear they should be thinned to approximately 8in apart for the frizzy types and 16in for the larger broad-leaved chicory. The plants must be kept well watered during dry periods or they could either wilt or bolt. They will

also benefit from a liquid feed every couple of weeks. Regularly hoe between the rows to prevent the developing plants from being smothered and diminished by competing weeds. The winter varieties should be covered with a tunnel cloche before the arrival of the fall frosts.

The leaves can be harvested like a cut-and-come-again plant, by snipping off a few leaves as and when needed. Alternatively the entire plant can be removed and taken into the kitchen.

**LEFT:** Chicory produces stunning, decorative flowers. These will appear on the plants if they are left to grow, and are very distinctive of the genus *Cichorium*.

# Endive
## *Cichorium intybus*

**Common name:** Endive, radicchio, chicory, chicons, Belgium chicory, witloof, sugar loaf chicory

**Type:** Perennial

**Climate:** Hardy, average winter

**Size:** 10in (25cm)

**Origin:** Northern Africa, Western Asia, Europe

**History:** Endive is one of the oldest recorded types of plants. Its cultivation is thought to have originated in Egypt in ancient times, later being grown by European monks in medieval times. In Europe during the 1820s endive roots were baked and ground then used as a substitute for expensive coffee beans. They are still used as an additive to coffee today. Some brewers also used roasted endive, adding it to their stout beers for extra flavor.

**Cultivation:** Seeds are sown in spring in shallow drills in a sunny, sheltered aspect in well-drained soil, with harvesting taking place in late fall or winter. To force the tender chicons during winter, a few plants should be dug up, taken inside, placed in a bucket, and covered with compost to be harvested three weeks later.

**RIGHT:** Belgium chicory is also known as witloof chicory and is grown for its crunchy green leaves. The plants is also used for forcing to make chicons.

**Storage:** Endive does not last for long in the fridge, but its shelf life can be extended by placing it in a paper bag to exclude light as this prevents the endive discoloring and turning even more bitter. Ideally the heads should be harvested as needed from the garden.

**Preparation:** Chop into pieces or leave whole. To cook, simply plunge the heads into salted boiling water for about 5 minutes.

E ndive is particularly popular in Italy and was enjoyed by the Romans. It is closely related to chicory and very often the two are confused. Both are grown for their bitter salad leaves and both supply useful winter leaves for the kitchen. However, the one main distinction is that the chicory is an annual whereas endive is a perennial, although it is often grown as an annual in the vegetable garden. Endive is also an attractive addition to the vegetable garden, particularly the radicchio types, and when allowed to flower provides a beautiful display of bright blue flowers. These should be removed before they seed otherwise the plants will seed themselves freely around the garden.

**BELOW:** The succulent leaves of this herbaceous perennial can be added to winter salads. Endive also produces a large tap root below the ground, similar to a dandelion, which persists after the leaves are harvested.

**ABOVE:** If allowed to flower, endive produces the most exquisite lavender-colored flowers. The roots of the plant are often dried and used to make a caffeine-free version of coffee.

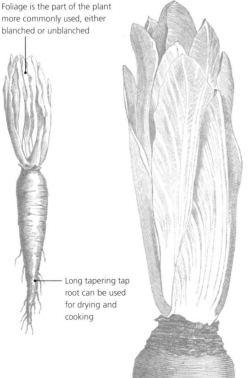

Foliage is the part of the plant more commonly used, either blanched or unblanched

Long tapering tap root can be used for drying and cooking

It is thanks to its perennial root system that it is also grown as a coffee substitute or mixed with coffee to bulk it up. Like dandelion, it can be dug up, and its root removed from the plant, washed, roasted, and made into a thirst-quenching hot drink. However, most gardeners grow endive for the leaves. There are three distinct groups: Belgium or witloof chicory, sugarloaf, and radicchio. Witloof chicory produces edible green leaves, but they are more commonly grown as the gourmet treat known as chicons (see box). Popular varieties include "Brussels Witloof" and "Witloof Zoom."

## FORCING CHICONS

Witloof or Belgium chicory can be forced indoors to create delicious tender, white chicon heads. To do this the leaves should be cut back hard in late fall, and the roots gently dug up out of the ground and taken indoors where they should be planted in the bottom of a bucket, container, or even a compost bag. They should then be covered with compost so that just the growing tips show, and then covered with another bucket or container and left in the dark for about three weeks. The emerging chicons can be harvested and the remainder of the plant can be covered again in order to repeat the process. Chicons should be harvested when they are about 6in long. The popular variety for forcing chicons and blanching is "Brussels Witloof."

Endive is harvested from late summer and into fall. Covering them up with cloches will extend the season.

Chicons are used in many gourmet dishes, but *Chicons au gratin* is particularly popular in Belgium and is best served with lots of strong-flavored cheese and a béchamel sauce. If you cannot get hold of chicons, then leeks make an equally suitable alternative.

The sugarloaf endives produce a rosette of broad leaves, looking similar to romaine lettuce with its large upright head. It is a useful crop as it is usually harvested in fall when many salad leaves aren't available, and if it is protected with a cloche will continue well into winter. Their upright habit means that the inner leaves are self-blanched by the outer ones, making them much sweeter. Reliable, tried-and-tested varieties worth trying include "Pan di Zucchero" and "Zuckerhut."

The radicchio types are probably the most ornamental of all the endives and are the ones often seen in mixed bags of salad from the grocery store. Sometimes called red-leaved endive it adds a beautiful splash of color to the kitchen garden. Radicchios also brighten up winter salads as they grow well under cloches, where they can survive well into winter. "Indigo" is a popular variety producing a dense head with red hearts and dark green outer leaves. "Palla Rossa" produces large heads and has impressive red hearts.

**LEFT AND ABOVE:** Red-leaved endive is also known as radicchio, and adds a splash of color to the kitchen garden. Usually harvested in the fall, the season can be extended further with cloches.

All the endives require a fertile soil in full sun. Plenty of organic matter should be dug into the soil before sowing. Witloof chicory is sown in late spring or early summer into shallow, ½in-deep drills 12in apart. After germination the seedlings should be thinned out to 6in and any emerging flower stems should be removed. To blanch the leaves outdoors, the leaves should be cut back in early fall and the remaining crown should be covered in a 6in-deep mulch. The young leaves should be picked as they emerge from the ground.

BELOW: Endive is a useful crop in the garden as it has attractive flowers, edible leaves for salads, and roots that can be dried to create an alternative hot drink to coffee.

### Broiled endive with pears and hazelnuts

The sweetness of pear and the slight bitterness of endive make them the perfect accompaniment to each other, while the hazelnuts put the crunch into this salad—an ideal appetizer for a casserole or stew.

**Preparation time:** 10 minutes
**Cooking time:** 10–15 minutes
**Serves:** 4 people

- 2 large heads of endive

- 2 tbsp olive oil

- 1 ripe pear

- 2 tbsp hazelnut oil

- 1½ tsp thyme, chopped

- Pepper, to taste

- 1oz (25g) hazelnuts

- 1 tsp thyme sprigs

Cut the endive lengthwise and remove core.

Brush with olive oil and place in a pan with cut side up. Broil for about 3–4 minutes. Turn and baste. Cook for 2–3 more minutes.

Halve, core, and slice the pear.

Turn the endive and top with the pear slices.

Brush with hazelnut oil, add the thyme and pepper, and broil for 5–6 minutes.

Garnish with hazelnuts and sprigs of thyme and drizzle with the remaining hazelnut oil.

# Sea kale
## *Crambe maritima*

**Common name:** Sea kale, *Crambe*, sea-colewort, scurvy grass, halmyrides

**Type:** Perennial

**Climate:** Hardy, cold winter

**Size:** 20in (50cm)

**Origin:** North and west coast of Europe

**History:** A wild plant that grows along many of the shorelines of Europe. Sea kale has been around for quite a time, the taste of which resembles cabbage. Louis XIV knew of it, and ordered its cultivation in the gardens of Versailles. It has been cultivated in English gardens since the 18th century and was mentioned in Thomas Jefferson's *Garden Book* of 1809. It was a popular food, often served at the tables of the very rich, until the early 20th century, but today it is no longer as popular.

**Cultivation:** Stems should be forced in late winter by excluding the dormant crown of the plant from light by placing a pot or forcing jar over it. A few weeks later there should be a crop of delicious, blanched white stems to harvest. Plants are usually discarded after being forced. Avoid forcing a plant in its first year as it will not have enough energy to grow properly.

**RIGHT:** Sea kale is a common plant in the wild, particularly in coastal areas, but is also used in herbaceous borders as it has attractive foliage and flowers.

**Storage:** Sea kale's moment of glory in the culinary spotlight is short lived. Blanched stems should be eaten immediately after picking as they turn to mush in the freezer and will only keep in the fridge for a few days.

**Preparation:** Simply trim the stalks and wash well. The young external leaves are edible too but, to ensure they lose their bitter taste, they should be blanched beforehand.

Sea kale is one of the simplest plants to grow, requiring very little work for the aspiring gardener. Its luxuriant, attractive, blue-green foliage makes it equally at home in the herbaceous border as the kitchen garden. Food aficionados enjoy it best when the early spring, blanched stems are lightly steamed and simply served up as a side dish

with butter. As the name suggests, it originates from coastal regions, which explains its ability to cope with poor, arid conditions and exposed sites, and its ability to combat whatever the harsh elements throw at it. Yet, while the plant might be super tough, beyond its hardy exterior lies a delicious treat providing one of the most sought-after delicacies appreciated by chefs and cooks worldwide. It is a native of Britain, again explaining how it can thrive in damp, maritime conditions, and it would have been harvested by coastal dwellers long before it became a popular ornamental and edible crop

**LEFT:** Despite its attractive, delicate-looking flowers, sea kale is a tough herbaceous perennial and is suited to growing in wild, exposed sites, coping with both damp and free-draining soil.

in the gardens of the rich. Nowadays, growing it at home is the only way to enjoy it—it is now a protected species, after the Victorians' passion for it exhausted the natural supply of this once abundant wild plant.

Not surprisingly, sea kale goes particularly well with fish dishes, but the blanched leafstalks or stems also can be eaten raw in salads or boiled and steamed. They can either be lightly steamed, where they retain their firmness with a slightly nutty flavor, or be reduced down to a spinachy texture, which tastes delicious when seasoned and flavored with garlic and a squeeze of lemon to accompany salmon or sea trout.

There is just one commonly grown variety called "Lilywhite," otherwise they appear in garden centers and catalogs simply as "sea kale." Plants can be difficult to source, so they can either be grown from seed, or even better they can be grown from root cuttings, sometimes called thongs, if a friend or neighbor has it in their garden.

Sea kale requires an open sunny position and free-draining soil, replicating the stony or sandy conditions it is used to in the wild. If the soil is heavy dig in plenty of grit or sand beforehand. Keep the area around the plant regularly weeded as it grows to avoid it becoming shaded or having to compete for nutrients. In fall, it should be treated like any other perennial and cut down close to ground level once the stems and flowers start to fade.

## FORCING SEA KALE

Although the foliage and stems of the plant can be harvested at any time of the year, the texture can be tough with a bitter flavor. The best way to enjoy sea kale is to force the plant into early growth by placing an upside down bucket, trash can, or a terracotta rhubarb forcing jar over the dormant crown in late winter. If using an old plant pot, then the drainage hole should be covered over to completely exclude the light. Place a brick on top of it to prevent it being blown away. A few weeks later there should be delicious pale white stems ready to harvest.

Use a knife to cut the stems just above the crown of the plant. Plants are often discarded after harvesting as they have expended their energy. However, do not to forget to take some root cuttings before you force as they will provide you with plants for the following year.

# Cucumber and gherkin
## *Cucumis sativus*

**Common name:** Cucumber and gherkin

**Type:** Climbing or trailing annual

**Climate:** Tender, cool or warm-temperate glasshouse

**Size:** 16in (40cm), spreading 6½ft (2m) or more

**Origin:** South Asia

**History:** The cucumber was first cultivated in India more than 3,000 years ago and was brought to England by the Romans, although it did not become established until the 16th century. According to Pliny, the Emperor Tiberius had the cucumber on his table daily during summer and winter. The Romans reportedly used artificial methods (similar to the glasshouse system) of growing to have it available for his table every day of the year.

**Cultivation:** Indoor cucumbers should be sown between late winter and early spring, and outdoor cucumbers from mid to late spring. They need regular watering as they have such a high water content. Keep harvesting the fruits to encourage them to crop more.

**Storage**: Cucumbers do not store for long and will keep in the fridge for about two weeks. Harvest baby ridge cucumbers as gherkins and store them in jars of vinegar.

**Preparation:** When using in salads, keep the skin on and cut into thin slices, dice, or chunks. Larger cucumbers or ridge cucumbers should be peeled thinly before eating.

**BELOW:** Ridge cucumbers are fairly hardy and can be grown outside in sheltered locations, but they will need a support system of wires and canes for the plants to climb up.

---

### GROWING GHERKINS

Gherkins are basically immature ridge cucumbers and are grown so that they can be pickled in jars of malt vinegar. Any ridge cucumber can be picked early although there are specific gherkin varieties that will perform better such as "Diamant" and "Venlo." Harvest them when they reach about 2½in in length.

---

Cucumbers have a history dating back over 5,000 years and were originally enjoyed in India before spreading toward Europe and the remainder of Asia. No green salad is complete without the cooling and refreshing texture of a cucumber. Alternatively, mix them with radish, feta, and nuts for a delicious crunchy salad. Lightly perfumed and very juicy, you almost drink the vegetable rather than eat it. Containing next to no calories, cucumbers are amazingly easy to grow, and yet strangely they are not that commonly grown in gardens. This is probably because they have a reputation for being difficult to grow, but they are actually surprisingly easy.

Not all cucumbers are long. There are lots of different varieties to grace people's gardens both outdoors and in the glasshouse. There are a range of different colors, including yellow and white, and round and oval shapes.

There are two types of cucumbers. First, there are the climbing types that include the ones commonly seen in grocery stores. They need to be grown under glass and varieties worth trying include "Carmen" and "Mini Munch." The other type of cucumbers are known as ridge types, and these are hardier so can be grown directly outdoors without the need for protection. Varieties include "Marketmore," which produces high yields and has a good trailing habit, and "Tokyo Slicer," which produces long, smooth fruits. For something a bit different try the quirky heritage variety "Crystal Apple."

**RIGHT:** Ridge cucumbers have slightly knobbly skins, which can be a bit tough and best if sliced off prior to eating.

It is best to choose F1 cucumbers when growing indoor varieties as they should not produce male flowers. Male flowers will pollinate the female flowers and this results in bitter-tasting fruits. If male flowers do appear they should be removed immediately. To distinguish between the two flowers, look just below the flowerhead. The female has a swelling (which eventually goes on to form the fruit) whereas the male has nothing.

### Growing indoor types

Indoor types should be sown in late winter in a heated glasshouse or in midspring in an unheated one. The large seeds should be sown on their edge, ½in deep to prevent them rotting, then transferred into pots filled with potting compost when they reach about 10in high. They require a bamboo cane or wire to train them upward. Once the plant has reached the top, the growing tip should be pinched out. The tips of side shoots should also be pinched out two leaves past female flowers. Trim back any other flowerless shoots to about 18in to prevent the plants expending valuable energy. Keep the plants regularly watered each day and feed with a liquid feed such as tomato fertilizer every 10 days from when they start to set fruit. The plants prefer humid conditions so damp the floor down once a day. It may be necessary to apply shade paint or hang a shade net up in the glasshouse to prevent the plants getting scorched from direct sunlight.

### Growing outdoor ridge types

For outdoor types the seeds should be sown under glass in midspring before being hardened off in cold frames for a few days and then planted outdoors 30in apart after the risk of frost is over. Alternatively, the seeds can be planted directly outdoors in early summer planting a seed 1in deep every 30in. A cloche can be placed over it to give it some initial protection during germination.

Cucumbers require a fertile, rich soil so add plenty of organic material prior to planting or sowing. The growing tip should be pinched out when it has produced about seven leaves to encourage the plant to form a bushy growth habit that will form lots of fruits. They can be trained up nets or tepees. The plants will need feeding about every 10 days with a liquid tomato feed. Keep the plants well watered and harvest the fruits regularly with a sharp knife every few days to ensure they continue to crop. Do not remove the male flowers on the outdoor types.

# TYPES OF KITCHEN GARDENS

There are a plethora of different types of kitchen gardens. Vegetables do not have to be grown in conventional, regimented straight rows following a strict program of crop rotation. Kitchen gardens can be modern and chic or rustic and informal. There is no right or wrong. Choosing a style or type of garden is a matter of personal taste and reflection of personality.

## WALLED GARDENS

Traditionally, mansion houses and palaces would have had large kitchen gardens that would have grown crops to provide food for the owners of the house, their guests, and their staff. They were usually grown in walled gardens as this provided extra protection from the elements, and imparted a warmer aspect enabling the gardeners to provide early crops to the kitchen and to extend the season into winter. Most people cannot emulate these grand gardens in their own back yards, but they are great places to visit and get inspiration for what to grow.

## POTAGER

This is a relaxed, informal type of garden that mixes ornamental plants with edible crops. It is named after the French word *potage* meaning soup, implying that the garden is a concoction of many different plants. Potagers usually have an artistic or creative element to the garden, where conventional crop rotation and formal straight rows are forsaken for esthetic purposes.

For people with a small garden, mixing ornamental plants and vegetables may be the only option anyway. However, vegetables are beautiful in their own right. Onions provide stunning flowerheads, and brightly colored cabbages and lettuces can form beautiful tapestries of texture. Wigwams with French and string beans scrambling up them provide height and a splash of color.

**LEFT:** Engraved frontispiece from Thomas Mawe (1760s–1770s) and John Abercrombie (1726–1806) *Every man his own gardener* dated 1800.

**ABOVE:** The Czech painter Antos Frolka (1877–1935) painted many folk scenes, this one showing a lady growing vegetables.

## COMMUNITY GARDENS

For many people without their own private outdoor space, Community Gardens offer a perfect solution. These are shared growing areas, often in towns, but not always, where people from the local community can create their own horticultural paradise. These areas are sometimes overseen by city authorities, other times by community organizations. Gardeners usually rent a "plot" but often end up sharing spaces with other community members. This is a useful method for people that do not have time to manage an individual space, or for beginners that want to learn from people with more experience.

Food produced from shared plots are usually distributed among its participants, commonly with the amount of fruit and vegetables given to an individual reflecting the amount of time that person has spent working in the garden. Members can then buy additional food at a discounted rate.

Not only are community kitchen gardens about producing food, it provides a valuable contribution to "greening up" urban spaces and creating greater biodiversity among "concrete jungles." Also, it is not just individuals who take part in community gardens as often organizations such as schools, preschools, and charities take part too. Surplus food or vegetables are sometimes distributed to local charities too.

**LEFT:** Community Gardens are the perfect solution for those people wanting to grow their own vegetables but do not have a garden. It is a great space for like-minded people to learn from each other about gardening and also an excuse to enjoy the fresh air and a spot of healthy exercise.

"For all things produced in a garden, whether of salads or fruits, a poor man will eat better that has one of his own, than a rich man that has none."

*An Encyclopaedia of Gardening*, (1822) **John Claudius Loudoun**

# Pumpkin and winter squash
## *Cucurbita maxima* and *C. moschata*

**Common name:** Pumpkin, winter squash

**Type:** Climbing or trailing annual

**Climate:** Tender, cool glasshouse

**Size:** 16in (40cm), spreading 6½ft (2m) or more

**Origin:** South and Central America

**History:** Pumpkins are the largest of the winter squashes. The word pumpkin originated from the Greek word *pepōn*, which means "large melon." The word was gradually morphed by the French, English, and then Americans into "pumpkin."

It is said that Columbus carried pumpkin seeds back with him to Europe from America. Without pumpkins many of the early settlers in America might have died from starvation. The following poem is a testament to the pilgrims' dependence upon pumpkins for food:

> For pottage and puddings
> and custards and pies,
> Our pumpkins and parsnips
> are common supplies.
> We have pumpkins at morning
> and pumpkins at noon.
> If it were not for pumpkins
> we should be undoon.
>
> **Pilgrim verse, (c. 1633)**

## NUTRITION

Pumpkin and winter squashes contain no saturated fats or cholesterol but are very rich in dietary fiber and antioxidant vitamins such as vitamins A, C, and E. They are also a source of potassium, which can help to stabilize blood pressure.

**LEFT:** Pumpkins are easy to grow but need very fertile soil to make them fruit and swell to a decent size. Their seeds are also edible and delicious when lightly roasted.

**Cultivation:** Pumpkins should be sown indoors into small plastic pots in spring and planted out after the risk of frosts is over. They require a rich, fertile soil with plenty of organic matter. Dig lots of compost into the soil prior to planting. Seedlings should be planted at 6ft apart and require regular watering and feeding as they grow.

**Storage:** In fall, the fruits should be left in the sun for a few days for their skin to cure as this will enable them to store for longer. If the weather is wet, then they should be brought in immediately to prevent them rotting. Store them in a cool, dark place such as a garage, cellar, or shed. The orange-skinned types will usually last for a few weeks in a frost-free location, whereas some of the blue-gray and green types will last right the way through winter. Chunks of pumpkin can be frozen, but the best method is to make them into delicious soups and pies and then put them in the freezer.

**Preparation:** Cut in half and scoop out the seeds. Then cut into sections and peel and chop the flesh into even-sized pieces. Simply cook in boiling salted water for about 15 minutes or until tender. Alternatively pumpkin can be steamed or roasted. If roasting, then treat like potatoes and add to the hot fat around a roasting joint. Pumpkins can also be stuffed and baked (like marrow) or used in soups and stews.

**RIGHT:** Pumpkins have a sprawling habit, providing lots of luxuriant growth. Give them plenty of space in the garden, planting them at least 6ft apart. The flowers appear just as soon as the plant has got established.

Whether you crave sweet or savory, there is a pumpkin recipe to please most people's palate. This chunky fall vegetable can be transformed into delicious food to sustain you throughout the following winter months, ranging from a thick warming soup to a delicious sweet pumpkin pie in a shell of filo pastry. It can also provide a tasty snack made from the chunky, crunchy seeds slammed in the oven for 20 minutes with a dash of paprika, nutmeg, or cinnamon and splash of olive oil. Even if there is not a recipe to tickle your taste buds it can still appeal to your creative side as everybody loves to carve a scary pumpkin face. And most people love the green-fingered challenge of trying to grow a huge pumpkin to impress friends and relatives in fall. And finally, if that doesn't satisfy you, then it can appeal to your practical side as the insides of the fruit can be scooped out, leaving the outer skin to act as a bowl

for your favorite fall dish. In the garden itself, pumpkins and winter squashes look resplendent with their impressive vines trailing through the vegetable patch and their brightly colored skins looking translucent in the fall hues. To both the gardener and cook there is not really any difference between the pumpkin and the winter squash, and both are grown in exactly the same way.

Pumpkins and winter squashes should be started off indoors from mid to late spring in small plastic pots. Sow one seed per pot, placing it on its side to prevent it rotting when it is watered. Keep them on a sunny windowsill or in the glasshouse until the risk of spring frosts has passed. They should then be hardened off in a porch or glasshouse for about a week before planting them outside.

TASTING NOTES

### Pumpkin pie

Capture the essence of fall with this classic pumpkin dessert.

**Preparation time:** 15 minutes
**Cooking time:** 45 minutes
**Serves:** 6–8 people

- 6oz (175g) shortcrust pastry

- 1lb (450g) pumpkin, cooked

- 2 eggs, separated

- 5 tbsp superfine sugar

- ¼ pint (150ml) milk

- Pinch of salt

- ¼ tsp ground ginger

- ¼ tsp grated nutmeg

Preheat a conventional oven to 400°F (200°C / gas mark 6 / fan 180°C).

Roll out the pastry, line a 7in (18cm) flan tin and prick with a fork. Cook for 10 minutes.

Sieve the cooked pumpkin to make ½ pint (300ml) purée.

Add the egg yolks and 3 tablespoons of sugar, then beat in the milk, salt, and spices.

Turn into the pastry case. Bake for 40 minutes.

Whisk the egg whites until stiff. Fold in the remaining sugar. Spread over the top of pie.

Turn off the oven, place the pie inside, and leave until the meringue is lightly brown.

Pumpkins and winter squashes require a sunny site in fertile soil. The soil has to be very rich to enable the plant to provide enough sustenance for its long trailing habit, luxuriant growth, and abundant fruit so that it can grow through to the end of the growing season. Such is the plant's hunger for fertile conditions that many gardeners grow it directly on top of the compost heap to maximize the amount of organic matter and moisture content that the plant craves.

Dig in lots of organic matter such as well-rotted horse manure or garden compost a few months before planting. Seedlings need lots of space to accommodate their rampant growth habit, so plant them 6ft apart. As the plants establish they will need watering regularly and the area around them needs to be kept weed-free. Some gardeners lay plastic down prior to planting and plant the pumpkins through it to help suppress the weeds and retain the moisture. When the plants start to flower, the plants should be fed with a potassium-based liquid fertilizer every 10 days , such as tomato feed, to help the fruit to set and develop their flavor and color.

The fruits are ready to harvest in fall when the foliage starts to die back and the pumpkins have reached their optimum size.

Leave them to dry in the sun for a few days after harvesting to cure and harden their skin before bringing them indoors to either cook or carve, or both.

### GROWING A GIANT PUMPKIN

Not everybody can grow pumpkins to match the world record-breaking weight that currently stands at a staggering 2,009lb (911kg). However, there are tricks of the trade that can produce fruits large enough to possibly win one of the popular "largest pumpkin" competitions that happen all around the world at harvest festivals and fall shows.

**BELOW:** A watercolor depicting a range of pumpkins and squashes dating from c.1800 and attributed to the Chinese artist and collector Wang Lui Chi.

Choose a large variety of pumpkin such as "Prizewinner" or "Dill's Atlantic Giant." Give the plants lots of space and add plenty of organic matter into the soil. As the plant starts to grow, allow the first couple of fruits to develop, but remove the remainder as they will deprive the plant of essential nutrients. Feed it regularly with a liquid feed high in potassium. Once you can tell which one of the two remaining fruit is going to be the largest, remove the smaller one and place the remaining potential prize winner on a patio slab or a bed of straw to prevent it from rotting on the soil. With a bit of luck, the remaining fruit will go on to be a record-busting giant pumpkin.

## SPAGHETTI SQUASH

This unusual squash is a real hit with children and a brilliant way of getting them to eat vegetables without them realizing. It is so named because when it is cooked the fibers break down to form distinctive long strands that look like orange spaghetti. To many people on health drives it is considered to be a low-calorie and healthy alternative to pasta with just 40 calories per portion as opposed to a gut-busting 200. Demand outstrips supply in stores for this rare gourmet novelty when it comes into season in fall, meaning that the only way to guarantee a supply of this dream nutritional snack is to grow your own. It can be baked, boiled, sautéed, and even microwaved but the simplest way to cook the fibrous strands is to throw them in a wok and stir-fry them with red onions, elephant garlic, and a pinch of paprika. Another option is to steam and serve with a bolognaise sauce and crusty garlic bread.

TASTING NOTES

*Pumpkin and squash varieties to try*

There is a huge range of different types of pumpkins and winter squashes to experiment with in the garden.

| | |
|---|---|
| "Rouge Vif D'Etampes" | A flattened ball shape with a beautifully rich orange-red skin—the classic Cinderella pumpkin. |
| "Potimarron" | These small French heirloom types of winter squashes are not much bigger than the size of a tennis ball. |
| "Crown Prince" | A smallish, quirky looking winter squash with steely blue skin, colorful rich orange flesh, and a sweet and nutty flavor. |
| "Turk's Turban" | Uniquely shaped squashes with stripy green, orange, and white skin. |
| "Butternut Harrier" | A classic with that distinctive large peanut shape ideal for cooking with rice to make a winter-warming risotto or simply roasted with seasonal herbs. |

"Well, there doesn't seem to be anything else for an ex-president to do but go into the country and raise pumpkins."

Chester A. Arthur, 21st President of United States, (1882)

# Zucchini, marrow, and summer squash
## *Cucurbita pepo*

**Common name:** Zucchini, marrow, courgette, summer squash

**Type:** Climbing or trailing annual

**Climate:** Tender, cool glasshouse

**Size:** 19½in (50cm), spreading 5ft (1.5m) or more

**Origin:** Mexico

**History:** Zucchinis are believed to have originated in Mexico about 7,000 years ago and archeologists have traced their development in cultivation from between 7000 to 5500 BC. About 500 years ago zucchinis were brought from Mexico to the Mediterranean by Christopher Columbus during one of his voyages. Before the 20th century, the zucchini was not a popular vegetable in Europe or the United States, but now it is widely recognized in kitchens and home gardens.

**BELOW:** Zucchinis are simply baby marrows, although varieties have been specifically bred that are more suited to being grown smaller. The flowers can also be fried in batter and eaten as fritters.

**Cultivation:** Start plants in plastic pots, indoors in late spring. Plant them out only after the risk of the spring frosts is over. Trailing types should be planted 4ft apart and bush marrow types require about 32in between each plant. Keep them well watered and harvest zucchinis frequently to encourage them to continue cropping.

**Storage:** Zucchinis do not last for long and should be cooked soon after harvesting, although they will keep in the fridge for a few days. Alternatively, they can be frozen but they lose their firm consistency. Marrows can be stored for a few weeks in a cool, dry, and frost-free location such as the garage or shed.

**Preparation:** Slice off both ends, wash the skin, and slice or dice as required. Small zucchinis can be steamed whole, sliced and boiled in salted water for about 5 minutes, coated in batter and deep fried, or sautéed in a little butter for about 5 minutes.

Zucchinis and marrows must be one of the most versatile vegetables in the culinary world. The flesh can be baked, puréed, fried, or broiled and then whipped up into any type of dish whether it be creamy, spicy, sweet, crunchy, smooth, or whatever takes your fancy. Roasting is a great alternative as it intensifies the flavors when the moisture evaporates and the natural sugars caramelize and the texture turns sweet and crunchy. Despite originating in North America, these fruits are associated very much with Mediterranean cuisine. On warm, balmy summer days nothing beats al-fresco dining while broiling or frying a few strips of herby zucchini on the barbecue. The attractive, large orange-yellow flowers are also edible and can be fried in batter to create a side dish of fritters.

In the garden, zucchinis and marrows look beautiful. The most common color is green, but there are attractive yellow zucchinis such as "Gold Star" and "Sunstripe" or the creamy light green color of "Alfresco." There are attractive looking marrows too, such as "Tiger Cross" with its unusual green and white stripes on its skin, and they are not always elongated: there are attractive ball-shaped zucchinis too, such as "Summer Ball." Some of the summer squashes also add interest to the vegetable garden, such as the colorful mix of "Patty Pan" with its quirky-shaped, scalloped fruits. These can be harvested throughout the season at various sizes from baby squash, for eating raw, to their mature size of 8in across.

Botanically there is no difference between the two vegetables. Marrows are simply oversized zucchinis. If a zucchini is left to mature on a vine it will get big, although specific varieties often have qualities better suited to whether they are grown as one or the other. Seeds should be sown indoors in

## NUTRITION

Zucchinis, marrows, and summer squashes contain no saturated fats or cholesterol. They are rich in vitamins A and C. They are a very good source of potassium and also contain moderate levels of the B-complex group of vitamins like thiamin and riboflavin and minerals like iron, manganese, phosphorus, and zinc.

**ABOVE:** This beautiful, colorful plate demonstrates the wide range of colors, shapes, and sizes of summer squashes, marrows, and zucchinis.

spring in plastic pots in general-purpose compost. Sow one seed per pot. As with all members of the squash family, it is better to place the large seed on its edge as otherwise it can be prone to rotting in the compost. Keep the pots on a sunny windowsill or glasshouse until the risk of late spring frosts is over. They should then be hardened off in a cold frame or the porch for a few days before being planted outdoors.

Zucchinis and marrows like to be bathed in sunlight from dawn until dusk, so plant them in a sheltered and warm, sunny spot in the garden. They require a fertile, well-drained but moisture-retentive soil so lots of well-rotted organic matter should be added to the beds a few months before planting. Plants with trailing habits will be happy sprawling on the ground, but they can also be trained up fences, hedges, and wigwam teepees. There are also bush varieties that produce the fruit from the central stem, and these require far less space, making them ideal for the smaller garden.

Zucchinis, marrows, and summer squashes can also be sown directly outdoors after the risk of frosts is over. Sow two seeds every 32in for bush types or 4ft for trailing types. A bell-shaped cloche or a transparent plastic container can be placed over the seedling for the first couple of weeks to speed up germination and give it protection. Thin the seed out to one plant per sowing station after germination.

Once the plants are fruiting check them over every couple of days and harvest zucchinis and baby squashes regularly to keep them productive and to prevent the fruits from getting too big. Both types of plant are thirsty and should be watered regularly and fed every 10–14 days with a liquid tomato fertilizer. Keep them weed-free, although often their rampant habit and large leaves suppress weeds anyway. Pick zucchinis when they are about 4in long. Cut through the stem with pruning shears about 1in away from the fruit. Zucchinis should be cooked immediately after picking as they do not keep for long, whereas marrows will keep for a few weeks if picked at the end of the season and left in a frost-free place either in net bags or in trays.

**BELOW:** Summer squashes are very easy to grow but should not be planted outside until after the risk of spring frosts has passed. Plant in full sun in fertile soil and keep them well watered.

TASTING NOTES

*Zucchini muffins*

A great recipe for an abundant crop, these muffins freeze well. Their flavor is slightly savory but the frosting adds a light, sweet twist.

**Preparation time:** 15 minutes
**Cooking time:** 25 minutes
**Serves:** makes 12 muffins

• 2oz (50g) grated zucchini

• 1 grated apple

• 1 orange, halved

• 1 egg

• 3oz (75g) butter, melted

• 11oz (300g) self-rising flour

• ½ tsp baking powder

• ½ tsp cinnamon

• 4oz (100g) golden superfine sugar

• Optional: 1 tub soft cheese mixed with
  3 tbsp confectioners' sugar, to make frosting

Preheat a conventional oven to 375°F (190°C / gas mark 5 / fan 170°C).

Squeeze the orange and add to the grated zucchinis and apple in a bowl.

Stir in the egg and butter.

Sieve in the flour, baking powder, and cinnamon.

Add the sugar, and mix well until combined.

Spoon the mixture into muffin tins. Place in the oven for 20–25 minutes.

# Cardoon
## *Cynara cardunculus*

**ABOVE:** Not only can the foliage of cardoons be blanched and eaten, but their flowerheads are also beautiful, making them suitable for the herbaceous border as well as the kitchen garden.

**Common name:** Cardoon

**Type:** Perennial

**Climate:** Hardy, cold winter

**Size:** 8ft (2.5m)

**Origin:** Mediterranean

**History:** The cardoon has been cultivated in the Mediterranean region for thousands of years. Roman gardeners are thought to have been responsible for taming this thistle into a garden vegetable, and it was a Roman custom to dip tender, young cardoon stems in a simple sauce of warm olive oil and butter and eat them raw. Cardoons were very popular in the Victorian era in Britain but are now grown mainly for their striking silvery foliage in the ornamental garden.

**Cultivation:** Wrap the stems up in late fall with cardboard or sacking to blanch. Remove three weeks later and harvest the succulent stems. Cut the plant down to ground level in early spring like any other herbaceous perennial. Remove the flowerheads that form during the year as this depletes the plant's energy.

They are easy to grow in the garden and although they can be grown from seed, it is quicker to buy plants from the garden center. A free alternative is to find a friend with this plant in their garden, as it can easily be divided in late fall by removing offsets with a sharp spade.

**Storage:** The stems do not last long and should be used within a few days of harvesting. They can be frozen but their flavor and texture will be lost.

**Preparation:** Cardoon can be eaten raw or cooked. When eaten raw it is important to separate the stalks and remove the strings and inner white skin. Cut the stalks into lengths and thinly slice the heart. To prepare for cooking, separate the heart and stalks and slice or cut into lengths and cook in boiling salted water with added lemon juice for 30–40 minutes or until tender. Peel away the string and skin and serve hot. May also be sautéed or braised.

This tall graceful plant with its large, purple thistle head and spiny, silvery foliage is one of the aristocrats of the traditional herbaceous border, yet it also provides a bounty for the dining table. Very closely related to the globe artichoke, cardoons are grown in the kitchen garden for their long, silvery-gray stems or stalks. This delicacy is a popular vegetable in Europe, particularly in France, Italy, and Spain, but it is considered in the UK as more of an edible curiosity rather than something delicious. The stems are usually boiled, steamed, or braised and taste great when served with a rich and strongly flavored cheese sauce or added to a creamy gratin. They provide a nutritional side dish as they are high in potassium, calcium, and iron; they can also be baked or roasted. In the Piedmont region of Italy the stems are eaten raw with the dipping sauce *bagna càuda*.

Cardoons are monsters growing upward and outward to at least 6½ft, so give them plenty of space in the vegetable garden. Plant them in a sunny, sheltered site in well-drained soil.

The stems should be blanched to enjoy eating them. By excluding the sunlight from the stems it reduces the bitterness and makes them tender and

**ABOVE:** Cardoons have a long history of being cultivated for their ornamental qualities as they have beautiful architectural foliage and attractive blue thistle-like flowerheads. In the vegetable garden however, they should not be allowed to flower.

succulent. To blanch them, in late summer the stems should be gathered up into the center of the plant and tied together with garden twine. Wear gloves to do this, as the stems can be quite prickly. Do it on a dry day as excess moisture will quickly rot the stems and foliage. Wrap a hessian sack or cardboard around the stems and put a stout stake in place to prevent the upright column being blown over in the wind. Leave the cover in place for about three weeks and the reward will be delicious cardoon stems ready for the kitchen. Cut the remainder of the plant down and repeat the process the following year. Avoid blanching the stems on newly planted cardoons.

> "A large garden vegetable in the luxury class, and not for small-space growing, the cardoon is as thistly in aspect as the globe artichoke."
>
> **Charles Boff,** *How to Grow and Produce Your Own Food,* (1946)

## NUTRITION

Cardoons are a good source of potassium, calcium, manganese, magnesium, copper, and folates. They are free from cholesterol, fat, and saturated fat. They also contain high levels of vitamin A, vitamin C, iron, and phosphorus, and are a very good source of dietary fiber.

# Globe artichoke
## *Cynara cardunculus* Scolymus Group

**Common name:** Globe artichoke, artichoke, French artichoke

**Type:** Perennial

**Climate:** Hardy, average to cold winter

**Size:** 8ft (2.5m)

**Origin:** North Africa

**History:** The globe artichoke was first cultivated over 3,000 years ago in the Middle East and was popular in the kitchens of ancient Rome. It was believed to be a potent aphrodisiac by the Romans. There is a Greek myth that the first artichoke was a woman of amazing beauty named Cynara, who lived on the island of Zinari. The god Zeus, who was there visiting his brother Poseidon, fell in love with her and decided to make her a goddess. Cynara missed her home and mother so much that she would sneak back to earth from Mount Olympus to visit her there. This infuriated Zeus, who in a fit of rage exacted his retribution by hurling her back to earth and transforming her into the first artichoke. It is from her name that we now get the botanical name for artichoke, *Cynara*.

**Cultivation:** Globe artichokes are best grown from plants or offsets as seed can give variable results. Plants should be spaced 29½in apart. They require a sunny, fertile soil. Add grit in the soil to make it less heavy. Mulch around the plant in spring to suppress weeds and keep the plants well watered. Harvest the flowerheads in summer when they reach the size of a tennis ball and before the flower opens.

**Storage:** Store globe artichokes in the fridge for a couple of days at the most because they do not last. Alternatively, they can be frozen but the stem and hearts should be removed. The hearts also can be stored in jars of oil or vinegar.

**Preparation:** Before cooking, cut the stalks off the artichokes and snip off a few of the rough outer leaves with scissors to remove any brown edges. Trim the tips of the remaining leaves.

**LEFT:** Globe artichokes are closely related to cardoons, but are grown for their edible flowerheads, which should be removed at this stage before they open.

If ever there was a delicacy that epitomizes a gourmet feast fit for a food connoisseur then this is it. Being regarded as a "posh crop" by most people due to the small yield from each bulky plant, once the base of the edible flower bud or "heart" has been tasted it is something that keeps chefs coming back for more, and it is not just foodies who love this plant—its beautiful, steely-gray ornamental foliage, statuesque purple flowerheads, and wonderful ornamental and architectural structure mean it is adored by ornamental gardeners too. If left unharvested, the wildlife also enjoy the heads as they attract a whole range of bees, butterflies, and other beneficial pollinators to the garden. Varieties of note include "Gros Vert de Lâon" for its superb flavor and "Carciofo Violetto Precoce," although this variety is not as frost hardy.

The globe artichoke flowerhead is usually boiled or steamed and then two parts of the plant are eaten, the main part being the plump green or purple-tinged young flower buds collectively known as the heart. The other edible part is the

base of the scale-like bracts. After boiling, these taste delicious when dipped in a hollandaise sauce or garlic butter, with the remainder of the bracts being discarded. Other popular methods of using artichokes include to chargrill them and add them to salads and risottos.

Globe artichokes require a fertile and well-drained soil in full sun. Because the plants are perennial, they will be in the same ground for a long time so it is important that the ground is prepared thoroughly prior to planting. Dig over the beds and

**ABOVE:** This decorative lithograph is by Anton Seder (1850–1916). The Art Noveau Print, called artichokes, clearly shows the decorative qualities of this attractive perennial.

**BELOW:** The edible part of the globe artichoke is the flower bud or heart in the center of the flowerhead. The base of the immature scale bracts can also be pulled off and eaten.

## NUTRITION

Globe artichokes are an excellent source of dietary fiber, magnesium, manganese, niacin, riboflavin, thiamin, vitamin A, and potassium. They are also a very good source of vitamin C and folic acid.

> "Life is like eating artichokes;
> you have got to go through so much
> to get so little."

**Thomas Aloysius (Tad) Dorgan, cartoonist**

break up any hard, compacted soil that may be below the surface. Remove any perennial weeds in their entirety and then dig in plenty of well-rotted organic matter. Artichokes are often propagated from suckers or side shoots, sometimes called "offsets," which are removed from the main plant in spring and potted up. Artichokes can be grown from seed in spring or fall but this does produce variable results, so it is best to buy small plants or propagate your own from offsets. Seeds should be sown in a seed tray at a depth of 1in. They should be potted on individually to 3½in pots a few weeks later and planted out in late spring. Plants should be spaced at least 29½in apart.

The globes are harvested with pruning shears when they are about the size of a tennis ball, before they open and start to flower. There is often a second flush of flowerheads after harvesting and these too can be harvested and eaten in the same way, or left to develop and open for ornamental effect. In fall the plant should be cut back to near ground level. Mulch around the plant each spring with a thick layer of mulch to suppress any weeds. Some of the less hardy varieties will need protection during the winter months.

**RIGHT:** Globe artichokes should be harvested when the head is about tennis ball size. They are ready for picking from mid to late summer.

TASTING NOTES

*Baked globe artichokes*

This classic appetizer is so quick and easy to prepare. Once baked they are delicious dipped in mayonnaise or added to salads.

**Preparation time:** 5 minutes
**Cooking time:** 50 minutes
**Serves:** 6 people

· 6 small globe artichokes

· 6 tbsp olive oil

· Salt and pepper, to taste

Preheat a conventional oven to 400°F (200°C / gas mark 6 / fan 180°C).

Trim the artichoke stalks.

Add the artichokes to a pan of boiled, salted water. Cover and simmer for about 30 minutes.

Drain and halve the artichokes lengthwise and remove the heart with a spoon.

Place the artichokes cut side up on a baking tray and drizzle with olive oil. Season and bake for about 15–20 minutes.

# Dahlia tuber (yam)
## *Dahlia*

**Common name:** Dahlia, yam

**Type:** Tuberous perennial

**Climate:** Tender to half-hardy, cool glasshouse or mild winter

**Size:** 4ft (1.2m)

**Origin:** Mexico

**History:** In 1525 the Spaniards reported finding dahlias growing in Mexico, but the earliest known description is by Francisco Hernández, physician to the Spanish King Philip II, who was ordered to visit Mexico in 1570 to study the "natural products of that country." They were used as a source of food by the indigenous peoples, and were both gathered in the wild and cultivated. It is believed that the Aztecs used them to treat epilepsy. The Plants were taken back to Europe by Spanish adventurers. During the 1800s the popularity of dahlias surged; thousands of ornamental varieties emerged and were documented. Dahlia tubers were used as a food crop to supplement potatoes, but after a brief time it was decided that they were better suited to decoration than food.

**Cultivation:** Plant tubers 4in deep in the soil in the spring. If growing them to harvest tubers later in the year, most of the flowerheads should be removed to allow the energy to be channeled into the root system. Harvest the tubers in fall when the first frosts have blackened the foliage.

**Storage:** Dahlias will store over winter if kept in a cool, dark, frost-free place. Cut back the stems and place the remainder of the plant in storage in boxes of sand or compost until ready to plant out again in spring. Check them over regularly for rot and remove those affected immediately.

**Preparation:** Wash and peel the tubers, then dice. To cook, simply place in salted boiling water for about 20 minutes or until tender. They can also be roasted, baked, or fried like ordinary potatoes.

**BELOW:** Dahlias originate from South America and were introduced to Europe originally as a possible blight-resistant alternative to the humble potato.

Putting the yum into yam, dahlias can be cooked just like a potato or a sweet potato to make sumptuous dishes. Considered by most gardeners to be a solely ornamental plant suitable for bedding displays or the herbaceous border, dahlia species were originally cultivated by the Aztecs for their tubers as an edible and nutritional food source. The dahlia species was introduced to the Western world by the 18th-century botanist Anders Dahl (hence the name dahlia), who considered the possibility that it would supersede the potato as part of the staple diet. Nowadays, dahlias are more of a curiosity than an edible treat and make a fantastic talking point at the dinner table. Of course, dahlias that are bought from garden centers and seed catalogs have been bred for their flowering ability, and not for their taste. Therefore, not surprisingly, many varieties of tubers can often be small, watery, and lacking in flavor. However, some of the older heritage varieties are closer to the original South American yam and are well worth growing.

Flavors vary and are often described as being nutty and similar to a water chestnut and the texture is slightly crunchier than a standard potato. They can be baked simply by being scrubbed and placed in the oven. If they taste bland, they can be livened up with creamy and garlic sauces or sliced and made into gratins. They can be made into chips or fries or roasted.

**RIGHT:** The edible part of the dahlias are the tubers of the root system. These should be dug up in fall, when the plumper ones can be removed for cooking.

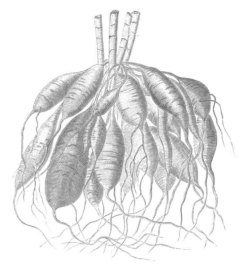

**ABOVE:** Dahlia tubers that are not to be eaten should be stored in a cool, dark, and frost-free place and replanted outside in spring once the risk of frosts is over.

If you suffer from potato blight each year in the garden, then this could be the tuber for you. Avoid eating dahlia tubers that have been bought that year from the garden center as they will probably have been chemically treated. Tubers should be planted in spring after the risk of fall frosts is over. They require a fertile soil in full sun. Add lots of organic matter prior to planting and as the plants grow they may need support with stakes to prevent them blowing over. Tubers should be harvested in fall when the foliage starts to die back. Dig the plants up carefully with a fork and remove about one third of the firmer, plumper tubers. Cut back the foliage and stems to about 4in away from the root system. Place unused tubers upside down in sand and store them in a frost-free place over winter. Plant them out the following spring.

# Carrot

## *Daucus carota*

**Common name:** Carrot

**Type:** Annual

**Climate:** Half-hardy to hardy, mild to average winter

**Size:** 6–8in (15–20cm)

**Origin:** Middle Asia (Afghanistan)

**History:** It is believed that the carrot originated as a cultivated plant some 5,000 years ago in Middle Asia around Afghanistan, then slowly spread into the Mediterranean area. The first carrots were mainly purple, with some white or black— but not orange. Their roots were thin and turnip shaped. It is believed the ancient Greeks and Romans cultivated carrots. For example, carrots are mentioned in the writing of Pliny the Elder and were prized by the Emperor Tiberius. Temple drawings from Egypt from 2000 BC show a purple plant, which some Egyptologists believe to be a purple carrot.

**Cultivation:** Sow seeds thinly in shallow drills between March and July. The early and late seasons can be extended by growing the plants under cloches. Thin them out to 6in apart and harvest about 9 to 12 weeks after sowing.

**Storage:** Carrots can be stored for a few months after picking if placed in boxes of sand or compost. Remove all foliage first. Alternatively, they can be frozen.

**Preparation:** Small new carrots should have their stalks removed and simply be scrubbed under cold water. Larger, older carrots should be peeled and have the ends cut off, then simply cut lengthwise into batons or slices. Carrots can be eaten raw or cooked in salted boiling water for about 20 minutes or until just tender, or steamed for about 30 minutes.

**BELOW:** Carrots prefer a light sandy soil in full sun. Soils that are stony or heavy will cause the roots to fork and twist.

## NUTRITION

Carrots are rich in antioxidants, vitamins A and C, and any B-complex vitamins such as folic acid, vitamin B6, and thiamine. They are also a rich source of carotenes. Its antioxidant property helps protect the body from diseases and cancers by scavenging harmful free radicals.

Carrots lend themselves to both savory and sweet dishes ranging from coleslaw to carrot cake. Boiled, steamed, or caramelized and roasted, there are so many dishes this popular orange root vegetable makes an appearance in. Yet, strangely, the orange carrot is a relatively new kid on the block and prior to the 16th century carrots were white, purple, and yellow with not an orange one in sight. It is supposed to have been the Dutch growers that developed the orange color, probably as a patriotic tribute to the House of Orange. It could now be said that carrots have returned to their roots, as there is a revival in some of the older varieties of colored carrots. "Purple Haze" is a popular purple one worth trying while "Rainbow" provides a selection of a few of the different colors all in one seed packet.

Carrots require a fertile, deep but light loamy soil that is free of stones as these can hinder the development of the tap root and cause forking. Carrots can also struggle to penetrate heavy clay soils, so they are better grown in raised containers and deep window boxes if space is a problem.

**ABOVE:** Orange is a relatively new color for these sweet root vegetables. Originally they were purple, white, and yellow. It was not until the 16th and 17th centuries that orange ones appeared.

**LEFT:** Carrots are biennial and if left in the ground for the second year, will produce an attractive flowerhead that can be used for garnishing dishes.

Alternatively, short "Chantenay" types of carrot can be grown such as "Carson" or the round, globe carrots called "Parmex."

There is a particular trend for baby carrots at the moment, and these are simply ones that have been harvested from the ground before they have had a chance to mature and are easy to grow at home.

Carrots can be sown as early as February under cloches if early varieties such as "Early Nantes 2" are

## Tasting notes

### *Carrots Vichy*

This is a classic French recipe using tender juicy carrots coated in a rich buttery glaze that makes a perfect side dish to many main meals. Substitute orange carrots for other colors such as purple or yellow to really make this dish stand out. This dish was named for the French town of the same name.

**Preparation time:** 5 minutes
**Cooking time:** 20 minutes
**Serves:** 4 people

· 20oz (600g) carrots, sliced julienned

· Knob of butter

· 1 tsp molasses sugar

· Salt and pepper, to taste

· 12floz (350ml) chicken broth

· Handful of mixed herbs, chopped

Put the carrots into a pan with the butter, sugar, salt, and pepper.

Add the chicken broth, bring to the boil, and cover and cook for about 10 minutes.

Remove the lid and furiously boil until the liquid evaporates and has produced a glaze—after about 10 minutes.

Tip into a warm serving dish and sprinkle with mixed herbs, such as parsley, cilantro, or chives.

chosen. Otherwise they should be sown between March and July. Sow seed thinly in shallow drills about ½in deep in rows 6in apart. Seedlings should eventually be thinned out to about 6in apart—do not forget to eat the thinnings. For growing baby carrots a spacing of about 2in between each plant is sufficient. Avoid using old seed as it tends to go stale quickly, so buy new to ensure that it is fresh and viable. Make sowings regularly every few weeks so that there are carrots to harvest regularly throughout the season.

> "Sowe carrets in your garden, and humbly praise God for them, as for a singular and great blessing."
>
> Richard Gardener, *Profitable Instructions for the Manuring, Sowing and Planting of Kitchen Gardens*, (1599)

**RIGHT:** Carrots have been cultivated for centuries. This picture in the *Vienna Dioscorides*, an early 6th-century illuminated manuscript, shows a yellow variety of carrot.

**ABOVE:** Carrots have attractive feathery or fern-like, serrated foliage and pale white flat flowerheads. Wild carrots are commonly seen in the countryside and are said to have medicinal uses too.

If the root tops start to poke above the ground they should be covered back with soil to prevent them turning green. Due to their fine foliage they are fairly drought resistant and only in extremely hot and dry conditions do they need watering. Early varieties of carrot should be ready for harvesting about 9 weeks after sowing, whereas main crops such as "Autumn King 2" will take about 12 weeks from sowing to maturity.

Main crop varieties will store for much longer than earlier varieties, but most can be stored in boxes in sand for a few months after harvesting.

### Friends and enemies

Not only do carrots and onions go well in the kitchen in dishes such as coleslaw and relishes, but they also make great companions in the garden. Carrots can suffer from a pest called carrot fly, which lays eggs at the base of the plant; later, maggots hatch from the eggs and infest and ruin crops. It is thought that by planting onions next to carrots the flies are prevented from landing as they get confused by the aroma. As if that is not good enough, carrots also help to deter the onion fly pest.

Another solution to avoiding carrot fly is to grow resistant varieties such as "Flyaway" and "Resistafly." Erecting a 24in-tall mesh barrier is perhaps the most effective method as it excludes the flies, which only fly low to the ground.

# WEEDING AND MAINTENANCE

Regular weekly weeding is vital if you are to get optimum growth from your vegetables, otherwise they will compete for water, nutrients, and, in the case of the taller weeds—light. Left untended, annual weeds will start to self-sow and perennial weeds will rapidly spread, making the job a lot harder to get on top of. If beds are to remain empty for a while then it is worth placing a black landscape fabric over the surface to prevent the germination of weeds. Where weeds are a real problem on the plot, it is worth permanently retaining the fabric, and planting vegetables through it. Regularly mulching the beds should also suppress weeds and encourage the vegetables to grow and out-compete their competitors.

> "I scarcely dare trust myself to speak of the weeds. They grow as if the devil was in them."
>
> **Charles Dudley Warner, (1876)**

### ANNUAL WEEDS

Annual weeds usually have a small root system and can simply be hoed off. Work along the rows, moving backward to avoid treading on areas already worked on. Push the hoe just below the surface of the soil, slicing through the roots and leaving them on the surface. The weeds can be left to desiccate in the sun during summer, but in less inclement weather they should be gathered up with a rake and added to the compost heap.

Annual weeds should be hoed off or pulled up before they set seed, otherwise they will rapidly spread throughout the vegetable plot.

Annual weeds include:
- Hairy bittercress
- Fat hen
- Shepherd's purse
- Goosegrass
- Annual meadow grass
- Groundsel

Annual weeds can also be burned off using a flame gun, taking care not to damage the vegetables.

**LEFT:** Shepherd's purse is a commonly found annual weed which can be hoed off and added to the compost heap. Try to catch it before is releases its seeds from its purse-like pods.

## PERENNIAL WEEDS

These weeds are the bane of the vegetable gardener's world. Once they have got their roots into the plot, they can be tricky to eradicate. Their root system can be invasive and quickly spread throughout the vegetable beds. Hoeing is ineffective as the deep, fleshy roots of perennial weeds will remain in the ground and quickly resprout new shoots.

For nonorganic growers a systemic weedkiller can be used, which will kill the roots. Alternatively, the plants can be dug out using a fork. A spade can be used but care needs to be taken not to slice through the roots as this will help the plants spread farther.

Fresh perennial weeds must not be added to the compost heap as they will rapidly spread. Instead, leave the weeds out in the sun to dry for a few weeks, which should kill the living material, and they can then be added to the compost heap. If there is no sun forecast, some plants can be seeped in water or placed in black bags and left for a few months before being added to the heap.

Perennial weeds include:
- Bindweed
- Ground elder
- Perennial nettle
- Creeping buttercup
- Dock
- Spear thistle
- Speedwell
- Dandelions

**BELOW:** Bindweed is one of the worst types of perennial weeds to find in the herbaceous border as it is so invasive and gets tangled up among the plants.

---

### USEFUL WEEDING TOOLS

There are a variety of different tools that can be used for removing weeds from the ground.

Two-pronged weeding tools are useful for prizing out perennials with long taproots. Ensure that each tine is on either side of the plant before lifting it out.

Narrow-bladed trowels can be used to lever out perennials or annuals in the vegetable bed without disturbing nearby roots

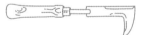

An L-shaped tool is suitable for scraping between narrow gaps such as paving slabs or brick paths on the allotment, to remove weeds or moss.

# Salad arugula

## *Eruca vesicaria* subsp. *sativa*

**Common name:** Salad arugula, rocket, rucola, Italian cress

**Type:** Annual

**Climate:** Half-hardy, mild winter

**Size:** 6in (15cm)

**Origin:** Mediterranean

**History:** In Roman times arugula was grown for both its leaves and its seed, and it was considered to be an aphrodisiac with added medicinal properties. It is one of the oldest vegetables cultivated. Arugula has become popular again recently and features heavily in the Mediterranean diet.

**Cultivation:** Seeds should be sown in shallow drills from late summer through to mid-fall. Plants need covering with cloches as winter approaches so that leaves can be regularly harvested throughout winter.

**Storage:** Leaves do not last long once picked, so harvest regularly from the garden as and when needed.

**Preparation:** To prepare, simply pick the arugula leaves and wash thoroughly under cold running water to remove any dirt or pests.

**ABOVE:** Arugula is a very fast-growing, leafy vegetable and can be grown on its own, but is also commonly found in seed mixes for cut-and-come-again cultivation.

## NUTRITION

Arugula is an excellent source of vitamins A, C, and K and is rich in the B-complex vitamins such as thiamin, riboflavin, niacin, and vitamin $B_6$. These vitamins help to promote a healthy immune system and good bone health.

There is a plethora of trendy salad leaves that are very much in vogue not just in restaurants but also in grocery stores where the shelves are full of vacuum-packed assortments. Leaves range from the bitter chicories and endives to the peppery Japanese brassicas such as mizuna and Chinese cabbage. Often these bags are very expensive and yet the leaves are so easy to grow at home. These plants hardly take up any space at all, and can even be sown in a window box just outside the kitchen so that handfuls can be cut, harvested, and thrown into a dish without even having even to step out into the garden. One of the most popular salad leaves is arugula because it is so easy to grow, and it has a unique spicy and peppery flavor. The older leaves are slightly hotter and are usually steamed or added to stir-fries. They make a superb spinach substitute. The younger leaves are usually eaten raw

TASTING NOTES

### Simple arugula and Parmesan salad

This is a versatile dish that will go with many different flavors. You can even add chopped, crispy bacon for some extra crunch.

**Preparation time:** 5 minutes
**Serves:** 2 people (as an appetizer)

· 1 large bunch arugula

· 1½oz (45g) Parmesan cheese

· 3floz (100ml) olive oil

· 4 tbsp lemon juice

· 2 tsp sea salt

· Black pepper, to taste

Wash the arugula and lightly pat dry.

Shave the Parmesan using a potato peeler.

Whisk together the olive oil, lemon juice, and salt in a large nonmetallic bowl.

Add the arugula leaves and toss together.

Simply arrange the dressed leaves on a serving plate. Scatter the Parmesan shavings over the arugula, add pepper, and serve.

**LEFT:** Arugula can be grown for most of the year but can be prone to bolting in summer, so is often sown in fall under cloches and treated as a winter and spring crop for salads.

## OTHER TYPES OF CUT-AND-COME-AGAIN SALAD LEAVES

Arugula can be grown on its own or as part of a seed mix. Browsing through seed catalogs enables you to pick out mixes that appeal to your taste buds. Other popular types of cut-and-come-again include land cress (*Barbarea verna*), white mustard (*Brassica hirta*), garden cress (*Lepidium sativum*), winter purslane, (*Claytonia perfoliata*) and lamb's lettuce (*Valerianella locusta*).

**ABOVE:** Garden cress (*Lepidium sativum*)

**RIGHT:** Arugula was grown by the Romans for both its aromatic leaves and its seeds. It was also considered to have medicinal qualities and was used as an aphrodisiac.

in salads or even sandwich fillings. The flowers are also edible. The leaves are often grown as cut-and-come-again leaves, which simply means that the leaves are cut with scissors near the base of the plant and it resprouts, providing numerous servings throughout the growing season.

Sow seeds regularly between April and September in fertile, well-drained soil or in a window box. Plants should be thinned out to a spacing of between 6in and 8in. As the alternate name "rocket" suggests, arugula is a fast grower and it is possible to start harvesting leaves just three weeks after sowing. Varieties worth trying include "Apollo" and "Runway."

### GROWING FOR WINTER

Arugula is a great fall and winter salad crop when lettuce crops are scarce. It loves it slightly cool to bring out the best of its flavors and will very often bolt and run to seed if the weather is too dry or hot. It should be sown thinly in late summer or early fall in shallow drills ½in deep in rows 12in apart. After germination the arugula can be thinned to 6in apart—remember to add the thinnings to the next salad. As cooler weather approaches, the plants should be covered with a cloche. Harvest throughout fall and winter by either snipping off individual leaves or by harvesting the individual plants.

# Florence fennel
## *Foeniculum vulgare* var. *azoricum*

**Common name:** Florence fennel, finocchio, or bulbing fennel

**Type:** Perennial

**Climate:** Tender, frost-free winter

**Size:** 24–31½in (60–80cm)

**Origin:** Mediterranean

**History:** The word "fennel" comes from the Middle English *fenel* or *fenyl*, meaning "hay." In Greek mythology, Prometheus used the stalk of a fennel plant to steal fire from the gods. Also, it was from the giant fennel that the Bacchanalian wands of the Greek god Dionysus and his followers were said to have come.

**RIGHT:** Contrary to popular belief, Florence fennel is not a bulb, but is a swollen stem. The attractive flowerheads produce seeds that can also be used as a flavoring in cooking.

**Cultivation:** Sow seeds from late spring to early summer and thin them to 10in apart in rows 14in apart. Do not sow too early as they have a tendency to bolt.

**Storage:** Fennel bulbs will not last for long after being harvested, and can only remain in the fridge for a few days.

**Preparation:** Florence fennel's bulbous root can be blanched or eaten raw. Fennel is also good braised. To prepare, simply trim both the root and the stalk ends. Chop or grate if it is to be eaten raw. To cook, quarter the bulb and cook in boiling salted water for about 30 minutes. Drain and slice. The slices can then be sautéed in melted butter.

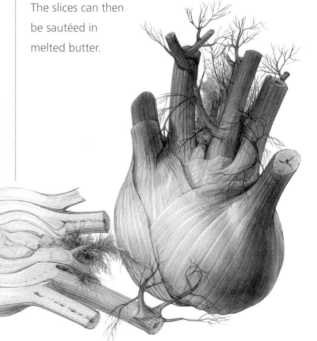

## NUTRITION

Fennel seeds and bulbs are a good source of dietary fiber and aid digestion. The seeds and bulbs are also a good source of vitamin C and other nutritious vitamins and minerals. Fennel also contains high levels of the B vitamin folate, which is especially helpful for maintaining the health of our blood vessels.

The name gives away the origins of this peculiar looking vegetable with a fat, swollen white stem at the base of the plant. Florence fennel, or finocchio as it is more commonly known in Italy, is very popular in their cuisine. It has a strong aniseed flavor that some may find overpowering when sliced or grated and served raw in salads, but when cooked the flavor becomes much milder. The vegetable goes particularly well with strong fish dishes such as salmon and sardines, and also combines well with celery and clean-tasting flavorings such as mint or lemon juice. The bulb is usually steamed or boiled but it can also be roasted whole. The strongly flavored aniseed foliage can also be used for flavoring stews and fish soup or simply used as an attractive garnish.

Fennel requires a fertile, light soil in plenty of sunshine. On heavy clay soils, it may be better to grow in raised beds. Alternatively plenty of grit should be added to help with drainage. Seeds can be sown indoors in pots or modules but they dislike root disturbance so directly sowing outdoors is a better option. There is no rush to sow the seeds, because if sown too early they have a tendency to bolt, although there are bolt-resistant varieties worth trying such as "Zefa Fino," "Cantino," and "Amigo." Aim to sow thinly between midspring and early summer in ½in drills in rows 14in apart. Thin the plants to 10in apart after germination.

**BELOW:** Florence fennel has a slight aniseed flavor, similar to star anise, and is often used to flavor fish dishes or poultry. The foliage can also be used for flavoring.

## NOT THE HERB

Do not get this plant confused with the closely related herb fennel, which is an attractive, billowing perennial that can grow up to 5ft in height. It too has aniseed-flavored leaves, which are used to flavor fish and chicken dishes. Its seeds are often used dried in breads and sauces. There is an attractive bronze-foliaged form.

ABOVE: The key ingredient to getting the stems to swell is plenty of water. If it is dry in springtime, the plants will need watering practically every day.

The two essential ingredients to getting a decent swollen stem from Florence fennel are water and sunshine. It needs lots of moisture to enable the stem to swell properly, so in dry spells it is essential that the plant is kept well watered. As the plant expands, the lower section of the stem can be earthed up with soil in order to blanch it and sweeten up the flavor.

Bulbs are usually ready for harvesting about 14 to 16 weeks after sowing. The bulb should be between the size of a golf ball and tennis ball. If cut about 1in above the ground, this will encourage a further flurry of feathery shoots to appear later, which can be harvested and used for aniseed flavoring and garnish.

### TASTING NOTES

#### *Simple roasted fennel*

Roasting fennel stems brings out their inherent sweetness. Delicious if served with roasted lamb, chicken, or fish dishes.

**Preparation time:** 5 minutes
**Cooking time:** 40 minutes
**Serves:** 4 people (as a side dish)

· 2 fennel bulbs, stalks cut off, bulbs halved lengthwise and cut lengthwise in thick pieces

· 2 tbsp olive oil

· 1 tbsp balsamic vinegar

Preheat a conventional oven to 400°F (200°C / gas mark 6 / fan 180°C).

Brush olive oil over the fennel pieces and sprinkle on some balsamic vinegar.

Grease a baking dish and lay out the pieces of fennel; roast for 30–40 minutes.

# Jerusalem artichoke
*Helianthus tuberosus*

**Common names:** Jerusalem artichoke, sunroot, earth apple, sunchoke

**Type:** Tuberous perennial

**Climate:** Fully hardy

**Size:** Up to 8ft (2.5m)

**Origin:** North America

**History** First cultivated by Native Americans, the French explorer Samuel de Champlain discovered plants cultivated at Cape Cod in 1605 and brought some back to France.

## MYSTERIOUS NAME

Bizarrely, the Jerusalem artichoke has nothing to do with globe artichokes. The name is attributed to the French explorer Samuel de Champlain, who sent plant samples back to France during his travels in the early 17th century, noting they had a similar flavor to globe artichokes. The vegetable also has nothing to do with Jerusalem. One theory behind its name is that it is a corrupted form of *girasole*, the Italian name for sunflower, to which it is closely related, as used by Italian settlers in North America.

By the mid 1600s, the Jerusalem artichoke had become a very common vegetable in Europe and reached its peak of popularity in the 19th century.

**Cultivation:** Plant tubers 2–4in deep in fertile, well-drained soil. Harvest in fall and winter as required.

**Storage:** Keep in the ground until ready to use. Avoid freezing as the texture deteriorates unless it's going to be puréed. After harvesting, store the tubers in a cool, dark, frost-free place, such as a fridge or shed during winter until ready for cooking.

**Preparation:** Par-boil the tubers before attempting to peel them as this makes the skin come off more easily. The flesh rapidly discolors when exposed to air, so immediately place them in water with a dash of lemon juice after peeling or chopping.

Closely related to sunflowers, this impressive perennial vegetable provides a dazzling display of attractive, tall yellow flowers, yet its real treat lies buried below the surface. Its knobbly, reddish-brown tuber is a gourmet delight in the kitchen. It is expensive to buy in stores and yet is probably one of the easiest vegetables to grow in the kitchen garden. If you have a tendency toward

**RIGHT:** Jerusalem artichoke enriches both the garden and the vegetable plot thanks to its striking yellow flowers, which appear from midsummer.

laziness in the garden, then this has to be the perfect plant for you. It out-competes surrounding weeds and thrives in most soils, requiring hardly any maintenance at all. It is incredibly easy to grow—in fact, almost too easy. If the plant is not kept in check, it can become large and unruly and smother other nearby plants. However, it will reward you with a bumper crop each year for minimum effort.

Cook with them as you would a potato. They can be boiled, roasted, sautéed, baked, and mashed. They have a distinctive nutty-yet-sweet flavor and unlike potatoes can also be sliced raw and added to salads or stir-fries. For total indulgence, try chopping them into chunks, dipping them in batter, and frying them.

Tubers for planting can be bought from good-quality grocery stores and specific varieties can be purchased from seed companies. Carefully

**LEFT:** A delight for the gourmet gardener, Jerusalem artichoke is an expensive vegetable to buy in stores, but this plant is remarkably easy to grow and its reddish-brown tuber is simple to cook.

select where you are to grow them, ideally avoiding the south and west sides of your plot as their 8ft height will cast shade onto the vegetable plants beyond. They should be planted out in early spring, burying each tuber 4in deep and 20in apart. Water the plants well after planting.

Tubers can just be left in the ground to regenerate each year. However, their quality will gradually deteriorate. Ideally the ground should be cleared every three or four years and the healthiest tubers selected and planted in a freshly dug patch. This is also a good way of keeping their spread in check.

Once the plants are about knee-height, pull the soil up around the base of each stem to about 6in to prevent them swaying about in the wind. As the foliage starts to turn yellow in fall, the stems can be cut back to just above ground level. Lay the stems over the soil to keep the frost off the ground, making them easier to harvest during the colder months. Tubers are ready for harvesting in fall and can remain in the ground throughout winter. Dig them up using a fork, taking care not to spear the tubers.

## NUTRITIONAL BENEFITS

The tubers are very high in iron, vitamin C, and both phosphorous and potassium. They also contain high levels of inulin, which is associated with intestinal health because of its probiotic properties or beneficial bacteria. However, do not overindulge with artichokes if you have a slightly sensitive stomach or a tendency for flatulence. Their effect on the body's gastric wind output is legendary!

# Daylily
## *Hemerocallis*

**Common name:** Daylily

**Type:** Rhizomatous perennial

**Climate:** Hardy, very cold winter

**Size:** 3ft (1m)

**Origin:** Far East

**History:** Daylilies were valued throughout Asia for medicine and food as well as for their beauty. They appear in a lot of Asian art and legends. Daylilies arrived in Europe from China, Japan, Korea, and Eastern Siberia during the 16th century, and by the 17th century had crossed the Atlantic to North America.

**Cultivation:** They need very little looking after. Keep them weed-free during the summer and watered in dry periods. Cut the flowered stems back down at the end of the growing season. They prefer full sun but will tolerate some shade. Divide the plant every few years by slicing through the rhizome root system.

**Storage:** Flowers do not last for long, but can be dried, which will extend their culinary life for a few days. Roots will store for a few weeks if kept in a cool, dark place such as the garage.

**Preparation:** To prepare simply cut the 1in long rhizomes from the roots and wash in cold water to remove the dirt. Boil in salted water for 15 minutes.

**LEFT:** Daylilies are a beautiful addition to the garden, with striking colored flowers coming in an array of colors including red, orange, and yellow. They are very easy to grow and low maintenance.

Daylilies are literally one of the perennial favorites in the garden for their gloriously colored flowers coming in fiery, reds, oranges, and yellows and their attractive, long strap-like leaves. However, unbeknown to many the entire plant is edible, stretching from the tallest leaf right down to its root system, making it not just a feast for the eyes but a feast for the stomach too. They have been grown for centuries in Asia as a food crop, particularly in China and Japan, and yet despite the worldwide popularity of daylilies as an ornamental plant, many people are missing out on a golden opportunity to sample an array of gourmet delights.

Daylilies' beauty is fleeting and in fact the botanical name *Hemerocallis* means "beautiful for a day." Individual blooms last for one day, opening in the morning and fading at night, hence their name daylilies. However, this unusual flowering phenomenon means that there are always plenty of tasty swollen, plump flower buds loaded up and ready to be harvested and used as a substitute in any recipe calling for green beans. Do not harvest all of the flower buds though as you want some of them to produce flowers, which are the highlight of the plant's edible prowess. These brightly colored blooms add a vibrancy and peppery zing to any salad. Use them for garnishing platters too. Alternatively they can be fried up in batter, a bit like a zucchini flower, and eaten as a side dish. Fresh flowers can

TASTING NOTES

*Edible parts of a daylily*

Daylily offers a part of its plant for cooking almost all year round, including winter when part of the roots can be harvested.

| | |
|---|---|
| Young shoots | Add emerging shoots to stir-fries and salads in spring. |
| Roots | Boil or bake them like a potato all year round, though they are best in the fall. |
| Leaves | Try in green salads and stir-fries in early to late summer. |
| Flower buds | Add to stir-fries in summer. |
| Flowers | Use in salads, stir-fries, or cook in batter in summer. |

also be stuffed with dried fruits, nuts, and cottage cheese with sweet herbs, tying the ends of the flowers together with chives stalks. The flowers have a slightly unusual chewy, thick texture that sets them apart from many other flowers. They can be dried and added to salads or stir-fries

The fresh emerging shoots have a very mild oniony flavor and can also be harvested, and can be chopped and added to stir-fries, or sautéed or steamed anytime in spring. Select shoots no longer than 5in tall as anything bigger will be too coarse.

**LEFT:** The flower petals are delicious when added to salads, but the swollen buds are equally tasty and can be used as a substitute for green beans in most recipes.

Very tender shoots can be used raw in salads or even as fillings for sandwiches. Daylilies require some sun to produce their abundant flower display but they will tolerate some dappled shade during the day. They require very little maintenance, not usually requiring staking or deadheading. They are simply cut back after the foliage starts to die back, but in milder areas its attractive strap-like leaves will remain above the ground. Every three or four years the plant should be lifted and divided, by slicing the plant into pieces with a sharp spade, throwing away the congested center, and replanting the fresher sections.

The best way to get daylilies growing in the garden is to buy young plants from the garden center and plant them in a sunny or partially shady location in spring. Alternatively, find a friend with a clump of it growing in their garden and slice through the root with a spade and take a section of it. It will not do their plant any harm at all. After planting simply water the plant and give the area around the root system a thorough mulching with organic matter such as garden compost.

In addition to dividing the plant every three or four years as part of the plant's general maintenance, it is possible at the end of each season to dig the plant up gently and harvest some of the roots. Daylilies are robust enough to tolerate this and once a few roots have been removed for the kitchen the plants can simply be planted back in their holes ready to flower again next year. There is no need to peel them; just give them a scrub and either bake or boil them like you would a potato or Jerusalem artichoke. Their flavor is reminiscent of turnips and nuts. They are recommended for detoxification diets.

**BELOW:** The name *Hemerocallis* means "beautiful for a day." Each flower lives and dies within the day, but thankfully they keep on producing flowers for most of midsummer.

## NUTRITION

Daylily flowers and tubers are high in protein and oils. The flower buds are good sources of betacarotene and vitamin C. They are very good in detoxifying the entire body system.

# Plantain lily
## *Hosta*

**Common name:** Hosta green shoots, plantain lilies, giboshi (in Japan), urui

**Type:** Perennial

**Climate:** Very hardy, very cold winter

**Size:** 25½in (65cm)

**Origin:** Japan, China, and Korea

**History:** Most of the species of hostas that provide the modern plants were introduced from Japan to Europe by Philipp Franz von Siebold in the mid 19th century.

**Cultivation:** Ideally hostas should be planted in shade in moist soil. However, they will tolerate sunshine. Keep them well watered during the year and watch out for slugs, which will quickly munch through the emerging shoots. Cut back the plant in fall and mulch around it in spring to help retain the moisture.

**Storage:** Hosta shoots will not last for long and the leaves quickly turn limp once they are picked. Harvest them from the garden in spring and early summer as and when they are needed.

**Preparation:** Hosta green shoots are best cut when young and tender, preferably in the early morning, and eaten as soon as possible. Similar in taste and texture to asparagus, they should be cut with a paring knife close to the soil. Then they need to be rinsed well under cold water.

The stems can be eaten raw or cooked but they are more bitter when taken from mature plants. If cooked place in salted boiling water and boil for about 3–4 minutes. Serve hot, smothered in melted butter and cracked black pepper.

Hostas are usually grown for their ornamental qualities with their showy, large foliage and long extended flower shoots. Perfect for woodland gardens and damp, shady corners, this popular herbaceous plant has yet another quality lurking among its attractive undergrowth. The baby shoots and leaves that emerge from the damp woodland soil are a popular springtime treat in Japan, where they are known as *urui*. The flavor has a taste reminiscent of a concoction of asparagus, lettuce, and spinach and they can be eaten raw or cooked. In addition the flowers are edible and can be added to salads or used as garnish.

There are various ways of using hostas in the kitchen, where their mild but crunchy texture can be used to enhance and complement a range of stronger flavors. The shoots and leaves are usually boiled or blanched and then added to salads and stir-fries. They work well with the sweetness of red onions, garlic, and fried tomatoes drizzled in honey or a Japanese sake wine dressing. They can also be fried up in batter as tempura and eaten dipped in a sweet plum sauce. Try them in wraps with a sweet-and-sour dressing and a goat's cheese filling with dried cranberries, or alternatively cook them up in omelettes with mushrooms, peppers, and sweet herbs. They can also be steamed in rice and wrapped up in seaweed or nori for homemade sushi.

*Urui* is incredibly hard to find in most stores and the only guaranteed way of a fresh harvest each year is to grow your own.

All hosta species appear to be edible, but *H. montana* and *H. sieboldii* are the most commonly used kitchen favorites as not only are they easy to grow but their leaves and shoots are also reputed to have the best flavor with the least amount of bitterness.

## GROWING HOSTAS

Hostas are associated with damp, woodland gardens but they will also tolerate sunnier locations and can be grown in an herbaceous border or even the vegetable patch, though it is important to keep the base of the plant moist. Prior to planting, dig over the soil and add plenty of organic matter, which will help retain the moisture. If possible add a barrow-load of leaf mold as this helps to replicate the conditions of a forest floor that hostas originally dwell in back in their native Asian woodlands. Plant hostas at about 24in apart depending on variety. Select a handful of plants if you plan on harvesting the young shoots, as just one plant will not provide much *urui* each year. Water the plant in thoroughly after planting. During the season keep the areas weed-free to avoid competition for moisture and keep an eye out for slugs and snails, which feast on the shoots (see p.218).

Every two or three years hostas benefit from being dug up and having their rootball divided, by ruthlessly slicing through it with a sharp spade. Discard the central congested section and replant the remaining fresh sections back in the soil. This not only reinvigorates the plants, but also

**ABOVE:** Hostas are the perfect ornamental foliage plant for a shady area of the garden, but they are also a gourmet treat and in Japan are a very popular delicacy. They flower in summer.

multiplies your stock, meaning in subsequent years there will be even more urui to harvest.

When the shoots emerge, resist the temptation to pick all of them as this will kill the plant. Remove no more than a third, although several pickings over time can be made from the plant as it comes into growth. It is generally considered better to harvest early in the morning as the moisture content is higher. Shoots should ideally be between 4½in and 6in long, but it is better to catch them while they are still rolled and have not unfurled, although larger leaves can be picked and cooked as a substitute for spinach. The summer flowers are pretty but very short lived.

# Sweet potato
## *Ipomoea batatas*

**Common name:** Sweet potato, Spanish potato

**Type:** Tuberous annual

**Climate:** Tender, frost-free winter

**Size:** 16in (40cm)

**Origin:** Central and South America

**History:** Despite its name the sweet potato is not related to the common potato. Its history dates back to 750 BC in Peruvian records and it was eaten in Europe well before the true potato. In fact, Columbus brought the sweet potato to England from the island of Saint Thomas in 1493. The Tudors considered them to be an aphrodisiac. The Spanish word for sweet potato is *batata* and in French it is *patate douce*. In the 1490s the English term "potato" referred to the sweet potato rather than the white potato.

**Cultivation:** Sweet potatoes like a fertile, well-dug soil in full sun. The ground should be cleared of weeds and dug over, incorporating lots of well-rotted manure. Place black landscape fabric on the ground to help retain warmth and moisture and suppress weeds and then cut holes in it, to plant the mature slips through at 12in apart with 29½in between rows. They should be planted deeply, partly covering the stems with

**ABOVE:** Sweet potatoes are harvested from the ground like common potatoes, but are completely unrelated. They are more closely related to bindweed and morning glory.

### NUTRITION

Sweet potatoes are low in sodium and very low in saturated fats and cholesterol. They are also a good source of dietary fiber and contain good levels of vitamin A, C, and B6, as well as potassium.

soil as this will encourage a larger crop. They do require a good growing season, so to help them on their way, place a cloche over them and water them regularly as they grow. If growing under a cloche, then this will need ventilating on warm days.

The tubers form underground and are harvested in a similar way to potatoes. After 12–16 weeks the foliage will start to die back, a sign that they are ready for harvesting. Lift them with a fork before the first frosts, and enjoy.

**Storage:** They will store for a few months if their skins are cured in the sun or glasshouse and then kept in a frost-free place, but can also be used immediately after harvesting.

**Preparation:** Scrub the sweet potatoes well and, if boiling, peel after they are cooked as the flesh is soft and rather floury. They can be boiled, baked, fried, or roasted like the potato.

These gourmet potatoes must be one of the most versatile vegetables available, being a sweeter alternative to the white potato. They can be used in so many dishes and are suitable for frying, boiling, roasting, and mashing, and they make the most amazing chips and fries. Try using mashed sweet potato as an alternative topping to a pie and you will never look back.

They can be grated and eaten raw, and even their leaves and stems can be picked and added to

### Sweet potato family

Despite their culinary similarities to the potato, the sweet potato *Ipomoea batatas* is not actually related to the potato family, but is instead from the same group as the bindweed *Convolvulus* and the beautiful ornamental climber, morning glory. Thankfully sweet potatoes lack the vigor of their cousins, and although they have a sprawling habit they are much more manageable.

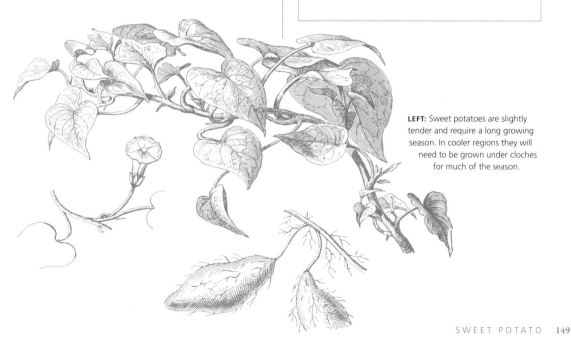

**LEFT:** Sweet potatoes are slightly tender and require a long growing season. In cooler regions they will need to be grown under cloches for much of the season.

### Sweet potato and beet

The color and flavor combinations of deep red beet and mellow orange sweet potato make them a delicious accompaniment to rich meats, particularly duck or venison.

**Preparation time:** 10 minutes
**Cooking time:** 2 hours
**Serves:** 10 people (as a side dish)

• 4 beets

• 6 sweet potatoes

• 3 tbsp olive oil

• Salt and pepper, to taste

Preheat a conventional oven to 375°F (190°C / gas mark 5 / fan 170°C).

Cover the beet with foil and place in the oven until tender—about 1–1½ hours.

Once cooled, peel the beet and cut into square chunks.

Cut the sweet potato into similar-size chunks.

Mix together, drizzle with olive oil, and season.

Place on a baking tray and into the oven; cook until tender, approximately 40–60 minutes.

stir-fries as an alternative to arugula or spinach. It gets even better, as they can also be used in desserts such as pies and cakes, and yet despite their sweetness they are low in fat, containing a mere 90kcal per 3½oz and are packed full of carotenoids and vitamins.

Most sweet potatoes are grown from slips, which are leafy cuttings without roots. They can be ordered through mail-order seed companies. The slips may look a bit withered when they arrive, so will need to be revitalized for 24 hours by placing them immediately into a jar filled with a little water to cover their bases. Then pot them on into multipurpose compost and keep them on the windowsill for a few weeks before planting them out after the risk of frost is over.

The variety "Beauregard Improved" has stunning bright orange flesh and one of the sweetest flavors. Other varieties worth trying include "Georgia Jet" and "O'Henry."

If you can resist cooking the entire crop after harvesting, save some tubers in pots of moist compost in the potting shed to use as next year's stock. Move them into the glasshouse or a sunny windowledge in spring; once they start producing shoots, these can be cut and planted up as slips for the new season.

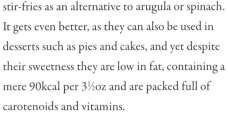

**LEFT:** These sweet potato tubers are packed full of healthy goodness and can be used in a wide range of dishes, being suitable for boiling, grating, baking, and making into fries.

# Lettuce
## *Lactuca sativa*

**Common name:** Lettuce

**Type:** Annual

**Climate:** Tender, frost-free winter

**Size:** 10in (25cm)

**Origin:** Europe and Mediterranean

**History:** Lettuce varieties appear as far back as 2700 BC, depicted on Egyptian tomb paintings. It is known to have been eaten by the ancient Greeks and the Romans cultivated several varieties including romaine and butterheads. The first lettuce was introduced into England in the 16th century.

**Cultivation:** Seeds can be sown from early spring onward in shallow drills. They are also ideal candidates for growing in containers, hanging baskets, and window boxes due to their short root systems. They will tolerate some shade but it is important they are kept well watered as they need the moisture to make their quick growth. Some varieties are ready to harvest just a few weeks after sowing.

**Storage:** Loose-leaved lettuces do not last for much more than a day after harvesting before they start wilting and should only be picked when they are to be used that day. Heart-forming lettuces such as iceberg will keep for a few days in the fridge—place in a damp plastic bag to revive limp leaves. Sow little and often so that all the plants are not ready for picking at the same time as they cannot be frozen or preserved.

**Preparation:** To prepare, trim the base stalk and remove any damaged outer leaves. Separate the remaining leaves and wash in a bowl of cold water. Dry thoroughly and tear the leaves into pieces. Lettuce is normally served raw in salads.

**BELOW:** Lettuce leaves are so easy to grow and can be used with almost any meal as either garnish, a side dish, or as the main ingredient in many different types of salads.

Lettuce has been a summer favorite for centuries. It was commonly grown during Roman times, but dates back even further. The original lettuces would have been more bitter than the mellower and sweeter flavors we have become accustomed to now. In the past the leaves would have required blanching to make them palatable, whereas nowadays there is a huge range of crisp and crunchy succulent leaves for people to enjoy. It is one of the most commonly used vegetables, possibly because it does not need cooking—making it an ultimate fast food, but also because its mildness does not clash with other flavors. It is ideal as a sandwich or burger filling, for garnishing just about any meal from around the world.

Lettuces are not only beautiful when used as garnish in the kitchen; they also add a decorative quality to kitchen gardens and potagers. The range of leaf textures, from frilly open-leaved varieties to dense hearting types, makes them a must for anyone trying to create beauty in the vegetable plot. Colors vary enormously too from deep green to bright reds, meaning they are often used to create patterns in vegetable beds in much the same way as bedding plants. There are lots of different varieties available, some of which form a center or heart, and others that are heartless.

**ABOVE:** Lettuce can be prone to bolting if sown too early and placed under stress early in the season. This causes it to flower prematurely and run to seed, resulting in bitter-tasting leaves.

## NUTRITION

Fresh leaves are an excellent source of vitamins A, C, and K, and betacarotenes. These compounds have antioxidant properties. Vitamin A is required for maintaining healthy skin and vision and vitamin K for healthy bone function.

Lettuces are fairly versatile in the garden; they can tolerate a range of different soils and actually prefer some shade during the heat of the day. The soil should ideally be moisture retentive to ensure the lettuces can form their succulent leaves, so plenty of organic matter should be dug in prior to planting. Because of their fast growing habit and the fact that they do not take up much room, they can be planted among other crops and quickly harvested before slower plants have had a chance to expand.

The simplest way to grow them is simply in ½in deep drills about 12in apart; thin them out after germination to between 6in to 12in depending on variety. Because lettuces do not keep for long, it is better to sow little and often throughout summer to avoid them all maturing at once. Because of their shallow rooting habit, they can also be grown in window boxes and containers in the same way. For earlier crops they can be sown indoors and planted outdoors under cloches. The season can also be extended into fall by picking winter varieties such as "Artic King," "Rouge d'Hiver," and "Density" (syn. "Winter Density") and planted under cover.

Heart-forming lettuces are ready for harvesting once they feel plump, whereas the loose-leaved types can be picked when small and harvested with scissors or picked later as a whole plant. Harvest the plants before they get too old as they quickly deteriorate, wilt, and provide a nourishing meal for slugs and snails.

**BELOW:** There are lots of different types of lettuce to try and they come in a range of different colors and textures, making them useful plants for creating attractive patterns in the vegetable garden.

TASTING NOTES

---

*Lettuce varieties to try*

There are lots of different types of lettuce leaves worth trying. Essentially a summer crop, it is possible to harvest almost all year round by carefully selecting early and late varieties and growing them under cloches.

| | |
|---|---|
| Butterheads | Fast growing and an open habit, with tender leaves but a soft succulent heart. Varieties include "Artic King," "Clarion," "Diana," "Roxy," and "Sangria." |
| Romaine | Sometimes called cos lettuces, these have an upright habit and are elongated. There are smaller semiromaine types too. Ones to try are "Little Gem," "Cosmic" "Tan Tan," "Corsair," and "Little Leprechaun." |
| Crispheads | As the name suggests, they have crisp succulent heads with a firm heart, the most commonly known lettuce being "Iceberg." They are less prone to bolting. Others to try are "Lakeland," "Sioux," "Robinson," and "Minigreen." |
| Loose leaf | These varieties do not form a heart and are often treated as cut-and-come-again types that are harvested with scissors and left to resprout. Types include "Red Salad Bowl," "Salad Bowl," "Frillice," Lollo Rossa," and "Nika." |

# CROP ROTATION

Long term planning is essential for the success of a vegetable garden. It is not just about thinking about the year ahead; it is considering what will be grown in each section of the garden for the next three or four years. Crop rotation is a popular system used by gardeners to plan what is going to be grown where. Vegetables are divided up into family groups and are then moved from one area of the garden to another each year.

There are no hard and fast rules, but the groups are usually divided as follows:

Group one:

### ROOT CROPS AND POTATOES

- Potatoes
- Root crops (such as carrots, parsnips, beet, radishes)

Group two:

### THE LEGUMES

- Peas, including snow peas and sugar snaps
- Beans including French beans, fava beans, string beans

Group three:

### BRASSICA FAMILY

- Kale
- Brussels sprouts
- Cabbages
- Broccoli
- Cauliflower
- Kohlrabi

Other vegetables such as lettuce, sweetcorn, squashes, and pumpkins are usually just slotted in among the beds. Tomatoes are often planted in the same rotation as potatoes as they are from the same family. Perennial crops such as rhubarb, globe and Jerusalem artichokes, and asparagus are not included in the rotation process as they stay in the same place from year to year. Nor does it include fruit trees and bushes, but it is important to take them into account when planning the vegetable beds.

**ABOVE:** Peas and beans are part of the legume family. They fix nitrogen from the air and leave it in the soil after they are removed, creating a fertile bed for the following group of vegetables, the brassicas.

## THREE- AND FOUR-
## YEAR ROTATIONS

Most people use a three-year crop rotation plan. Occasionally a four-year plan is used, and this would involve splitting out potatoes from the root crops.

The rotation order in one bed for a three-year plan would be:

Year 1:    Potatoes/tomatoes
           and root crops
Year 2:    Legume family
Year 3:    Cabbage family

The rotation order in one bed for a four-year plan would be:

Year 1:    Potatoes
Year 2:    Root crops
Year 3:    Legume family
Year 4:    Cabbage family

## BENEFITS OF CROP ROTATION

By moving the crops into a different growing space each year, it prevents the buildup of soil-borne pests and diseases. Many of the problems in the soil are specific to one group of plants, such as club root affecting brassicas, or onion white rot affecting the onion family. Growing a different

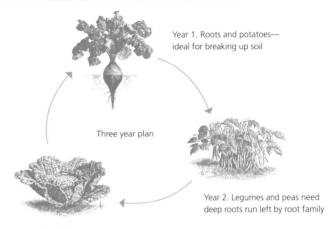

Year 1. Roots and potatoes—ideal for breaking up soil

Three year plan

Year 2. Legumes and peas need deep roots run left by root family

Year 3. Cabbages require rich soil left by pea family

**ABOVE:** Most people operate a crop rotation with three groups of plants.

type of crop in the soil each year avoids ongoing problems. In three or four years' time when the group of plants returns to the same soil, hopefully you will be one step ahead of the pests and diseases.

Crop rotation also assists with the fertility of the soil. Moving crops around avoids the constant depletion of the same nutrients. Different plant groups have specific requirements and can benefit from being planted following another crop. For example, the pea and bean family require a deep root run and therefore benefit from the space vacated by the root family such as carrots and potatoes. Likewise brassicas, which need a fertile soil, do better when planted after the pea and bean family as the soil is enriched with nitrogen left by the legumes' root system.

"Seeing a fruitful and pleasant Garden, can not be had without good skill and diligent minde of the Gardener on matter of the ground."

Thomas Hyll, *The Gardener's Labyrinth*, (1577)

# Asparagus pea
## *Lotus tetragonolobus*

**Common name:** Asparagus pea, winged lotus

**Type:** Annual

**Climate:** Tender, frost-free winter

**Size:** 16in (40cm)

**Origin:** Europe, Mediterranean

**History:** Little archeological evidence has been recorded on the early history of the plant or its uses, but it is mentioned in many Renaissance herbals. There are records of its cultivation in Sicily from the mid-16th century.

**Cultivation:** Either sow them directly into fertile soil in full sun or in modules. Wait until the risk of spring frosts is over. Keep them well watered and weed-free and harvest the pods regularly to encourage more pods to develop.

**Storage:** The pods will last a few days in the fridge, but the best way to preserve their summer flavor is to cook them in soups and freeze them, use them instead of beans in pickles and preserves, or make a type of piccalilli relish from them.

**Preparation:** Only the very young seedpods, when less than 1in long, can be used in the kitchen either raw or cooked. They can be added to salads, lightly steamed as a vegetable and served with melted butter, or added to soups and stews.

Capture the essence of asparagus in a pea pod produced by a beautiful-looking plant that really will put the wow factor into the vegetable patch. It is a small shrubby-looking plant that produces stunning red-maroon flowers with dark centers that look a bit like sweet peas. The blooms are followed by strange, quirky-looking winged seed pods, which are the parts of the plant that are cooked. Popular but expensive to buy in Asia, and practically impossible to purchase closer to home, the only way to get hold of these delicious but curious-looking seed pods is to grow your own.

The benefits of growing this plant do not end there. As it is a legume or member of the pea and bean family it means the roots of the plant fix nitrogen from the air. This is great for the environment as it means less need to fertilize and therefore nutrient hungry plants such as members of the cabbage family can be planted in this fertile-rich soil the following year. It is a much easier plant to grow than standard asparagus as it does not mean having to wait a couple of years for it to crop, and does not take anywhere near the same amount of space as the perennial plants. So if you want to flavor your dishes with asparagus but do not have the room or patience, then asparagus pea is an absolute must.

The simplest way to cook the pods is to lightly steam them, adding butter and salt, although they can be enjoyed raw. However, they can be used in a whole range of dishes and used as a substitute for pea or asparagus in recipes. They should be sliced and can then be sautéed, broiled, or fried and are delicious when used as an appetizer by dipping them into rich and spicy sauces such as sweet and sour or mango chutney. Their crunchy texture also goes well with fish, prawns, and chicken dishes and frying them with a slice of goat's cheese, red onion, garlic, and a handful of herbs brings out the flavor. A delicate soup can also be made from these pods.

Seeds should be sown in 3in pots or modules in potting compost under glass from mid to late spring and left to germinate on a sunny windowsill or glasshouse. After a few weeks they should be hardened off in a cold frame or even the porch for

**ABOVE:** The edible part is the winged seed pod, which is very popular in Asian cuisine. Harvest the pods when they are about 1in long. Any longer and they become unpalatable.

about 10 days before planting them out after the risk of spring frosts is over. Plant them in a sunny, sheltered spot at 12in apart. They prefer light fertile soil that is well-drained and a generous helping of garden compost to be added to the soil to get them started.

Alternatively, they can be sown directly outdoors after the risk of spring frosts is over. Placing a glass or plastic cloche for the first few weeks after sowing will get the plant off to a quick start. Sow them every 12in and give them a good watering afterward. Depending on their vigor they may need twiggy supports but it isn't usually necessary. Plants should be kept weed-free although their trailing habit does form a useful mat that helps suppress encroaching weeds.

Due to their attractive trailing habit they are also suitable for growing in a hanging basket or window box, but it will need regular watering.

Harvest the pods when they reach about 1in. Do not allow them to get much longer because they lose their texture and become stringy and unpalatable. Like sweet peas or string beans it is important to keep picking the pods because otherwise they stop cropping. When they have finished cropping they should be chopped down at ground level and the nitrogen-enriching roots later dug over into the soil.

**LEFT:** Considered to be a curiosity rather than a staple vegetable in the garden, asparagus peas are very easy to grow and in addition produce attractive flowers.

# Watercress
## *Nasturtium officinale*

**Common name:** Watercress

**Type:** Perennial

**Climate:** Very hardy, very cold winter

**Size:** 8in (20cm)

**Origin:** Europe

**History:** Watercress has a long history dating back to the Greeks, Persians, and Romans and is the most ancient of green vegetables known to man. It was not until the early 19th century in England that watercress was cultivated on a large scale.

**Cultivation:** Grow in moist fertile soil or in a container such as a washing-up bowl. It can be grown in compost in a container or trough sitting on a saucer filled with water. Sow seeds in situ during spring or summer, or in trays indoors during winter.

**Storage:** Leaves do not last for long so pick as required. Alternatively, make into soup and freeze.

**Preparation:** Wash well and trim off the tough stalks before use.

**ABOVE RIGHT:** Watercress is very easy to grow and has a strong, peppery aroma. Try to keep plants contained if planting directly into damp ground as they will rapidly spread.

You do not need a vast riverbed to enjoy the peppery flavors and health benefits of watercress. All that is needed is a shady corner of the garden and a container to hold the water in. Suddenly the world of home-grown watercress soup is available to anyone with the smallest of gardens. This peppery, leafy herb with its straggly habit is a fantastic accompaniment to strong-flavored meats such as boar and venison, but works equally well in poultry dishes. It is usually served raw as garnish or healthy sandwich fillers. Watercress combined with orange segments and a splash of olive oil is a classic side dish or salad.

Watercress must be kept permanently damp for it to thrive but it does not have to be permanently submerged in water, and can instead be planted in boggy soil in the garden. However, in the right conditions, it will quickly spread and take over, so think carefully before doing this. The easiest method of obtaining home-grown watercress is to grow it directly in a container filled with compost. It can be anything from a washing-up bowl to an

## GROWING WITHOUT A GARDEN

If you do not have a garden and still crave some of these peppery leaves then do not despair. They can be grown on a windowsill and regularly harvested as baby leaves throughout the year. Lightly scatter them on a seed tray containing compost, cover with a clear plastic bag, and leave to germinate. Keep the tray well supplied with water and regularly topped up. Regularly harvest leaves when they are big enough to handle and add to salads or sandwiches.

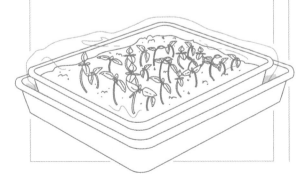

old sink. If the container has drainage holes then it should be placed on a saucer filled with water so that it can absorb moisture. Seeds should be sown on the surface of damp compost during spring or summer in a container. Keep the container or saucer regularly topped up with water. Occasionally pour water through the container to keep the water fresh and regularly change in the saucer to prevent it going stagnant.

It is very tough and will supply leaves throughout the year, staying green until about 28 or 26°F .

# Parsnip
## *Pastinaca sativa*

**Common name:** Parsnip

**Type:** Annual

**Climate:** Hardy, cold winter

**Size:** 10in (25cm)

**Origin:** Eastern Mediterranean

**History:** Archeological evidence has shown parsnips to have been around since prehistoric times. Parsnips grew wild in Europe and were considered a luxury item for the aristocracy in ancient Rome. The Emperor Tiberius accepted part of the tribute payable to Rome by Germany in the form of parsnips.

**Cultivation:** Parsnips require a long growing season so seeds should be sown directly outdoors from early to midspring. They require a fertile, well-drained soil. Sow rows 12in apart and thin so that they are 6in apart within the rows. Keep them regularly watered as they tend to split if it rains heavily after a dry period. Harvest from fall onward.

**Storage:** Parsnips can remain in the ground throughout winter, but in very cold areas it might be difficult to dig them up if the soil freezes over. They should therefore be lifted in fall and buried in trays filled with sand or compost and kept in a cool, dry place such as a garage.

**Preparation:** Scrub well, trim the top and root ends, and peel thinly. Either leave young parsnips whole or slice large parsnips into quarters and remove the central core. Boil in salted water, steam for 15–20 minutes, or roast around a joint of meat after parboiling.

Not offering much above ground in terms of beauty in the garden, this winter root crop does all its talking below the surface as it is the aromatic and sweetly flavored tap root that gardeners and chefs love. It is one of the classic vegetables to accompany a traditional pot roast when glazed with honey and roasted, but there is so much more to this old favorite. They can be made into fancy herby fries, or thinly sliced, drizzled with chilli oil and baked in the oven to make crunchy chips. They can also be mashed and mixed with maple syrup or grated into a rosti and fried. They can also be curried or added to traditional hotpots, casseroles, soups, and winter stews and combined with other winter vegetables such as leeks, turnips, and rutabaga.

There are lots of varieties to chose from but it is worth choosing one that has some canker resistance as it can be heart breaking to dig up the roots in fall and discover they are all split and rotting. Resistant varieties include "Gladiator," "Albion," "Palace," and "Archer." One of the best flavored varieties is called "The Student," which is an old heritage type dating back to the 1800s and also has canker resistance. For those who enjoy a

**RIGHT:** The chromolithograph plate from the *Album Benary* of 1876 shows a range of parsnip and other root varieties.

gourmet treat then try the variety "Arrow," which has narrow shoulders, meaning they can be grown closer together at high density, which will provide the sweet "baby" parsnips that are so popular in good-quality restaurants.

Often it is advised that seed can be sown as early as February because parsnips do need a long growing season, but unless it is an exceptionally mild spring and the soil is not cold and heavy, the seed is likely to languish and eventually rot in the soil. It is better to wait until late March or early April. Seed should be sown in shallow drills 12in apart. Sow three seeds at stations every 6in or 8in; gently rake back over the soil and water. Thin the seeds out to one seed when they are about 2in tall. As they can be slow to germinate, it is possible to sow a row of radishes in the row too as this helps mark out the row and they can be quickly harvested without affecting the emerging parsnip crops.

Like carrot seed, avoid using old stock as it quickly goes stale. Instead buy fresh seed each year to ensure reliable germination and a bumper crop. Avoid freshly manured soil as this

can cause the parsnips to fork. Instead, if possible use fertile, free-draining ground that has been manured in a previous year. Stony soil should be avoided as well as this prevents the root from developing fully. One technique to encourage a deeply rooted parsnip and to avoid the problem of stones is to use a crow bar at each sowing station to push it down deeply into the soil; then fill it up with compost. Keep the plant well watered throughout summer and keep the area weed-free. In very cold areas it may be necessary to protect the tops of the parsnips with straw, but they are generally very hardy.

Parsnips are ready for harvesting from fall onward, although it is possible to lift them earlier in the year for smaller roots. Most connoisseurs insist on waiting until the first fall frosts before digging them up as they are supposed to taste sweeter. Use a fork to loosen the ground, taking care not to damage the root, and then lift them out by hand.

"The parsnip is a very nourishing and valuable vegetable for winter food, and is highly esteemed by those who like vegetables of a sweetish, agreeable flavour."

T. W. Sanders, *Kitchen Garden and Allotment*, (c.1920)

# String bean

## *Phaseolus coccineus*

**Common name:** String bean, scarlet runner, runner bean, or stick bean

**Type:** Annual

**Climate:** Tender, frost-free winter

**Size:** 6½ft (2m)

**Origin:** Central America

**History:** They were introduced to Europe from Mexico in the mid 17th century. However, string beans have been known as a food crop for well over 2,000 years. They were introduced to Britain in the 17th century by the plant hunter John Tradescant (gardener to King Charles I) and were grown as a decorative plant before being used as a food. Today they are eaten in each of the five continents.

**Cultivation:** Beans should be sown in full sun in fertile soil. Seeds should be sown from mid to late spring under cover and planted out after the risk of frosts has passed. Keep them well watered and harvest when the beans inside the pod have started to swell and have reached about 6in long, depending on variety.

**Storage:** Beans do not last for long after they are picked but they can be frozen or preserved in relishes.

**Preparation:** Cut off the ends and remove the strings from the sides by running a sharp knife down each side of the bean. Cut diagonally into 1in lengths or slice into lengths. Steam or cook in salted boiling water for about 10 minutes.

**BELOW:** String beans can also be grown as an ornamental annual climber. Because of their attractive flowers and rapid growth they make a decorative and edible screen.

A rustic wigwam smothered with brightly colored flowers and strings of tender beans is a quintessential kitchen garden image. It is not hard to see why the first plants introduced to Europe in the 16th century were grown more for their ornamental value, before people realized how delicious the seed pods were. String beans not only add height, color, and structure to the otherwise flat-looking vegetable plot but home-grown varieties also taste so much better than the ones bought in stores. There is a huge variety of dishes that string beans can be used for in the kitchen. They should be eaten cooked, usually steamed or boiled, and thinly sliced to maximize their flavor. Their flowers

are also edible and are commonly added to bean salads or used as garnish.

One of the reasons for their popularity on the vegetable plot is for the huge gluts that they provide during summer. Not only will they keep cropping if regularly picked, but any excess can also be frozen, meaning there is hardly any wastage and nothing needs to get slung on the compost heap. Despite their height, they can also be grown on small balconies and patios as they can be planted in deep containers that are at least 19½in in diameter and have plenty of drainage holes. Containers should be filled with good-quality compost. The plants will need watering daily and feeding once a week once they start to flower.

String beans require a sunny, well-drained plot with plenty of organic matter added to the soil to improve its ability to retain moisture and to add some nutrients. A string bean trench can be created the fall before planting, which involves digging out a 12in trench where the beans are to be planted later. It should be filled up over winter with kitchen waste and other organic matter, gradually letting it rot down so that when it comes to planting out the string beans they have a beautiful, fertile soil to grow in. String beans should be grown in a sheltered spot, partly to prevent the tall climbing structures being blown over.

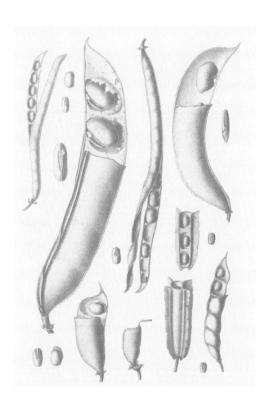

**LEFT:** Left to mature, the pretty seeds can be dried and stored for sowing the following year.

## CREATING A CLIMBING STRUCTURE

String beans are climbing plants and use their tendrils to scramble up structures. To make it easier for picking, they are usually trained up tepee or wigwam structures made from bamboo canes or hazel sticks. They are usually about 6½ft tall although most string beans will climb much higher if allowed, but this makes picking harder.

To make a tepee 8ft canes should be pushed into the ground in a circle, leaving about 10in between each one. The tops of the canes should be pulled tightly together and lashed with gardening twine. Alternatively, they can be trained on a pair of parallel rows of canes, whereby they are joined by a horizontal cane at the top running parallel with the row. Rows need to be 24in apart with canes spaced 8in apart.

**RIGHT:** Left to climb, string beans will keep going and may pull over the entire support. Stop them when they reach the top.

Seeds can either be sown indoors in midspring or outside after the risk of the frosts. The advantage of growing them indoors to start with is that it gives them a head start for the season ahead. Sow one seed per 3in pot at 1½in deep in a multipurpose compost. Water the seeds and leave them to germinate on a sunny window ledge or in the glasshouse. Before planting them directly outside they should be hardened off in a cold frame for a few days to gently acclimatize them to the outside weather. Plant them at the base of each bamboo support and water them well. Pay particular attention to watering once the flowers start to form.

Alternatively, the seeds can be sown in early summer by using a dibber to push two seeds 1½in deep at each cane support. Once germination has taken place the weaker one of the two seedlings should be removed. The plants will need regular watering to help them maintain their vigorous, climbing growth habit. On dry soil it is also beneficial to mulch around the root system with garden compost to keep the root system moist. Harvest the beans regularly and do not let them get too long as they become stringy and tough.

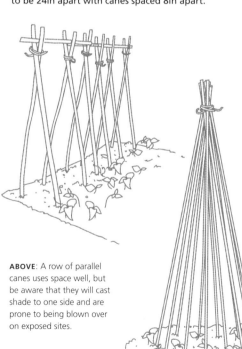

**ABOVE**: A row of parallel canes uses space well, but be aware that they will cast shade to one side and are prone to being blown over on exposed sites.

**LEFT:** Wigwams make solid supports but slightly less space efficient as they present less of a surface area for the beans.

# GARDEN TOOLS

M an has toiled the soil for thousands of years, yet many of the tools remain the same today as back in the old days. Having the right tool for the right job is essential, as it increases efficiency and can save hours of backbreaking work. When purchasing tools it is important that they are suitable for your height and strength. Otherwise you run the risk of overextending and injuring yourself. If good-quality tools are looked after properly, they should last a lifetime.

Soil dibbers                    String lines

## SHEDS AND TOOL CARE

Garden tools should be stored under cover when they are not being used, ideally in a shed as it provides plenty of space. A shed can also double-up as a potting area or simply somewhere to shelter from the rain and have a cup of coffee. It should have lots of shelves and racking so that tools, pots, bags of compost, and other garden implements can be secured safely.

Wipe mud and dirt off all tools before storing them. Metallic material will benefit from being wiped down with an oily rag, while wooden handles can be occasionally rubbed with linseed oil. Regularly sharpen implements used to cut, such as pruning shears, loppers, and hoes.

Below are some of the essential tools required for creating and maintaining a vegetable garden.

### DIBBER

This slender hand tool is pushed into the ground to make holes for seed sowing. It can either be bought, or simply made from offcuts from bamboo canes and sticks.

### STRING LINE

Vegetable gardeners love their straight lines. A string line is used prior to digging out a trench, making a seed drill, or making holes with a dibber. It can also be used for marking out paths or rasied beds.

### SPADE

Probably the most essential tool for vegetable gardening. Use it for digging over the soil but be aware—it slices through perennial weed roots, which increases the problem.

## SHOVEL

An invaluable tool used for moving loose materials such as garden compost, manure, and wood chippings around the vegetable plot. When purchasing one, check the weight and balance so that you do not damage your back.

## FORK

Used for digging, breaking up the ground, particularly on heavy soils, and reducing compaction. The back of the fork can be used for breaking up clods of earth.

## RAKE—LANDSCAPE

Landscape rakes are regularly used on the vegetable plot for leveling out the soil after digging and spreading compost and manure. They have a larger head than traditional rakes, making leveling easier.

## WHEELBARROW

Where would gardeners be without this essential bit of kit for moving plants, compost, and garden waste around the garden? Paths should be wide enough in the kitchen garden to accomodate a wheelbarrow.

Dutch hoe

Pruning shears

## DUTCH HOE

This essential tool is used for removing annual weeds between rows of vegetables. It cuts on both the pushing and pulling motion and the long handle avoids backbreaking weeding.

## PRONGED CULTIVATORS

These strange-looking implements can be used to scratch at the surface of the soil, breaking up compaction and allowing water to penetrate beneath the surface.

## SOIL SIEVE

If you make your own compost then a soil sieve is useful for removing large uncomposted material. It can also be used for removing stones in the soil.

## PRUNING SHEARS

These are used to cut back garden foliage and to harvest vegetables. Bypass-type shears are more expensive but give a better cut than the anvil types. A pocket knife is also useful.

## WATERING CAN

All seeds and seedlings should be watered after planting. A rose can be fitted to the watering can's nozzle so that the water does not wash away recently sown seeds or emerging seedlings.

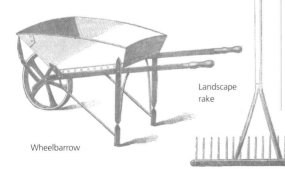

Landscape rake

Wheelbarrow

# French bean
## *Phaseolus vulgaris*

**Common name:** French bean, common bean, snap bean, green bean, navy bean (dried)

**Type:** Annual

**Climate:** Tender, frost-free winter

**Size:** 6½ft (2m)

**Origin:** South America

**History:** These beans have been grown as a crop for thousands of years in South America. Archeologists working in Peru have dated bean remains to about 5000 BC. They were first introduced to Europe in the 16th century by Spanish and Portuguese explorers.

**Cultivation:** French beans are frost tender so should only be grown during the summer months. Train climbing beans up tepees or climbing structures. They require lots of moisture, sunshine, and organic matter for them to grow successfully.

### TASTING NOTES

#### *Attractive varieties to try*

Although there is not much difference in flavor between French beans, their range of color adds a visual vibrancy to any dishes.

| | |
|---|---|
| "Borlotto Lingua di Fuoco" | A dwarf variety with flat pods and speckled with red. |
| "Purple Teepee" | A dwarf variety with purple pods that go dark green when cooked. |
| "Cobra" | A climbing type with tender green pods but attractive purple flowers. |
| "Selma Zebra" | An heirloom climber with quirky looking green streaky pods. |
| "Golden Gate" | A climbing variety with impressive bright yellow pods. |

**Storage:** French beans are best eaten fresh but will store in the fridge for a few days. They can be frozen but should be blanched first. If the pods are left to swell and dry these navy beans can be stored in sterilized, airtight containers for months.

**Preparation:** Choose slim french beans that break with a crisp snap. The beans should be young and only need topping and tailing, but if they are a little coarse then they may need their stringy sides removed. They can then be steamed or cooked in boiling salted water for about 10 minutes.

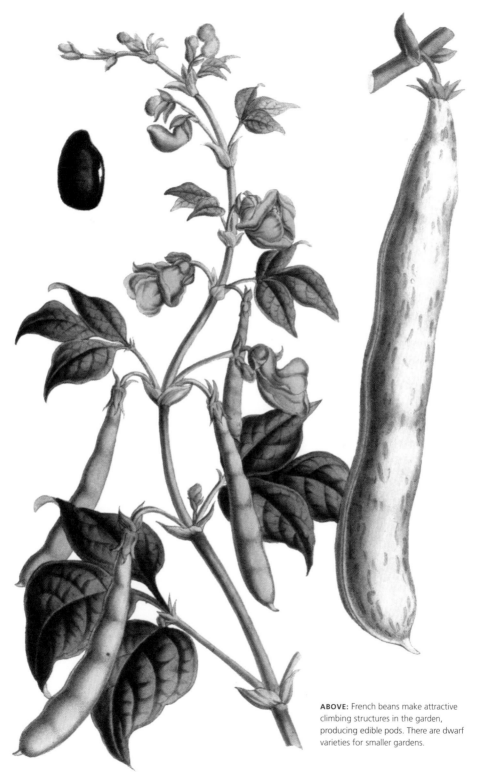

**ABOVE:** French beans make attractive climbing structures in the garden, producing edible pods. There are dwarf varieties for smaller gardens.

French beans have been grown for over 7,000 years and are more popular now than ever before. They are so easy to grow and yet are very often overlooked in summer for their closely related cousin, the string bean. Yet for those who find string beans too stringy, these are the answer as they are far less likely to go that way. They are usually grown for their pods and, unlike string beans, these come in a range of bright colors, which is ironic really considering their other common name is "green bean." Look out for varieties coming in yellow, purple, cream, and speckled. These brightly colored pods make them a sight to rival any ornamental flower display and some gardeners grow the plants for that reason alone. One other advantage French beans have over string is that they

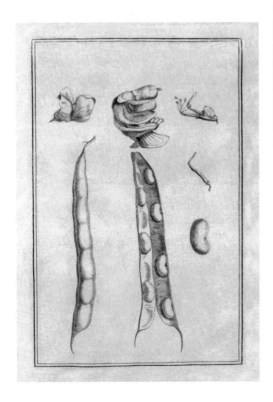

come into cropping earlier, sometimes as quickly as seven or eight weeks after sowing, making them useful for filling that summer bean gap in the harvest calendar after the fava beans have been harvested. There are dwarf or bush varieties too, only growing to about 19½in high, meaning they can easily be grown on a sunny patio or balcony without having to overstretch. The shorter versions are great in small veggie patches where shading neighboring plants can be a problem.

French beans are so easy and quick in the kitchen too. Simply pick them fresh from the garden, top and tail them, and boil them in salt water for three or four minutes. Afterward run them under cold water to prevent them overcooking or going soggy, slice and toss them into salads, and add a dressing. Their flavor is versatile, meaning they will go with anything from a lemon-based vinaigrette to something stronger such as a soy sauce-based mix. Combine them with fried chillies, garlic, peppers, and a pinch of flaked almonds for a delicious quick and healthy snack.

To produce navy (sometimes called haricot beans) the pods are left until the end of the season and then cut down and left to dry in a frost-free place such as a garage. Once they are "rattle dry" they can be shelled and stored in airtight containers. They have a mild flavor, meaning they are a perfect accompaniment for bulking up stronger flavored foods. They are commonly added to cassoulet and other slow-cooked dishes, but can equally be used in bean salads, soups, or even in purées.

**LEFT:** French beans are usually harvested when reasonably young, but the beans inside the pod can be left to swell and then picked, dried, and stored as navy beans.

French beans like to be in full sun and require the same fertile and nutrient-rich conditions as string beans. A "string bean trench" can be dug the fall before planting to enrich the soil (see p.164). Alternatively dig in plenty of garden compost in spring. Seeds can be sown indoors in plastic pots in midspring and kept on a sunny windowledge or glasshouse for germination. They shouldn't be planted out until after the last of the spring frosts. Acclimatize the plants to the outdoors by placing them in a porch or a cold frame for a few days before plunging them outside into the elements. Climbing varieties will need a structure to scramble up (see p.165), and they should be planted out at 8in between each plant and 35in between rows. The dwarf beans should be 3in apart in rows 18in apart.

Alternatively seeds can be sown directly into the soil. Sow two seeds per 1½in deep hole using a dibber at the spacing mentioned above; once they have germinated the weaker one should be removed, leaving the other to grow away strongly. The growing tip should find the climbing structure on its own and start to twist its way upward, but it sometimes needs help to find the canes at the early stages of development. Once attached it should romp up those canes. Then, when it reaches the top of the structure, the growing tip should be pinched out, which will encourage it to channel its energy into producing beans.

Harvest the beans regularly. This can start as early as seven or eight weeks after sowing. If you want to produce navy beans then leave them to mature and swell, and harvest them right at the end of the season.

TASTING NOTES

*French beans with garlic*

French beans taste best when cooked immediately after harvesting, as this captures those fresh flavors that are quickly lost if stored in the fridge. For a milder flavor, substitute garlic for elephant garlic or fried red caramelized onions. This simple dish brings out the natural herbaceous flavors of the beans, and only takes minutes to prepare.

**Preparation time:** 5 minutes
**Cooking time:** 5 minutes
**Serves:** 4 people (as a side dish)

· 25oz (700g) French beans, ends removed

· 1oz (30g) unsalted butter

· 1 tbsp olive oil

· 2 garlic cloves, crushed

· Salt and pepper, to taste

Blanch the French beans in a saucepan of boiling salted water for just 1½ minutes.

Drain and immerse in a large bowl of ice water to stop the cooking. When they are cool, drain and set aside.

Heat the butter and olive oil in a very large pan over a medium heat and cook the garlic for 1–2 minutes, or until lightly browned.

Add the French beans, sprinkle with salt and pepper, and toss together.

Reheat the French beans and serve.

# Pea
## *Pisum sativum*

**Common name:** Pea, snow pea, mange tout, sugarsnap pea

**Type:** Annual

**Climate:** Tender, frost-free winter

**Size:** 4ft (1.2m)

**Origin:** Middle Asia

**History:** Peas are one of the oldest cultivated vegetables and are believed to have grown at least as far back as 7800 BC. Archeological remains of Bronze Age villages in Switzerland contained early traces of peas dating back to 3000 BC. The Greeks and Romans were cultivating peas from about 500 to 400 BC.

**Cultivation:** Sow early varieties in late fall and other types in spring. Sow them in flat-bottomed trenches in fertile, well-drained soil in full sun. Provide twiggy pea sticks cut from hazel or birch trees to support the plants.

**ABOVE:** Peas are one of the most popular vegetables in the culinary world, but their young emerging tendrils and shoots can also be eaten as a delicacy with herbaceous flavors.

### NUTRITION

Peas are very high in fiber and can help lower cholesterol. They provide an abundance of nutrients, including iron in good levels. Peas are also rich in vitamin C, which helps maintain your immune system.

**Storage:** Peas must be one of the best vegetables for storing. They are without doubt best when eaten fresh from the plant, but their sweetness can be captured when frozen. They can also be dried although this is less common these days.

**Preparation:** Very full pods may have tough peas inside. Remove the peas from their pods and discard any that are blemished or discolored. Wash under cold running water. Boil in lightly salted water, with a sprig of mint if desired, for about 10–15 minutes. Drain well and add butter. If steaming, then do so for about 3–5 minutes.

Peas are one of the oldest cultivated vegetables in existence and they are just as much loved today. Fresh peas in a pod straight from the garden provide a flavor that is impossible to replicate from store-bought ones and just for that reason alone they should be given pride of place in the vegetable patch. Many kitchen gardeners even struggle to get their pods as far as the kitchen before giving in to the heavenly delight of devouring the seeds from a freshly opened pod seconds after picking them. The reason why store-bought ones just do not taste anywhere near as good is because as soon as they are picked the sweet sugars immediately start to transform into starch. Therefore, for lovers of the finest fresh peas, only home-grown ones will do.

Despite their delicious fresh flavors they are included in countless recipes from around the world, ranging from pea soups to mushy peas with mint. They are used in dishes in Europe, the Americas, and particularly Asian cuisine such as classic Indian dishes including Mutter Paneer or Aloo Mutter (*Mutter* meaning "pea").

For those who like a real gourmet treat the fresh shoots and tendrils can also be eaten early in the season and have a spinach-like flavor. Despite being a common sight at the markets in Asia they are practically impossible to get hold of farther afield. To maximize their flavors the shoots should be picked before they have a chance to open. There are lots of different types of peas to choose from,

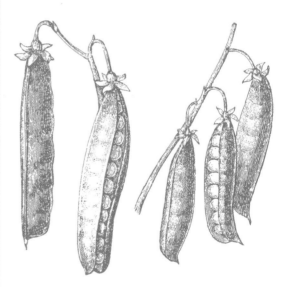

**ABOVE:** Most pea varieties need to be shelled from the pod before eating, but other varieties such as snow peas and sugarsnaps are eaten entirely, pod and all.

"The culinary pea is universally acknowledged to be the king of vegetables. It has been grown from time immemorial on the Continent and in this country, and it is regarded as one of the most delicious, as well as the most nutritious, of vegetables."

T. W. Sanders, *Kitchen Garden and Allotment*, (c. 1920)

### Pea varieties to try

There are several different types of peas. Round peas, sometimes called smooth-seed types, are hardier and suitable for earlier sowings of seed. However, they do not taste as sweet at the less-hardy wrinkled types. The small, sweet-tasting peas that are so popular in the frozen aisles of the grocery store are known as petit pois and they can also be grown in the garden.

| Round types | "Bountiful," "Feltham First," "Meteor," and "Pilot" |
|---|---|
| Wrinkled | "Early Onward," "Little Marvel," "Hurst Green-shaft," and "Onward" |
| Petit Pois | "Peawee" and "Waverex" |
| Snow peas | "Delikata," "Oregon Giant," and "Snow Wind" |
| Sugarsnap | "Sugar Ann" and "Sugar Bon" |

The true gourmet fan will love snow pea "Shiraz." These unusual pods are purple with bicolored flowers. Not only do they look great in both the garden and on the plate, but they are also packed full of nutritional goodness including anthocyanin (antioxidants) pigments. They are best eaten raw, such as in a salad, but will retain some of their unique color if steamed. If they are boiled they will lose their color but still taste fantastic.

with some of the traditional types now making room for some of the new kids on the vegetable block, such as the sweet snow pea and sugarsnap. These must be the ultimate healthy fast food, simply being picked from the plant and eaten immediately to maximize their crunchy, sweet, and herbaceous flavors. Both are eaten whole, as the French name "*mange tout*" suggests.

Peas require an open but sheltered site in full sun. The soil should be thoroughly dug over before sowing and plenty of garden compost added. The early varieties can be sown in fall and will overwinter but may need a cloche in cold areas. Alternatively, seed sowing should start in late winter or early spring and can continue through to early summer for some of the main crops.

The simplest way to sow the seed is to draw out a flat-bottomed trench using a draw hoe. The trench should be about 6in wide and 2in deep. Peas are sown in parallel rows either sides of the trench in a zigzag pattern. The soil should gently be raked back over the seeds and the area should be watered. Supports such as twiggy sticks or pea netting should be added when the plants have reached about 3in high, taking care not to damage the plants.

Early peas have a speedy turnaround and are ready for harvesting about 11 weeks after sowing. The later varieties take a bit longer to mature. The podding types are ready for picking when the peas feel plump inside their pods. Picking should begin at the bottom of the plant, and work upward as the season progresses.

Snow peas are picked when the pods reach about 3in and should be caught before the seeds have swelled. Sugarsnaps should be about the same length but the pods should feel plump and the peas developed inside.

At the end of the season, cut down the plants to ground level and add to the compost heap. Chop up and dig the roots into the soil, though, as they are a valuable source of nitrogen.

## Tagliatelle with mint and pea pesto

A perfect combination of herbaceous fresh mint and pea flavors with the comforting background flavor of tagliatelle make this a wonderful light snack.

**Preparation time:** 5 minutes
**Cooking time:** 20 minutes
**Serves:** 4 people (as an appetizer)

· 14oz (400g) fresh egg tagliatelle

· 2 garlic cloves, crushed

· 3oz (75g) pine nuts

· 6oz (175g) fresh or frozen peas

· Handful of fresh mint leaves

· 2oz (50g) Parmesan, grated

· 4 tbsp olive oil

· Salt and pepper, to taste

Cook the pasta in boiling salted water until al dente, then drain.

Place the garlic, one-third of the pine nuts, peas, mint, and Parmesan in a food processor and whizz to a paste, gradually adding the oil.

Stir this pesto through the pasta and season.

Sprinkle with shavings of Parmesan and the remaining pine nuts.

**LEFT:** The anatomy of the humble pea plant is fascinating, with its keeled flowers, delicate yet strong tendrils, and pinnate leaves—all of which are edible.

# Radish
## *Raphanus sativus*

**Common name:** Radish, common radish, wild radish, garden radish

**Type:** Annual

**Climate:** Tender, frost-free winter

**Size:** 6in (15cm)

**Origin:** Mediterranean

**History:** There are records of radishes being grown in ancient China. Later they became popular in ancient Egypt where it was the staple diet for the laborers who built the pyramids. The radish was domesticated in Europe

> "Ah! And here's the surprise, something dainty, some pretty little pink radishes. Just fancy! Radishes in March; what a luxury!"
>
> **Emile Zola, Paris, (1898)**

in pre-Roman times. The Greek name of the genus *Raphanus* means "quickly appearing" and refers to the rapid germination of these plants. The common name "radish" is derived from the Latin meaning root.

**Cultivation:** Seeds should be sown thinly, ideally in drills ½in deep, between March and mid April, although they can be sown earlier under cloches. Rows should be 6in apart. Winter radishes should be sown 10in apart and sown in late summer.

**Storage:** Radishes should be picked as soon as they are ready to be eaten because they will not store for much longer than a couple of days. Winter radishes should remain in the ground until needed, although they can be lifted and stored in boxes filled with sand and kept in a cool place.

**Preparation:** Trim off the tops and root ends. Wash, then slice or grate for use in salads, or cut into decorative shapes for garnishes.

**LEFT:** Radishes come in all sorts of shapes and colors including the traditional bright red but also white, yellow, and pink.

If you are new to growing your own crops, and want to walk before you can run, then this is the crop to try. Not only is it probably the easiest, but it is also one of the quickest to grow, meaning you can test both your gardening and gourmet cookery skills within a few weeks of getting started.

Crunchy, peppery with mustardy overtones, radishes are usually eaten raw and are perfect for pepping up the dreariest and limpest of salads with their vibrant, spicy flavors. They go best with mild ingredients because they otherwise clash with other strong flavors. In salads radishes go well with

## GROWING THEM AS A "CATCH CROP"

Take advantage of the fast-growing habit of radishes by sowing them quickly in among slower growing crops such as onions, potatoes, and peas. This avoids wasting valuable space in the garden. They can even be used to mark out rows by planting them in the same drill as parsnips, so you do not lose sight of where this slow-to-germinate winter vegetable is, and so accidentally hoe or weed through them.

## TASTING NOTES

### *Attractive varieties to try*

Brightly colored radishes to brighten up a salad.

| | |
|---|---|
| "Sparkler" | A pink variety with a white base. |
| "French Breakfast 3" | Red with a white tip. |
| "Ping Pong" | Attractive pure white roots. |

Sow these seeds regularly through the season. They only take about 25 days from sowing through to harvesting. Sow little and often about once a week to ensure that there are crops to harvest regularly, rather than sowing one long crop and having to deal with a glut when they are all ready for picking at the same time. If they are left in the ground they quickly turn woody and become unpalatable.

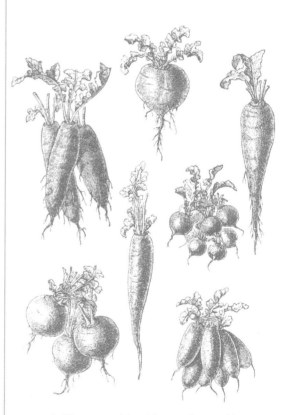

**ABOVE:** Radishes are one of the quickest growing vegetables in the gardening world. They are also one of the easiest and are simply sown in shallow drills every few weeks during spring and summer.

**ABOVE:** Radishes are the perfect vegetables for the weight watcher as they contain less than 5 calories per serving, meaning you probably expend more calories eating them than are consumed.

TASTING NOTES

*Simple radish salad*

This is a salad for those who like a hot and spicy side dish. If you want something less intense, then add milder flavored ingredients from the kitchen garden such as cucumber, tomato, or avocado.

**Preparation time:** 20 minutes
**Serves:** 2 people (as a side dish)

· 10–12 radishes, thinly sliced

· 1 tbsp salt

· ¼ tsp ground black pepper

· 2 tbsp fresh lime juice

· 1 tbsp fresh orange juice

Combine the radishes with the salt in a bowl and cover with water. Let it sit for 15 minutes.

Meanwhile, stir together the pepper and fruit juices.

Drain the radishes and then toss in with the dressing.

Add more salt, pepper, or fruit juices to taste as needed, and serve.

celery, beans, crispy lettuce, apples, and raisins. They also brighten up poultry dishes such as chicken and turkey. Try a wrap with pea guacamole, turkey, and sliced radishes for a simple lunchtime snack that brings out the best of this spicy vegetable's qualities. Interestingly, the heat of radishes is affected by the weather. In hot summers they will taste really spicy, whereas in milder seasons they taste less so. For the weight watchers among aspiring gourmet cooks, radishes are a godsend as they only contain 5 calories per serving. Water is about the only thing less, but the spicy flavors are bound to get that metabolism moving too, as well as burning calories while crunching through it.

It is a root crop and related to mustard, which explains the impressive heat that can be mustered from such a small vegetable.

The red-skinned types are the most commonly grown ones in the garden although they come in other colors too. There are also winter radishes, which are hardier and remain in the ground during fall and winter until needed for harvesting.

Radishes should be grown in a sunny location and only require a shallow soil and one that is not too rich. The soil should also be free-draining but have some moisture-retentive qualities because otherwise they quickly will run to seed and taste woody.

# Mooli

## *Raphanus sativus* var. *longipinnatus*

**Common name:** Mooli, daikon

**Type:** Annual

**Climate:** Hardy, average to cold winter

**Size:** 6in (15cm)

**Origin:** Asia

**History:** Closely related to the common summer radish, there are records of radishes being used in ancient China around 800 BC and later in Japan where the long, white daikon radish or mooli became a major food.

**Cultivation:** Grow them in nutrient-poor soil in full sun. Sow from late summer and harvest in fall and winter.

**Storage:** They keep for much longer than summer radishes, and as they are winter hardy they can be kept in the ground until they are needed (usually no later than early winter) in the kitchen. If it is likely that the soil is going to freeze, they can be lifted and stored in boxes of sand or compost.

**Preparation:** In Japan, mooli is known as daikon and is frequently pickled and served as a crunchy accompaniment to rice at mealtimes. It can also be chopped and put into salads or made into crudités to serve with dips. It can also be steamed and grated or added to stir-fries.

**LEFT:** Mooli radishes are grown in the same way as winter types and are not suitable for containers.

Good things come to those who wait and this gourmet vegetable is worth waiting for. If you want something to spice up your dishes toward the end of the season then give this giant Asian root vegetable a try.

Mooli is the Hindi word for this large crunchy white radish that is used all over South and East Asia and known as daikon in Japan and by various names in China. They are not as pungent as the smaller radishes and have a high water content. The seed pods are called mongray, and these are eaten as a vegetable too. Mooli is known as "white ginseng" in China, so is known for its invigorating properties. It purifies the blood and can detoxify the organs and is great for hangovers. In some rural areas of Pakistan it is cultivated for both food and medicine along with other plants such as aloe vera, ajwain, okra, fennel, and nightshade (for ear infections).

Mooli is very closely related to the much smaller and more commonly grown red radish that is so popular through the summer months in salads. However, this has a different season of interest, being ready for harvesting as the first fall frosts

arrive in the garden. It gives the gourmet gardener an exciting ingredient to harvest from the vegetable patch that is not one of the stalwart winter crops such as leeks, kale, and parsnips. Mooli is far larger than the traditional radish and can be used in a wide range of cuisine. It can be eaten raw but also cooked and is perfect for adding spicy flavors to stir-fries. It can be sliced raw and used as a radish substitute in salad—alternatively, the root can be grated and used as an ingredient in rostis. It is one of the key ingredients in Kimchi, the Korean fermented pickle, but is also often added to Indian curries and Chinese dishes and is a key ingredient for Dim Sum. The most commonly grown color of mooli is white but there are lots of other colors to try too.

Like the usual summer radishes, mooli do not like rich soil, too much fertilizer, or to have been recently manured, as this causes an excess of leaves to sprout and roots to become distorted and forked. However, due to the larger size of the root they need a much deeper soil than standard radishes, which will happily grow in just a few inches of top soil. Before planting, dig over the soil thoroughly, breaking up any hard pans just below the surface. Add some grit or sand to ensure there will be a decent root run for them. Rake the soil level and then sow the seeds at about 8in apart between each plant and between each row. Seeds should be sown in later summer because if they are sown too early they will bolt and quickly turn to seed. After sowing keep the seedlings free from weeds and keep them well watered.

## TASTING NOTES

### Chinese pickled mooli

Mooli is not has hot as the traditional radish, but its natural crunch makes it a great ingredient for pickling and using as a relish.

**Preparation time:** 5 minutes, 30 minutes soaking, 8 hours pickling
**Serves:** 2 people

· 6oz (175g) chopped mooli

· ³/₄ tsp salt

· 1 tbsp rice vinegar

· ¹/₄ tsp freshly ground black pepper

In a mixing bowl, toss the mooli with salt. Cover and refrigerate for about 30 minutes.

Drain and rinse, to remove the salt.

Pat dry with a paper towel, and return to bowl.

Stir in rice vinegar and pepper. Cover and refrigerate for at least 8 hours.

# Rhubarb
## *Rheum × hybridum*

**Common name:** Rhubarb

**Type:** Perennial

**Climate:** Hardy, average winter

**Size:** 3ft (1m)

**Origin:** China

**History:** Rhubarb was first cultivated in Siberia around 2700 BC. It was the dried root of Chinese rhubarb that was highly prized for its medicinal qualities. It was not until the 13th century that Marco Polo brought the root to Europe but little is known of it in Britain until the 14th century. At this time, the price of rhubarb root commanded even more than opium.

**Cultivation:** Rhubarb can be grown from seed but is easier from crowns or from established plants bought from the garden center. It needs a rich, fertile

soil and shouldn't be harvested the first year after planting. Keep the plant well watered and mulch around its base each year, being careful not to cover up the crown as this can cause it to rot.

**Storage:** Stems will last for a few days in the fridge but it is best to keep picking them during the season as and when they are required. It can be cooked and then frozen to use in dishes later in the year.

**Preparation:** Rhubarb is always cooked for eating and can be used in pies, fools, desserts, and jams. The leaves must not be eaten as they are poisonous. Cut off the leaves, then wash in cold water and chop the stems into cubes. Just eat the red or white parts of the stems—the greener parts of the stem are much tarter.

**BELOW:** The emerging shoots of forced rhubarb are a real treat in early spring. The crowns are covered over during winter to encourage them into growth early on in the year.

---

### NUTRITION

The stems of the plant contain multiple vitamins and minerals. Rhubarb is a nondairy source of calcium and promotes healthy bones and teeth. Vitamins A, C, E, and K are also present in high levels, helping the body repair and protect its immune system and develop and repair tissues.

With just the perfect amount of acidity and sharpness to cut through the sweetness of pie crust or custard, yet bursting with flavor, rhubarb is a springtime gourmet treat. One of the mainstays of the vegetable garden with its large ornamental leaves and its spreading habit, rhubarb is popular with gourmet gardeners for the beautiful, pink, succulent stems that are forced over winter. Even when the stems have not been forced they are still delicious, with enough sharpness to contrast well with sweet creamy dishes that use yogurts, ice cream, or crème fraiche. Stems must be cooked before eating and rhubarb leaves are poisonous and should not be eaten.

It needs to be grown in rich, fertile soil with lots of organic matter dug in to feed its huge luxuriant leaves and its rampant growth habit. It needs plenty of moisture but it dislikes waterlogged conditions, where the crown will quickly rot. Think carefully about the positioning of the plant—the plants do not mind a bit of shade, and it makes them useful for a shady spot in the garden. Because it is a perennial it will occupy the same spot for a few years, so make sure it is not going to interfere later with crop rotation. Rhubarb is best started from dormant crowns, which should be planted out between fall and spring. Space plants 30–36in apart. For those with a small garden or patio, they can be grown in large containers but they should be at least 19½in deep and wide.

To harvest, the stems should be grabbed near the base, twisted, and pulled upward. Harvesting unforced rhubarb usually starts in spring, with the last crops being collected in mid July. Picking any later can harm the plant as it needs to recover for the following year.

After a few years the center of the crown will need dividing into sections because it becomes woody and congested. To do this, it should be dug out of the ground in fall and the rootball should be sliced into sections with a sharp spade. The center should be discarded, but other sections with growing tips should be replanted in the garden. This helps to reinvigorate the plant and is a great way of getting extra plants for free. Allow it a year to recover.

## FORCING RHUBARB

The best-tasting stems are forced during winter by covering up the crown with clay forcing pots, or alternatively an upturned trash can. This excludes the light, which forces young, tender shoots to grow upward. In the gardening world this is called "forcing." The bright red stems taste much sweeter

### TASTING NOTES

#### Three of the best

If you want rhubarb with the finest taste, then sometimes some of the older, traditional varieties are the best.

| | |
|---|---|
| "Timperley Early" | The most popular variety for early forcing. |
| "Champagne" | An old favorite which produces long pink-tinged stems when forced. |
| "Victoria" | A traditional variety with deep, fleshy stems and superb flavor. |

and more flavorsome than when grown in normal conditions. The technique of forcing rhubarb into early growth was allegedly discovered at the Chelsea Physic Garden in London in 1817 when somebody accidentally covered a dormant crown with soil. A few weeks later, when the soil was uncovered, it revealed these delicious blanched stems that were sweeter, redder, and better flavored than when grown under usual conditions. The technique of forcing rhubarb was born. However, it was not until the 1870s that people started growing it commercially, by taking the crowns inside and growing them in the dark in warm forcing sheds.

## Not just a spring treat

Until recently rhubarb has always been something to enjoy from spring until midsummer. However, thanks to a new variety called "Livingstone" it is now possible to keep harvesting right through until fall. Summer dormancy, which causes conventional varieties to stop producing stems in midsummer, has been eliminated in this new strain. Now it is possible to combine rhubarb with fall fruits such as apple and blackberry to create amazing new seasonal combinations of dessert.

With stems being produced by forced rhubarb through winter, and "Livingstone" producing stems in fall, it seems that rhubarb is becoming an ingredient for all seasons.

### Rhubarb cobbler

Rhubarb crumble is a splendid treat from early spring to midsummer. Ready in the garden before most soft fruits, rhubarb is known as the first "dessert" ingredient of the year.

**Preparation time:** 20 minutes
**Cooking time:** 40 minutes
**Serves:** 6 people

· 10oz (300g) all-purpose flour

· 5oz (150g) unsalted butter

· 5oz (150g) Demerara sugar

· 8floz (250ml) orange juice

· 2oz (60g) superfine sugar

· 1lb (500g) rhubarb, chopped

Preheat a conventional oven to 350°F (180°C / gas mark 4 / fan 160°C).

Rub together the flour, butter, and sugar until mixture resembles breadcrumbs.

Mix the orange juice with the sugar in a pan and bring to the boil. Add the rhubarb, reduce the heat, and simmer until it is softened.

Spoon the rhubarb into a baking dish and cover with 6 tablespoons of poaching liquid.

Add crumble mixture on top and bake for 30–40 minutes.

**LEFT:** Rhubarb is a large vigorous perennial plant with huge leaves, requiring plenty of space in the kitchen garden. It should be mulched each year to retain moisture around the root system.

# EXTENDING THE SEASON

It is possible with careful planning to extend the season and to keep the kitchen garden productive for the majority of the year. There are various techniques for doing this including regular or successional sowing and using protection such as cloches or glasshouses to keep plants growing during colder weather.

## SUCCESSIONAL SOWING

Some plants such as lettuces, radishes, and carrots can be sown regularly throughout most of the year and will keep producing a crop. Other plants such as cabbages have winter, spring, summer, and fall varieties and will crop depending on when they were sown.

Other examples include:

Fava beans—sow in fall for early spring crop; sow in early spring for late spring crop.

Carrots—sow from March until September for regular harvesting through that period.

String beans—do three sowings, two weeks apart, from mid-May to extend the season.

Garlic and onion sets can be sown in the fall for early summer harvesting and throughout the following months until early spring to stagger the harvest time.

**ABOVE:** There are different types of cabbage including spring, summer, fall, and winter types. By selecting the right varieties it should be possible to have cabbages all year round.

**ABOVE:** Carrots can be enjoyed from early spring through to the end of the season, if they are sown successionally from early spring.

## CLOCHES

The word cloche means bell in French and traditionally they were shaped as such so that they could fit snugly over individual plants to protect them either from the spring frosts or from the fall cold at the end of the season. Bell-shaped cloches are still commonly used today and are usually made from glass or plastic. If using the latter material it is necessary to peg them down to prevent them blowing away.

For long rows of vegetables, tunnel cloches are a popular option. They usually consist of plastic stretched over hoops and placed over rows of vegetables, a bit like a mini polytunnel. Some cloche tunnels are made from corrugated plastic, which is stronger and less likely to get damaged in the wind.

In hot weather it is important to vent the cloches as otherwise the plants will quickly dry out and the foliage will get scorched in the sun. This is not the case for tunnel cloches with open ends. Cloches will need additional watering compared to plants grown directly outdoors, though plants under plastic or glass will rely on you entirely for their water supply. Cloches are also useful for placing over the soil, prior to sowing, to warm the ground up, which will promote earlier germination in the season.

---

### MAKE-DO CLOCHES

Recycled homemade mini-cloches made from plastic bottles cut in half are a popular option on allotments and are used to protect vulnerable seedlings such as zucchinis and pumpkins when first planted out.

---

## COLD FRAMES

These are essentially a wooden or brick box with a sloping glass roof. The roof is usually hinged, enabling plants to be lifted in and out, and meaning it can be easily watered and ventilated on hot days. They are usually used for hardening off plants that have been grown indoors, enabling them to acclimatize for a few days before being planted directly outdoors. This is done by gradually opening the cold frame for progressively longer periods over the course of two weeks. They can also be used like a cloche to extend the growing season.

**ABOVE:** A wooden-sided cold frame with a sloping glass roof is ideal for hardening off plants that have been started indoors.

## GLASSHOUSES

These are a useful addition to any vegetable garden as they enable crops to be sown earlier in the year, getting them off to a good start without having to wait for the weather to warm up outdoors for direct sowing. They also enable more tender crops such as eggplants, chillies, and indoor tomatoes to be grown. Glasshouses must have plenty of ventilation as they can quickly get too hot on sunny days. Shade netting can be used to moderate the heat in summer.

# Scorzonera
## *Scorzonera hispanica*

**Common name:** Scorzonera, black salsify, Spanish salsify, viper's grass

**Type:** Biennial

**Climate:** Hardy, very cold winter

**Size:** 14in (35cm)

**Origin:** Mediterranean

**History:** Scorzonera was first cultivated in the 16$^{th}$ century in Italy and France. The name scorzonera is derived from the Italian words *scorza*, meaning "bark," and *nera*, meaning "black." Also the word scorzone in Italian means a venomous snake, and the root has been used for a long time to treat snakebites. By 1660, the plant was being cultivated as a vegetable in Italy and France.

**Cultivation:** This Mediterranean plant is very hardy, but does require a sunny site in well-drained soil. Seeds should be sown in spring for a harvest the following fall and winter, but they can also be sown in late summer for harvesting the following year. Sow seeds thinly in a shallow drill. Rows should be 12in apart, and be thinned to 6in between each plant after germination.

**Storage:** Keep the roots in the ground until needed for cooking. Once harvested they will store in a fridge for a couple of weeks.

**Preparation:** Scorzonera is often roasted or boiled, used in a gratin, or in soups. It can be cut into large pieces and cooked, unpeeled. Once cooked, the outer black skin slides off pretty easily. You might want to wear gloves when preparing and cooking scorzonera as it can discolor your fingers.

**BELOW:** This ancient root vegetable is rarely seen in kitchen gardens these days, but is easy to grow, has attractive flowers, and can be used in a variety of different recipes.

Scorzonera and salsify are often grown together as they are very similar root crops requiring the same growing conditions, both coming from the daisy or *Asteraceae* family. It is still quite rare to find these vegetables either in a store or restaurant, but they are enjoying something of a renaissance among foodie fans looking for something a bit different in the culinary and horticultural world. Scorzonera is often referred to as "black salsify," due to the color of the outer layer of the root. When the skin is peeled back it reveals an attractive pure white flesh. It is a biennial and, if left in the ground for a second season, it will produce flowers, and the seeds can be collected and resown the following year. They are very easy to grow with no significant pests and diseases. They just need to be kept well watered during dry periods and regularly weeded around to avoid competition for moisture. Roots should be ready for harvesting in fall, but are fully hardy so can be kept in the ground throughout winter and

**LEFT:** Bundles of scorzonera roots make for an unusual harvest. As the roots are quite fragile, it helps to bundle them up to prevent damage.

harvested the following season. Each plant produces one long tap root about 12in in length. Like parsnips, their flavor is said to be enhanced and sweetened once it has been hit by frosts. Take care not to snap the brittle root when digging it up with a fork. In addition to the root, the plump flower bud can also be picked, steamed, and eaten. Flower petals can also be added to salads.

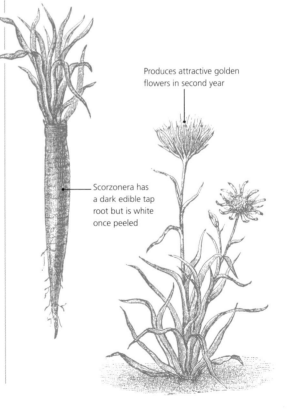

Produces attractive golden flowers in second year

Scorzonera has a dark edible tap root but is white once peeled

## NUTRITION

Scorzonera is very low in calories and is a concentrated source of nutrients such as iron, potassium, thiamin (vitamin B1), and phosphorus. It is also a good source of vitamin C, folate, copper, and magnesium.

# Tomato
## *Solanum lycopersicum*

**Common name:** Tomato, love apple, pomme d'amour

**Type:** Annual

**Climate:** Tender, warm glasshouse

**Size:** 6ft (1.8m)

**Origin:** Peru, Ecuador

**History:** Tomatoes were first harvested and consumed by the Incas and Aztecs. These tomatoes were the early wild form of the vegetable that grew in the valleys of the Peruvian Andes. It was not until the 16th century that tomatoes were brought to Europe by Spanish explorers. John Gerard's *Herbal* published an article in 1597 describing them as poisonous. They were not widely eaten until the mid 18th century because of this misconception.

**Cultivation:** Tomatoes can be grown in the glasshouse or outdoors. Seeds are sown in early spring. They should not be planted outside until late spring or early summer, when there is no risk of frost. Plants can be grown in grow bags and will need daily watering during the summer and a liquid tomato feed once a week when the trusses start to form.

**Storage:** Tomatoes will store for about a week in the fridge but there is no doubt that their flavor

**BELOW:** Tomatoes vary in size and color from tiny cherry types which can be eaten whole, to large beefsteak types that can be sliced up and either cooked or eaten raw.

is at its best when stored at room temperature on the table, like fruit, and eaten as soon as possible after picking from the vine. They do not freeze well as they end up watery and mushy. Try drying them in the oven and then packing them into jars of olive oil where they can keep for months when stored in a dark, cool cupboard. They can of course be made into tomato sauce or chutney, or made into soup and frozen.

**Preparation:** If using raw, slice or quarter the tomato. For using in cooked dishes, tomatoes will often need skinning. For this simply cover with boiling water for about 30 seconds, then plunge into cold water and the skins will peel off.

Biting into a sun-ripened tomato picked fresh and warm from the vine is the epitome of Mediterranean living and alfresco dining. There is a whole range of different types to try, from the huge and chunky "Flame" beefsteaks to the tiny yellow "Sungold" that simply explode in your mouth with summer sweetness. If ever there was a vegetable (technically a fruit) that exemplifies the difference in flavor between a store-bought vegetable and one eaten directly from the garden, then this is it. It is used in so many dishes, either uncooked in salads, concentrated, puréed, or in sauces. It appears everywhere, from popular Italian favorites such as lasagna, bolognaise, and pizza topping through to fast-food restaurants with bottles of tomato ketchup. It is used across the world to flavor dishes including Indian, Thai, and Mexican. If you want it in a can then the ubiquitous tomato soup or baked beans must be the two most preserved vegetable dishes in the world.

Just as popular in the garden as the kitchen, tomatoes can be grown in the tiniest of spaces.

They can be grown in growing bags and containers and there are trailing types such as "Tumbling Tom Red" that are suitable for hanging baskets. In the garden they are a wonderful ornamental addition with the brightly colored red, yellow, and green fruits often making a greater splash than many flowers. For those lucky enough to have a glasshouse, there is a wider range of tomatoes available and the season is extended by a few weeks on either side of summer.

## NUTRITION

Tomatoes are low in sodium, and very low in saturated fat and cholesterol. They are also a good source of vitamins A, C, and E, and are high in fiber. High levels of the antioxidant lycopene, present in tomatoes, has been shown to lower the risk of cardiovascular disease.

One medium sized-tomato provides over a third of the recommended daily allowance of vitamin C, and nearly a third of the recommended daily allowance of vitamin A.

**BELOW:** Gardeners usually refer to tomatoes as vegetables, yet botanists know of them as a fruit because the seed is contained within their succulent flesh.

There are still plenty of varieties to choose from
to grow outdoors provided that the site is sunny
and sheltered and they are kept watered and fed.
If planting them directly in the ground then lots
of garden compost should be added to the soil.
If placing in a growing bag then limit to two
tomatoes per bag.

## TASTING NOTES

### *Tomato sauce*

This tomato sauce should last for a few weeks
or even months and provide a supply of sauce
to accompany your meat and pasta dishes.

**Preparation time:** 5 minutes
**Cooking time:** 20 minutes
**Serves:** 4 people (for a pasta dish)

• 14oz (400g) chopped skinned tomatoes

• 1 tbsp mixed herbs, chopped

• 1 tbsp tomato purée

• ½ tsp sugar

• ¼ pint (150ml) dry white wine
  or vegetable broth

• Salt and pepper, to taste

• 1 large garlic clove, crushed

Place all the ingredients in a saucepan.

Bring to the boil, then simmer, uncovered, for
15–20 minutes or until mixture has reduced
and thickened. Season.

**ABOVE:** Tomatoes need regular feeding, at least once a month,
once they start to produce flowers. Sub laterals should be pinched
out to concentrate the plant's energy into the fruit.

Tomatoes are usually grown as cordons, with a
central leader that is trained up a cane. There are
shorter bush types too that do not need a support.
Seeds for growing outdoors can be started in March
or early April, whereas plants for glasshouses can be
started in April. Sow them in small plastic pots
indoors and keep them on a sunny windowledge
or a propagator. Plant them out in the glasshouse
when they are about 8in tall. Outside varieties
should only be planted out after the risk of spring
frosts is over. Continue to tie up the central leader
to the wire or cane as it grows. When it reaches the
top, the growing tip should be pinched out.

Keep the plants watered regularly. Irregular
watering will cause the skins to split. Tomato plants
should also be given tomato feed once a week. You
will soon notice that tomato plants put out lots
of sideshoots that extend from the leaf axils. For
cordon tomatoes, these must be pinched out as

soon as they appear. You do not need to do this with bush types. Water the plants in the evening or morning because otherwise the water will quickly evaporate and splashed leaves could get scorched.

Plants should be picked regularly as soon as they ripen. They will usually turn red although there are different colored varieties. They feel soft to the touch and when ready, pull away from the vine easily when gently twisted. At the end of the season the green tomatoes can be brought inside and ripened on a sunny ledge. Placing them next to banana skins speeds up the ripening process. If they do not turn red then a green tomato chutney can be made from them.

Watch out for the dreaded tomato blight, which causes the leaves and stems to turn yellow and brown before the entire plant rapidly starts to die back. There is very little that can be done to prevent it, although choosing modern, disease-resistant varieties can help. Remove the plants as soon as the symptoms are spotted to prevent the disease from affecting neighboring plants.

"A world without tomatoes is like a quartet without violins."

Laurie Colwin, *Home Cooking*, (1988)

## "TomTato"

If you are short of space in the vegetable garden and cannot decide whether you prefer to grow tomatoes or potatoes, then this could be the answer for you.

A plant called a "TomTato" can be grown, which produces tomatoes above the ground, and potatoes below the ground—a potato and tomato on the same plant!

The plants are not genetically modified, they are simply a potato plant and a tomato plant that are grafted together. It works because they are closely related, both belonging to the *Solanaceae* family. The plants last for one growing season, and by the time the tomato harvest is over at the end of summer, the plant can be dug up and the potatoes harvested.

**RIGHT:** There are so many different types of tomato to try that it is bewildering. Browse specialist seed catalogs and attend summer tastings to find the best ones.

# Skirret

## *Sium sisarum*

**Common names:** Skirret, suikerwortel (Netherlands), crummock (Scotland), zuckewurzel (Germany)

**Type:** Perennial

**Climate:** Hardy, very cold winter

**Size:** 3ft (1m)

**Origin:** Asia

**History:** Its name comes from the Middle English word skirwhite, perhaps from the Scots *skire*, meaning "bright," "clear," and "white." Skirret was eaten throughout the Middle Ages and its taste was improved by the addition of wine and honey until it was supplanted by the growing popularity of the potato. By the end of the 18th century, the use of skirrets in cooking had mostly vanished.

Pliny the Elder mentions skirret as being a favorite vegetable of the Emperor Tiberius, who would request a fixed amount of the plant every year from Germany, where it grew especially well despite the cold climate.

**Cultivation:** This perennial should be planted between fall and winter. Avoid harvesting its roots in the first year. Plant them at 16in apart in fertile soil. Their natural habitat is by streams and rivers, so they will need lots of watering during the summer. Harvesting takes place during fall and winter when the foliage has died down.

**Storage:** Treat them like carrots. They can be stored in the fridge for a while but can also be placed in "carrot clamps," which are simply holes dug in the ground outdoors and covered with soil and straw. They can also be kept in boxes or trays covered in slightly moist sand and stored in a garage, shed, or cellar.

**Preparation:** Simply scrub the roots and cut them into suitable lengths for cooking.

**LEFT:** Skirret is an easy-to-grow perennial root vegetable and is closely related to carrot and parsley. It can be used in many recipes as a carrot substitute.

This one-time popular root vegetable has fallen from grace, and from the dinner table, among gardeners and cooks alike over the last 200 years. Yet it is remarkably easy to grow and in addition produces attractive plumes of white flowers that look beautiful in the vegetable patch—far prettier than the dull foliage from other root vegetables such as carrots and parsnips. These also play a role in attracting pollinating and beneficial insects such as bees, butterflies, and lacewings. The root tastes like a cross between parsnip and potato but is packed full of sweetness. In fact the name "skirret" is actually derived from the dutch word meaning "sweet root," *Suikerwortel*.

It is a medium-sized perennial belonging to the same family as the carrot and parsley (*Apiaceae*). It produces sweet and aromatic thin white roots, usually longer than a carrot's and suitable for crunching on raw. In fact, skirret can be substituted for just about any carrot recipe and can be used peeled, sliced, and grated in salads. It is also suitable for boiling, roasting, creaming, and mashing. Try making a "carrot" cake from its roots and using it interchangeably with other fall vegetables such as parsnips, pumpkins, and both sweet or standard potatoes. Like other root vegetables they can also be baked with cooking oil to make fries; although they will be a lot thinner than the chunky fries produced from thicker rooted vegetables such as sweet potato, they will taste just as good.

Skirret prefers full sun, but will grow in dappled shade. It was once a popular waterside plant so it will tolerate a degree of moisture and it prefers a light soil for the roots to be able to penetrate

**LEFT:** Skirret is a perennial closely related to carrots, and produces an abundance of edible roots underground that can be harvested and cooked.

downward. However, it will benefit from having organic matter added, so add plenty to the planting hole. It is possible to sow seeds of skirret but results can be patchy and it takes a long time to establish. It is far easier to buy young plants from specialist suppliers and herb nurseries for immediate planting. In addition to compost, add sand or grit to the planting hole on heavy soils to help the plant establish well.

## Taking root cuttings

If you want more of these plants in the garden they are very simple to divide and propagate from root cuttings. Simply dig up the root system between late fall and early spring and cut away sections of the plant's roots and replant them elsewhere in the garden. Place the remainder of the plant back in the hole where it should continue to grow.

Avoid harvesting the root in the first year after planting, which will give the plant a chance to send down some roots and get itself established in the garden. The following year, between fall and winter, once the foliage has died back, dig up the plant and remove sections of the root with a sharp knife before taking it indoors for eating raw or cooking. Do not harvest all the roots or the plant will not survive into spring. Place the plant back in the ground and recover the rootball with soil and compost.

# Eggplant
## *Solanum melongena*

**Common names:** Eggplant, aubergine, brinjal, melongene

**Type:** Annual

**Climate:** Tender, warm glasshouse

**Size:** 29½in (75cm)

**Origin:** There is debate as to exactly where the eggplant originates from, with some historians believing it comes from India, although it would also appear to have been grown in China in the 5th century.

**BELOW:** Eggplants are easier to grow than most people think. They are usually grown in glasshouses or cold frames unless in a very warm and sheltered garden.

**History:** The eggplant was first cultivated over 2,000 years ago in southeast Asia. In China by 500 BC eggplants had became a culinary favorite to generations of Chinese emperors. The Moors introduced the eggplant to Spain where it received its Catalonian name "Alberginia." The vegetable soon spread throughout Europe and by the 16th century Spaniards believed the eggplant to be a powerful aphrodisiac, an "apple of Love."

**Cultivation:** Eggplants require a warm site to survive. Ideally this is in a glasshouse or cold frame but they can survive outdoors in sunny, sheltered spots. Plant two per growing bag and keep them well watered during summer. They can be started by seed in spring, which will give a better choice of variety, but are readily available from garden centers too.

**Storage:** Eggplants do not last for long and should be used within a few days of harvesting. They do not freeze well because of their high water content.

**Preparation:** Before cooking, cut off the stems, trim the ends, and halve or slice the eggplants. Place in a colander, sprinkling the layers with salt, and leave for 30–45 minutes.

To many people, the eggplant probably looks like more of a curiosity with its funny looking white or purple shaped fruits, rather than something appetizing and appealing to the taste buds. It was treated with skepticism when first introduced to England, not just because of its relationship to the deadly nightshade family (incidentally so are potatoes and tomatoes); it was also blamed for a variety of sicknesses ranging from piles to leprosy. Today it is treated with a similar contempt and skeptical attitude, not for the same reasons but because people think that they are tricky to grow in the garden, and hard to cook in the kitchen. Neither of these is the case, and in the garden it is just as easy to grow as some tomatoes. In the kitchen with a bit of imagination it can be transformed into many sumptuous and simple dishes other than the ubiquitous but delicious moussaka. It can be cooked as part of many other dishes such as ratatouille and as a side dish in its own right. It has a lovely rich texture and can be roasted and puréed. It tastes great when combined with garlic and onions. They can also be thinly sliced and fried to make eggplant chips. Try stuffing them with a cheese and onion filling or slicing them down the center and baking them in the oven with

**ABOVE:** The attractive leaves and flowers look very similar to some of its closely related cousins, particularly potatoes and the very poisonous deadly nightshade.

TASTING NOTES

*Eggplant varieties to try*

There are a huge range of different eggplant types to try. Here are some of the best and most interesting for lovers of gourmet cuisine due to their colors and flavor:

| | |
|---|---|
| "Pintung Long" | Long lavender-purple fruit packed full of flavor. |
| "Rossa Bianca" | A gourmet treat with white, rose-tinted fruit with rich creamy flavors and texture. |
| "Bonica" | Flavorsome fruits with glossy purple skins. |
| "Galine" | Ornamental and with very tasty, smallish fruit. |

a bed of tomato bolognaise and topped with goat's cheese or mozzarella and herbs.

Eggplants originate in Asia, probably India, and do require warmth and a degree of humidity in the garden. They add a touch of the exotic and beauty to any planting display with their purple-tinted stems and their soft, velvety luxuriant leaves. They also have attractive potato-like bluey flowers but it is their impressive fruit that gives them the wow factor. They are usually dark purple or white, but they also come in other colors including pink, striped, yellow, orange, and green. Shapes range from the traditional "egg shape" to elongated 12in-long types or round. For small patios or balconies, try a dwarf variety in a container. "Mini Bambino" is a curious form that only reaches 12in in height and produces tiny 1in fruits.

Plants require a warm and sheltered site. Ideally they should be grown in a glasshouse, but they can be grown outdoors in mild areas in full sun. Start seeds off indoors in spring into individual pots or modules. Soaking the seeds overnight before sowing can help with germination. Leave them on a warm windowledge or in a heated propagator. They like warm conditions to germinate, at about

LEFT: Eggplants are so-called because some varieties have fruits of that shape. They are usually white or dark purple, but can also be stripy, yellow, and even pink!

70 to 77°F. Once they have germinated they can be planted into growing bags or containers filled with good-quality compost. If growing outdoors they will need hardening off for about two weeks in a cold frame or porch before moving the growing bags outdoors.

When the plants reach about 16in high, the growing tips should be pinched out to encourage branching and a bushier habit, as this will promote more fruits. The fruiting sideshoots should be pinched out when no more than five or six fruits have set. The plants will need watering daily during the summer and will benefit from a liquid tomato feed every 10 days from when they start to set fruit. They will need canes and string for support, particularly when the large fruits start to swell.

Eggplants will be ready from midsummer onward if grown in a glasshouse or cold frame. If they are grown outside then they will not ripen until late summer or early fall. The fruit should be picked before the skin loses its attractive sheen and glossiness. Use pruning shears to cut the fruit from the plant, retaining a bit of the stem on the eggplant.

"That in Italy and other hot countries, where they [the fruits] come to their full maturity, and proper relish, they [the people] doe eate them with more desire and pleasure than we do Cowcumbers."

John Parkinson, English 17th-century horticulturist

# Potato

## *Solanum tuberosum*

**Common name:** Potato, spuds, taters, tatties

**Type:** Annual

**Climate:** Tender, frost-free winter

**Size:** 29½in (75cm)

**Origin:** Central America

**BELOW:** Potatoes are edible tubers produced under the soil. To increase yield and prevent them turning green the soil is earthed up around the stems as the plants start to grow.

**History:** It is thought that the potato was cultivated in the Andes as early as c. 5000 BC. Spanish adventurers took the domesticated potato back to Europe in the 16th century, although it was not until the late 18th century that it began to be widely consumed.

**Cultivation:** Potato tubers are planted below the surface of the soil in spring. As they grow, the soil should be "earthed up" around the base of the shoots to protect them from the frost, to prevent the tubers near the surface turning green, and to increase the potential yield. Potatoes should be grown in a sunny, sheltered site and they like a rich soil.

**Storage:** Early potatoes should be eaten soon after harvesting to capture their unique flavors, although they will keep if stored in paper bags in the dark, such as an understairs cupboard. Do not keep them in the fridge or leave them in the light as they will turn green and therefore poisonous. Maincrop potatoes should also be kept in the dark and will store for many months in the right conditions.

**Preparation:** Wash and scrub the soil off with a brush. Early potatoes and those larger ones intended for baking are usually cooked with their skins on. Maincrop potatoes intended for boiling, mashing, and frying are usually peeled. Roast potatoes are usually peeled, but some people think they're crunchier and have better flavor when roasted in their skins.

Ranging from French fries and chunky wedges to creamy mashed potato and dauphinois gratin, there is a dish to suit everybody's taste contained within these versatile underground tubers. They are the classic staple food for so many people and can be grown in a variety of different ways. It is hard to imagine a traditional pot roast being served without crunchy roast potatoes and equally hard to conceive of a fast-food restaurant without a side order of fries. Whether you crave chips, waffles, or Irish potato bread there is a recipe for everyone. Although they taste delicious and have a wide range of different flavors depending on variety, they are fairly neutral tasting, meaning they make a perfect accompaniment to more powerfully

## NUTRITION

Potatoes are fat free, a natural source of fiber, and contain several vitamins and minerals, such as vitamins C and B6. Vitamin B6 helps to contribute to normal red blood cell formation, normal functioning of the nervous system, and the reduction of tiredness and fatigue. All potatoes contain vitamin B6, whatever way they are prepared.

## TO CHIT OR NOT TO CHIT

Traditionally, gardeners have always "chitted" their potatoes to get them off to an early start in the season. This involves starting them into growth about four or five weeks prior to planting by placing the seed tubers in a light, frost-free place to encourage small shoots or "chits" about 1in long to form. However, more recently, people are claiming it does not speed up the process, and the warmth of the soil and amount of sunshine are the determining factors in getting an early crop.

flavored ingredients, which is why they are the number-one addition to so many dishes. It also explains the popularity of the baked potato filled with just about anything imaginable. Society's dependence on the humble spud reached devastating proportions during the 18th century when many of the Irish starved, partly due to the successive failures of their potato harvest when it became affected by potato blight between 1841–1845.

Despite its popularity as an edible crop it is related to deadly nightshade, and apart from the underground tubers, the rest of the plant is actually poisonous. However, the tubers themselves are very healthy and contain C and B complex vitamins and are packed full of iron, calcium, and potassium. The skins are loaded with fiber and are therefore far more nutritious when cooked unpeeled.

Potatoes are classified into three different groups depending on their season of planting and harvesting, which are first earlies, second earlies, and maincrops. First earlies are planted in late winter, second earlies in early spring, and maincrops in midspring. If space is short, then focus on growing the early varieties as they have the best flavor, take up less area, and are expensive to buy in the store. To plant the tubers, a trench should be dug that is about 6in deep, with lots of well-rotted organic matter dug into the bottom. Plant the potatoes with their shoots facing upward (if they have been chitted, see box). Early potatoes should be spaced 12in apart with 20in between each row; second earlies and maincrops should be 16in apart with 30in between each row. Cover the tubers over gently with a mix of the soil and compost, being

**BELOW:** Many varieties of potato produce an attractive flower spike. Early varieties are usually ready for harvesting just after the plant has finished flowering.

### The perfect roast potato

The perfect roast potato should be crisp and golden on the outside with a fluffy interior. Red-skinned potatoes, such as "Desirée," are particularly good for roasting, but any floury type like "Charlotte" will do.

**Preparation time:** 20 minutes
**Cooking time:** 50 minutes–1 hour
**Serves:** 6 people (as a side dish)

· 2lb (1kg) potatoes

· 10oz (300g) goose fat or lard (alternatively sunflower oil or groundnut oil)

· Salt and pepper, to taste

Preheat a conventional oven to 475°F (240°C / gas mark 9 / fan 220°C).

Peel and cut the potatoes into egg-sized pieces.

Place in a large pan and pour on cold water until they are just covered and add salt.

Bring to the boil and cook for 5–8 minutes until they are parboiled, then drain.

Toss the potatoes to smash the edges so they become crispy during cooking. Leave to cool.

Place the fat in a large roasting tin and heat in the oven for a few minutes until sizzling hot.

Very carefully tip the potatoes into the tin. Add salt and pepper and turn them over so they are well coated in oil.

Roast in the oven for approximately 45–60 minutes, turning occasionally, until they are soft inside with crispy skins.

"What can the world do without potatoes? Almost as well might we now ask, what would the world be without inhabitants?"

Samuel Cole, The New England Farmer, (1852)

careful not to break the chits. As the shoots start to emerge from the ground, use a draw hoe or rake to form a ridge in the soil along the row that is between 6in and 8in high.

There is usually a period of about 12 weeks from planting tubers to harvesting first early types of potato, depending on the quality of the season and the variety. The sign that they are ready for digging up out of the ground is just as they finish flowering, but it is always worth scraping away some of the soil and investigating to see whether the tubers are big enough. Otherwise they can stay in the ground for longer. Maincrop potatoes can be harvested any time after flowering and it is usually at least 20 weeks until they are ready to be lifted from the ground. If they are intended to be stored over winter, they should be left in the ground until the foliage starts to die down. If potato blight strikes, turning the stems black and quickly spreading, then cut down the foliage and begin to harvest the crop. Blight is a problem in wet summers, and if you find it is affecting you year after year, then grow second earlies instead, which should mature before blight strikes.

**ABOVE:** The potato world has a rich heritage and there have always been lots of varieties to choose from as demonstrated in *Watercolor of Potatoes* by Pierre François Ledoulx c.1790.

**ABOVE:** On harvesting, you will notice that the original seed potato will have withered, with lots of new potatoes in its place. Take care when harvesting them as they are easily spiked with a fork.

## Choosing varieties

There are literally hundreds of potatoes to choose from. Some are more suitable for boiling while others are better for baking or roasting, so choose ones that will suit the type of dishes you enjoy cooking. "King Edward" and "Maris Piper" are the traditional best varieties for a baked potato, as well as roasting. "Red Duke of York" is a versatile variety that can be harvested early and enjoyed like a new potato or left to mature to make a delicious baked potato with red skin and creamy white flesh. The variety "Golden Wonder" is great for making chips. It has a dry and floury consistency, but disintegrates when boiled. There are lots of "salad" type potatoes that have a lovely waxy skin and make perfect salad potatoes. If you suffer from blight in the area, then try a resistant variety such as "Sarpo Mira."

# Spinach

*Spinacia oleracea*

**Common name:** Spinach, common spinach

**Type:** Annual

**Climate:** Tender, frost-free winter

**Size:** 10in (25cm)

**Origin:** Ancient Persia

**History:** The English word "spinach" dates to the late 14th century, and is from the French word *espinache*, which means "of uncertain origin." Spinach is thought to have originated in ancient Persia, and it first appeared in England and France in the 14th century, probably via Spain, and became a popular vegetable. During World War One, wine fortified with spinach juice was given to French soldiers weakened by hemorrhage.

**Cultivation:** Sow seeds in spring in shallow drills in fertile soil in full sun. Keep the soil moist to prevent the plant from bolting. Sow again in late summer to harvest during fall and winter. Overwintering spinach should be protected with horticultural fleece or a plastic cloche to keep the leaves tender.

**Storage:** Spinach leaves do not last for long at all, and should be picked from the garden or allotment as and when needed that day. They can be frozen for cooking with later in the year.

**Preparation:** Wash spinach leaves well to remove dirt and pests. Spinach is best steamed for about 5–10 minutes.

**RIGHT:** Spinach should be sown in early spring but can be prone to bolting and going quickly to seed if the soil is not kept moist during its early stages of development.

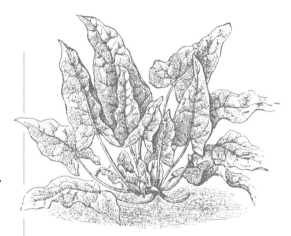

**ABOVE:** Spinach is a commonly grown leafy vegetable. The young leaves are often eaten raw, whereas the mature leaves are usually boiled, steamed, or added to stir-fries.

Feared by children yet loved by the cartoon character Popeye, spinach alongside Brussels sprouts are the vegetables that everybody loves to hate, and shudder with eye-watering magnitude when placed in front of them on a plate. Yet not only is spinach one of the healthiest vegetables available, packed full of vitamins and antioxidants, it can also taste superb if grown properly in the garden, and prepared well in the kitchen. There are countless dishes that use spinach: a spinach roulade filled with cream cheese and crunchy peppers or spicy chillies is delectable, while spinach and goat's cheese muffins are one of the tastiest savory cakes out there.

It can be used to make scrumptious Indian dahl soups with yogurt and served with naan bread or used in a poached egg Florentine breakfast dish. A spinach and ricotta cheese cannelloni is a must for anyone who wants to take their first tentative steps to tasting this gourmet vegetable. Spinach leaves can be eaten raw when young and are often chopped up in salads. But they come into their own when cooked and the leaves break down into a versatile texture that enables them to be spread, baked, and easily mixed with other ingredients.

Spinach should be grown in a sunny, sheltered site in well-drained soil. It requires lots of organic matter to help retain moisture, which will help prevent the plant from bolting in dry weather. Sow the seeds thinly in shallow drills 12in apart, doing so little and often, about every couple of weeks, in short rows to ensure a plentiful supply throughout the season. Once the seeds have germinated they can be thinned out to 6in between each seedling, but do not throw the seedlings on the compost

### NUTRITION

Spinach is a rich source of omega-3 fatty acids and contains a good amount of minerals like potassium, manganese, magnesium, copper, and zinc. Potassium helps the body to control heart rate and blood pressure. Spinach is also a good source of vitamins A, C, and K.

3½oz of farm fresh spinach has 47 percent of daily recommended levels of vitamin C—a powerful antioxidant, helping the body develop resistance against infectious agents.

"I'm Popeye the sailor man, I'm Popeye the sailor man. I'm strong to the finish because I eats me spinach. I'm Popeye the sailor man!"

"I'm Popeye The Sailor Man," composed by Sammy Lerner (1933)

### Spinach and bacon salad

This simple salad is a mix between the healthy, fresh leaves of young and tender spinach and the crunchy bacon.

**Preparation time:** 5 minutes
**Cooking time:** 5 minutes
**Serves:** 2 people (as a side dish)

· 4oz (110g) spinach leaves, washed

· 6oz (170g) bacon, chopped

· 2oz (50g) croutons

· 1 tbsp cider vinegar

Place the spinach leaves in a bowl.

Fry the bacon in a frying pan until crisp and then add this to the spinach.

Add the vinegar to the pan, stir well to soak up the juices, and pour over the salad.

Toss quickly, sprinkle croutons over the top, and serve immediately.

heap as they can be tossed into salads or used as fillings for sandwiches and wraps.

Sowing can begin in early spring and can continue through to early summer. Avoid sowing during the middle of summer as the heat will cause the plants to bolt. Start sowing again in late summer to provide a crop for overwintering. They will need covering with a cloche when the fall frosts arrive. This will not just protect the plants but will also ensure the leaves are delicious and tender when harvested during those cold winter months.

Harvest the leaves when they are young and tender for salads. They are a quick-growing crop and can usually be picked about 8 weeks after sowing. Do not pick off all the leaves at once, but make regular harvests from it until the plant matures and starts to flower and seed.

**RIGHT:** Spinach is easy to grow and requires a fertile soil in full sun. Regular, successional sowing will guarantee a plentiful supply of leaves but avoid sowing in summer due to bolting.

Watch out for the fungus-downy mildew, which can cause the leaves to go moldy in warm, humid conditions. Ensuring the plants are spaced out enough should allow the air to circulate around the foliage, which should hopefully prevent this problem. Alternatively there are modern mildew-resistant varieties.

Also, keep an eye out for birds, which can quickly ruin a crop of spinach seedlings. Either grow seedlings in a fruit cage or cover them with a fine gauge netting or horticultural fleece. Once the plants are established the protection can be removed.

There are a number of varieties to try but "Atlanta" is one of the hardiest and is ideal for growing through winter. "Monnopa" is also suitable for fall or summer, and is useful because it tends not to bolt. It produces thick tasty, strong-flavored leaves. "Palco" is another good variety that has some resistance to bolting and also to downy mildew. "Fiorano" is great for containers and has attractive dark green, rounded leaves. It also has high resistance to downy mildew and good bolting resistance, making summer sowings possible. "Bloomsdale Long Standing" is a heritage variety that produces high yields of tender, dark green savoyed leaves.

## ALTERNATIVES TO SPINACH

Spinach prefers a cool summer and has a tendency to become stressed and bolt, which means it is quick to flower and go to seed. Keeping the plant watered should help to avoid this problem. However, if it continues to be an issue, there are some leafy alternatives. Try Swiss chard or perpetual spinach (see p.48), which has a similar

**ABOVE:** The hardy annual *Atriplex hortensis* is delicious when added to salads, but also looks interesting in the ornamental garden, with red or green leaves and a purple flower spike.

flavor. Alternatively, try growing the more drought-tolerant New Zealand spinach (*Tetragonia tetragonoides*) or mountain spinach (*Atriplex hortensis*), which is simple to grow and the red forms add an attractive splash of color to the plate.

# STORING VEGETABLES

Feast or famine is a common problem for vegetable growers, but by careful planning it should be possible to fill the periods of famine on the plot with vegetables that have been stored during the peak harvest season.

Gluts of fresh vegetables during harvest time are a lovely problem to have on the vegetable plot, but it is not necessary to sling them on the compost heap. One obvious solution is to swap them with friends and family for crops that you may not have grown yourself. Alternatively there are various methods of storing them until ready to use later in the kitchen.

## FREEZING

Chest freezers are almost essential for vegetable gardeners these days as there are so many crops that can be frozen. Although most vegetables taste better fresh, some crops such as peas actually taste sweeter when they have been frozen as the freezing process ruptures their cells, imparting more flavor. In addition to freezing vegetables, cooked vegetable dishes can also be placed in the freezer for a delicious instant meal later in the year. Save up plastic boxes and bags so that there are plenty of containers to freeze the vegetables in, and label them clearly.

## PRESERVING

Many vegetables can be preserved and made into the most delicious chutneys and pickles (see box). There are fantastic, simple recipes such as picallilli, which uses lots of vegetable ingredients from the garden. Onions and beet taste delicious when stored in a jar of quality vinegar and will keep for years in that form.

**LEFT:** Most vegetables are best eaten fresh, such as corn on the cob. Sweetcorn also freezes easily, once separated from the cob.

"It is a very good idea to string onions with baler or binder twine. Then hang them in a cool airy place. In many peasant communities the tradition is to hang them against the wall under the eaves of the house."

*The Complete Book of Self-sufficiency*, **John Seymour, (1975)**

## DRYING

This old traditional method is ideal for preserving chillies and herbs. They can simply be left hanging on strings indoors, with plenty of air circulation, to dry out and be used later in the year in dishes.

Onions and garlic also benefit from being dried out before using. They can be plaited or tied together and left in a dry, rodent-free place for months before using. Alternatively they can be stored in a stocking and hung up on a peg in the garage or shed.

**ABOVE:** Hardneck garlic does not store for as long as softnecked types. Both types can have their stems plaited together and kept in a dry, frost-free place for a few months.

---

### Sterilizing jars

- First wash the jars and lids in soapy water and rinse in clean, warm water.

- Allow to drip dry, upside-down on a rack in the oven heated at 275°F (140°C / gas mark 1 / fan 120°C) for about 30 minutes.

- Remove by holding with oven gloves.

- Fill with your preserve and cover with lid while still hot.

---

## STORED IN THE DARK OR EVEN THE SOIL

Most vegetables will last longer if stored in a dark cool place, such as a cellar, or a building in the shade. Potatoes will keep for longer if kept in a dark cupboard in paper bags.

Some plants can be stored in the ground over winter until they are needed. This is a common method for storing carrots, often called a carrot clamp. A hole is dug in the ground; the carrots are placed in the center and are then covered over with soil. They are then dug up as and when required. Other root vegetables such as parsnips and salsify can also be stored using this method.

**BELOW:** Winter squashes, gourds, and pumpkins will store for a few months after harvesting if their skin has been cured by leaving to dry in the sunshine for a few days before harvesting.

# Chinese artichoke
## *Stachys affinis*

**Common name:** Chinese artichoke, crosnes, Japanese artichoke

**Type:** Perennial

**Climate:** Hardy, average winter

**Size:** 16in (40cm)

**Origin:** China

**History:** Chinese artichoke is native to and grown in China and Japan. It is also called the Japanese artichoke. In Europe it is called *crosnes*, which, according to legend, was also the name of a small town in France where the Chinese artichoke was introduced in 1822.

**Cultivation:** Plant tubers in a fertile, well-drained site in full sun at 10in apart in early spring. Keep them watered during dry periods and harvest in October. Leave some tubers in the ground to regenerate the following year.

**Storage:** Keep them in the ground and harvest them as required in the kitchen.

**Preparation:** Chinese artichoke tubers do not need to be peeled and simply need to be scrubbed prior to eating raw or cooking.

The tubers of Chinese artichoke are a rarity in stores and plant nurseries, which is a shame as these plants are so easy to grow and are the ultimate in gastronomic indulgence. They can be enjoyed raw and crunchy in salads, or stir-fried in Asian dishes and boiled and steamed. Alternatively their crunchy, nutty texture can be enjoyed when chopped up and fried in garlic butter. They are occasionally found in high-quality or Asian restaurants, but the best way to get your hands

**RIGHT:** An easy-to-grow plant that is popular in Asia, but very hard to find to find closer to home. They can be added raw to salads or cooked in stir-fries, boiled, or steamed.

### Yacon root that tastes a bit like pear
### (Smallanthus sonchifolius)

Try yacon for another alternative tuber. It is a large perennial plant, hailing from South America and related to sunflowers, with small yellow flowers. It is simple to grow and requires very little maintenance. In fall the plant is dug up and the tubers are harvested. Replant some of the tubers with growing tips to ensure there is a crop for the following year.

The tubers have a crunchy texture and their natural sweetness goes nicely when eaten raw in salads (peel tubers first) or added to stir-fries. They make a good substitute for water chestnut recipes. The knobbly growing tips can be divided and replanted, so you do not need to buy additional plants.

The tubers are quite juicy, in fact Yacon means "water root" in the Inca language. They can be pressed to extract a sweet juice that is then reduced down by boiling to make a sweet syrup, a bit like maple syrup. Quickly cover with croutons over the top and serve immediately.

on these delicious roots is to grow your own. Do not let the look of them put you off; the best way to describe them is like the Australian witchetty grubs with a white, crinkly skin, about 3in long!

Plant the tubers out between fall and winter at 3in deep and 10in apart in rows. The tubers should be planted horizontally and the rows should be 18in apart. They are ready for harvesting from October onward after the foliage has started to blacken and die back. Like Jerusalem artichokes, they can be harvested throughout winter, and once established they should be self-perpetuating so long as some tubers are left in the ground each year after harvesting. Mulch the beds with well-rotted garden compost each spring as this will help to retain the moisture. Water the plants during dry periods.

## OCA (OXALIS TUBEROSA)

Tubers are one of the staples of people in Bolivia and Peru. They come in the most amazing bright colors and the taste is like potatoes dipped in lemon juice.

They are very easy to grow as long as you have a moderately long season. Just cook as you would a potato, either boiled, baked, or fried. Tubers start to form in fall and should be harvested in early winter. The leaves are also edible and delicious.

# Salsify
## *Tragopogon porrifolius*

**Common name:** Salsify, goat's beard, vegetable oyster

**Type:** Biennial

**Climate:** Hardy, cold winter

**Size:** 14in (35cm)

**Origin:** Southern Europe, Mediterranean

**History:** Salsify was probably first cultivated in Italy in the 16th century but it was not known specifically as a kitchen garden plant. It became very popular in Europe in the late 16th and 17th century and was grown in gardens, together with black salsify (see p.186).

**Cultivation:** Sow in spring into shallow drills in rows 12in apart. Thin the seedlings out after germination so that there is 6in between each plant. They prefer to be grown in full sun in a well-drained soil.

**Storage:** Salsify is very hardy and the roots can remain in the soil throughout winter until required. Salsify will last two weeks if stored in the refrigerator, but do not remove their skins.

**Preparation:** Prepare salsify by scrubbing with a brush, removing the skin, rootlets, and all dark spots. Trim the tops and bottoms and slice as you would a carrot or leave whole. Avoid overcooking this root as it will quickly turn into mush. Salsify can be steamed, sliced and added to soups and stews, or simply mashed and served instead of potato. Salsify goes very well with roasted beef.

**RIGHT:** Salsify was a popular root vegetable in Europe in the late 16th century, but is less well-known these days. It has a distinctive flavor sometimes compared to oysters.

## NUTRITION

Salsify is very low in calories and is a concentrated source of nutrients such as iron, potassium, thiamin (vitamin B1), and phosphorus. Vitamin C, folate, copper, and magnesium are also present in high levels, making it an exceptionally healthy vegetable.

Closely related to scorzonera, this root crop is back in fashion in the vegetable patch, as well as the kitchen, after years of it being overlooked by cooks and gardeners in favor of carrots and parsnips. Yet, this quirky vegetable really does have a distinctive flavor that explains why it is having a resurgence, and is well worth trying.

The taste is reminiscent of oysters, hence one of their common names "vegetable oyster," meaning that it goes well with a range of meat and seafood dishes. It also makes a delicious soup by puréeing the roots, adding herbs and spices, and serving it with wholegrain rolls for a satisfying and healthy lunchtime snack.

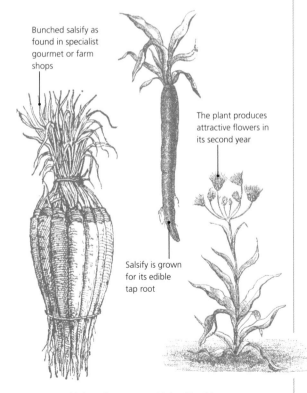

Bunched salsify as found in specialist gourmet or farm shops

The plant produces attractive flowers in its second year

Salsify is grown for its edible tap root

**ABOVE:** This lesser-known vegetable is a biennial but is usually treated as an annual as the plant is dug up at the end of its first year, in order to harvest the flavorsome roots.

Salsify is a biennial, meaning it will flower in the second year. However, for most people it is treated as an annual because it is dug up at the end of the first year and the root is harvested. Seeds can be sown from late winter until midspring, meaning that the roots will be ready by fall. They can remain in the ground throughout winter though and if the roots are not large enough they can be left to grow on the following year too. During the growing season, keep the area around the roots watered during dry periods, and weed-free. Harvest as and when required in the kitchen, being careful not to snap the root when digging it out of the ground.

"Salsify is a root of high quality, the growing of which is generally considered a test of a gardeners skill."

**Suttons & Sons,** *The culture of Vegetables and Flowers,* (1913)

# Fava bean
## *Vicia faba*

**Common name:** Fava bean, broad bean, faba bean, horse bean, Windsor bean

**Type:** Annual

**Climate:** Half-hardy to hardy, mild to cold winter

**Size:** 18in (45cm)

**Origin:** Middle East

**History:** This is one of the most ancient of beans, with a history dating back to the Bronze Age. By the Iron Age, fava beans had spread to Europe.

**Cultivation:** Sow hardy fall varieties in November for an early harvest the following year. Otherwise sow in late winter or early

spring. Tall varieties may need supports to stop them collapsing. Keep them well watered during dry periods and harvest when the pods feel plump.

**Storage:** Fava beans are best when shelled and eaten fresh, but they can be frozen. Alternatively they can be dried and stored in sterilized, sealed jars.

**Preparation:** When very young and tender the pods can be cooked whole but usually they are shelled. As the plant matures its beans develop a gray outer skin that gradually becomes tougher. This is easily removed after cooking by blanching in boiling water or the beans can be slipped out of their skins after cooking. Cook beans in boiling salted water for about 15–20 minutes.

## NUTRITION

Fava beans are rich in phytonutrients such as isoflavone and plant-sterols. They are also very high in protein and energy as are other beans and lentils. They also contain plenty of health-benefiting antioxidants, vitamins, and minerals. Fava beans are also one of the fine sources of minerals like iron, copper, manganese, calcium, and magnesium. They also contain high levels of potassium, which helps look after the heart and reduce blood pressure.

Reckoned to be the oldest and original bean, this is one of the first vegetables of the season and is worth savoring and celebrating for that reason alone. You should choose a hardy variety, and good examples are "Aquadulce" or "Aquadulce Claudia." For those with aspirations for self-sufficiency it is an important crop as it fills the gap between the end of the winter crops and the start of the new season. They are usually shelled and can be enjoyed steamed or boiled and are at their best when simply served up with fried onion, garlic, and freshly picked mint. They can also be added to soups, stir-fries, casseroles, and stews. For a real treat the fava bean pods can be picked when very young and tender, chopped and tailed, steamed, and eaten whole. The beans can also be made into a light green purée and, when mixed with Dijon mustard, make a delicious accompaniment to ham, pork, or crispy bacon. Alternatively, try mixing with fried garlic, olives, and chillies with crumbled feta cheese and served on a crostini.

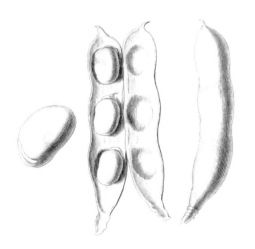

## TASTING NOTES

### *Fava bean varieties to try*

There are lots of different varieties of fava bean to try, but the ones listed below are considered to have the best flavor and are particularly easy to grow.

| | |
|---|---|
| "Aquadulce Claudia" | This variety is an old favorite among vegetable growers. Good for fall planting, it produces an early crop of large pods with white beans. |
| "Medes" | A tall and compact variety with pods producing 5–6 white beans and excellent flavor. |
| "The Sutton" | A popular dwarf variety that produces an abundance of pods each containing five white tender beans. A good variety for freezing. |
| "Crimson Flowered" | For a curiosity try this fava bean variety that has deep red flowers followed by small pods filled with small beans of great flavor. |

To get an early crop in spring, seeds can be sown in fall where they will quickly germinate in the soil. In cooler locations they may need protection with a cloche during winter. Alternatively, they can be sown in late winter or early spring, meaning they will crop later on in the season. To get a regular crop through spring and into early summer, sow seeds once a month. They should be grown in a fertile well-drained site that has been enriched with plenty of organic matter.

Seeds should be sown 2in deep and 12in apart in the row, and 18in apart between rows. They can also be sown in double rows which should be 10in apart with 24in between the next row. Rows should be weeded regularly to prevent them competing for nutrients with the seedlings. Growing them in double rows should mean they do not need staking as the plants support each other, but taller varieties in single rows may need tying up with string and stakes being run to the row. The beans will need watering regularly once they start flowering. The tops should be pinched out when the first pods

**ABOVE:** Fava beans are very easy to grow, but require a fertile soil in full sun. Their spring flowers are always a welcome sight as it means your first crop of the year is on its way.

start to form as this will channel their energy into producing beans rather than growing. It also helps mitigate one of their main weaknesses, their susceptibility to black fly, which tend to attack the tip of the plant where it is most tender. For the gourmet gardener the spring tips from these fava beans are worth saving and adding to a stir-fry, but leave them if they have been attacked by black fly, which can be a problem in some years.

The pods should be picked when they start to look plump. Harvest the lowest pods first and do not leave them for too long because the smaller beans are by far the most tender and sweet. Do not forget to pick very young pods to steam and eat whole.

### TASTING NOTES

#### *Color for the plate*

Fava beans are usually green or white (although really these are just very light green beans) with the green ones considered to be best for freezing. There are also mahogany red varieties that are worth trying for something different at the dinner table. Try "Red Epicure," which retains its color best if steamed rather than boiled.

# Sweetcorn
## *Zea mays*

**Common name:** Sweetcorn, corn on the cob

**Type:** Annual

**Climate:** Tender, frost-free winter

**Size:** 5ft (1.5m) or more

**Origin:** Americas

**History:** Sweetcorn has a very ancient history and is believed to have been domesticated over 8,000 years ago. It was recorded as being the staple food in diets of the Mayan tribes around 2000–1500 BC. In the 16th century it was brought to Europe by the Spaniards.

**Cultivation:** Sow seeds indoors from mid to late May and plant out after the risk of frosts. They should be planted in a grid system as they are wind-pollinated, so avoid planting in long rows. They require a sheltered, sunny site on fertile soil.

## NUTRITION

Sweetcorn is gluten free and is low in saturated fat, and very low in cholesterol. Sweetcorn is not particularly nutrient-dense, but does contain folate, which is a B vitamin. Sweetcorn is also surprisingly high in protein and is a good source of fiber, which is essential for bowel health.

**Storage:** Cobs are best eaten directly after harvesting from the garden, and will not store in the fridge for much more than a few days. The corn can be removed from the cob by scraping it with a sharp knife and stored in bags in the freezer.

**Preparation:** Remove the outer leaves, silky fibers, and stem. If the corn is to be served off the cob then remove it by holding the cob upright and cutting off the corn with a sharp knife, working downward. Cook in boiled unsalted water for 5–10 minutes or until a kernel comes away from the cob easily.

**BELOW:** Sweetcorn was introduced to Europe by the Spaniards in the 16th century but its origins can be dated back a lot further with evidence of cultivation over 8,000 years ago.

Fresh cobs of sweetcorn are hard to find in the store and their season is fleeting. When they do become available they are usually expensive and the taste and the flavor are disappointing. One of the reasons for the blander taste of store-bought corn is because once the cob is cut from the plant, the kernel's natural sugars change to starch and the sweetness is quickly lost. Growing your own plants ensures a plentiful supply and their fresh flavor and sweetness always seem to taste so much better. The simplest way to cook them is simply lightly steamed and then smothered in butter with cracked black pepper, but they can also be used in salads and stir-fries. Yellow varieties are the most common, but it is possible to procure some of the more wacky

## TASTING NOTES

### Colored sweetcorn to try

There are quite a few colored sweetcorns worth trying. They are always a good talking point whether in the garden or around the kitchen table.

"Hopi Blue"    This was developed by the Hopi Indians, a Native American tribe from Arizona. It has a sweet, distinctive flavor. Similar alternatives include "Blue Jade" and "Red Strawberry."

"Bloody Butcher"    This variety has blood-red kernels in wine-red husks. When young it can be eaten like sweetcorn, but as the cob matures it can be ground to make red corn flour.

colored varieties, some of which are multicolored. However, they can also be transformed into soups, fritters, chowder, and the thick savory porridge known as polenta. The latter can also be used to make gnocchi.

In the garden they do take up a lot of room, but their sweet flavor definitely makes it worth the effort. They make attractive features with their lofty

**LEFT:** Yellow varieties are the most commonly seen types in the grocery store, but there are a whole range of edible and ornamental corns available including red, blue, and multicolored.

flower spikes and large glossy strap-shaped leaves. Sweetcorn likes a sun-drenched aspect in order for the corns to develop their full sweetness. They need a fertile well-drained soil with lots of garden compost added prior to planting.

Sow sweetcorn at the same time as you are sowing your French and string beans from mid to late spring. Sow seeds indoors in 3½in pots in general-purpose compost and leave them to germinate on a sunny windowledge or inside the glasshouse. Plant them out after the risk of frost is over, but harden them off first in a cold frame or porch to acclimatize them to the outdoor weather. They should be planted in blocks or grids because they are wind pollinated, meaning that the pollen from the higher male flowers should be able to blow from one plant to another and onto the lower female flowers. Avoid planting them in single rows as they are less likely to get pollinated and therefore will not produce a crop. When the plants are over 3ft high the base of the stems can be earthed up. Plants should be kept well watered during dry periods and the area should be kept weed-free, being careful not to damage the shallow roots.

**LEFT:** To tell whether the corn cob is ready for harvesting, the sheath or outer layers should be peeled back. Push your thumbnail into a kernel, and it will exude a milky sap when ready.

Cobs are ready for harvesting toward the tail end of summer, when the tassel at the end turns brown. Milky sap should squirt out if a fingernail is pushed into the kernel. Cobs should be twisted and pulled to remove them from the plant.

### THREE SISTER METHOD

This is a traditional space saving method of growing squashes, beans, and sweetcorn in the same space. This method originates from the native North American Iroquois people, who believed these three vegetables were inseparable sisters.

The three sisters technique saves space as three crops are planted together. The squashes sprawl on the ground and their large leaves smother out competing weeds, while the beans use the upright stems of the sweetcorn to train themselves up on. The beans also help prevent the corn from flopping onto the ground, and the roots from the beans fix nitrogen from the air, which helps to sustain the growth of the corn.

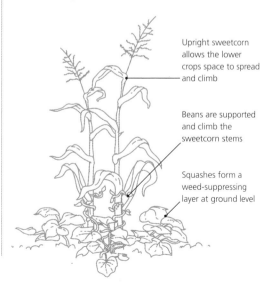

Upright sweetcorn allows the lower crops space to spread and climb

Beans are supported and climb the sweetcorn stems

Squashes form a weed-suppressing layer at ground level

# PESTS AND DISEASES

It can be heart-breaking to walk into the vegetable garden to discover that all your hard work has been destroyed by a pest or infected with a disease. A garden will never be completely free of problems but there are certain precautions that can help reduce them.

## GOOD HORTICULTURAL PRACTICE

A healthy plant stands a much better chance of combating pests and diseases than an unhealthy one as its strong growth is more resilient.

- Do not import infected plant material into the garden. Carefully check over plants, whether they are from a garden center or given by a friend, as a new pest or disease can be very hard to eradicate once it establishes itself.
- Remove diseased plant material as soon as it is spotted. The longer it stays, the more time it has to spread.

**CHOOSE RESISTANT VARIETIES**

Some varieties have resistance to specific pests or diseases. For example "Sarpo Mira" potatoes have resistance to blight, and carrot "Flyaway" has resistance to carrot fly. Careful selection of vegetable varieties could help mitigate many garden problems. Varieties of parsnip such as "Albion" or "Palace" have good resistance to parsnip canker.

- Keep on top of the weeds as they will weaken the vegetable plants, depriving them of water and nutrients, which makes them more susceptible to pests and diseases.
- Fungus can spread rapidly if there is poor air circulation between plants, so it is good practice to remove weeds that could be smothering vegetable plants.
- Keep the plants well watered and fed, but avoid overwatering and ensure the foliage does not stay damp as this can cause problems with fungus such as downy mildew.
- Practicing crop rotation (see p.154) can reduce a buildup of problems in the soil.

**LEFT:** Potato blight can be a major problem for vegetable growers, and the fungal disease can rapidly destroy a crop. Foliage should be cut down and removed as soon as blight is spotted to prevent it spreading.

## RABBIT PROTECTION

Unfortunately, rabbits like feasting on vegetables just as much as humans and the crops therefore need protecting. Vegetable plots should be surrounded with chicken wire dug down to at least 6in and turned outward to prevent rabbits from burrowing underneath.

## SLUGS AND SNAILS

Slugs and snails are the number one pest to a vegetable gardener. There are numerous methods of control available, some of which are more effective than others particularly early in the year when there are a lot of young and vulnerable seedlings and juicy new shoots. Slug pellets are usually the most effective control, used sparingly, but feel free to adopt some of these other methods.

- Make a trap, such as an upturned, scooped-out orange or grapefruit, or a half-filled bowl of beer that has been half buried so that the top of it is level with the surface of the soil. The theory is that the slugs and snails fall in the trap and drown.
- Create a barrier: slugs and snails do not like traveling over coarse material such as grit and sand. Surrounding plants with these materials can prevent them from attacking the vegetable plants.
- Nematodes: these are microscopic organisms, which can be mixed in a watering can to make a solution that is then poured over an infected area. The nematodes attack the slugs and snails, helping to reduce their number.
- Picking them by hand: go out with a flashlight at night and slugs, snails, and caterpillars will often by found gorging on plants and seedlings. Dispose of them in salt water.
- Encourage hedgehogs into the garden as they love eating many of the pests. Building a simple hedgehog home in fall when they are looking for a place to hibernate might be enough to get them to consider making the garden its permanent residence.

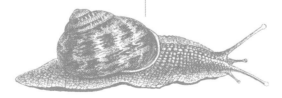

"Shutting one's eyes to trouble due to pests or diseases and hoping for the best is the short cut to serious losses."

**Charles Boff,** *How to grow and produce your own food,* (1946)

# BIBLIOGRAPHY

Akeroyd, Simon. *A Little Course in Growing Veg and Fruit*, DK, 2013.

Akeroyd, Simon. *The Allotment Handbook*, DK, 2013.

Akeroyd, Simon, Hodge, Geoff, Draycott, Sara, Barter, Guy. *Allotment Handbook*, Mitchell Beazley, Royal Horticultural Society, 2010.

Boff, Charles. *How to Grow and Produce Your Own Food*, Odhams Press Ltd, 1946.

Clevely, Andi. *The Allotment Book: Seasonal Planner*, Collins, 2008.

Davies, Jennifer. *The Victorian Kitchen*, BBC Books, 1989.

Davies, Jennifer. *The Victorian Kitchen Garden*, BBC Books, 1987.

Furner, Brian. *The Kitchen Garden*, Arthur Baker Limited, 1966.

Gammack, Helene. *Kitchen Garden Estate*, National Trust Books, 2012.

Halsall, Lucy. *RHS Step by Step Veg Patch*, DK, 2012.

Harrison, Lorraine. *A Potted History of Vegetables*, Lyons Press, 2011.

Hessayon, Dr.D.G. *The Vegetable and Herb Expert*, Expert Books, 2001.

Klein, Carol. *RHS Grow Your Own Vegetables*, Mitchell Beazley, 2007.

Larkcom, Joy. *Creative Vegetable Gardening*, Mitchell Beazley, 1997.

Laws, Bill. *Spade, Skirret and Parsnip: The Curious History of Vegetables*, The History Press, 2004.

Pavord, Anna. *Growing Food*, Francis Lincoln Limited, 2011.

Pavord, Anna. *The New Kitchen Garden*, DK, 1996.

Pollock, Michael. *Fruit and Vegetable Garden*, DK, The Royal Horticultural Society, 2002.

Raven, Sarah. *The Great Vegetable Plot*, BBC Books, 2005.

Shepherd, Allan. *The Organic Garden*, Collins, 2007.

Smit, Tim, Mcmillan-Browse, Philip. *The Heligan Vegetable Bible*, Victor Gollanez, 2000.

Stickland, Sue. *Heritage Vegetables*, Gaia Books Limited, 1998.

Whittingham, Jo. *Grow Something to Eat Every Day*, DK, 2011.

Whittingham, Jo. *Vegetables in a Small Garden*, DK, 2007.

# INDEX

## A

Album Benary 22, 63, 161
*Amaranth leaf pasta* 37
annual weeds 132
arugula 91, 134–136
asparagus 43–45
asparagus pea 156–157
*Asparagus soup* 45

## B

*Baked globe artichokes* 125
Bauhin, Gaspard 57, 58
beans 46, 217
beet 51–53, 90, 91, 154, 206
*Beet brownies* 53
Benary, Ernst 22, 63
bindweed 133
bitterness, reducing 100
blanching 39, 100
bok choi 82–84
bolting 86
broccoli 81, 90, 154
brownies 53
Brussels sprout
  72–74, 154
bunching onion 27–29
buttercup 133
butterhead lettuce 153
butternut squash 116

## C

cabbage 63–65, 67, 154
calabrese 78–81

*Canna chips* 88
canna lily 87–89
cardoon 121–122
carrot 46, 67, 128–131,
  184, 207
*Carrots Vichy* 130
catch crops 80, 177
cauliflower 68–71, 154
*Cauliflower cheese* 69
celeriac 40–42
*Celeriac remoulade* 42
celery 38–39
Champlain, Samuel de 140
cheese 24, 49, 69
*Cheesy chard gratin* 49
chicory 101–104
chilli pepper 47, 93–95
Chinese artichoke
  208–209
*Chinese pickled mooli* 180
chips 88
chitting 198
chives 91
choice 10
chop suey greens 96–97
chutneys 206
climbing structures 165
cloches 24, 185
Cock-a-leekie soup 18
cold frames 185
community gardens 111
companion planting 131
composting 30–31

containers 66, 90–91
*Creamy coleslaw* 64
creeping buttercup 133
crisphead lettuce 153
crop rotation 154–155, 218
Crown Prince squash 116
cucumber 107–109
"cut-and-come-again" crops
  90, 91, 136
cuttings 193

## D

dahlia tuber 126–127
dandelion 133
daylily 143–145
dips 24
direct sowing 46
diseases 218
dock 133
drying 207

## E

eggplant 90, 194–196
Egyptian onion 28
elephant garlic 15–16
endive 98–100
*Endive and prawn omelette* 99
extending the season 184–185

## F

fat hen 132
fava bean 154, 184, 212–214
finochiio 137–139

# PICTURE CREDITS

By the same author

*Why Read?*
*Teacher*
*Nightmare on Main Street*
*Literature Against Philosophy, Plato to Derrida*
*Wild Orchids and Trotsky* (ed.)
*Towards Reading Freud*

# The Death
# of Sigmund Freud

# The Death
# of Sigmund Freud

*The Legacy of His Last Days*

Mark Edmundson

BLOOMSBURY

Published by Bloomsbury USA, New York
Distributed to the trade by Holtzbrinck Publishers

All papers used by Bloomsbury USA are natural,
recyclable products made from wood grown in well-managed
forests. The manufacturing processes conform to the
environmental regulations of the country of origin.

LIBRARY OF CONGRESS CATALOGING-IN-PUBLICATION DATA
Edmundson, Mark, 1952–
The death of Sigmund Freud : the legacy of his last days / Mark Edmundson.
p. cm.
Includes bibliographical references and index.
ISBN-13: 978-1-58234-537-6 (alk. paper)
ISBN-10: 1-58234-537-6 (alk. paper)
1. Freud, Sigmund, 1856–1939. 2. Psychoanalysts—Austria—Biography. I. Title.
BF109.F74E36 2007
150.19′52092—dc22
[B]
2007006634

First U.S. Edition 2007
1 3 5 7 9 10 8 6 4 2

Typeset by Hewer Text UK Ltd, Edinburgh
Printed in the United States of America by Quebecor World Fairfield

*For Willie, fellow maker*

# I
# Vienna

In the late autumn of 1909, two men who would each transform the world were living in Vienna, Austria. They were in almost every way what the poet William Blake would have called "spiritual enemies." One was Sigmund Freud, the creator of psychoanalysis, who would become the most renowned and controversial thinker of the twentieth century. In 1909, Freud was in vigorous middle age, fifty-three years old and at the height of his powers. The other man, whose impact on humanity would be yet greater, was young.

The young man had come to Vienna in hopes of making his fortune as an architect and an artist. He lived with a friend in a small apartment, and there he spent his time reading, drawing, writing, composing music, and dreaming of future triumphs. The young man had inherited a small sum of money when his mother died, and on these funds he lived frugally, eating little and paying modest rent. His main indulgence was opera, Wagner's opera in particular. There were disappointments: he was rejected not once but twice by the state-sponsored art school, and this infuriated him. He had never gotten along well with teachers, and the faculty at the art school was no exception—they sneered at his work and told him that he had no real talent. The young man decided to take up a bohemian life and to succeed brilliantly as an architect, and perhaps as a painter, poet, and composer too, despite Austria's corrupt establishment.

Before he left for Vienna, the young man fell in love with a woman named Stefanie, whom he saw on the evening walks he took back in his home city of Linz. Though he never spoke a word to Stefanie, the young man was faithful. All the glories he would achieve in the city, he hoped to lay before her in tribute. So even in decadent Vienna, he tried to lead a moral life: he stayed away from prostitutes; he stayed away from women in general, despite the fact that they often found him alluring. They stared at him at the opera and sent him notes requesting liaisons. But the young man was determined to keep what he called his "Flame of Life" pure.

From his boyhood, the young man was hypersensitive, prone to tantrums and bouts of weeping. He loved animals and could not bear to hear about any cruelty being inflicted on them, much less to see such a thing. He never drank and was sure that tobacco destroyed a person's health. He thought of himself as a humanitarian with a poetic nature. One of his major projects in Vienna was to design spacious, light-filled housing for the workers who lived in the city's slums, but no one outside his household ever saw the plans.

Soon the one friend that the young man had in Vienna went back home to the provinces, and by the time his friend returned, the young man had left their shabby apartment, giving the landlady no forwarding address. He became lost, lonely, and his money all but ran out. For a while he lived on the street, sleeping in doorways and on park benches. Perhaps at times he was compelled to beg. Finally, he found a home

in a men's shelter, a strictly run, almost monastic establishment. Here he lived until a year before the beginning of the
First World War, taking a certain kind of pleasure in the
simplicity and order that now surrounded him. He made his
living by painting postcards, which sold at kiosks on the
street. He read a great deal, though he did not always
understand what he read, and he gave speeches to the other
residents of the shelter. He stood in the dayroom and held
forth about the Jews and the Communists and about Germany's exalted destiny among nations. Sometimes one of his
fellow residents would secretly tie his coat to the bench he
was sitting on, and then provoke him with a political
question. The young man would leap up then, and begin
pacing around the room, declaiming, while the bench
clunked along behind him. People who met the man sometimes had doubts about his sanity: none of them imagined
that Adolf Hitler, for that, of course, is who the young man
was, would ever be of consequence in the world.

Sigmund Freud was in the prime phase of his life when Hitler
was living in Vienna. In middle age, Freud was a robust, full-
faced man with a burgher's well-insulated body and a dense,
regal brown beard, streaked with gray. His usual facial expression somehow conveyed both contentment and ambition. He
had a hawk nose and bright, all-consuming eyes. Freud was not
tall, only about five feet, seven inches, but his presence was
formidable: he seemed to be more than a match for life. In his

fifties, Freud looked like a field marshal of intellect—worldly, urbanely humorous, and self-aware.

In the fall of 1909, when Hitler was living on the streets, Freud was emerging from a protracted period of isolation. He had undergone an intense self-analysis; he had composed and published his first major work, *The Interpretation of Dreams*; and he was well begun in his exploration of the unconscious. Now Freud was writing constantly: he believed that once one understood the nature of the id—or the "it"—and its conflicted relation to the conscious mind, many previously puzzling matters in human life became understandable. Freud could offer unexpected truths not only about dreams, but also about jokes and slips of the tongue and pen. He had illuminating ideas about art, religion, the sources of human identity, and a great deal more. Now, after Freud had struggled for many years to distinguish himself, brilliant younger men, and some gifted women as well, were gathering around him. He was creating something like a movement.

As a young man, Freud confessed that he wanted to take on the major questions. He secretly aspired to be something of a philosophe, in the manner of Diderot, Rousseau, and Voltaire, and to make original contributions on matters like free will and fate, just government, love and death, and the good life. Finally, Freud believed that he had put himself in a position to begin doing precisely that. Mapping the dynamics of the unconscious brought him to the threshold of great things, giving him something new and consequential to say on all the questions that had preoccupied the West since at least Plato's time. At the end of the first decade of the twentieth century, Sigmund Freud was looking forward to life, and more life, with an intensity that not all men of fifty-three can muster.

In the fall of 1909, when Hitler was walking confused and lonely through Vienna, Freud had recently returned from a triumphal visit to the United States. Accompanied by his closest disciples, Carl Jung, Sándor Ferenczi, and Ernest Jones, he'd spent a week in New York touring the city, then gone off to Worcester, Massachusetts. There, at Clark University, he gave a celebrated set of talks, which were attended by, among others, America's preeminent philosopher and psychologist, William James, and by Emma Goldman—the formidable anarchist intellectual, who found herself in agreement with a good deal of what Freud had to say. Freud even received an honorary degree at Clark. Thinking back to the trip, he would write: "In Europe I felt as though I were despised; but over there I found myself received by the foremost men as an equal. It seemed like the realization of some incredible daydream." Freud returned from America with his confidence and his energies redoubled, ready to do what he believed would be great work.

The work that Freud did do, following the American sojourn, went in an unexpected direction. Up until 1909, Freud, to speak broadly, had been fascinated with the dynamics of desire. He wanted to know how the unconscious, the seat and source of desire, worked and in particular how it expressed itself in neuroses and dreams and in works of art. It was during this period that Freud was inclined to see erotic urges—and also, less consequentially, aggressive drives—at the root of human behavior. But as time went on, Freud became more and more preoccupied with the issue of authority, and with the agency that he thought of as the center of authority in the human psyche, the superego, or over-I.

In a few years, Freud would begin to write a sequence of books and essays that focused on authority that had become toxic, authority gone bad. He would become preoccupied with tyranny—with the human hunger for power and the human desire to be dominated. In *Group Psychology and the Analysis of the Ego, Totem and Taboo, The Future of an Illusion,* and many other works, Freud would reflect on what makes human beings respond to tyrants—not just obey them, but honor and love them. He would, in a certain sense, soon start to think in depth about the man that the young Adolf Hitler, his fellow resident of Vienna in 1909, would become, and also about all the tyrants who have followed Hitler through the twentieth century and on into the twenty-first.

If Hitler and Freud passed each other on the street on an afternoon during the cold late autumn of 1909, what would each of them have seen? In Hitler, Freud would have seen a rank denizen of the crowd, a street rat. (Freud was no populist.) But he probably would have felt sorry for the unfortunate man as well. For his part, Hitler would have seen a Viennese burgher (he despised the upper middle class) and probably would have recognized Freud as a Jew. Hitler would have drawn back in shame at his threadbare overcoat and his broken-down shoes. If things were bad enough, he might have extended a hand to beg. Whether Freud gave or not—he could well have; he was generally good-hearted—would have made little difference; the encounter would still have left the young Adolf Hitler seething.

*   *   *

But time passed and the world changed. Almost three decades later, in 1938, the former street rat was the chancellor of Germany and one of the most powerful men in the world. In 1933 he had been elected—no coup was involved (though some devious machinations were)—to the most important office in his nation. Twenty-five years after his desperate period in Vienna, Adolf Hitler achieved the ascendancy he dreamed about when he was giving his speeches to the disbelieving crowd at the men's shelter.

During the First World War Hitler had come into his own. He became a dispatch runner in the German army, serving with stunning bravery and twice winning the Iron Cross. After the war, he joined a small political party in Munich—at the beginning there had been only a handful of members—and he turned it into a powerful alliance. He attempted a coup in 1923, failed, and was sentenced to prison. While he was there, he wrote *Mein Kampf,* where he described his past life and laid down his program for Germany's future. There followed a decade of astonishing work, campaigning, speaking, brawling, writing, forming and destroying alliances, until, at the end of it, Adolf Hitler was the preeminent man in Germany. Of course he had further ambitions: he wanted the world. But in 1938, Adolf Hitler desired one thing above all others, and that was Austria.

Soon Hitler would be headed again to Vienna, the city where he had been so badly abused and humiliated, but this time he would not be coming with a sketchbook and a pittance in his pocket. He would arrive instead with thousands of troops at his back. On the first page of *Mein Kampf*, Hitler had announced that Austria must be made part of the German nation, and now that he was in power, he was determined to bring this event to pass. Even in middle age, after he became chancellor, Hitler recalled time and again how he had spent the worst years of his life in Vienna. He said that he had come to the city as a mother's boy, and that Vienna had made him hard. Sometimes he joked with his intimates about how satisfying it would be to destroy the entire city and to start again from scratch.

Waiting for Hitler in Vienna in that winter of 1938 was an old and desperately ill Sigmund Freud—as well as a hundred and seventy-five thousand other racial enemies. The Nazis hated Freud with a particular vehemence. When they burned his books at their outdoor rallies in Germany in 1933, the presiding officer had shouted out an indictment: "Against the soul-destroying glorification of the instinctual life," he cried, "for the nobility of the human soul! I consign to the flames the writings of Sigmund Freud." Freud, hearing the news about the book burning, remarked, "What progress we are making. In the Middle Ages they would have burnt me; nowadays they are content with burning my books." Five years later, the Nazis who were preparing to invade Austria, and the ones who lived there themselves—there were many—might not be content with merely the burning of books.

Sigmund Freud did not appear to be ready for strife of any sort. He was eighty-one years old and he seemed smaller than his modest height; he was bent and brittle and precariously thin. His beard had gone completely white, and was cropped close to his cheeks; he wore black-framed oval glasses that gave him an owlish appearance. His skin, which was blanched and seemed thin as rice paper, stretched taut against his face. He could no longer speak with force and clarity because of the prosthesis implanted in his jaw to replace the teeth and bone that had been removed during the many operations for his cancer. His eyes, as almost everyone who knew him during those days attested, remained potent: at times, Freud did not stare at things, so much as through them to the other side. Overall, his presence was unnerving: by 1938, deep into old age, Freud looked like a dark fairy-tale version of Death himself.

Adolf Hitler's Austrian aggression—and the drama that composed the last two years of Sigmund Freud's life—began when Hitler summoned Kurt von Schuschnigg, Austria's chancellor, to his compound at Berchtesgaden. (Now the onetime street rat had the leaders of nations at his beck and call.) An introverted, scholarly man who wore rimless glasses and chain-smoked, Schuschnigg was no match for the führer. Hitler issued ultimatums. He demanded that Austria legalize the Nazi Party; he demanded that Nazis be installed in the government; he demanded a military treaty between the two nations. He also required that Austria hold a plebiscite so its citizens could vote on unification with the grand German nation. Schuschnigg, nervous, badly in need of a cigarette, yet aware that no one, under any conditions, smoked in the presence of the führer, had not gone to Germany expecting an easy interview. (Before leaving, he remarked that he should be bringing a psychiatrist along to help him contend with Hitler.) Still Schuschnigg was shocked by what he heard.

"You don't seriously believe that you can stop me or even delay me for half an hour, do you?" the führer asked. "Perhaps you will wake up one morning in Vienna to find us there—just like a spring storm. And then you'll see something. I would very much like to save Austria from such a fate, because such an action would mean blood."

Hitler had been brooding on Austria for some time and he had a great deal to impart to Schuschnigg. "The whole history of Austria," Hitler told the chancellor during the meeting, "is just one uninterrupted act of high treason. That was so in the past and is no better today." Schuschnigg was so anxious that he refrained from reminding Hitler that he himself had been born in Austria. The führer went on, his rage expanding: "And I can tell you right now, Herr Schuschnigg, that I am absolutely determined to make an end of all this. The German Reich is one of the great powers and nobody will raise his voice if it settles its border problems."

"I have a historic mission," Hitler said, "and this mission I will fulfill because Providence has destined me to do so. I thoroughly believe in this mission; it is my life . . . Look around you in Germany today, Herr Schuschnigg, and you will find that there is but one will." Hitler told the Austrian chancellor that his triumph was inevitable: "I have made the greatest achievement in the history of Germany, greater than any other German." When Schuschnigg informed Hitler that France and

England would not stand by and allow him to absorb Austria, the führer laughed.

Over the past decade, Hitler had nearly consolidated his power over the German people; he had done away with his party enemies in a quick, bloody purge, the Night of the Long Knives (Freud, hearing the news of the purge, expressed a wish that the Nazis might have killed each other off to the last man: that was just an hors d'oeuvre, he said, where is the main course?); Hitler had earned the friendship of Mussolini, the only national leader that he respected; he had become certain that the democracies were weak, irresolute, and would not risk war against him. Now he could look out to the world at large with an unlimited sense of possibility. In vigorous middle age, Hitler had never felt so potent, so much a man of destiny.

Freud's own situation was much more precarious. On January 22, he had been forced to undergo yet another operation for the cancer of the jaw that had been tormenting him for fifteen years. This time the tumor was hard to reach, because it was close to Freud's eye socket, so his surgeon, Hans Pichler, had to create a special implement to get at it. Freud spent two days in the sanatorium, and then, still in great pain, made his way home to rest. Freud knew that the cancer was the result of his incessant cigar smoking, and he had been told many times to stop, but he wouldn't. He loved cigars too much: at the height of his consumption, he smoked twenty a day. When things were especially bad, he sometimes used a clothespin to open his frozen, aching jaw so as to wedge one more into his mouth.

The January operation was especially brutal, and it was followed by another, on February 19, a few days after Hitler's meeting with Schuschnigg. In this operation, Pichler cut out a suspect wart in the cancerous region, and fortunately, the bioposy on the new growth was negative. This operation was less painful than the previous one, but the patient was eighty-one years old, and physically at least, he was very frail. It wasn't at all clear how many more such ordeals Freud could take.

Freud left the clinic and spent his time resting and recuperating at Berggasse 19, the apartment where he had been living for fifty years and that he now shared with his wife, Martha; her sister, Aunt Minna; and Anna, the Freuds' daughter. Here Freud had developed his psychoanalytical practice, raised his six children, and written the books and papers that made him known throughout the West.

Berggasse—literally Hill Street—deserves its name; it's a frequently steep thoroughfare that begins at the Tandelmarkt, Vienna's flea market, and runs to the Votivkirche, a modern Gothic cathedral. By Viennese standards, Freud lived in a respectable, though not truly distinguished, neighborhood. Berggasse 19 was built in the 1870s; the lower part of the building is Renaissance style, the upper features classical revival work. Downstairs to the left of the apartment house was Siegmund Kornmehl's butcher shop, on the right a food cooperative, the Ersten Wiener Consum-Vereines. The Freud family lived on the mezzanine, the second floor of the building.

Though from the outside it looked conventional enough, the

Freuds' apartment at Berggasse 19 was actually a place like none other in Vienna, and in fact like none other in the world. In the back of the dwelling, Freud had fashioned himself a private kingdom of two rooms, and it was here that he retired during the bad days in February and early March, after the two operations, to nurse his aching jaw, to gather his powers, and to see what Adolf Hitler would do.

Throughout his life, Freud had been a ferocious worker, able to push on through intense pain, but now he was spending much of his time lying down on the couch that his patients used when they came in for analysis. This was the famous divan that he had sat at the foot of during so many sessions over so many years, out of sight of his patients—"I cannot put up with being stared at . . . for eight hours a day (or more)," he once said— smoking his cigars, keeping himself in a state of evenly suspended attention, and listening, listening. The couch, Freud ruefully said, was "meant for others," but these days he needed it himself.

Yet however weak and uncertain Freud may have appeared in those hard days in March of 1938, however much he may seem to have declined from the confident, ambitious figure who strolled through the streets of Vienna in 1909, he was still Sigmund Freud, and that meant a number of things. It meant that he was an extremely rebellious and passionate man who would say things, write things, and even sometimes do things that his contemporaries found shocking. He was self-reliant and daring and, when it came to action, ultimately consulted no one but himself.

But as rebellious as Freud could be—and delighted in being—he was also a man who was attracted to convention.

Freud was interested in conventional success, in money, in fame, in having a sterling reputation, in maintaining an impeccable bourgeois household. (There were few apartments more bland than Berggasse 19—until one reached Freud's inner sanctum.) He wanted to fit in and he wanted to succeed, even as he was committed to a mode of thought that was genuinely revolutionary.

Freud's passion was manifest time after time in his life. When he fell in love with his future wife, Martha Bernays, he fell furiously in love. He wrote her wildly adoring letters; he fumed with jealousy. Somewhat in the mode of a medieval troubadour, he dreamed up an image of Martha that was exotic, erotically rich, complex—and at some variance with the sweet, decent young woman he actually married. The two were apart for much of their long engagement, and in his letters Freud was a writer of romantic fiction par excellence. "Martha is mine," he cried to her in one letter, "the sweet girl of whom everyone speaks with admiration, who despite all my resistance captivated my heart at our first meeting, the girl I feared to court and who came toward me with high-minded confidence, who strengthened the faith in my own value and gave me new hope and energy to work when I needed it most."

Freud was also prone to fall for men. His involvements with his mentors, men like Wilhelm Fliess and Josef Breuer, have a lover's intensity, and his eventual breaks with them have the drama of erotic terminations. He brought the same passion to his relations with his disciples. Jung, whom he hoped would inherit his role as the head of the psychoanalytical movement— Freud liked to refer to him as the "crown prince"—was

genuinely beloved by Freud. When they quarreled and eventually went separate ways, Freud's world shuddered.

He was a similarly passionate thinker: it sometimes appears
that there was nothing that crossed his mind that he would not
write down and publish. It's not only that Freud declared the
existence of the Oedipal complex, shocking the world with the
view that all children want to have sex with their mothers and
do away with their fathers; not only that he believed that infants
were sexually alert and sexually responsive beings. These ideas
were central to Freud's vision of human life: he could hardly
suppress them. But at times expanding the broad wings of his
imagination, Freud seemed incapable of holding anything back.

How did mankind gain control over fire? Freud believed that
he knew. In prehistoric times, fire came to earth through
lightning storms. A branch would flame up and drop to the
ground. But generally, when men saw this happen, they would
approach the flames and urinate on them until they went out.
This was, according to Freud, a source of great pleasure. "The
legends that we possess," he said, "leave no doubt about the
originally phallic view taken of tongues of flame as they shoot
upwards. Putting out fire by micturating—a theme to which
modern giants, Gulliver in Lilliput and Rabelais's Gargantua,
still hark back—was therefore a kind of sexual act with a male,
an enjoyment of sexual potency in a homosexual competition."
At some point, a man capable of instinctual renunciation came
along and was able to refrain from dousing the flames. He
brought the fire back to his cave and experimented with it,
finding that he could use it for heat and for cooking. Thus did
mankind conquer fire. This fable—a remarkable twist on the

Prometheus story—occurs not in a letter or a conversation, but as a footnote in what is perhaps Freud's best-composed book, *Civilization and Its Discontents*. Why did Freud write such a thing? Because he thought it was true—and what Freud thought to be true, he wrote and published, period.

Time after time in his work, Freud changed course, revised himself, came up with ideas stranger and more off-putting (and often more brilliantly illuminating) than the strange, off-putting ideas of his already in place. At one point he decided, based on very thin evidence—assuming there was any evidence at all—that something called the "Death Drive" is a force in all organic life. All beings, Freud declared, have an urge to return to an earlier state of things, to seek destruction and decomposition and to do so after their own fashion. "The aim of all life," Freud famously declared, "is death." Looking around him and pondering as deeply as possible, Freud simply concluded that this was true, and rather than suppress the idea, he did all he could to develop it—and damn the consequences for his reputation and the reputation of psychoanalysis. Until the end of his life, the Death Drive was for Freud an open hypothesis: from his point of view, he simply ran out of time to confirm it.

Yet the same Sigmund Freud, being asked if he raised his children according to the tenets of psychoanalysis, simply grunted and replied that he raised his children as children— that is, pretty much according to convention—and that was all there was to it. Freud lived his whole life through as a conventional bourgeois: he was well dressed at all times; his hair and beard were always trimmed; he paid his debts and got places on time. While to many he was the great advocate of

Eros, his own erotic life seems to have been almost entirely conventional. Speculations to the effect that Freud had a love affair with his sister-in-law, Minna Bernays, remain just that— speculations.

Then there was the matter of Freud's intellectual identity. He fought to attain the rank of Professor, not only because it would help him to earn more, but because it added to his quotient of respectability. Though on some level Freud surely knew that the kinds of books and essays he was writing were without any obvious precedent and that in many ways they were closer to literature than to anything else—"the drives," he once said, "are our mythology"—he went on insisting that he was a scientist and demanded for psychoanalysis all the prestige that science possessed. He sought prizes and honors—though he sometimes claimed not to—and he quietly cherished them when they came his way. Though Freud declared time and again that he hated to be photographed, it sometimes seems that there were times in his life when he did little but. In his photos, Freud seems to be trying to look ever more wise, stable, authoritative, and com- manding.

Freud is at his best when his two potent drives, the drive to rebellion and the drive to logic and respectability, animate each other. The result then is thinking that is rigorously presented, is well argued, and takes account of myriad objections, but that is also astonishing in its originality. Among such performances are books like *Civilization and Its Discontents, The Ego and the Id, Group Psychology and the Analysis of the Ego, Totem and Taboo, Three Essays on the Theory of Sexuality, The Interpretation of Dreams,* and *Beyond the Pleasure Principle.* There are also major essays in this mode, pieces like "On Narcissism," "Mourning and Melancholia," "Analysis Terminable and Interminable," "Humour," "The Uncanny," and the best of the articles on therapy and technique that Freud wrote to guide future analysts. Here Freud is not only as bold in his conceptions as any poet, but clear, shrewd, and impressively self-critical.

From at least the time he set out on his professional road, in his twenties, Freud was both a cannily and rigorously conventional man and something on the order of a visionary. The tendencies shifted all the time—sometimes one dominated, sometimes the other, and sometimes they entered a rich synergy. But Freud's intellect was always intense and inventive. Sigmund Freud at eighty-one and Sigmund Freud at thirty-one were, despite appearances, not drastically different beings, at least internally. Close to the end of his life, William Blake, whose poetry anticipates Freud's thinking in certain ways, observed in a letter that he has been near death and has returned "very weak & an Old Man feeble & tottering, but not in Spirit & Life not in The Real Man The Imagination which Liveth for Ever. In that I am stronger & stronger as this Foolish Body decays." In 1938, Freud was surely feeble enough in body, but The Real Man in him was still alive.

On February 20, the day after Freud's operation, Hitler addressed the German Reichstag on the Austrian problem and the speech was broadcast not only in Germany but in

Austria as well. The many concessions he had compelled Schuschnigg to make at Berchtesgaden would not be enough, Hitler declared. Austria was continuing to mistreat its German citizens: it was "intolerable," the führer declared, "for a self-conscious world power to know that at its side are co-racials who are subjected to continuous suffering because of their sympathy and unity with the whole German race and its ideology." The speech went on for hours, with Hitler rising to a frenzy of rage against Germany's oppressors. After the speech, Austrian Nazis began to gather in the streets of Vienna and to chant "Sieg Heil! Sieg Heil! Heil Hitler! Heil Hitler!" G. E. R. Gedye, a newspaper correspondent, described the sound coming from the German legation. "As one first caught it in the distance it was just a rhythmic throb, like the beating of a feverish pulse, which as one approached seemed to change into the inarticulate but disciplined cawing of some militarized rookery—'A-a-a-ah—AAAH! A-a-a-a-h—AAH–A-a-a-ah—AAH!,' and finally into audible words." Soon the brownshirts were in the streets and rioting.

On the day of Hitler's speech, Freud's daughter Anna wrote a letter to Ernest Jones, Freud's most trusted disciple next to Anna herself, sizing up the situation. "There was an atmosphere of panic in Vienna," she said, "which has now calmed down a little. We have not joined in the panic. It is too early, one can not yet fully assess the consequences of what has happened. For the time being everything is as it was. It is perhaps easier for us than for others who are more mobile, we do not need to consider many decisions since for us hardly any come into consideration." What Anna Freud meant was that her father was too old and too sick to try to escape, and that in any event, he would probably never consent to leave Vienna.

Things had been turbulent in Vienna before, and Freud had never contemplated leaving. This was not the first Nazi threat to the city, and in fact, ever since 1918, with the end of the First World War and the collapse of the Austro-Hungarian Empire, Vienna's situation had been precarious. There was massive inflation in the 1920s, then deflation, followed by the great economic depression of the 1930s. There had been a socialist uprising in the working-class districts of Vienna in 1934, which had been brutally suppressed, with the leaders barely escaping through Vienna's famed sewer system. All through the 1930s, the once small Austrian Nazi Party grew. In July 1933, the Christian Socialist chancellor Engelbert Dollfuss outlawed it, but by then, the party, made up of tradesmen, small shop-keepers, veterans, recent university graduates, and many po-licemen, counted seventy thousand members. The Nazis were bound together by anti-Semitism (as virulent as any to be found in Germany), anti-clericalism, anti-Catholicism, and the desire for unification with Germany. During the months after it was banned, the party picked up twenty thousand new members.

In the summer of 1934, with Hitler now chancellor of Germany, a small group of Nazi SS men dressed themselves in Austrian army uniforms and invaded the Chancellery. There they caught Chancellor Dollfuss attempting to escape through a side door, shot and killed him. They took over the radio station and announced to the country that the government had resigned. But there were potent divisions in the Austrian Nazi

Party at the time—it was just after the Night of the Long Knives—and most Nazis refused to join in the putsch. Hitler, who had approved the attempt, was compelled to back off and disown it. Soon afterward, Dollfuss's killers were hanged in the yard of the Vienna regional court, and some of the other plotters went to jail. For a while, Nazi activity in Vienna quieted. But by 1938 the Austrian Nazi Party was growing stronger again. The Nazis wore their swastika pins on the inside of their lapels, ready to turn them out at the right moment; they greeted each other with "Heil Hitler," and sometimes on the street, they exchanged the salute.

Yet even now, with the situation worsening, Anna Freud was quite right to suggest that her father would not consent to leave, for Sigmund Freud loved—and despised—the city a great deal. Vienna was where Freud had lived for nearly all his life and where he had, against no little resistance, done his work. The resistance in Vienna to Freud was twofold: he had difficulties because he was a Jew and difficulties because of his ideas. From the time that Freud went into medicine and biological research, almost everyone around him recognized his vast talents. Nonetheless his advancement through the professional ranks was slow. It took Freud a long time to secure the title that he wanted—the title of "Professor"—to attract patients, and to generate a solid income. This had no little to do with the fact that Freud was a Jew and a Jew who, irreligious as he was, had no inclination to deny his origins. In fact, he thrust them forward aggressively.

When Freud was very young, his father told him a story about how he had gone for a walk one Saturday, decked out in a new fur hat. Along came a Christian, who with a single blow knocked the cap off Jacob Freud's head and into the mud. "Jew! get off the pavement," the Christian hollered. "And what did you do?" Freud asked. He wanted to hear about how his dear papa stood up to the bigot and put him in his place. But that is not what Jacob told him. "I went into the roadway and picked up my cap." The young Freud—he couldn't have been more than ten or twelve—was outraged. "This struck me as unheroic conduct on the part of the big strong man who was holding the little boy by the hand," Freud reflected years later. "I contrasted this situation with another which fitted my feelings better: the scene in which Hannibal's father, Hamilcar Barca, made his boy swear before the household altar to take vengeance on the Romans." From then on, Hannibal had a major place in Freud's imaginative life. Freud resolved that he would never be humiliated by the bigots who surrounded him and his family in Vienna. In the future he would struggle with the gentiles when he had to, and never step aside.

But it wasn't only Freud's Jewish identity that created trouble for him; his ideas themselves, once they began to attract attention, caused scandals. When Freud published his book on the theory of sexuality, with its insistence that infants lived thriving erotic lives (they could devolve into "polymorphous perverts," he believed), respectable people crossed the street in order to avoid him. Freud's response was not only to keep the book in print, but also to update it and revise it regularly, a distinction he conferred only on texts that mattered a great deal to him, such as his first major book, *The Interpretation of Dreams*.

But Freud, if never exactly happy in Vienna (Freud did not put much of a premium on happiness per se), nonetheless knew that it provided him one of the things he most needed, which was productive conflict. Like certain contentious, passionate poets, such as Milton, whom Freud read and admired, and Blake, whom Freud would have admired had he read, Freud understood that he did his best work when he had opposition in front of him. And work was to Freud the ultimate goal: he measured every day by how much and how well he produced. He once remarked that for all to go well, he needed to have a close friend to confide in and a spirited enemy to oppose. "My emotional life has always insisted that I should have an intimate friend and a hated enemy," Freud said. "I have always been able to provide myself afresh with both." In fact, Freud's close friends often obligingly transformed themselves—or were transformed by Freud—into inspiring enemies. But Freud thrived against collective opposition too. He loved good intellectual fights and he believed that he owed his power to sustain those fights and use them to generate more work to his Jewish background. Jews, he said, are accustomed to being in opposition; it's a part of the legacy. "It was only to my Jewish nature," he wrote once, "that I owed the two qualities that have become indispensable to me throughout my difficult life. Because I was a Jew I found myself free of many prejudices which restrict others in the use of the intellect: as a Jew I was prepared to be in the opposition."

Yet as a mental warrior, Freud was not usually white-lipped, vindictive, or bitter. He proceeded with high spirits, possessed by an intellectual form of what heroic cultures call "battle joy." "I am not really a man of science," he wrote once, "not an observer, not an experimenter, and not a thinker. I am nothing but by temperament a *conquistador*—an adventurer, if you want to translate the word—with the curiosity, the boldness, and the tenacity that belong to that type of being. Such people are apt to be treasured if they succeed, if they have really discovered something; otherwise they are thrown aside. And that is not altogether unjust."

Freud found in Vienna what he needed: many spirited opponents, some people open-minded enough to come to him when no other doctor could help, and a small minority of students, and then disciples, who were truly interested in his ideas. But the opposition he was looking at in the winter of 1938 threatened far more than denying him the professional standing that was his due, denouncing his ideas, or ruining his reputation.

On March 9, the mild Kurt von Schuschnigg defied Adolf Hitler. During the conference at Berchtesgaden, when Hitler had delivered his threat of invasion, he demanded that Austria hold a plebiscite so the Austrian people could decide whether or not they wanted to unite with Germany. Hitler was sure he would win and had reason to be, for the Austrian Nazi Party was gaining strength with each passing month.

After a couple of weeks' lull, Schuschnigg gave a speech calling for the referendum to be held almost immediately—on Sunday, March 13. He was doing exactly what Hitler demanded, but with a twist: citizens had to be at least twenty-four years old to vote in Schuschnigg's referendum. The Austrian Nazis were young: the National Socialists were the party of choice for anyone who wanted to rise in the world and be part of an imperial nation. Without young people voting, the chances were that the plebiscite would go in favor of Austrian independence. Holding the vote soon would also ensure that Hitler and Goebbels didn't have the time to initiate a lavish propaganda campaign. In the speech on March 9, Schuschnigg, decked out in the traditional Austrian gray jacket and green waistcoat, looked out at his audience and asked, "Are you in favor of a free and German, independent and social, a Christian and united Austria?" The crowd of twenty thousand roared assent. Schuschnigg finished the speech with the words of the Austrian hero Andreas Hofer, calling on his countrymen to resist Napoleon. "Men—the hour has struck!" For Hitler, this was not to be borne.

But Hitler was now concerned not only with the Austrian nationalists but also with Mussolini, who was, supposedly, Austria's protector. Hitler wrote to him immediately, requesting the right to do what he liked about his former home country: "In my responsibility as Führer and Chancellor of the German Reich and likewise as a son of the soil . . . I am now determined to restore law and order in my homeland and enable the people to decide their own fate according to their judgment in an unmistakable, clear and open manner." Hitler made various professions of fealty to Il Duce, then dispatched Prince Philip of Hesse to deliver the letter as quickly as possible. The prince boarded a plane to Italy carrying the critical message, along with a basket of plants for his garden in Rome.

In Vienna, Schuschnigg's speech provoked action: on Thursday afternoon, trucks equipped with speakers rolled through the streets, announcing the plebiscite and urging people to vote "Ja" on Sunday. Austrian patriots ranged all over Vienna, chanting, "Heil Schuschnigg!" "Heil Liberty!" and "Sunday is polling day: We vote Ja!" For a while, it seemed as though Austria might actually be able to stand alone against Germany. By evening, though, the Nazis were on the streets too. They walked four abreast through the center of Vienna, sounding their war cry: "One People! One Nation! One Leader!" At first the Austrian patriots looked on benignly: they outnumbered the Nazis at least three to one. But then scuffles began and the police jumped in on the side of the Nazis and started beating the nationalists. Before long, the streets belonged to the storm troopers.

Early Friday morning, Hitler, still having heard nothing from Mussolini, made his decision: he issued invasion plans to his staff. "If other measures prove unsuccessful," he said, "I intend to invade Austria with armed forces in order to establish constitutional conditions and to prevent further outrages against the pro-German population." At five thirty that morning, Schuschnigg received a phone call letting him know that the Germans had closed their border with Austria; soon the chancellor discovered that German troops were being mobilized in Munich. At ten o'clock, demands came to Schuschnigg from

Berlin: he must resign his office immediately and turn it over to a member of the Nazi Party, and he must postpone the plebiscite for at least two weeks.

If he did not do so, the Germans would "act accordingly." Backed to the wall, Schuschnigg sent a telegram pleading for help to the British prime minister, Neville Chamberlain, who, as chance had it, was at a lunch on Downing Street in honor of the German ambassador, Joachim von Ribbentrop. Confronted with the reports from Vienna, Ribbentrop lied. He said that he knew nothing about a crisis in Austria and said that the reports might well be mistaken. It did not take Chamberlain long to decide what it was that he and England would do: nothing. He had Lord Halifax send a cable off to Schuschnigg, telling him as much. "His Majesty's government cannot take responsibility," the communiqué began. Ribbentrop stayed late into the afternoon, satisfied that things at home were going well. Winston Churchill, who was present at the lunch too, recalls how "the Ribbentrops lingered on, so that most of us made our excuses and our way home. Eventually I suppose they left." But then Churchill adds a sentence: "That was the last time I saw Herr von Ribbentrop before he was hanged."

With no help coming from England, France, or anywhere else, it became clear to Schuschnigg that there was nothing he could do.

Shortly after Schuschnigg's March 9 speech, help came Freud's way from a most unexpected source, the United States of

America. America: there was no nation that Sigmund Freud disliked more. Despite his having been so well treated there when he visited in 1909, and despite the early success psychoanalysis enjoyed in the United States, Freud never ceased to detest the country. To him, America represented a social catastrophe nearly as dire as the one embodied by the Nazis gathering along Austria's border. Virtually everything he knew—or thought he knew—about the United States irritated Sigmund Freud.

Americans, first off, were obsessed by money. Everyone in America, Freud believed, was dully materialistic, without cultivation, without subtlety, without the capacity to enjoy life's higher pleasures. The word "dollars" shows up in almost all of Freud's denunciations of the United States. In America, they compete with each other bitterly and worship the almighty dollar, and that alone, Freud said, time after time. They're all afflicted with a hideous disease: "dollaria." As he put it in a letter to Ernest Jones: "The Americans are really 'too bad.' . . . Competition is much more pungent with them, not succeeding means civil death to every one and they have no private resources apart from their profession, no hobby, games, love, or other interests of a cultured person. And success means money. Can an American live in opposition to the public opinion as we are prepared to do?" It is an unfortunate fact, but nonetheless true: when Freud fulminates about American obsessions with wealth, he can sound uncomfortably like an anti-Semite grousing about Jewish money-hunger. Yet no such awareness ever stemmed Freud's feelings about American dollaria.

Freud was also convinced that Americans were prudes. He believed that their interests in moneymaking absorbed the libido that they could have invested in sensuous pleasure. All their energy was devoted to the pursuit of cash; for the pursuit of pleasure, nothing was left. Freud conceived of psychoanalysis as a way to relax what he called "civilized sexual morality," which expected far too much repression from individuals. Americans, in Freud's understanding, loved damming up their erotic energies, the better to rechannel them for the pursuit of prosperity. Freud even castigated American love affairs, rare occurrences that they presumably were, for being slight and fleeting. Why did they lack passionate depth? Because, presumably, Americans were so keyed to the present that when they fell in love, if you could call it that, they didn't activate the old parental prototypes—there was nothing deeply Oedipal, that is, ambivalent, tormented, strange—about their erotic encounters.

But what most disturbed Freud about America was its politics. Americans suffered from what Freud liked to call the "psychological poverty of groups." Much like de Tocqueville, but with far less sympathy, Freud saw America as a nation where the group tended to rule over, and often to crush, the individual. Not only did America always teeter close to mob rule; it was doomed to mediocrity because the lowest common denominator would always prevail. In America, there was no room for true leaders. The crowd, mesmerized by democratic propaganda, believed that it was always in the right. The people never needed to change or develop their vision of life. "My suspicion of America," Freud said, "is unconquerable."

When associates pointed out to Freud, as they often did, that no nation outside of Germany and Austria was more hospitable to psychoanalysis than America, Freud's inevitable reply was that Americans had no idea what psychoanalysis was actually about. "We are bringing them the plague," Freud purportedly said when he and Jung and Ferenczi disembarked in New York in 1909. "We're bringing them the plague, and they don't even know it."

Yet when the Nazis threatened Vienna, Americans rushed forward to help Freud. On March 10, Freud had a visit from John Wiley, the chargé d'affaires at the American Embassy in Vienna. Wiley, a man of the world, never seen without his extralong cigarette holder, inquired about Freud's welfare, asked about the rest of the family, and made it clear that the United States would do all it could to protect them. Wiley was a close colleague of William Bullitt, who was then the American ambassador to France, and Bullitt considered himself to be a particular friend of Freud's. Bullitt was a charming, affable man from a wealthy Philadelphia Main Line family; there was no one in the diplomatic world he didn't know. Bullitt had worked for a while with Woodrow Wilson, and then broken with the president over the Versailles Treaty. After the war, he made himself notorious by criticizing Wilson and the treaty to the Senate Foreign Relations Committee.

Bullitt had come to Freud in the mid-1920s, attempting to find a cure for what he took to be his self-destructive behavior. (Testifying against the president to the Senate probably began to look like precisely that in retrospect.) Then Bullitt reappeared at Freud's doorstep in 1930, with an idea for a project. He wanted to collaborate on a book about Woodrow Wilson, a psychological study, and Freud, surprisingly, agreed. Freud was constantly being approached with schemes like this, and they tended to come from America. The publisher of the *Chicago Tribune* offered Freud twenty-five thousand dollars to travel to Chicago to psychoanalyze the killers Leopold and Loeb. The producer Samuel Goldwyn claimed that he was ready to give Freud a hundred thousand dollars to come to Hollywood and collaborate on making movies. After all, Goldwyn observed, who knows more about laughter and love—the staples of good movies—than Sigmund Freud? To both offers, Freud said no: he almost always turned such opportunities down, despite the fact that he was usually short of money. Freud had been very taken with Bullitt, though, and agreed to the collaboration; and in fact the Wilson book was, in time, published. Now Bullitt was going to do all he could for the man he so admired. Largely because of Bullitt, Freud would soon have the sympathetic attention of the president of the rogue republic himself, Franklin Delano Roosevelt.

The day after Wiley's visit, Friday, March 11, 1938, Sigmund Freud did something that he disliked: he listened to the radio. His son Martin Freud says that this was the only occasion that he could recall his father doing so. What Freud heard that evening was the voice of Kurt von Schuschnigg, but now Schuschnigg's defiance was gone. The chancellor was canceling the plebiscite on Austrian independence and resigning from office. In the hopes of avoiding slaughter, Schuschnigg encouraged the Austrian army not to fight back when the German troops came rolling across the border, as they now seemed certain to do. "We have yielded to force," the chancellor said. "Because under no circumstances, not even in this supreme hour, do we intend that German blood shall be spilt, we have instructed our army to retreat without offering any resistance." Schuschnigg's final words to the country were grieving: "Thus I take leave of the Austrian nation with a German farewell which also expresses my heartfelt wish: God save Austria!"

As soon as the speech was over, Vienna came alive again with chants of "One People, One Nation, One Leader!" as well as cries of "Death to the Jews!" William Shirer, the American reporter, saw young men heave paving blocks through the windows of Jewish shops. The crowds egged them on and roared with pleasure as the windows shattered and the glass dropped like great ice chunks into the street.

"As I crossed the Graben," G. E. R. Gedye recalls, "the Brown flood was sweeping through the streets. It was an indescribable witches' Sabbath—storm-troopers, lots of them barely out of the schoolroom, with cartridge-belts and carbines, the only other evidence of authority being Swastika brassards, were marching side by side with police turncoats, men and women shrieking or crying hysterically the name of their leader, embracing the police and dragging them along in the swirling stream of humanity, motor-lorries filled with storm-troopers clutching their long-concealed weapons, hooting furiously, trying to make themselves heard above the din, men and women leaping, shouting and dancing in the light of the smoking torches which soon began to make their appearance, the air filled with a pandemonium of sound in which intermingled screams of: Down with the Jews! Heil Hitler! Heil Hitler! Sieg Heil! Perish the Jews! Hang Schuschnigg!"

Nazis began to mobilize all over Austria. An SS group took control of the headquarters of the Tyrolese provincial government. In Linz, not far from the führer's birthplace, twenty thousand people gathered to cheer the news that Schuschnigg was gone. The Nazi high command in Berlin told their colleagues, newly installed in the Austrian government, that it was time to make a formal request for Germany to "step in and restore order"—the order that Germany was destroying. By ten past nine that evening, the communiqué asking for German assistance was out. At ten forty-five, Prince Philip of Hesse, who had gone to Italy in Hitler's behalf, phoned the führer to let him know that all was in order and that Il Duce endorsed the invasion. "Please tell Mussolini I will never forget him for this," Hitler said, "Never, never, never, whatever happens."

At five thirty the next morning, Saturday, March 12, 1938, the German troops that had gathered along the border in Bavaria crossed over into Austria with no opposition. The Annexation—the Anschluss—had begun.

Later that Saturday, Freud made a two-word entry in his journal, "Finis Austria": the end of Austria. That morning, Freud's paper, *Neue Freie Presse*, announced that Arthur Seyss-Inquart, a "moderate" Austrian Nazi, was now in control of the government. But it was the evening's paper that enraged Freud. Martin, Freud's son, remembered how his father gently took the paper from the maid and read through the headlines. He sat for a while, pondering. Then the old man crumpled it all up in a ball and hurled it across the room. Freud was, at home as he was abroad in the world, an extremely self-contained man who did not readily show emotion. Martin had never seen his father act this way. No one dared ask Freud a question; no one dared to speak. After a while Martin softly crossed the room, picked up the sheets, unfolded them, and read. In the paper was Hitler's proclamation justifying the invasion; it ended with the words "Long Live National Socialist Germany-Austria!"

Freud may have been enraged at what was happening in Austria, but he was not entirely unprepared for it. Writing to his son Ernst in 1934, the year after Hitler came to power, Freud said, "The future is uncertain: either Austrian fascism or the swastika. . . . Our attitude to the two political possibilities for Austria's future can only be summed up in Mercutio's line in *Romeo and Juliet*: 'A plague on both your houses.'" By 1936, things looked, if possible, more dire to Freud: "Austria seems bent on becoming National Socialist," he wrote to Arnold Zweig. "Fate seems to be conspiring with that gang. With ever less regret do I wait for the curtain to fall on me."

In 1937, a year before Hitler made his move on Austria, Freud felt nearly certain how things would go. "Our political situation seems to become more and more gloomy," he told Ernest Jones. "The invasion of the Nazis can probably not be checked; the consequences are disastrous for analysis as well. The only hope remaining is that one will not live to see it oneself. The situation is similar to that in 1683, when the Turks were outside Vienna. At that time military reinforcements came over the Kahlenberg; today—nothing like that is to be expected. . . . If our city falls, then the Prussian barbarians will swamp Europe." This time Freud ended with a dream of travel and change—and of hope: "I should like to live in England . . . ," Freud said, "and travel to Rome, like you."

The Nazi troops who entered Austria that Saturday morning enjoyed a glorious welcome. Crowds swarmed the streets to greet them, throwing flowers in their path. Troops eventually received orders to keep their goggles down lest the flowers harm their eyes. All through Austria members of the once-banned Nazi Party began turning their swastika lapel buttons outward and exchanging the salute with each other on the street. Hitler himself flew to Munich and from there began driving to the Austrian border in an open-topped Mercedes, accompanied by a bodyguard of SS troops. At ten minutes of four in the afternoon—close to the time Freud was reading the newspaper headlines and throwing the paper across the room—Adolf Hitler arrived at his birthplace, Braunau am Inn, where screaming crowds met him.

Four hours later, Hitler was in the city of Linz. Church bells rang and a mob gathered in front of the town hall, and began the chant: "One People! One Nation! One Leader! / One People! One Nation! One Leader!"

"Any further attempt to tear the people apart," Hitler cried from the balcony of the town hall, "will be in vain." The führer laid flowers on the graves of his parents and, after visiting his old home, went back to his hotel to dream the future.

The reception he got in Linz shocked Hitler. He had hoped that the Austrians would acquiesce to the German takeover. He planned to form a confederacy with Austria, in which Germany would be the dominant partner. But far from being merely compliant, the Austrians who greeted Hitler along the road and who gathered beneath his balcony in Linz were in ecstasy. They saluted the führer as if he were their savior: they knew that Hitler would deliver them from their poverty and their weakness and from the chief source of all their troubles, the Jews. That night in the hotel, Hitler saw that he could hope for more than a confederacy: he could annex the entire nation and do what he liked with its resources and its inhabitants. He could make Austria what he would eventually want every sovereign state in the world to be, a dependent province of Germany. His ambitions burning, Hitler set out for Vienna, Sigmund Freud, and a hundred and seventy thousand other Jewish men and women and children.

"Vienna was scarcely recognizable this morning," wrote Shirer of that Saturday. "Swastika flags [were] flying from nearly every house. Where did they get them so fast?"

Finis Austria, the End of Austria—the words Freud wrote in his journal that Saturday meant something specific and painful to their author. They meant the end of a culture, centered in Vienna, that was cosmopolitan, at least ostensibly tolerant, not lacking in sophistication, devoted to art and science—and relatively safe for the Jews. During Freud's boyhood several

Jews had actually served in the Austro-Hungarian ministry. Looking back, Freud said that, at the time, Jewish schoolboys went around with ministers' portfolios stashed in their schoolbags—a sign of their possible destinies—much as common soldiers in Napoleon's army had gone off to war carrying field marshal's batons. Freud's life had unfolded in a city that some people have described as Wittgenstein's Vienna. It was a city that, from the end of the First World War and the dissolution of the Austro-Hungarian Empire until March of 1938—until the moment, one might say, when Sigmund Freud threw his newspaper across the room—had been a center of art and learning. This was the Vienna of Karl Kraus, perhaps the most brilliant satirist of the modern period. It was the Vienna of Robert Musil, author of the modernist masterwork *The Man Without Qualities*. Here Arnold Schoenberg made his breakthroughs in twelve-tone musical composition. In Vienna, Adolf Loos developed his version of a modernist architecture. And in Vienna, perhaps most consequentially, Ludwig Wittgenstein offered a new start for philosophy, attempting to sweep away virtually all prior work in the field, and getting back to basic problems and basic propositions.

Vienna hummed with new and consequential happenings everywhere, of innovations issuing from the artists and intellectuals directed toward an alert, intelligent public. No doubt the atmosphere was at times an inspiration to Freud. But while many—and perhaps even the most gifted and original—of his contemporaries were seeking clarity, elegance, and mathematical precision, in perfect aphorisms, geometrically precise architectural designs, and pared-down philosophical treatises, which passed over all things that could not be rigorously said in silence, Freud moved in a different direction. His work was a dramatic contrast to the international, Apollonian style that characterized a significant quotient of the Viennese revolution in culture.

Freud's thinking moved backward into the dark past—rather than forward into the highly reasoned future. "He would have us remember most of all," as Auden put it in his beautiful elegy for Freud, "to be enthusiastic over the night." Freud was absorbed by what was old, atavistic, uncanny, and heretofore undecipherable. He was fascinated by things that most of Vienna's elite artists and thinkers would have considered ridiculous. (Wittgenstein, probably the most gifted and original of the group—and rightly renowned for his intellectual honesty—found Freud's work to be both alluring and misleading: he called it "a very powerful mythology.") After his book on dreams, Freud wrote one about slips of the tongue and the pen; soon afterward came a full-length book about jokes. He brooded on childhood eros in his notorious *Essays on the Theory of Sexuality*. Childhood, folktales, dreams, eccentric day-to-day behavior, the unwell, the marginal and the misunderstood—Freud was intrigued by the kinds of people and things that grandmothers sitting around the hearth gossiped over.

To Freud, the only way to move forward as a civilization was to face the repressed—the disordered accumulation that was packed down in the cellars and crypts of the psyche. It would be hard to argue that any of Freud's prominent contemporaries in art and intellectual life, with the possible exception of the satirist Karl Kraus, were doing work that could have prepared Vienna and the world for what would happen in March of 1938. There is nothing to be found in the *Tractatus* of Wittgenstein—who actually went to school with Hitler for a while and may be referred to in a passage in *Mein Kampf* about an aloof Jewish boy—that looks ahead to the horror of the 1930s.

To many middle-class Viennese, Wittgenstein's Vienna (which was in some measure Freud's Vienna too) was an exhilarating place. They took themselves to be at the heart of the intellectual and artistic world. But Vienna in the 1930s became socially and politically an extremely turbulent place. The depression of 1929 hit Austria particularly hard: in May of 1931, Vienna's largest commercial bank, the Creditanstalt, declared itself insolvent; by February of 1933, a quarter of the labor force was unemployed. A year later, came the February uprising, in which the Social Democrats and Bolsheviks of what was called Red Vienna rebelled, only to be murderously put down by the government of Engelbert Dollfuss. Less than six months later, in July of 1934, came the attempted coup, in which Dollfuss himself was killed by the Nazis and Hitler nearly invaded.

Though Freud's financial situation was relatively secure in the early and mid-1930s—he had foreign patients who paid him well—many of the people around him in Vienna were suffering. "The human cost [of the depression] was incalculable," Peter Gay observes. "Personal tragedies—promising careers aborted, sudden poverty, educated men selling shoelaces or apples on street corners, proud bourgeois taking handouts from their relatives—became commonplace everywhere."

The Viennese were encountering a version of the world that Karl Marx was expert at describing: this is the world of capitalism amok, in which the preeminent values are monetary values. In this world there are no stabilities, because nothing that cannot produce profits, or somehow lend itself to profit production, will stay intact for long. As Marx put it, in lines that for many would have characterized Vienna from the end of the First World War until the day that Hitler and his troops crossed the border: "Constant revolutionizing of production, uninterrupted disturbance of all social conditions, everlasting uncertainty and agitation distinguish the bourgeois epoch from all earlier ones. All fixed, fast-frozen relations, with their train of ancient and venerable prejudices and opinions are swept away, all new-formed ones become antiquated before they can ossify. All that is solid melts into air, all that is holy is profaned."

Freud was both old and new. What he said about the psyche was shockingly novel and, as such, a part of the Viennese cultural revolution. Yet what he said also drew on old wisdom; Freud compounded his work not only from clinical observation, but from reading Sophocles, Shakespeare, and Milton. He also drew on fairy tales and folk wisdom, as well as that fund of information—to him often closer to the truth than the educated believe—everyday common sense.

Freud's response to the crisis of the age was complex: look backward in order to look to the future, he seemed to say. Hitler and the Nazis had a way of dealing with the world where "all that is solid melts into air" too. Their way was to bring the present under control through the triumph of one leader, one party, one race, and one nation. They insisted on oneness in a world that seemed to be flying apart into unmanageable fragments. The Austrians who, on those March days, began turning their swastika lapel buttons out for the world and their Jewish neighbors to see, were hoping for many things, but one of them was deliverance from the world that Marx had so aptly described into a world of comforting, if brutal, simplifications. Hitler, who, on Monday, March 14, was heading to Vienna (and to Freud), seemed to many the man best able to solve the problems of modernity.

For his part, Freud began to make preparations. The night before the führer's arrival in the city, Freud called a meeting of the Vienna Psychoanalytical Society at Berggasse 19. There he shook hands individually with each of the members, saying, quite simply, "There is nothing one can do about it." The decision was to disband the society, with the possibility of reforming it wherever Freud might settle, assuming he could— or wanted to—find a way out of Vienna at all.

The Nazis had not, as one might have expected, closed the Berlin Psychoanalytical Institute when they gained power in 1933. Rather, they had taken it over, begun discharging the Jewish analysts, and put it under the direction of one M. H. Göring, a cousin of Hermann Göring, Hitler's eventual Reichsmarschall. The Nazis associated with psychoanalysis generally thought that Freud was right, almost word for word. All he had written was valid: psychoanalysis was in fact a science. However, they added one qualification. Psychoanalysis was a Jewish science, which meant not only that a Jew had created it and other Jews had developed it, but that by and large its findings applied to Jews and to Jews only. Jews, it seems, were people beset by the Oedipal complex; possessing—and possessed by—a violent, sexually charged unconscious; prone to infantile sexuality. All that Freud said was so—but it was so about the Jews. Not long after the Nazi takeover, Carl Jung gave a sequence of lectures at the new institute in Berlin in which he made some theoretical observations about the singularity of the Aryan psyche and its contrast to what he thought of as the psyche of the Jews. "The Aryan unconscious," Jung observed, "has a higher potential than the Jewish; that is the advantage and the disadvantage of a youthfulness not yet fully estranged from barbarism." The theoretical work of the Göring Institute was to compound a comprehensive theory of Aryan psychology, given that a Jewish psychology was already so well in place.

On the afternoon of March 14, Adolf Hitler returned to the great city of his youth. He rode through the streets of Vienna in the open-topped Mercedes, standing up, holding on to the car's windshield with his left hand, with his right returning the salute to the crowds massed to greet him. Almost every prominent building was draped with the German flag. There were swastikas everywhere and the crowds were screaming. Yet Hitler was distracted. He gave little indication that he even took the people in. His salute appeared to be halfhearted, perfunctory; he seemed to be hardly holding on to the windshield. What's striking is how vulnerable the führer allowed himself to be. He was completely exposed to the crowd and at the mercy of any halfway able assassin. Yet he proceeded with an absolute, if somnambular, confidence; he was sure, it seems, that no one in Vienna could mean him serious harm.

Hitler's car stopped in front of the Imperial Hotel, a place that he had often dreamed of entering when he was living at the men's shelter. Now it was decked with a huge red banner emblazoned with the swastika. Even after Hitler entered the hotel and made his way to the royal suite, the crowd stayed outside, chanting a variation on an old German drinking song: "We won't go home, we won't go home," they cried, "until the führer speaks!" The mob sang on into the night, and Hitler showed himself again and again from the hotel.

As the evening passed, Hitler began reminiscing about the feelings he had for the Imperial Hotel when he lived in Vienna thirty years ago. He fell into one of his amazing bouts of speech: Hitler, as a Don DeLillo character says, "called himself the lonely wanderer out of nothingness. He sucked on lozenges, spoke to people in endless monologues, free associating, as if the language came from some vastness beyond the world and he was simply the medium of revelation." And so the führer seems to have spoken that night.

"I could see the glittering lights and chandeliers in the lobby," Hitler said to his companions in the suite, "but I knew it was impossible for me to set foot inside. One night, after a bad blizzard which piled up several feet of snow, I had a chance to make some money for food by shoveling snow. Ironically enough, the five or six of us in my group were sent to clean the street and sidewalk in front of the Imperial Hotel." Members of the royal family, the Hapsburgs, were at the hotel that night, and Hitler remembered them well. "I saw Karl and Zita step out of their imperial coach and grandly walk into this hotel over the red carpet. We poor devils shoveled the snow away on all sides and took our hats off every time the aristocrats arrived. They didn't even look at us, although I still smell the perfume that came to our noses. We were about as important to them, or for that matter to Vienna, as the snow that kept coming down all night, and this hotel did not even have the decency to send out a cup of hot coffee to us." The music that Hitler heard coming from inside was so beautiful that it made him want to weep, but it also made him rage about the injustice of what was happening to him. "I resolved that night," Hitler said, "that some day I would come back to the Imperial Hotel and walk over the red carpet in that glittering interior where the Hapsburgs danced. I didn't know how or when, but I have waited for this day and tonight I am here."

The next day, Tuesday, March 15, which would be a sadly memorable one for Sigmund Freud, Hitler woke up without the stomach cramps that had bothered him in Linz. The führer had a tender digestive system and unaccustomed food could play havoc with it. In the afternoon, a quarter of a million Viennese gathered in the Heldenplatz, the Hero's Square, and Hitler exuberantly announced that Austria was now part of the German Reich; the nation had a new name, Ostmark. "A Legitimist leader," Hitler declared, "once described the task of Austria's so-called independence as that of hindering the construction of a really great German Reich. I now proclaim for this land a new mission. The oldest eastern province of the German people shall from now on be the youngest bulwark of the German nation."

Finally, in front of the 250,000, he congratulated himself: "I can in this hour report before history the conclusion of the greatest aim in my life: the entry of my homeland into the German Reich."

As soon as the German troops crossed the border into Austria, Jews in Vienna began coming under attack. All through the streets, Jews were being stopped by gangs of storm troopers who kicked, punched, and humiliated them. Nazis broke into Jewish homes and businesses, beat up everyone on the premises, and took what they wanted. The streets became a sort of black carnival, an urban hell, where all the bottled-up racial hatred of the last decades exploded into the open. Shirer, the American journalist, saw Jews on their hands and knees scrubbing nationalist slogans off the sidewalk as jeering storm troopers stood over them and crowds taunted. "Many Jews killing themselves," Shirer observed. Hundreds of Jewish men and women were taken into custody to clean latrines for the Nazis, sometimes with implements, sometimes with their hands. The storm troopers rounded up elderly white bearded Jews, brought them to the synagogues and compelled them to do deep knee bends, while they chanted "Heil Hitler."

Franz Danimann, who lived in Schwechat, a suburb of Vienna, recalled what happened to the Jewish businesspeople in his district. They were driven onto the street by Nazis, given toothbrushes, and told to get down on their knees and clean. Finally, the Nazis said, the Jews would learn how to work. "They were heartbreaking scenes," Danimann recalled. "The victims were often old people, but despite the fact that they were forced to kneel down to the work, they managed to retain their dignity."

Danimann, who was a Social Democrat and not a Jew, accosted one of the storm troopers, asking if he wasn't ashamed of his behavior. The Nazi replied, "Ah, so you are a friend of theirs, are you? Well for you we can find another toothbrush. Get down on your knees and start scrubbing." Danimann jumped onto his bicycle and rode away. Not much later, he was arrested; ultimately he went to Auschwitz.

Shirer's wife, Tess, was in the hospital to deliver a baby. A Jewish woman she met there was grieving for her brother-in-law, who had committed suicide the day Hitler entered Vienna. She left the hospital in black mourning dress, holding on to her newborn child. Another woman, about to give birth, learned that the Nazis had taken away her husband's business and looted their apartment. "She fears her husband will be killed or arrested," Tess told Shirer, "and weeps all night long."

A few days earlier, Shirer and his fellow correspondent Edward R. Murrow had gone out late for a drink. They stopped into a bar and sat down, but Murrow was obviously uncomfortable. He told Shirer that they had to leave. Why? Shirer liked it there and wanted to stay. Finally Murrow explained. Last night, he had been at the same place and "a Jewish looking fellow" standing at the bar took an old-fashioned straight razor out of his pocket and slashed his throat with it.

Jews were trying to leave the city, but almost as soon as the German troops crossed the border, young Austrian storm troopers dispatched themselves to the train stations and intercepted most of them. The Jews who tried to escape were sent back to Vienna and often put under arrest. Then the Nazis made for their homes and began stealing what they could. In all, the Nazis arrested 21,000 people during the first days of the Anschluss and sent them off to Dachau. By the end of the year, all but 1,500 had been released, though many who went free then would be captured again and sent to the concentration camps.

From those early days of the annexation, certain photographic images stand out. One is a picture of a large man, his belly pressed tight against his fully buttoned jacket. He wears lace-up boots, knee socks with knickers, and a soft hat. He looks to be a man who enjoys mountain climbing, beer, and his breakfast. On his face is an expression of surpassing distaste, as though he takes himself to be an important executive of some sort, overseeing a highly consequential but rather repulsive project. Behind the man and to his right, a crowd of eight or so people is gathered, looking on with approval. A young boy about ten years old kneels in front of the man, facing the wall of a building. The boy's flexible posture, one knee bent almost gracefully outward, is in marked contrast to the man's stiff, stolid presence. The boy has a can of paint in his left hand and with his right he wields a brush. A rectangular block protrudes slightly from the face of the building, and on that block, the boy is painting the word *Jude*, Jew. He is painting the front of his father's business, at the insistence of the stolid man, so that the people will know it is a Jewish business and avoid it.

Another image. A Viennese crowd is in the street and scuffling with police. The police have linked their hands to form a human rope. They are holding on tight, but the mass of people is pushing hard against them, making it difficult to maintain order. The police are well turned out in jackboots and neat military caps. One of them, probably an officer, directs them as effectively as he can, but their case may be hopeless. Behind the human lines there are some men, but most who have made it to the front are women. Some of the women are smiling, some laughing, some seem nearly ecstatic. Clearly, the police are only pretending to disapprove of the crowd's passion; really they are enjoying it, playing the role of authorities, when in fact they're as happy and excited as the crowd. Behind them is a Nazi flag, about twenty feet high, hanging on a lamppost. The people are waiting for Hitler to come and address them and they are showing all the vitality and mock rebelliousness that girls and boys at rock concerts, about thirty years and a world away, will show.

The Nazis threw Jews in prison; they confiscated businesses that had taken generations to build; they invaded apartment buildings, tossed the residents out on the street, and moved in themselves. They insulted and spit on mothers and fathers in front of their children. But they also visited smaller indignities on the Jews, banning them from certain park benches, restricting their movements. Matters of dirt and contamination obsessed the Nazis. They wanted the Jews to be cleaning things, streets and latrines. They wanted to limit the contact between Jews and gentiles, lest the Jews pass them some sort of infection. This obsession with cleanliness and hygiene, this concern with purity, which took off so violently in Austria, would eventually come to dominate the Nazis. In time, Jews were not to clean, or sanitize on their own, but to be cleaned away.

Many who observed the events in Austria after the Anschluss were shocked by them. They could not imagine that anyone, not even the Nazis, could act so brutally. The Germans, it seemed, had embraced anti-Semitism much more slowly. It had taken five years, the years since Hitler came to power, for the Germans to commit themselves fully to race hatred. Even now, in March of 1938, it was probably safer to be a Jew in Berlin than to be one in Vienna. (One observer declared that the Germans were excellent Nazis but rather poor anti-Semites; but that the Austrians, though inept enough as Nazis, were highly accomplished in their anti-Semitism.) The Viennese, purportedly among the most tolerant people in all of Europe, rose to rabid violence against the Jews in just a few days. Stefan Zweig, a friend of Freud's, and himself a Jew, was horrified by the events of March: "All the sickly, unclean fantasies of hate that had been conceived in many orgiastic nights found raging expression in bright daylight."

Zweig's shock is not difficult to understand. Vienna's more refined residents were not only proud of their city's culture, they also took Vienna to be a center of enlightened social tolerance. The city was multiracial and multinational: here one found not only Germans, but Czechs, Slovaks, Poles, Ruthenians, Slovenians, Serbo-Croats, Magyars, Romanians, and Italians. Certainly there were a number of anti-Semitic publications, which carried stories and cartoons depicting Jews in ways that were, to say the least, distasteful. From 1897 to 1910, Vienna had an anti-

Semitic mayor, Karl Lueger, whom Hitler greatly admired, calling him "the mightiest mayor of all time." (Freud detested Lueger, once celebrating one of his political reversals with a forbidden cigar.) Still most liberal observers thought of pre-Anschluss Vienna as a relative paradise for European Jews.

Anyone who had been reading Freud though would not have been terribly surprised at the events of March 1938. Ever attentive to the sadistic side of humanity, Freud believed that even the most apparently civilized people nurse fantasies of violence, rape, and plunder. To Freud, we are all in our hearts criminals. "Our dreams convince us that these things are so," he said, in one form or another, time after time. The forces that divide us from our most disturbing desires—the ego, reason, civilization—are potent, to be sure. But their potency is diminished when unconscious desires are inflamed by external events. Freud believed that what we dream at night we can, given certain circumstances, enact in waking life. In his reflections on the Anschluss, Freud shows irritation, impatience, and occasionally something approaching a dark bemusement, but he is never shocked. He had been studying the unconscious for too long.

Nor does Hitler seem to surprise him much. It is strange but true: Freud is always scandalized by the thought of America, but he often seems to take Hitler and the Nazis as simple facts of life. Perhaps that is because for twenty-five years, authority, and particularly the sort of authority that Hitler embodied, had been at the center of Freud's concerns as a writer and thinker, and also of his practice as a therapist. Reflecting on the Nazis, well after the takeover of Austria, Freud told Arthur Koestler that they were merely expressing a commonplace sort of human aggression. "Something like this was inevitable," Freud said. "I am not sure that from my standpoint I can blame them."

Up until 1914, Freud had been transfixed by the workings of the unconscious. He was absorbed in his studies of dreams and folktales, slips of the tongue and the pen, jokes, children, fantasies, and art. He was absorbed, too, in his case studies. He told the stories of the Wolf Man and the Rat Man, Dora and Emma, and all the rest. Freud was always a relatively dark writer, but one can find a certain measured optimism in his developing view that in the simple, often-forgotten corners of human life, there is meaning to be found—and that in such meaning there lies hope for freedom from psychological misery. By becoming more conversant with their desires, Freud suggested time and again, human beings might expect a little less renunciation from themselves and so might become a little freer, more at peace. We need not act out every repressed desire—Freud was too much a realist to believe that we should. But simply by attaching words to out deepest wishes, making conscious what had been repressed, we might achieve a level of self-acceptance that would lead to some tranquility and—who knows?—maybe a glint of happiness from time to time. Where "it" was, Freud said, there "I" shall be, and in saying as much he gestured toward an intellectual and spiritual path that would lead not to salvation, to be sure, but to a better life. This was the Freud who, as Peter Gay acutely observed, taught the world that there was more to understand and less to judge about people than most had previously imagined.

But beginning in about 1914, traces of optimism become less

and less common in Freud's work. For he had, he thought, hit upon a fundamental difficulty in human life: the problem of authority. Human beings, Freud came to believe, are addicted to authority and often to destructive authority at that. Frequently our strongest desire, oddly enough, is to find a figure who will control our desires. We wish to be dominated. We wish to submit.

Freud saw this hunger for domination manifest in many areas of experience, but nowhere so potently, or so dangerously, as in politics. In 1921, when Hitler's political career was just beginning, Freud published *Group Psychology and the Analysis of the Ego*, a study of crowd behavior that lays special emphasis on the role of the leader. The world, in this vision, is a disturbing, complex, sometimes chaotic place where everything that has been solid and sound melts into the air. Values, if they exist at all, are in flux. But then comes the leader, who appears to be certain about all things. "His intellectual acts," Freud wrote, are "strong and independent even in isolation, and his will need[s] no reinforcement from others." Where others are buffeted by doubts, the leader is always sure that his vision is the one true vision. His ego has few emotional ties; he loves no one but himself and to others he gives away no more than the bare minimum of affection or recognition. "Members of a group," Freud continued, "stand in need of the illusion that they are equally and justly loved by their leader; but the leader himself need love no one else, he may be of a masterful nature, absolutely narcissistic, self-confident and independent. We know that love puts a check on narcissism"—and the leader is the ultimate figure of self-enclosed self-love. In his insistence on the centrality of the leader and the dynamics of his relation to the group, Freud pressed beyond the work of predecessors like Gustav Le Bon, who, to Freud's way of thinking, overemphasized the power of the collective mind in and of itself. Le Bon believed that when a group forms, a special consciousness rises up, one that is markedly different from individual consciousness, but not determined by the presence of the leader. To Freud, crowds on their own can be dangerous—he was as wary of them as two of his favorite authors, Charles Dickens and Mark Twain, were—but he suggested that crowds only constitute a long-term murderous threat when a certain sort of figure takes over the leader role in ways that are both prohibitive and permissive.

The description that Freud offers of the leader eerily anticipates the kinds of descriptions that Hitler's followers began to offer about him, starting in the 1920s. Here, finally, was a politician with an uncompromising way of seeing the world and a clear program. He knew what he hated: Jews, the Versailles Treaty (he called it "the stab in the back"), Marxists. He knew what he wanted: the unification of the German people, a strong army, complete dedication to the state, an empire. He said that for Germany to come into its own, the people would have to look to a great leader and find in him the sublime expression of their will. He was that leader. Providence had appointed him. Such a leader did not need to consult the people or their representatives from moment to moment. No, his relation to them was nearly mystical, for he embodied their will. He embodied all of their highest aspirations, *whether they were aware of those aspirations or not.* Hitler was never in doubt. He always knew the Truth and proclaimed it with absolute conviction.

In another sense, of course, Hitler was an absurd figure. The man who so fiercely endorsed the Aryan ideal was himself short, dark, and homely, with a ridiculous mustache. He spoke in mangled sentences; his writing was full of misspellings and puerile grammatical errors. His idea of the good life consisted of sitting around a lunch table with a collection of lackeys, eating sweet pastries and holding forth on his two favorite subjects, his war experiences and the loyalty of dogs. In the evening he watched operettas on film, then, when they were over, went back to talking about his war experiences and praising the loyalty of dogs. In private he could be astonishingly emotional—he was prone to weep—and out of focus. But when he needed to, Hitler was highly accomplished at playing the role that Freud describes, the role of the masterful man who knows the truth and is untroubled by doubts. (Hitler's biographer, John Toland, speculates that Hitler may have read *Group Psychology* and used it to guide his performances. Yet there is no hard evidence for this; nor is there evidence for Hitler having read any intellectually demanding book and taken in its meaning. He claimed to adore Schopenhauer, but he misunderstood *The World as Will and Representation* almost entirely.) Hitler was especially appealing to young people and to women; when they heard him, they seemed to feel, as Goebbels, the most devoted of Hitler's sycophants, observed, that a new messiah had come at last into the world.

*     *     *

On the day that Hitler addressed the citizens of Vienna, announcing to them and to the world that he had absorbed Austria into the Reich, a gang of Nazis invaded the Verlag, the printing press that published Freud's books. The press was at Berggasse 7, just a few doors away from Freud's apartment, and Freud's son Martin, a lawyer, was there already, doing what he could to dispose of the records, when the Nazis arrived. Papers stored at the Verlag revealed that Freud, like many Viennese Jews, had placed money in foreign accounts. This was now illegal. If the Nazis discovered it, they would surely confiscate the funds, and perhaps jail Freud and his family too.

Martin had not been at the Verlag long when the gang broke in. There were about a dozen of them, Martin recalled, shabbily dressed, not in uniform, but well armed. Almost all carried rifles, except for one small, worn-out-looking man, who came in with a drawn pistol. When Martin seemed uncooperative, the small man pushed the pistol into his belly and said, "Why not shoot him now and be finished with him? We should shoot him on the spot." Quickly the Nazis got into the safe, emptied its contents on the desk, and began combing through them.

The situation was dangerous, but also rather grotesque. The men facing Martin Freud that day were not, it appears, hard-core Nazi ideologues. Rather they were anti-Semitic thugs looking to get what profit they could in the confusion that reigned everywhere in Vienna. It was open season on Jews and Jewish property and they were not going to be left out. The encounter with Martin vacillated from raw threat, with the disheveled man poking his victim with the pistol, to something bordering on dark comedy. At a certain point, Martin petitioned the group for a cup of tea. This was put to a vote, and it was decided that yes, it would be all right, provided that Martin wash his own cup and saucer. Martin requested that the office boy wash them, and this too was put to a vote and approved, even though the office boy had converted to Nazism at about the moment the gang arrived.

Suddenly Ernest Jones, Freud's devoted disciple, appeared in the office. Jones had flown in from London as soon as he heard about the Anschluss and had rushed to the press to see what he could do. Nothing, it turned out: the men wouldn't listen to him and so he went off to find what Martin Freud rather optimistically called "a more responsible Nazi authority."

In the early afternoon, Martin was left alone with one of the Nazis, a melancholy-looking, middle-aged man, who seemed more like a headwaiter than a soldier. The guard told him a tale about the hardships and privations he had endured in recent years and soon it became clear to Martin that what he most wanted was money. Martin gave him all he had in his pockets, some gold coins and a roll of notes. The guard was so grateful that he began honoring Martin's multiple requests to use the bathroom. Time after time, Martin went down the corridor, on each visit scooping up a handful of compromising documents and flushing them away.

It turned out that across the street from the Verlag lived a Nazi who was watching the proceedings through his window. He saw that when Martin and his guard left the room, other members of the gang crept back in and pocketed the coins and bills that were lying on the table. A disgrace to the party, this was inexcusable. The outraged Nazi called party headquarters and in time the district commander of the SA made his way to the press, huffing and puffing. Apparently he had run all the way. "Young and erect of stature," Martin recalled, "he radiated an authority which had an immediate effect on the rabble that had been tormenting me for so long. They fell in at his sharp command and after one or two had been ordered to remain to clear up the mess in the office, the main body marched off." Left standing in the corner was the original guard, the headwaiter manqué, who had been frisked and found with Martin's money in his pocket.

While the Nazis were breaking up, Anna Freud arrived and received all the courtesy of the Reich. The commander gave Anna and Martin a pass they could use to make their way to Nazi headquarters the next day without being stopped and harassed on the street. The last thing the commander did was to dismiss the melancholy waiter, giving him back his rifle, but not the coins and currency that Martin had passed his way.

There is a semi-farcical quality to the events of that afternoon, or at least to Martin's account of them. But what seemed absurd could quickly have become dangerous, maybe deadly. All over Vienna similar gangs, armed and decked with swastikas, were making the rounds. Often all they did was steal. But some Jews were badly beaten, some Jews murdered. And of course all this was only a prelude to deeper horrors.

Freud was surely disturbed to learn of the threat to Martin that day, but the thought of his daughter Anna being on the scene and in danger would have been almost more than he could bear.

Freud's love for Anna was by now nearly beyond description. She was his Cordelia and, as he often said, his Antigone as well. Anna was the great comfort of his old age and also his hope for the future. What Freud wanted was not to live on and on; he was tired and sick now and at times seemed ready to leave the world. What he wanted was to depart life convinced that the movement he founded would live on through time. Freud was obsessed with the continuity of his work and lately he had come to see that Anna might be the one who could do the most to achieve it.

He had not always held his youngest child in such esteem. Anna was not pretty and she was not precocious; as a girl, she was dutiful, thoughtful, and thorough, with a capacity for work that wasn't unlike Freud's. Over time, though, Freud came to see that what Anna lacked in quickness of understanding, she made up for in depth. She immersed herself in his work and in his world—when she was still a girl, she sat in on the seminars Freud held for his disciples at Berggasse 19 in a room blue with cigar smoke—and became as well versed in his thought as any of his followers. Her relation to Freud's vision was never what could be called creative. She took it all in; she learned its terms by heart; but it never seems to have occurred to Anna that her father's thinking required anything by way of revision or even much development.

Freud's authority with Anna was absolute and he had established it early in her life in part by psychoanalyzing her himself. Looking back on the psychoanalysis, Anna said that her father never permitted her to indulge in half measures. He compelled her to offer the whole truth about everything, including her erotic life. She shared with him her sexual fantasies and her forays into masturbation, and Freud took it all in with his characteristic equanimity. Anna emerged from the analysis grateful to her father and more committed to him than ever. From that time on, Freud's attitude toward his daughter was protective in the extreme, especially when sex was the issue. Even as Anna reached her twenties and began to attract men, including the devoted womanizer Ernest Jones, Freud continually proclaimed that she was too young and not at all ready to leave the family. Once, during the period of Anna's analysis, when she had gone off on vacation and left her mother and father, Freud wrote to Lou Andreas-Salomé, saying that "I have long felt sorry for her for still being at home with us old folks . . . but on the other hand, if she really were to go away, I should feel myself as deprived as I do now, and as I should do if I had to give up smoking!"

Anna Freud's closest relationship aside from the one with her father was with Dorothy Burlingham, an American woman who arrived in Vienna in 1925, where she was analyzed by Theodor Reik and then by Freud. She also had her four children analyzed and was so impressed by the results that she herself trained to be a child analyst. Dorothy Burlingham became attached to the Freud family and particularly to Anna: the two of them traveled together in Italy in 1927. Yet as close as Dorothy came to Anna, as constant as was their companionship, it is almost certain that there was no overtly sexual relation between the two. Anna was and remained her father's.

By 1938, Anna had virtually displaced her mother, Martha, in Freud's life. Anna took care of Freud, she got his medicine, she helped him remove and clean the prosthesis on the right side of his jaw, she made sure that he was comfortable. And, also, Anna sustained him intellectually, for he talked his ideas over with her as much as he did with anyone. He sought her comfort, yes, but he also sought her intellectual advice. Anna had become Freud's great stay against the world. In a letter to Ernst, Freud's architect son who was living in London, two months before the Anschluss, Freud said, "Anna is splendid in spirits, achievement, and in all human relationships. It is amazing how clear and independent her scientific work has become. If she had more ambition . . . but perhaps it is better like this for her later life."

Freud loved his daughter for all she was and all she brought to him day after day, but there was also a pragmatic dimension to his attachment. Part of Freud's genius lay in knowing that to be a genius was not enough. Freud had a comprehensive and brilliant vision about what life was and, implicitly, of how it might be lived. Good: so had others. The pressing task now, in 1938, was to make certain that the vision would survive over time. Freud could look back into recent German intellectual history and see two thinkers, Schopenhauer and Nietzsche, whose achievements were comparable to his own—perhaps they were even more original. But would their work live on? Both had left academia early in life. Neither had founded a school;

neither had created disciples in significant numbers or set up an institutional structure to ensure that their ideas would outlive them and circulate throughout the world. Freud did not want to make such a mistake.

For at least the past thirty years, Freud had sought inheritors, younger men (it would preferably be men) who could devote themselves to him and continue his legacy. He gathered around him talented figures like Karl Abraham, Sándor Ferenczi, and Carl Jung. He seated them at the table, with himself at the head, like a monarch surrounded by his knights. In time, he gave some of them rings, to seal the fellowship. He called them his sons. (His actual sons were, Freud had to admit, solid and sensible young men, but without the kind of intellectual talent that he most valued.) Freud, in other words, behaved something like the primal father he described in *Totem and Taboo* and also not entirely unlike the leader he described in *Group Psychology*, the man with the masterly aura. He lorded it over a horde of surrogate sons. And then, what he said in *Totem and Taboo* about the dynamics of tribal authority proved to be true, or nearly true, even in the purportedly civilized world of Vienna.

In *Totem and Taboo*, the climax of the tribal story comes when the sons rise up, kill the father, and eat him. (They believe him to be magic and want to internalize his supernatural powers.) Their guilt at what they have done causes them to idealize his image and to worship him in the time to come. Thus is religion founded. The book comes close to describing—in melodramatic enough terms—the dynamics of Freud's own urge to achieve authority. Freud managed to mesmerize his adoptive sons, not only with his originality and brilliance, but also with his frequent willingness to play the role of the patriarch. The sons, eventually, revolted—or at least the most talented of them usually did. Jung, the "crown prince," was the most promising of the inheritors and also the most rebellious, for Jung demanded to think for himself. He disagreed with Freud on many things, perhaps most significantly about his vision of the unconscious. To Jung, the unconscious was not the seat of repressed and dangerous desires. Rather, the unconscious was a repository of collective wisdom. Here one found figures—wise men and women, wizards, tricksters, the cast of the world's mythology—who offered wisdom to the individual locked in a repressive existence.

That Jung, who had learned all he knew from Freud, was ready to announce, in his gypsy way, that the unconscious was more sane and creative than the conscious mind—to Freud, this was too much to bear. Look outside in the street now, look into Vienna, where the unconscious, unmediated by any sane authority, is having its day, and see what you think, Freud might have reflected during those March weeks, for his thoughts, even many years after the break, were often full of Jung.

Over time, in fact, Freud could not bear much of any intellectual disagreement from his followers. The story goes that when a disciple once disputed a point with him during a seminar, Freud tried to quash him. "But," the disciple replied, "a dwarf sitting on the shoulders of a giant can see farther than the giant." Freud took this in. He gestured with his cigar once, then again. "Fine," the founder replied, "but a louse sitting on the head of an astronomer, what can he see?"

Carl Jung was creative; he was a visionary and a mystic and he impressed Freud and disturbed him in about equal measure. To break with Jung, as Freud did beginning around 1912, and to choose Anna as the guardian of the legacy was a great shift. In making it, Freud chose caution over imagination, continuity over creative disjunction. That Anna's best-known book is *The Ego and the Mechanisms of Defense* is entirely apt, for Anna was becoming a defense mechanism, not only for the ego that was Freud, but for his entire legacy. In time, she would set out to turn her father's work, which was sometimes nearly as speculative and wild as anything Jung ever wrote, into a coherent, stable, and sensible doctrine.

Freud loved Anna for herself; he passionately wanted her happiness—that much is certain. But he also loved her as a guarantor of the only kind of immortality that Freud, the self-professed godless Jew, could believe in.

Soon another group of Nazis—some of them perhaps from the gang that had invaded the Verlag—appeared at the door of Berggasse 19, where they were met by Martha Freud. Martha looked them over, stood aside, and let the Nazis into the apartment. Ever the good Viennese housewife, she asked the men as they entered if they might care to leave their rifles in the umbrella stand set by the door. This courtesy they declined.

When the Nazis arrived on that March day, Freud was sequestered at the back of Berggasse 19, in his private domain. To regather his strength, Freud had taken to lying on his famous couch atop a thick, richly woven oriental rug, propped up with a half dozen or so pillows. There was a second carpet fastened to the wall behind the couch, giving Freud, the convalescent, what it gave his patients, a sense of enclosure and warmth. At the foot of the couch where Freud lay, a small stove burned to fend off Vienna's winter chill. Close by the stove sat Freud's beloved dog, his chow, Lün, snoring and panting and filling the air with her rich canine scent.

Here Freud was surrounded by his massive collection of antiquities and by tributes to great civilizations past. Over Freud's head hung a large colored rendering of the Egyptian cliff temple of Ramses II at Abu Simbel. At the head of his couch, directly behind him in the corner, was a bust of an earnest Roman citizen, and above the bust, Pompeiian-style wall paintings of a centaur and of the great god Pan. At the couch's foot, close by the stove, were a number of pictures, including a reproduction of the famous painting by Ingres that depicts Oedipus interrogating the sphinx. When Freud celebrated his fiftieth birthday, his disciples gave him a medallion that showed Freud himself conducting an exchange with the creature.

When Freud turned right from where he lay on the couch, he saw a bookcase full of his antiquities, small statues, busts, and vases from ancient Egypt, Greece, and Rome, as well as a few from China and India. Freud had over two thousand such pieces and they were posed everywhere, including on the floor, in his section of the house.

On the bookcase was a large Chinese camel from the Tang dynasty, a classical terra-cotta Greek head, and several Buddhas from the Far East. On the left side of the bookcase stood the Egyptian warrior goddess Neith, a figure Freud found especially fascinating. The effect of all the antique art and the couch with its pillows and complexly colored rugs, like a barge for a journey through remote spirit realms, was to make the consulting room look like a shaman's lair. It was a mystical space, haunted by the past and alive with promises of revelation.

The study, next door to the consulting room where Freud lay, was the place where Freud wrote his books and essays and talked with visitors, often far into the night. This room too teemed with antiquities and also held Freud's library, about twenty-five hundred books. The volumes were in English, which Freud read and spoke fluently, in Italian and French and Spanish, as well as in German. They covered almost every conceivable subject, including religion, anthropology, and history. The library was full of literary works, with books by Goethe and Schiller, whose styles he greatly admired, as well as by Shakespeare and Milton and Mark Twain. Freud had collected numerous volumes on archaeology, which he followed with a passion; he once said that he had read more archaeological studies than works of psychology, which is entirely likely. Freud did not think much of psychology until he himself intervened in the field.

On the crammed bookshelves, Freud had posed photographs of some of the women in his life. Freud and Martha stopped having sex after the birth of their last child, Anna, and Freud became a grand celibate, though a celibate intensely steeped in eros. Freud displayed a picture of Lou Andreas-Salomé, the most notorious woman in the intellectual world of nineteenth-

and early-twentieth-century Europe. Rilke and Nietzsche had both courted Lou, and Nietzsche, who did not generally think much of women, went so far as to ask Lou to marry him. Lou eventually became a disciple of Freud's and an analyst as well. Of Princess Marie Bonaparte, Freud had two photographs. "Our Princess," as Freud often called her, was a descendant of Napoleon, and like Lou had become a practicing analyst. It was to the princess that Freud had addressed his most famous query: "The great question which has never been answered," Freud said to her, "and which I have not yet been able to answer, despite my thirty years of research into the feminine soul, is 'What does a woman want?'" The third member of Freud's erotic trinity was the Parisian singer and actress Yvette Guilbert, another beauty, famously painted by Toulouse-Lautrec. Freud, who did not often go out, always did what he could to attend her concerts when she came to Vienna.

The center of the study was Freud's desk, where he usually sat after a day of seeing patients, smoking—for he could not think without his cigars—and writing his essays and his books in longhand. At the desk was a strange modernist chair—it looks like a homunculus—designed for Freud by Felix Augenfeld. When he read at the desk, Freud had the habit of slinging his leg over the side of the chair and twisting himself around corkscrew-style.

On top of the desk would no doubt have been the manuscript of Freud's book on Moses, which he had been struggling for a long time to finish. Some years before, Freud had written a brief essay—its first publication was oddly anonymous—about Michelangelo's sculpture of the prophet. It was clear from the essay that Freud had some vital, but still undefined, connection with Moses that he wanted to work out. Now he was about two thirds of the way through his book, which was as bold and speculative a piece of work as he had ever attempted. Freud had spent his career saying things that the public did not want to hear, but perhaps nothing he had published was as potentially inflammatory as this volume—he liked to think of it as his "historical novel." He wondered if he would ever be able to finish this strange project, which might serve as something like an intellectual last will and testament for Freud, and for psychoanalysis.

On the front of the desk, facing Freud like a chorus when he sat there, were thirty-five or so more figurines, perhaps the ones that inspired him most. They varied in size from the height of Freud's fountain pen, which he employed constantly—during the good times, Freud often wrote for four or five hours a day—to the size of a large wineglass from one of the family cupboards, which he would hardly have used at all; Freud was abstemious, and in fact highly suspicious of intoxication, whether from alcohol, religion, or romantic love. Here Egyptian figures predominate: Osiris, Isis, Neith. Few cultures were more mysterious, their secrets harder to crack, than Egypt's, and that fact drew Freud's intense interest. Behind the desk, was an urn, a south Italian bell krater, from the fourth century B.C., depicting the god Dionysus, which in time would hold Freud's ashes.

\*     \*     \*

When the Nazis arrived at the door, Martha did not feel it necessary to summon her husband from his rooms. She was prepared to deal with the intruders on her own.

Martha and Sigmund had by now been married for over fifty years. She had raised six children, attended them in their many illnesses, guided them through personal crises, and created a smoothly running domestic sanctum, where the Professor—as almost everyone who knew and admired Freud called him—went about his intellectual business unbothered. Martha was highly organized and punctual, rare traits in relaxed Vienna; her house was always clean; the meals came on time. She had been just barely pretty as a girl—Freud informed her once that she had no claims on beauty—and now was stout, rather bland in appearance, and deliberate in all she did. Martha lived to make Freud's work possible, but as to what that work was, she had virtually no idea. She read a little for pleasure—but only after dinner, when the day's chores were done—and never entered into intellectual conversation with her husband. That was the domain of his male friends, of Anna, and sometimes too of Martha's sister, Minna, who had more aptitude for such things.

After asking the Nazis to deposit their rifles in the umbrella stand, Martha asked them if they might care to sit down. This too they refused. As the Nazis began to search the house, Martha went off, fetched the household money, and placed it on the dining room table. "Won't the gentlemen help themselves?" she suggested, and this time the gentlemen complied. They also, it appears, got the passports of the entire Freud family.

Anna Freud, seeing that the household money wasn't going to be enough for the Nazis, escorted them to the safe and removed the contents, six thousand Austrian schillings. The raiders fell on it quickly and began splitting it up. All was going according to the Nazis' design, but then, as Ernest Jones tells it, something unexpected happened.

From his sanctum at the back of the apartment came Sigmund Freud. He tottered into the front rooms, bent and frail, and he looked at the Nazis. Or, more precisely, he gave them a version of the stare that he had used time upon time to put his antagonists in disarray. It was the stare that he'd employed to respond to bitter criticism of his work and the stare he'd used to extinguish flare-ups of rebellion among his followers. It was the stare that he used when, a psychoanalytic session completed, the patient issued a disparaging or a discouraged remark. Freud aimed his stare at the Nazis and, the story goes, they scattered like mice.

Ernest Jones refers to the stare as a look of Old Testament rebuke and Freud's look that afternoon perhaps was akin to the one that Moses gave to the Jews when he came down from Sinai with the commandments in his hands and saw them worshipping the golden calf. Freud believed that Michelangelo's statue depicted the prophet at precisely that moment. The statue was about prohibition and power. But it was about power of a contained sort: in Freud's interpretation, Moses never throws down the tablets in rage. He provides an image of contained, sublimated anger.

After the Nazis had gone, Freud asked Martha how much they had taken. When Martha told him, Freud, never at a loss, replied, "Hmmm, I have never gotten so much for a single visit."

Freud's American friends were now rallying around him. On the day the Nazis searched his home and the press, John Wiley, the American chargé d'affaires in Vienna, aware of the threat to all Viennese Jews, sent a cable to Cordell Hull, the American secretary of state. "Fear Freud, despite age and illness, in danger." Hull not only sent a copy of the message off to William Bullitt, Freud's collaborator on the Wilson book, in Paris, but he also spoke to President Roosevelt about the situation. The president of the United States then took the time to learn that Freud would be well received in Paris, by Princess Bonaparte, if the French would only issue him a visa. Roosevelt ensured that Hull sent a message to Hugh Robert Wilson, who was the American ambassador to Germany. The message read, in part, "Wiley reported in a telegram from Vienna yesterday that he fears that Dr. Freud despite age and illness is in danger. The President has instructed me to ask you to take the matter up personally and informally with the appropriate officials of the German Government and desires you to express the hope that arrangements may be made by the appropriate authorities so that Dr. Freud and his family may be permitted to leave Vienna." Soon Cordell Hull knew that Freud's house had been invaded, his money stolen, and his passport confiscated, which only caused the Americans to step up their efforts to help.

Ernest Jones was as active as the American diplomats in the struggle to assure Freud's safety during the early days of the Anschluss. Jones—who had shown up at the Verlag to try to assist Martin, and then later saw the Nazis scurrying in disarray at Berggasse 19—was, aside from Anna, Freud's closest disciple. In his photographs, Jones cuts a rather elegant figure; he can look like a smooth Chicago gangster, one of Capone's lieutenants. He had a determined, manly face, with a prominent nose, and brought with him an aura of businesslike capability that seemed almost American. Early in his career, Jones had to leave England, where he was born, because he was accused of indecent behavior with child patients. Jones, for his part, argued that they were projecting their own fantasies onto him. From England, Jones went to Toronto and began to lecture on psychoanalysis. In 1911, he contributed to founding the American Psychoanalytic Association. Two years later, Jones returned to England and began practicing analysis.

Freud never had a more loyal follower than Ernest Jones. Though he disagreed with Freud on one or two matters, saliently on female sexuality, Jones invested himself completely in Freud's genius. Jones was a superb organizer, excellent at putting together conferences and at getting psychoanalytical work translated and published. But as Jones admitted time after time, he was not an original thinker. He defended Freud; he elaborated Freud's ideas, but he had little of his own to add. He seemed to want to guard Freud in the way that Huxley, Darwin's bulldog, guarded the intellectual legacy of the great theorist of evolution. Jones was constantly letting Freud know who was king and who was merely a servant to the cause. In a letter to Freud he wrote that "the originality-complex is not strong with me; my ambition is rather to know, to be 'behind the scenes,' and 'in the know,' rather than *to find out*. I realize that I have very little talent for originality; any talent I have lies rather in the direction of being able to see perhaps quickly what others point out: no doubt that also has its uses in the world . . . To me work is like a woman bearing a child; to men like you, I suppose it is more like the male fertilization." Then Jones, true to form, apologized for the style of his genuflection. "That is crudely expressed," he said, "but I think you will understand what I mean." Jones was tireless in Freud's cause; he was tireless in general. Having fulfilled his duties as Freud's intellectual defender, he found time to write a treatise on one of his favorite diversions, ice-skating. (In it, he recommends practicing in one's bedroom, surrounded by an ample supply of cushions.)

There were few people now in Vienna who could do more for Freud than Ernest Jones. But if Freud were to survive the occupation, he needed help not only with the Nazis, but also in overcoming his own feelings. When Jones sat down with Freud after the invasion of the Verlag and of Berggasse 19 and began to talk with him about leaving Vienna, it became clear that Freud was determined to stay. Jones insisted that Freud was not alone in the world, that there were many people who cared for him and who badly wanted him to live. "Alone," Freud answered. "Ah, if I were only alone I should long ago have done with life." Freud was sick of living for other people; he was tired and might not at all mind making an end to things. He told Jones that he could never travel; that he could not manage to make his way onto a railway compartment; and that, moreover, no country would be likely to take him. Jones countered that France might and that England probably would. Freud, pushed to the limit, told Jones that if he left Vienna, it would be much like the captain of a ship abandoning his post. Hearing that, Jones told the story of the second officer of the *Titanic*, a man named Lightoller. Lightoller was blown to the surface of the ocean when the boiler exploded on the ship and accordingly survived the wreck. He was interrogated afterward and asked, "At what moment did you leave the ship?" He answered, "I never left the ship, Sir; she left me." So Austria had detonated and ceased to exist. Freud would not be leaving Austria; Austria had left Freud.

Maybe. Maybe after a lifetime of Freud telling Jones what to do and (by and large) what to think, Jones finally took charge. Stranger things have happened. But it's much more likely that the events of Tuesday, March 22, which was to be one of the worst days in Freud's life, were the main influence on Freud's plans. By that bad day, though, the day that he almost lost Anna, Freud would have another ally, Ernest Jones's equal and perhaps more than that, on the scene.

This was Princess Marie Bonaparte, the woman Freud referred to as "our Princess," and whose two photographs were on display in his study. The princess was a descendant of Napoleon, a great-granddaughter of his brother Lucien. She was also married to Prince George, who was the brother of Constantine I, the king of the Hellenes, and first cousin to Christian X, king of Denmark. The princess was extremely rich and knew everyone in Europe, or at least everyone of a certain class. In her youth she had been a spectacular beauty, with many lovers.

Now in middle age, she was an impeccably handsome woman and relentless in her devotion to Freud. He had analyzed the princess, spending two hours a day with her, over a two-month period. Freud hadn't been able to solve the princess's sexual problems—she described herself as "frigid"—but by the end of the analysis, she had developed the power to work in a focused, productive way: the "energy devil," Freud came to call her. She became an analyst herself, wrote multiple papers and books, including a detailed study of Edgar Allan Poe, corresponded constantly with Freud, sent him money to bail out the always precarious Verlag, and generally used all her resources in the interest of the Professor and his cause.

The princess was smitten by Freud from the first time that she met him. She told him that he combined the powers of Einstein and Pasteur. "Do you really think so?" said Freud. "I'm very flattered. But I can't share your opinion. Not that I'm modest, no. I have a high opinion of what I have discovered, not of myself. The great discoverers are not necessarily great minds. Who has changed the world more than Christopher Columbus? Now who was he? An adventurer."

Freud was taken with the princess as well. He informed her that she was bisexual and could see the world through a man's eyes as well as a woman's. "Lou Andreas-Salomé," he told the princess flirtatiously, comparing her to the most seductive woman in the intellectual life of nineteenth-century Europe, "is a mirror—she has neither your virility, nor your sincerity, nor your style." The princess, Freud proclaimed, had "no prudishness whatsoever." Then Freud said, "Nobody understands you better than I. But in my private life, I am a petit bourgeois. . . . I would not like one of my sons to get a divorce or one of my daughters to have a liaison." Later, the princess recalled, "I dared to say to Freud that he must have a supernormal sexual development." "Of this," Freud told her, "you will not learn anything; perhaps not so super."

About his financial desires, Freud was much more forthcoming than about his erotic ones. He told the princess how he had lost his entire life savings in 1918: 150,000 crowns invested in Austrian state bonds, and 100,000 in life insurance. "He too little, I too much," the princess wrote in her journal, brooding on Freud's money woes. "Would he keep me [as a patient, as a friend] if I were ruined?"

Freud certainly would have. He respected the princess, liked her, and was drawn to her erotically, in his own peculiar way. The only occasions he seems to have shown prolonged impatience with her was when she insisted on having a pair of operations to move her clitoris closer to her vagina, the better to achieve arousal. (The operations did not work.) A few days after the Anschluss, the princess came to Vienna, took up residence at the Greek legation, and began eating meals with the Freud family. Like Ernest Jones, she was ready to do absolutely anything that could be done to protect Freud from the Nazis. And in 1938, when the Nazis were just making their way to international power, a figure like the princess could actually intimidate them. Her money and her lineage impressed them and she could, at least for the present, stand up to them with relative impunity.

On March 17, the day that the princess arrived at Berggasse

19, Hugh Robert Wilson reported that he had been in touch with German state secretary Ernst von Weizsäcker of the Foreign Office and had let them know about his concern for Freud. "I told him that I had received a telegram from Washington informing me that Doctor Freud, now an old man and ill, was desirous of leaving Vienna with his family for Paris, where he has friends who could take care of him. I added that he was widely and well known in the United States and that a permission accorded to him and his family to leave could not but create a favorable impression upon American opinion." Weizsäcker told the ambassador that he would do what he could.

But the person who may have had the most to do with Freud's eventual fate in Vienna was neither Jones nor the princess, nor any of the members of the American diplomatic corps, but a much more enigmatic figure, Doctor Anton Sauerwald. After the Anschluss, the Nazis appointed what they ingenuously called a "commissioner" for every Jewish business in Vienna, and Sauerwald was the man responsible for Freud and for the psychoanalytic publishing house. Sauerwald was thirty-five years old when he took charge of liquidating the Verlag's assets and turning them over to the Nazi government. He had been a student of science, medicine, and law at the University of Vienna and had graduated in 1929. Soon afterward, he went into business for himself, opening up a chemical laboratory in Vienna.

In the mid-thirties, Sauerwald played two roles. The Austrian government hired him to investigate and report on the numerous terrorist bombs going off in and around Vienna, many of them planted by the then-outlawed Nazi Party. (Sometimes as many as forty bombs a day went off.) This Sauerwald did with remarkable success: he was very quick to submit reports on the kind and amount of explosives used. Over time, he gained a stellar reputation with the Viennese police force for the accuracy of his reports. But this was only so because Sauerwald was manufacturing the explosives for the Nazis in his own laboratory. He built the bombs in the afternoon and reported on them the next morning.

When Sauerwald first took on the oversight of the Verlag, he comported himself like a fierce and dedicated Nazi. He insulted the staff, and in particular the gentiles who worked for the press, asking them again and again what they were doing consorting with Jewish swine. Sauerwald swaggered, fired invective, but in time he grew bored. And then he did something unexpected: he sat down and began to read Freud's books and papers at the Verlag. In them, he discovered some things that surprised him a great deal.

On Tuesday, March 22, the Gestapo came to Berggasse 19 and took Anna. They were persuaded that the International Psychoanalytic Association was a front for some antifascist political movement. Surely the person they most wanted to arrest and question was Freud. Anna told them that it was not possible for her father to leave the apartment building because he was ill and too frail to manage the stairs. She was willing to go in his place and to answer any questions the Gestapo might have about the association, as was Marie Bonaparte, who was also there in the apartment that day. But even though the princess asked to be arrested, the Nazis refused to take her, perhaps not wanting to risk the publicity that would come their way from arresting a royal personage. They were willing, though, to take Anna. Before she left with them, Max Schur, Freud's personal physician, gave her Veronal, a poison that would have allowed her to kill herself if the Nazis decided to torture her. Freud did not know about the Veronal, and if he did, he would no doubt have been enraged at Schur. But mostly now he was furious at the Nazis. All over Vienna, Jews were disappearing: some were killed, many were taken off to the concentration camp at Dachau.

The first thing that Anna did was to keep her head. Her brother Martin remembered her leaving with complete composure. He recalled "Anna being driven off in an open car escorted by four heavily armed S.S. men. Her situation was perilous; but far from showing fear, or even much interest, she sat in the car as a woman might sit in a taxi on her way to enjoy a shopping expedition." Soon Anna was being questioned at Gestapo headquarters.

No one now knows for certain what Anna said or did not say in her encounter with the Nazis. But she had observed her father well over the years, and he had provided her—just as he had provided himself—with something close to a perfect cover story to use in case of this kind of emergency. When the officers asked her if her father was political or subversive, or if any of his ideas might be an affront to the Reich, Anna had a whole grammar and vocabulary of response at her disposal. This language of exculpation was both radically misleading and absolutely true.

My father, she might have said, has always involved himself in science. He has labored for years in conditions as close to laboratory conditions as he can find in order to draw valid conclusions about the dynamics of human behavior. He has tried to write up these conclusions in dispassionate, clear language. Some of the conclusions, to be sure, are provisional, but, as he has himself said many times, he is waiting for further developments in biochemistry to confirm, or perhaps to modify, what he has learned.

Moreover, my father is a medical doctor with impeccable credentials. He is licensed to practice, to heal the sick, and he attends particularly to the sick no one else can help. He has taught at the university. He holds the rank of Professor.

As to day-to-day politics, they hardly interest my father at all. He reads the newspaper as others do; he follows events. But he is far too old, at eighty-one, and he is far too sick—his jaw has been operated on time and again for cancer—to be a rabble-rousing Austrian nationalist. When the Great War came in 1914, he dutifully sent his sons off to fight; he hoped for their safety and he hoped for the victory of Austria-Hungary and of its ally, Germany.

Granted, my father is a Jew, as I of course am myself. But Papa's commitment to Judaism has never consisted of much more than going to the B'nai Brith every couple of weeks and playing a spirited game of Tarok with other old men. He is not a Zionist and he is no Jewish rebel. And as his writings will show you, should you chance to read them, he is anything but a

Communist. Though it is true, my father will never deny his Jewish heritage. He is above all things an honest man. When he is healthy, he leads a regular life: breakfast and his patients; dinner, his walk, his beard trim, his paper, more patients; supper with the family, then work, work, late into the night.

My father has worked ceaselessly his whole life and over time this work, which is, as I say, of an impeccably scientific nature, has won him many admirers and many friends, some of whom do not lack influence in the world. He is an aged, peaceful, and overall harmless man, but, with all respect due, one would not lightly disturb the tranquility of what are almost certainly his final years. For such a disturbance would not be without consequences.

At home, waiting for his daughter, Freud paced the floor and smoked one forbidden cigar after the next. He did not speak; he was too distressed to utter a word, and he knew that nothing he could possibly say there in the front room of Berggasse 19, with his family around him, could have been of any actual help. Freud was an instinctive pragmatist in his external life: if something did not advance his cause, he did not do it. So there was nothing to say. But surely during those bad hours, Freud thought a great deal. Anna was so much to him. She was his intellectual confidante: Freud never wrote down an idea now that he not had tried out on Anna, discussed with her. She was his hope for the future. She was also his nurse and in this their relations were painfully intimate. Anna was the one who helped him take out the enormous prosthesis—"the monster" was what they called it—that sat in his mouth like a stone. She knew the harsh secrets of his old man's body, blighted by disease, and still loved him without qualification. Could he live in the world without her any longer than old Lear could after he lost Cordelia? Would Anna come no more—never, never, never?

At Nazi headquarters, Anna was no doubt telling the most blandly respectable story she could about her father—and he had left her plenty of resources to do so. But she might also have been thinking more candidly about the bearing her father's work actually had on the Nazis.

My father, she might have thought, as the dull questions came and came again, knows you far better than you know yourself. For years he has been writing about your ridiculous leader—the half monster, half clown—and all the others who've come before and all who will come later in his image. (For the hunger for this kind of man will last for all time.) He knows why you need the leader the way you do. He sees the God-shaped hole in your heart. And here is the strange thing: he sympathizes with the need. He knows it not to be alien but all too human.

To him, Hitler is not a special invention of the Germans, not their unique contribution to the world. My father understands that your Hitler is what everyone, man and woman and child, pines after. He is the answer to almost every human question, just as he is the destruction of everything that makes being human worthwhile. All the fiery joy you felt when you saw the glorious führer ride in state through Vienna—the apotheosis of the will—my father has foreseen. You are nothing new and wonderfully rebellious, as you imagine, but part of the endless recurrence of the same sad hunger for Truth, the Center, the King, and the Law. By understanding as much and making it plain for all who care to see it, my father is the one who has brought something new into the world.

It's possible that there was some intervention on Anna's behalf, perhaps help from the American embassy. Anna recalled a phone call that seemed to change the atmosphere. It could have come from the Americans; it could have come from Italy. Edoardo Weiss, an Italian analyst who knew Mussolini, said that Il Duce had intervened personally on Anna's behalf. Four years earlier Freud actually inscribed a book to Mussolini; it was the volume *Why War?* which Freud and Einstein authored together. The dedication ran as follows: "From an old man who greets in the Ruler the Hero of Culture." (In all probability what Freud was referring to in the dedication were the archaeological excavations Il Duce was sponsoring in Italy, which Freud, as a student of past civilizations and past architecture, greatly valued.) It seems clear that if Mussolini actually read the book, he was not taking it to heart. In all likelihood, it was Anna herself who worked her way out of the Nazis' trap. More and more the Nazis were realizing how little the world cared about what was happening in Austria and how much they could do as they pleased. In significant matters they were becoming ever freer to make up their own minds.

At home Freud walked and walked, smoked and smoked. At noon he could not eat. He did not acknowledge anyone and said nothing. When Anna finally walked in the door early that evening, exhausted from her ordeal, the restrained Freud did something, we're told, that almost no one had ever seen him do. Sigmund Freud showed emotion; the great stoic may even have wept.

Perhaps it was during the black days around the time that Anna was arrested that Freud went furthest in considering suicide. His thoughts about suicide took two forms. The first was quite overt: the whole family might do what a number of Jews throughout Germany and Austria were doing, administering poison to themselves (Freud was a medical doctor after all; he knew something about making the matter as painless as possible) and so leaving the world that Hitler and the Germans were creating. But though Freud considered this option, he finally came out strongly against it. When Anna brought the matter up, Freud answered, with exasperation, "Why? Because they would like us to?"

Freud might also have committed a different kind of suicide, simply by staying where he was, refusing to budge. Freud and his entire family could easily have been taken off to Dachau and murdered. Yet Freud, old and sick as he was, could nonetheless be spurred on by Jones and by the princess, by the future of the psychoanalytical movement and by the prospect of one more battle in his long war with tyranny. The Moses book was still unfinished; the crucial third chapter, where Freud could add an installment to his critique of perverse authority and its uncanny appeal, still had to be finished.

There was also the fact that Freud had a very clear idea of what suicide was: he had written perceptively about what drove people to what Hamlet, the literary character who probably fascinated him the most, calls "self-slaughter." In "Mourning and Melancholia," Freud suggests that the main cause of suicide is an internal imbalance in the psyche. The over-I has become too strong, at the expense of the poor, depleted ego. The internal agent of authority rails at the self for its manifold inadequacies. But only when the ego is weak and unable to defend itself does it surrender to the over-I and do away with itself. If Freud were to commit suicide, overtly by taking poison, or covertly by staying put and letting the Nazis do as they would, he would be showing weakness. He would be showing that his sense of self, or ego, his confidence in who he was and what he had achieved, was not strong enough to fight against whatever forces were telling him that life, *his life*, was not worth living. He would, perhaps, be surrendering to the Nazi version of who Sigmund Freud was—a troublemaking Jew who'd written noxious books. "After the destruction of the Temple in Jerusalem by Titus," Freud told his Viennese colleagues at the meeting on March 13, the day before Hitler arrived in Vienna, "Rabbi Jochanan ben Sakkai asked for permission to open a school at Jabneh for the study of Torah. We are going to do the same. We are, after all, used to persecution by our history, tradition and some of us by personal experience." When he told his colleagues this, Freud was still not entirely determined to leave. But after the episode with Anna, Freud seems to have become convinced that the fight wasn't over and that he had something more to do in the world. Now, though, it was a matter of getting out.

On March 28, 1938, Freud and his family received good news. Ernest Jones had been in England, working on Freud's behalf, and he had gotten permission from the British government not only for Freud and his family but for others in the world of Viennese psychoanalysis to leave Vienna and to emigrate to England. In all, there could be eighteen adults and six children in the party—the number that Freud had insisted upon. Jones achieved this near miracle partly through the influence of his brother-in-law, William Trotter, who was the secretary of the Royal Society. Through Trotter, Jones got himself an introduction to the society's president, the physicist Sir William Bragg. Jones met with Sir William on March 23; Jones was taken aback, he said, to find out how naïve a distinguished scientist could be. When Jones told Sir William about Freud's plight, the scientist asked, "Do you really think the Germans are unkind to the Jews?" Yet whatever the limits of his moral imagination, Sir William immediately gave Jones a letter to Sir Samuel Hoare, the home secretary, endorsing Freud's case for immigration. (Jones already knew Hoare slightly: they belonged to the same ice-skating club.) Jones met with a member of Hoare's staff and two days later was able to write in his diary, "Saw Hoare's Secretary, A.S. Hutchinson, re Immigration. Success! First rain for 24 days. Amazing March."

England was willing to take Freud and his family but that did not mean the Nazis would be willing to let them go; there were still obstacles in the path. Most of the democratic nations were anything but hospitable to Jewish refugees—even those in a position to pay a high price for their freedom, as Freud and his family, with the help of Princess Bonaparte, were ready to do. Now, the Freuds would need to get the Nazis to issue an *Unbedenklichkeitserklärung,* a "statement of no impediment," which said that the government had no more claims to make on the family. To obtain the statement, the Freuds would have to pay a very large refugee tax, which would require Freud to liquidate many of his assets. Yet whether that, or anything else, would be enough for the Nazis was still open to question.

The Nazis had been aware of Freud's pernicious influence for some time. On May 10, 1933, young Nazis had broken into the main libraries of Germany and hauled out the works that Goebbels detested most. They brought the books out by carloads and set them on fire, chanting "*Brenne* Karl Marx! *Brenne* Sigmund Freud!" They burned Heine and Remarque, Mann, Zweig, and Gide. "This is a strong, great and symbolic act," Goebbels declared. "Never, as today, have young men had the right to cry out; studies are thriving, spirits awakening, oh, century, it is a joy to live!" Into the flaming pile went what were to become some of Heinrich Heine's most famous lines, "Wherever they burn books, sooner or later they will burn human beings also."

Before the Nazis took control in Austria, Martin Freud had shipped copies of his father's works away from the Verlag to Switzerland and presumed safety. But the Nazis found the record of the shipment and demanded that the books be sent back at the Verlag's expense. They were, and naturally, the Nazis destroyed them.

In the meantime, as the Freuds negotiated with the Nazi officials, Doctor Anton Sauerwald was growing impatient. The Freud case was moving slowly enough and his own political situation was still unresolved. During the days before the Anschluss, Doctor Sauerwald wore his Fatherland Front pin on the outside of his lapel, in apparent fealty to Schuschnigg and the party in power, while he wore his swastika on the inside, waiting for the great day to come. Sauerwald was devoted to playing both sides of the game, much as he was when he provided the Nazi terrorists with bombs *and* investigated their attacks on behalf of the police. Now, with the Nazis fully in power, Sauerwald was at a disadvantage because he could not claim the highly esteemed status of "illegal Nazi." That is, he had not made himself a member of the party before the Anschluss took place. The "illegal Nazis" were the ones who got preferment: chances for office, economic privileges, enhanced opportunities to loot their Jewish neighbors. Sauerwald applied to the party after the Anschluss, but was put on a waiting list because active recruitment was over. So Sauerwald sat and hoped for good news from party headquarters.

While he waited, Sauerwald read the works of Sigmund Freud. Virtually all that Freud had written on psychoanalysis was there to peruse, and as the long days passed, Doctor Sauerwald immersed himself. He had reason to be curious about Freud, not only because of Freud's notoriety in Vienna, but also because he had been a student of one of Freud's good friends, a Professor Herzig, who recommended Freud highly. So now Sauerwald was not only plunging into Freud's work, but also reading through all the private papers on file at the Verlag, among them papers that Martin Freud should have sent down through the intricate sewer system of Vienna.

During the days of March and April as he himself waited for news, Freud was not idle either. He was working on the Moses book, giving the project his most alert, composed hour each day. "Moses won't let go of my imagination," he had informed Arnold Zweig in a letter three years earlier, and it was still true. He would eventually tell Ernest Jones that his obligation to get the book written tormented him "like a ghost not laid." One of the things that drove him on was that in the character of Moses, Freud believed he could find the secrets of Jewish identity. "Several years ago," he observed, "I started asking myself how the Jews acquired their particular character, and following my usual custom I went back to the earliest beginnings. I did not get far. I was astounded to find that already the first so to speak embryonic experience of the race, the influence of the man Moses and the exodus from Egypt, conditioned the entire further development up to the present day." What Freud does not mention here, though, is that, to his mind, understanding Jewish character is integral to understanding human character and its promise for the future, however precarious such promise might be. For the Jews had given the world a great gift and also a great danger: the belief in an invisible god.

But during those weeks, Freud was also devoting time to

another literary pursuit. He and Anna were collaborating on a translation, from French to German, of Marie Bonaparte's book about her dog, Topsy. The book, which the princess published in 1937, was called *Topsy, chow-chow au poil d'or* (Topsy, the golden-haired chow). Freud was also a dog lover. Like the princess, he was devoted to chows, long-haired, handsome, highly intelligent dogs—"little lion-like creatures," as Freud's patient, the American poet H.D., described them.

Freud's first chow was Lun-Yug, who he acquired from Dorothy Burlingham, Anna's friend, in 1928. But after only fifteen months, Lun-Yug dropped out of sight in the train station in Salzburg while being taken to Vienna. A few days later, she turned up dead on the tracks. In March of 1930, Freud acquired his most famous chow, Jo-Fi (who was Lun-Yug's sister). Jo-Fi was Freud's constant companion, sitting at the foot of his consultation couch while analysis was in session, panting away rhythmically. Sometimes Jo-Fi received more attention than the patient. Said H.D.: "I was annoyed at the end of my session as Yofi would wander about and I felt the Professor was more interested in Yofi than he was in my story." Many patients noticed that the combination of Freud's cigar smoke and Jo-Fi's dog smell made the consulting room a place with a singular and memorable, though not entirely agreeable, scent. Bad smells or not, Freud adored his dog: after Freud underwent an especially painful surgery, he wrote to Marie Bonaparte, "I wished you could have seen with me what sympathy Jofi shows me during these hellish days, as if she understood everything." Freud's deep affection for dogs sometimes resembles that of his great precursor, Schopenhauer, who said that he would rather converse with his dogs than he would with most people.

Like Schopenhauer's, Freud's dog obsession probably arose in part from a mild misanthropy. (Hitler's dog obsession signaled a misanthropy that was not so mild.)

On January 11, 1937, Jo-Fi entered the hospital to have a pair of ovarian cysts removed. She came through the operation well enough, but on January 14, she died unexpectedly of a heart attack. Freud was crushed—"one cannot easily get over seven years of intimacy," he wrote to Arnold Zweig—and on the following day he acquired another chow, Lün. Originally Lün had belonged to him, but when it was clear that Jo-Fi could not deal with a rival, Freud packed Lün off to Dorothy Burlingham. In March of 1938, when the Nazis invaded, the beloved Jo-Fi was gone, and Lün reigned supreme in the Freud household. Freud greeted the manuscript of the princess's book about Topsy ("Teaupi" was the dog's formal name) with real delight: "I love it," he said. "It is so movingly genuine and true. It is not an analytical work, of course, but the analyst's thirst for truth and knowledge can be perceived behind this production, too."

About dogs, Freud had a very odd belief: he thought that they were creatures whose natures were entirely pure—untouched by civilization. Speaking of the princess's book, he said, "It really explains why one can love an animal like Topsy (or Jo-Fi) with such extraordinary intensity: affection without ambivalence, the simplicity of a life free from the almost unbearable conflicts of civilization, the beauty of an existence complete in itself. . . . Often when stroking Jo-Fi I have caught myself humming a melody which, unmusical as I am, I can't help recognizing as the aria from *Don Giovanni*: 'The bond of friendship / Unites us both.'"

The princess's book, highly impressionistic, sometimes operatic in style, was not the sort of thing that Freud was generally drawn to read. "Topsy," the princess cries at one point, "the greatest philosopher, strive as he may, will never know the visions which pass through your little golden head." Freud usually preferred his writers as tough, and relatively unadorned, as he was. But Freud adored this book and it was not only because of his affection for the princess and his love for chows, but also because of the story, which is the story of an illness. Like Freud, Topsy has cancer: both are afflicted with tumors on the right sides of their mouths. Like Freud, Topsy has surgery, and is treated, as Freud will be, with roentgen rays and radium. The princess was slightly embarrassed to take her dog to a clinic that was usually for people and dismayed at having to submit Topsy to the fierce regimen. But her love for the dog was so great that she went through with it.

The conclusion of the book is all that the princess—and Freud—might have hoped: Topsy is cured. "She runs along by the sea, inhaling the wind and the storm. Topsy, Topsy little healed dog, looking at you I am prouder to have almost magically prolonged your little life, than if I had written the *Iliad*." Topsy recovers; Topsy is alive and well after her struggle with cancer. She romps in the garden, she smells the ocean: Topsy is reborn. Freud, sitting with Anna in his study, going over their translation of the princess's book, had the chance to think about recovery and even perhaps about resurrection, albeit indirectly. Freud and Anna together, telling the story of Topsy, could brood on the possibility of more life.

"Does Topsy realize that she is being translated?" Freud

asked the princess in a letter. On April 9, the day that Adolf Hitler returned to Vienna to begin building enthusiasm for his upcoming Austrian plebiscite, Sigmund Freud wrote a simple sentence in his journal: "Topsy translation finished."

For Hitler, in early April of 1938, things were going splendidly. His success in Austria had enhanced his popularity even more among the Germans. Middle-class nationalists, who before had their doubts about Hitler, were now wild for him. In the German army, where there had been skepticism about the little corporal, there grew a sense that he was simply too popular to oppose. Though quite a few members of the officers corps believed that he was going to lead them all to ruin, they concluded that there was nothing to be done about it, at least for now. Hitler's speeches were full of celebrations of himself as the man chosen by divine providence to lead Germany's rebirth. He was so confident that he decided to go through with the plebiscite on Austrian unification with Germany that Schuschnigg had scheduled for March 13, and that the invasion canceled. The führer wanted to show the world that what he'd done in Austria was entirely legitimate and that the Austrians had embraced him as the figure of destiny he was.

On April 8, Hitler was back in Linz to campaign for the referendum, and there appeared in the lobby of his hotel, Gustl Kubizek, his best friend (and perhaps his only friend) from the time when he was scraping by in Vienna before the First World War. They had not seen each other for thirty years. The next day, the friends had lunch together at the Weinzinger Hotel and they looked out the window at the Danube and the iron bridge across it, which Hitler had always detested. "That ugly thing, still there!" the führer groaned. "But not much longer, you can be sure of that, Kubizek."

What had happened to Kubizek since the war, Hitler wanted to know. Had he gone on to become a great musician, as he had hoped? Alas, Hitler's old friend was now a town clerk in Eferding, but there was a municipal orchestra and its program was ambitious.

"What, Kubizek," Hitler asked, "you even give symphonies in this little Eferding. But that's marvelous. Which symphonies have you played?"

Kubizek told his former roommate that they performed Schubert's Unfinished, Beethoven's Third, Mozart's *Jupiter* Symphony, and Beethoven's Fifth.

Hitler, whose love for art and music was undiminished, told his old friend that he would do what he could to help the orchestra. And what about Kubizek's personal life? Did he have a family? Gustl now had three boys, all of whom were interested in music.

"So you've got three sons, Kubizek," Hitler sighed. "I have no family. I am alone. But I should like to look after your sons."

Gustl told his old friend everything about his sons, two of whom were, as Hitler fancied himself to be, gifted draftsmen. Hitler listened intently and asked for every detail about the boys.

"I shall make myself responsible for the training of your three sons, Kubizek," Hitler finally said. "I don't want gifted young people to have such a hard time of it as we had. You know best what we had to go through in Vienna. But the worst time came for me later on, after we parted. Young talent must no longer be allowed to perish through sheer poverty. Whenever I can help personally, I do, and all the more when it's a question of your children, Kubizek!"

An hour later, Hitler left his friend and was on his way to Vienna to create the future for Kubizek's sons—whose musical education he did, in fact, arrange—and for the rest of the world besides. Again he was greeted by joyful crowds. The Nazis had transformed Vienna into a giant election theater. The trolleys were covered in red bunting with swastikas in front and on top, and everywhere there were placards proclaiming that Adolf Hitler was the man for Vienna—he creates work and bread. Party headquarters in individual districts were emblazoned with banners and slogans. In the Jewish quarter, Nazi flags flew everywhere and a huge banner shouted out the words "We remain true to the honor of our blood and give our voice to Adolf Hitler."

Saturday, the day before the plebiscite (and the day that Freud and Anna finished the Topsy translation), Hitler and Goebbels faced the crowd in Vienna. "Dr. Goebbels steps onto the balcony," a Nazi newspaper said, "and announces 'Germans, I proclaim the day of the Greater German Reich. Up flags.' Sirens howl. Flags rise on their masts. And the hundreds of thousands stand there with heads bared. Their silence is prayer. If we were asked to shout our joy out loud we could not. The tears running down the cheeks tell our creator infinitely more than storms of joy could say." Later that day, Hitler, comparing himself implicitly to Jesus, told the people how proud he was to have been born in Austria: "I believe that it was God's will to send a boy from here into the Reich, to raise him to be the leader of the nation so as to bring back his homeland into the Reich. Otherwise one would have to doubt God's providence." Close to tears, Hitler cried out to the crowd, "I believed in Germany at the time of its deepest humiliation."

Now it was the time for Austria to believe in Hitler. The next day, Sunday, came the plebiscite: In Austria, 99.73 percent of the voters approved unification. In Germany, 90.02 percent voted *Ja* and 99.8 percent approved Hitler's list of candidates for the new Reichstag. Only 11,281 Austrians voted against Hitler, 4,939 of those in Vienna. "For me," Hitler said, "this is the proudest hour of my life."

Many of the people who witnessed the events in Austria could not believe what they saw before them, an entire nation moving into barbarism. They believed that every monstrous step backward would be the last. And as a result, many of them stayed in Vienna and suffered the consequences. But Freud, again, had suggested why what was happening in Germany and Austria, as well as in Italy and Japan and Spain, might be close to inevitable. Freud, it is true, never applied his reflections to the immediate political situation in front of him, but he must have taken some dark, quiet satisfaction in having anticipated the horrible events at hand so well.

Fascism begins, Freud suggests, with the allure of the leader, the man of a masterly and charismatic nature who appears to be absolutely certain of himself and all that he does. However eccentric, volatile, and strange Hitler may have been in his private life—and he was all of those things—when he stood before a crowd, he was superb at playing the role. Here, finally, was a real man, a true force, all of whose energies flowed in one direction. But for Freud, the crucial question is why exactly the absolute leader should be such an important and, often, a necessary figure for human beings. Why did a figure like Hitler inspire such mad reverence?

At the center of Freud's work lies a fundamental perception: human beings are not unified creatures. Our psyches are not whole, but divided into parts, and those parts are usually in conflict with each other; for Freud the psyche is often in a state of tension that borders on civil war. The "it," or the "id," wants what it wants and does not easily take no for an answer. The over-I, or the superego, the internal agent of authority, often looks harshly upon the id and its manifold wants. The superego, in fact, frequently punishes the self simply for wishing for forbidden things, even if the self does not act on those wishes. Then there is the I, or ego, trying to broker between the it and the over-I, and doing so with the greatest difficulty, in part because both agencies often operate outside the circle of the ego's awareness. And Freud claims that the over-I can be unconscious, just as the it. Then too the "poor ego" must navigate a frequently hostile outside world. It is easy to see how, for Freud, life is best defined as ongoing conflict. In a well-known passage in *The Ego and the Id*, Freud observes that the ego is a "poor creature owing service to three masters and consequently menaced by three dangers: from the external world, from the libido of the id, and from the severity of the super-ego. Three kinds of anxiety correspond to these three dangers, since anxiety is the expression of a retreat from danger."

Humanity, Freud said, has come up with many different solutions to the problem of internal conflict and the pain that it inevitably brings. Many of these solutions, he believed, are best described as forms of intoxication. What the intoxicants generally do is to revise the superego and make it milder, less harsh in its judgments, and so more bearable. We like to have one glass of wine and then two, Freud suggests, because for some reason—he's not quite sure what it is in scientific terms—alcohol relaxes the demands of the over-I. "Why do we not get drunk?" Freud asked in a letter to his fiancée, Martha. The answer that Freud's later work suggests is because the pain that follows the next day is too hard to bear. This pain may not only be caused by the toxicity of alcohol, but also by the angry  reassertion of the superego, which punishes the ego for deposing it and for acting (and thinking and desiring) in such shameful ways the night before.

Falling in love, claims Freud, and a thousand or so years of Western poetry, has a similar effect. Love—romantic love, the full-out passionate variety—allows the ego to be dominated not by the wishes of the demanding over-I, but by the wishes and judgment of the beloved. The beloved supplants the over-I, at least for a while, sheds glorious approval on the lover, and creates a feeling of almost magical well-being. Take a drink or two, take a lover, and suddenly the internal conflict in the psyche abates. A divided being becomes a resolved, unified, and temporarily, happy one. But these forms of inebriation have their built-in limits: after liquor comes the hangover, after love comes marriage.

Freud had no reservations about calling the relationship that crowds forge with an absolute leader erotic. (In this he was seconded by Hitler, who said that in his speeches, he made love to the German masses.) What happens is that the members of the crowd are hypnotized (and that is the word Freud uses) by the leader. The leader takes the place of the over-I, and for a variety of reasons, he stays there. What he offers to individuals is a new psychological dispensation. Where the individual super-ego is inconsistent and often inaccessible because it is unconscious, the collective superego, the leader, is clear and absolute in his values. He is associated with things that are permanent: with God, or destiny, or with absolute truth. He satisfies the human hunger to rise above time and chance and join with something more powerful and more enduring than merely transient, mortal enterprises. By promulgating one code, one set of values, the leader wipes away the differences between people, differences that can be a serious source of anxiety. Now everyone in Germany—and, the plebiscite over, in Austria as well—loves the fatherland, believes in the folk, blames the Jews, and has a grand imperial mission to fulfill.

But the leader is also permissive. Where the original superego prohibited violence and theft and destruction, the new super-ego, the leader, enjoins those things, though under certain prescribed conditions. So the day that Hitler arrived in Vienna, gentile Viennese, who had been so urbanely tolerant, could turn on their Jewish neighbors—and do so with a good conscience. When they broke into Jewish apartments and stole, when they trashed Jewish shops, when they made Jewish children scrub the sidewalks, they were doing two things at once: they were satisfying their most aggressive urges, and they were helping create a society based on higher values, one where the Jews were no longer in control. They did everything with a sense of righteous conviction: they were operating in accord with the new superego. All the energies that had been bound internally by normal human ambivalence could now be released. The anxiety that arises from both wanting to do something forbidden and not wanting to do it could be discharged. The result was a tremendous collective burst of passion—along with corresponding barbarism. Thus on the streets of Vienna, one saw in the new-formed Nazi mass exactly what Freud, in *Group Psychology*, predicted one would: "the weakness of intellectual ability, the lack of emotional restraint, the incapacity for moderation and delay, the inclination to exceed every limit in the expression of emotion and to work it off completely in the form of action."

Freud was no historicist and did not reflect on how some historical moments are more conducive to this sort of explosion than others. But it follows that when the world seems most disordered, incoherent, and inconsistent, and when humanity seems to be drowning in its own confusion, then the advent of a figure who can satisfy both the need for order *and* the need for indulgence is especially sharp. It was now such a time in Vienna. Just so, the last decades in Germany had been a time when Marx's phrase applied surpassingly well: all that was once solid had melted into air. As the historian Alan Bullock puts it, "Between 1918 and 1923, the German people . . . suffered a cumulative series of . . . shocks: defeat after the heavy losses of the war, Versailles, reparations, the collapse of the monarchy, revolution, near-civil war, and inflation. All the fears and insecurity of the postwar period were revived and made the harder to bear by the brief interlude of recovery, now [with the onset of the Depression] seen to be a treacherous illusion. In the early 1930s, millions of German men and women felt like survivors of an earthquake starting to put their homes together again, only to see the fragile framework of their lives cracking and crumbling around them a second time. In such circumstances human beings lose their bearings and entertain extravagant fears and fantastic hopes."

Freud tells us that we all long for inner peace. He says at one point in *The Ego and the Id* that it's probable that one of the reasons we need to withdraw regularly to sleep is that the work of maintaining the tensions within, among the various agencies of the psyche, is so taxing. When we sleep and dream, those tensions relax a little. But we want, quite understandably and also dangerously, to have the inner tensions dissolve not just at night but through all of our waking life as well. And we find dozens of ways to accomplish this. When we hear a joke or tell one, our forbidden desires break through, if only for the briefest moment. When we contemplate something beautiful, the tumult inside can still itself too. When we fall in love, when we play with a child, or (as Freud so much loved to do) pet a favorite dog, we experience a measure of inebriation. We get a little high. But that of course only sharpens our appetites to find a way to stay there, to get high and not come down.

We long, in particular, to replace our inconsistent, inscrutable over-I with something clearer and ultimately more permissive. We want a strong man with a simple doctrine that accounts for our sufferings, identifies our enemies, focuses our energies, and lets us indulge our forbidden desires with the best of conscience. This sort of man, appearing at the right moment, mouthing the right deceptions, rams life full of meaning and gives us, more enduringly than wine and even than love, a sense of being whole. Suddenly we are not at war within ourselves. The sense of anxiety departs and we feel free. The man who delivers this kind of intoxication must, as Freud says, appear completely masterful. He must seem to have perfect confidence, to need no one, and to be entirely self-sufficient. Sometimes this man will evoke a god as the source and guarantor of his authority, sometimes not. But in whatever form he arrives— whether he is Hitler, or Stalin, or Mao, or any one of their ilk past or to come—he will promise to deliver people from their confusion and to dispense unity and purpose, where before there had been chaos.

Easter Sunday, April 17, was the fifty-second anniversary of the beginning of Freud's practice as a psychoanalyst and it was a sad occasion, not least because Freud, who often thought of himself first as a healer, could no longer see patients. After the Anschluss, he dismissed his last two, finding it impossible to practice psychoanalysis because of the disturbances around him. "When the conscious mind is troubled," he said, "one cannot be interested in the unconscious mind." Freud had much to look back on in his career as an analyst but he must have done so now with some pain. Patients came to him, often in despair, because they were suffering and no one could help them. Faced with the neuroses, the average physician simply threw his hands up. Men and women who could not eat, who could not walk outside into the city square, who could not bear to be in a room with their mothers or fathers, who were so committed to ritual behaviors that they had no life beyond their sad obsessive acts—such people and many more like them made their way to Freud. He did what he could to acquaint them with the complexities of their desires and the strengths of their inhibitions. He told them stories about themselves that disturbed them dramatically—you're in love with your sister's husband; you wish your beloved brother were dead—and that they found disgusting, appalling. But then, over time, those patients often discovered that Freud had a point. They did desire forbidden things, but—as they also learned from the Professor—so did everyone else. Their desires may have been more potent than the norm, or their inhibiting energies might have surpassed those of other people, but the fact remained that there was nothing monstrous about them. "We are all sick," Freud used to say. Part of what psychoanalysis teaches is that there is no such thing as an original desire: Freud had seen it all before, or imagined it. He freed people so that they could bear at first just to glance at their strangest wishes, and then to stare with a spirit of calm toleration and even humor. Because of Freud the therapist, Auden said, "The child unlucky in his little State, / Some hearth where freedom is excluded, / A hive whose honey is fear and worry, / Feels calmer now and somehow assured of escape."

Surely Freud could be a dominating, even a domineering, analytical presence. The early case studies, in particular the stories of Dora and Emma Eckstein, sometimes make dispiriting reading. At one point in Dora's analysis, Freud, caught in what he would call the "counter-transference," the web of fantasies the analyst spins about the patient, concluded that what she wanted most was a kiss—and from no one other than himself.

Freud could also be dismayingly detached from his patients. Sometimes he was capable of suspending his belief that in analysis all was to be tolerated, and judged his more damaged patients as being barely worthwhile. The consulting room was Freud's laboratory and he occasionally regarded patients as though they were concentrations of data, fascinating data, to be sure, but no more than that.

Yet this condescension was infrequent for Freud the therapist. At his best, he saw himself as an educator. He taught people how to describe themselves in new ways. He helped them talk less moralistically and more tolerantly about themselves, and the result was to free them—sometimes a little and sometimes more than that—from their confusion and self-hatred. Overall, Freud loved his patients, though in his peculiarly severe way. That he no longer could see them surely left a void in his emotional life, as well as cutting him off from what was probably his major source of inspiration as a writer and thinker. Freud believed that neurotics extend and exaggerate normal human behaviors. They are not alien from the healthy ones. By seeing into neurotic patients, he believed that he could see into himself and humanity at large. Their sorrows were in a sense both his and everyone's.

It was not only patients that Freud was compelled to give up. On April 19, he gave his brother, Alexander, his stock of cigars. "Your seventy-second birthday finds us on the verge of separating after long years of living together," he wrote. "But the future, always uncertain, is at the moment especially difficult to foresee. I would like you to take over the good cigars which have been accumulating with me over the years, as you can still indulge in such pleasure, I no longer." Freud had been smoking since the age of twenty-four, beginning with cigarettes and moving quickly on to cigars. His father had been a heavy smoker, hanging on to the habit through to his eighty-first year, Freud's age when he gave his stock to Alexander. At the height of his commitment to tobacco, Freud was not only a user but a committed advocate. When his nephew Harry was seventeen, Freud offered him what would probably have been his first cigarette. The young man was judicious enough to refuse and Freud said, "My boy, smoking is one of the greatest and cheapest enjoyments in life, and if you decide in advance not to smoke, I can only feel sorry for you."

Freud called smoking "a protection and a weapon in the combat of life," and he was devoted to it for the great balance of his existence. When in 1923, he discovered a cancerous growth on his jaw and palate, he refrained for some time from letting his doctors know because he was aware that they would tell him that he had to give up his cigars. Freud did eventually let the doctors see the growth and they gave him the expected medical advice. But Freud being Freud, he ignored the doctors and went on smoking. At times his jaw became nearly frozen shut with pain, so Freud would use what he could to lever it open and insert his beloved smoke.

Cigar smoking gave Freud, who, despite an early fling with cocaine, almost never touched other drugs, the combination of energy and tranquility that he needed in order to write. Smoking calmed his nerves and let him focus his attention onto the field of inquiry at hand. His cigar unified him. When his onetime confidante Fliess convinced him to think psychoanalytically about smoking, Freud was compelled to admit that, like all addictions, cigar smoking was probably a substitute for the most common and most regressive addiction there was: masturbation. In all probability, Freud did not apply this diagnosis to himself. He was, he believed, a relatively sane man able to love and work—though over time it perhaps became clear to him that work was the thing that he loved most in life.

Committing oneself to smoking is a way to acquire a strong and persistent desire; because of tobacco's addictive power, the desire for it is nearly as potent as the desire for love or for fame. But the smoking desire can be met readily; the satisfaction of the desire to smoke depends by and large on oneself and oneself alone. Acquiring love or fame involves the capitulation of others. One needs a willing partner, an adulatory crowd. Freud's hunger for cigars was about as strong as any human hunger could be, and he himself was in control of satisfying it. "You actually do feel best," Freud's disciple Ferenczi once said to him, with a combination of admiration and concern, "when you can be independent of the whole world."

Even after he gave his cigars to Alex, Freud would continue to smoke. If food was the stuff of life, *Lebensmittel,* then cigars were to Freud *"Arbeitsmittel,"* the "stuff of work," and Freud, by his own estimation, still had a good deal of work to do. If he could somehow emerge intact from his encounter with Hitler and the Nazis, Freud had another struggle planned. This one was against a longtime adversary: Yahweh, God himself.

While Freud was surrendering his practice and at least pretending to surrender his dear cigars, Adolf Hitler was thriving. Elated by his victory in Austria, Hitler, who for a while displayed a genius comparable to Caesar's and Napoleon's for knowing the next move and when to make it, turned in a new direction: toward Czechoslovakia, an artificial country, an imposture created by the Allies after the First World War. The German General Staff had concocted a plan for invading the small nation—Case Green, it was called—but the plan had sat virtually unconsidered for more than two years. Now, seeing how smoothly things had gone in Austria, Hitler began to look for an excuse to invade. That was not hard to find: there were three and a half million Germans in Czechoslovakia, and they, as the Germans of Austria had done, were complaining ever more vehemently about persecution.

Hitler was still mildly afraid that France, England, and even the United States might intervene to stop him, so early in May, while Freud was waiting for his exit visa, and on the verge of celebrating his eighty-second birthday, Hitler went off to Italy accompanied by a staff of five hundred, all in uniform, to win Mussolini's blessing for the new adventure.

From Hitler's point of view, the visit to Italy was one protracted insult. He and the grand entourage were met not by Mussolini himself, but by King Victor Emmanuel. And Hitler was transported not in a motor car—he loved all modern conveyances and was ever ready to jump into an airplane, no matter what the weather—but in a coach drawn by four horses. At dinner, he was forced to accompany the queen, who towered over him, making him look absurd; she wore a crucifix around her neck, another attempt, surely, to diminish him. The king, for his part, spread rumors that Hitler was injecting himself with narcotics daily, and also that at bedtime he required a woman—not for any overtly sexual purposes, but simply to turn down the covers of his bed. Without this, the führer was purportedly unable to sleep. After an evening at the opera, Hitler appeared in public wearing a tuxedo, which was not, it seems, flattering dress for him. "The German Fuhrer and Reich Chancellor," one observer said, "looked like a headwaiter at the peak of business in a restaurant."

Mussolini stayed in the background, scheduling Hitler and his enormous party for one inane event after the next. But Hitler persevered. At last he made his way into Il Duce's company and managed to bring up the question of Czechoslovakia. Mussolini let Hitler know that the small nation was of no consequence to him, and that Hitler could proceed as he liked. As to the Allies, Hitler guessed that they were planning to do what they had done after each of his other bold moves: absolutely nothing. (He had taken to referring to the leaders of England and France as "the worms.") On this matter, as on many others that arose during the spring of 1938, Hitler turned out to be right. The British prime minister, Neville Chamberlain, wrote to his sister: "You only have to look at the map to see that nothing that France or we could do, could possibly save Czechoslovakia from being overrun by the Germans if they wanted to do it. . . . Therefore, we could not help Czechoslovakia—she would simply be a pretext for going to war with Germany. That we could not do, unless we had a reasonable prospect of being able to beat her to her knees in a reasonable time and of that I see no sign." Stalin professed endless loyalty to the Czech government, but what he truly wanted was for France and England to protect Czechoslovakia, not Russia. All of this Hitler quickly surmised. He had paid a price in humiliation during his trip to Italy—for which Mussolini would in time be compelled to pay—but now he was ready to expand the empire.

Freud's empire at the time was sickness and age and anxious boredom. While Anna and Ernest Jones and the princess negotiated with the Nazis, Freud sat and waited. He wrote an hour a day, working still on the Moses book; he read what he could; he tried to manage his correspondence; but mostly he waited and suffered. On April 26, Freud had an attack of deafness. For some time he had been having trouble with his hearing; postoperative infections had damaged his capacities on his right side, the cancerous side, so badly that he sometimes had to reverse the position of his chair to hear his patients. But now Freud's hearing faded out altogether for a brief span. It was perhaps fortunate that it did, for on May 1, Freud would have been compelled to hear the shouting in the streets that accompanied the Nazis' celebration. This was in all probability the day that the swastika went up over the exterior doorway of Freud's apartment, Berggasse 19, along with a banner that read, "The First of May shall document that we do not wish to disrupt but mean to build." The disrupters, presumably, were the Marxists of what had once been called Red Vienna; May 1 had been their day, the day that the workers massed to celebrate. Now this holiday, like everything else, was Nazi property.

On May 6, Freud, ill and disgruntled, marked his eighty-second birthday. Freud had never cared for his birthdays—they brought intimations of mortality—and was always at least moderately annoyed when the people around him made a fuss. Two years before, when Freud turned eighty, there had been a profusion of good wishes, which he had barely expected. When, in 1936, Ernest Jones told Freud that the British Psycho-Analytical Society was planning a major celebration for May 6, Freud told him that it made no sense to celebrate round-figure birthdays, especially when the person in question wasn't close to being intact. There was also talk about getting Freud the Nobel Prize for his eightieth year. That too irritated him: Freud, after all, was a renegade and renegades don't win major prizes.

But despite Freud's protests, eightieth-birthday salutations came to him from all over the world. He heard from Albert Einstein, Thomas Mann, H. G. Wells, Romain Rolland, Albert Schweitzer, and many others. Brooding on all the recognition, Freud wrote to Stefan Zweig that "although I have been uncommonly happy in my house, with wife and children and especially with a daughter who satisfied in rare measure all of a father's demands, I cannot reconcile myself to the wretchedness and helplessness of being old, and look forward to the transition into nonbeing with a kind of longing."

It is highly unlikely, though, that the birthday letter from Einstein failed to move Freud; for Einstein was what Freud often wanted more than anything else to be, a scientist. Einstein wrote to say that he had always been impressed by Freud's speculative power and by his cultural influence. However, he had lately come upon a case that brought home to him not only the intelligence, but the accuracy of Freud's way of thinking. "This gave me pleasure," Einstein said, "for it is always a source of pleasure when a great and beautiful idea proves to be correct in actual fact." Anna gave Freud her recently completed book, *The Ego and the Mechanisms of Defense*, in which he also took considerable satisfaction. Still, Anna could observe that, from her father's perspective, the best thing about the eightieth-birthday celebration was the fact that, eventually, it came to an end.

The coming of Freud's eighty-second birthday disturbed him yet more, so he decided to ignore it completely. To Ernest Jones, he wrote, "I am sitting here in my study being absolutely idle and otherwise useless. We have decided to disregard this birthday and to [postpone it until] 6 June, July, August, etc., in short, to a date after our liberation, and indeed, I have not acknowledged any of the letters, telegrams, etc. that arrived. Now it seems that we shall land in England in May after all. I say 'it seems' for, despite all promises uncertainty is the all-controlling factor." Freud's determination to get out of Austria was gathering force. To his son Ernst, Freud, not long after his birthday, wrote, "Two prospects keep me going in these grim times: to rejoin you all and—to die in freedom." To die in freedom: those words, written in English, declared Freud's developing allegiance to what he hoped would be his new home, and signified his deep determination to leave Vienna and Hitler, and with all the dignity that befit his age and his achievement.

Yet many members of the Gestapo had other ideas. All through Vienna, prosperous Jews like Freud were having their property confiscated and being taken off to Dachau, often with their entire families. Why should Freud be any different? In fact, his doctrines—"his obscene emphasis on sex" in particular—made him especially repugnant to the new regime. Why not create an example of Sigmund Freud?

At the Verlag, Doctor Anton Sauerwald, aspiring member of the Nazi Party, was making discoveries. He was reading Freud's work and finding out what a fascinating thinker the old man who had come under his charge was. And he was also discovering that he rather liked Freud: the Professor struck him as dignified, thoughtful, perhaps even brave. Sauerwald began to treat Freud and his family with a certain politeness. When a member of the Gestapo was rude to Freud, Sauerwald apologized later to Anna. "What do you expect?" he said. "These Prussians don't know who Freud is."

At the same time, reading through Freud's private papers at the Verlag, Sauerwald realized that Freud was breaking the law. He was keeping money stashed in foreign banks and not reporting it to the Nazis. The crime was punishable, at least nominally, by death. Surely it occurred to Sauerwald that if he reported Freud's financial situation, he would be able to advance his own fortunes; he could, perhaps, be officially inducted into the party. On Freud's birthday, May 6, the American ambassador to Berlin, Hugh Robert Wilson, reported to the secretary of state, Cordell Hull, that there was only one more matter to clear up, the settling of Freud's debts to the Verlag, before Freud would be allowed to emigrate. But that one matter was under the discretion of Doctor Anton Sauerwald.

A week after his birthday, Freud and his family received new passports from the Nazis. Their Austrian passports, which Freud and his family had used in the past to travel through Europe, were confiscated by the SA raiders on March 15, the day that Freud tottered out from the consulting room—the story goes—to scatter them like mice. But the old passports would have been no good anyway; they were Austrian and Austria no longer existed. The new documents that arrived on May 12 were German passports and bore the eagle and the swastika conspicuously on the front. In the passport photo, taken by Edmund Engelman, Freud wears a dark suit, with shirt and tie. Freud's shirt collar is loose around his neck, a sign that he had recently lost a good deal of weight. He looks overwhelmingly weary, and also mildly puzzled and mildly annoyed. He does not at all seem ready for a new start in a new country, a new life.

On May 5, Aunt Minna, ill though she was, had made her way to London; on May 24, Freud's daughter Mathilde and her husband, Robert, departed. On May 14, Freud's son Martin left Vienna for Paris, where his wife and two children had already fled. Though Martin had flushed many incriminating papers from the Verlag down into the Viennese sewer system, the Nazis nonetheless had left with a few compromising documents, probably about undisclosed funds of Martin's. It turned out that the vice president of the police, a man with an extensive criminal record of his own, was a good friend of Martin Freud's cook. Through the cook, Martin was able to buy back most of the documents, but apparently not enough of them. He soon learned that he was to be arrested; on Saturday, the fourteenth, he boarded a train for Paris.

Martin understood that it was forbidden to take any money out of Germany, so he sent back what currency he had and kept all of his coins in his pockets. But even that money might be too much. Martin was told that another Jew was recently taken from the train and shot for the crime of carrying a few stamps with him. Martin decided to take with him just enough money to buy food on the train.

After boarding, Martin went to the dining car and ordered up a whole roast chicken, asking the attendant to refrigerate it for him for the morning. "I filled that worthy . . . Nazi, with deep suspicion," Martin recollected. "He said the unusual request was a breach of customs regulations and that he would have to report me to the Gestapo." Martin canceled the request, took the chicken immediately to his compartment, and ate it all, while the dining car attendant watched from the corridor. As it turned out, there was no inspection at the border, and Martin Freud, stuffed with suspicious chicken, crossed the Rhine Bridge at Strasbourg unmolested.

Back in Vienna, Freud waited: he waited on the German authorities in general and without quite knowing it on Doctor Anton Sauerwald, who might at any time decide that it was in his interest, and the Reich's, to expose what he knew about Sigmund Freud. Though Freud had his passport, he also needed his "statement of no impediment," which indicated that all of his debts and taxes had been paid. On May 21, Freud received a statement about the value of his precious collection of antiquities, a statement that would be the basis for the tax he would have to pay to take them out of the country. The collection was valued—or rather, generously undervalued—at thirty thousand Reich marks; Hans von Demel, the curator of the Viennese Museum of Cultural History, had done Freud the good turn of pricing the antiquities at a low rate, so as to keep the tax on them within Freud's means.

Freud's obsession with his antiquities, never minor, had

increased that spring. He spent a good deal of time putting his books and statues in order, and he even began to catalog them—odd for someone as relatively unsystematic about such things as Freud was. One can only imagine Freud's thoughts as he went through his artworks for what he felt might be the last time. Creating the collection had been one of Freud's major avocations, even though he was always pressed for money and quite strict with himself about what he could and could not buy. One day a week, Freud held an open consultation period, when anyone who wanted to could come and get treatment or advice. With the money from those sessions, Freud pursued his passion.

Looking at the pieces now he perhaps recalled how he'd acquired each one and how much he'd paid. Freud was a very hard bargainer and knew the field well, so he was not often cheated. Probably too he thought a little about the authenticity of the work, for though he had a good eye, there were a number of forgeries on the market and in fact Freud did buy a few. (In the nineteenth and early-twentieth centuries, the sort of antiquities that Freud loved didn't generally command a high enough price to be worth forging.) Still he must have asked himself, Which are the most valuable? Which the most worth saving?

The antiquities had for many years been Freud's teaching tools. He told patients that the unconscious could preserve the past just as the dry sands of Egypt preserved this or that statue now standing intact on the bookshelf. Freud and the patient worked together to excavate the trauma or the dream and take it into the light of day, much as archaeologists dug deep for the treasures buried where ancient cities had been. Freud liked to tell his patients that a past memory, though as strange and disturbing as a statue of Toth was on first encounter, was nonetheless, like the statue, susceptible to analysis. What archaeologists and students of ancient history and religion could bring to understanding the icon, Freud and the new art of psychoanalysis might bring to interpreting a dream or a once-repressed memory.

But of course the collection had private resonances for Freud too. Many consequential thinkers and writers in the nineteenth century were drawn, as Freud was, to the pagan world and particularly to its religion and myth. One thinks of Nietzsche and his fascination with Dionysus and Apollo; Shelley and his great poem on Prometheus; and Keats in his ode to Psyche and the "Ode on a Grecian Urn," among many other writers. For these writers, pagan antiquity was a world beyond and before the Judeo-Christian world that they often found oppressive. By returning to the classical era, the poets and thinkers could reject the prevailing religious norms, but without surrendering to sterile skepticism. The pagan worldview allowed them to sustain their sense of wonder at the variety and strangeness of nature and at the miracle of their own being. Rome, as the formidable Edward Gibbon indicated, worshipped many gods, was hospitable to many religions, and that polymorphous worship was a source for the empire's urbanity and tolerance—and also for its amazing vigor. Perhaps Freud was one of that breed of modern pagans who would not give up pondering rich mystery, even as they repudiated the all-knowing sky god. The collection had been valued—good; there were promises that it would follow Freud into exile—also good. But surely the Nazis could confiscate it any time, prevent it from reaching him, if indeed he ever left.

Marie Bonaparte, who sat on the stairs every day after Anna was arrested to make sure that the Gestapo did not come and take away the Professor, and who often seemed to know what Freud needed, sometimes better than he knew himself, soon smuggled away his favorite treasure: a bronze statue of Athena, a little more than four inches high. Athena's left hand is poised to grip a spear, which was lost; in her right hand she holds a libation bowl. She is wearing a Corinthian helmet, set far back on her brow, and a breastplate, decorated with the figure of Medusa, though in this rendition, Medusa is without her snakes. The statue had a special place in Freud's heart, symbolizing both wisdom and martial prowess; it was an icon of the mind as warrior, the intellect combatant. Marie Bonaparte held it for Freud at her home in Paris to present to him when he was finally free.

Still Freud did not have his *Unbedenklichkeitserklärung*, the statement of no impediment. The Germans had put Freud in the same position in which they put many Jews: they took all he had on hand and then demanded that he pay taxes on it. They had seized the press, and they had seized Freud's Viennese savings. So they put Freud in an impossible situation. You must pay taxes and all of your supposed debts; but we've confiscated your funds. What will you do? The Nazis claimed that Freud owed a debt to his publisher, the Verlag, which was now in their hands: the sum was 32,000 schillings.

What Freud needed at this point was ransom money, pure and simple. The resources that he himself had had on hand were all but gone. Now Marie Bonaparte was compelled to do more than rescue the statue of Athena for Freud. Now she stepped in and paid off the criminals masquerading as officials, and finally, Freud seemed to be free to go.

Freud was far luckier than most Jews in Vienna. To reach the verge of emigration, he had the help of the American government (including President Roosevelt himself); the British government (which had to agree to accept him); his well-connected and wealthy friend, the princess; the analyst Ernest Jones, who was born for bureaucratic intrigue; intrepid and levelheaded Anna; his dutiful son Martin; and a dozen others.

Yet there was still one more factor: Doctor Anton Sauerwald. Anxious and unhappy, sitting in the Verlag, hoping to advance his career and become a figure of note in the new Austria, Sauerwald commanded the destiny of Freud and his family. All he needed to do to have them arrested was to reveal the information he had about the funds in foreign banks. There were figures high in the Nazi Party who reportedly would have been happy to do away with Freud, even now at this last minute. The story goes that Hermann Göring, whose cousin had taken over the Berlin Psychoanalytical Institute, supported letting Freud go. But against him were arrayed both Goebbels, the propaganda minister, and Himmler, who would in time be a key figure in implementing the Final Solution. A phone call to the office of either man, placed by Sauerwald, would almost certainly mean the arrest of Freud and his family.

\*      \*      \*

On Saturday, June 4, Sigmund Freud boarded the Orient Express, with Martha, Anna, Doctor Josefine Stross, the housemaid, Paula Fichtl, and Lün, his chow. Doctor Stross was a late addition, for, as Freud said, "Dr. Schur, our family doctor, was to have accompanied us with his family, but at the eleventh hour he was unfortunate enough to require an appendix operation, with the result that we had to content ourselves with the protection of the lady pediatrician, whom Anna brought along." The train made its slow way across Germany and to the border of France, and Doctor Anton Sauerwald, for whatever strange complex of reasons, did not intervene. Whether it was loyalty or laziness or hopes for some later relations with Freud—in fact, Sauerwald would appear again in Freud's life—one cannot know. When the train crossed the Rhine River, Freud offered a simple remark, "*Jetzt sind wir frei.*" Now we are free.

Behind him, Sigmund Freud left Berggasse 19, soon to be empty of its furnishings, and the Verlag, stripped of its assets; he left Vienna, the city he both hated and loved, in the control of Adolf Hitler; he left four sisters, too old to travel, under the care of friends; he left a population of Jews that would soon be virtually destroyed; he left his life, his history, and the site of all of his major achievements. But he left something else, as well. Before Freud boarded the train, the Gestapo required him to sign a document. It said, "I Prof. Freud, hereby confirm that after the Anschluss of Austria to the German Reich I have been treated by the German authorities and particularly by the Gestapo with all the respect and consideration due to my scientific reputation, that I could live and work in full freedom, that I could continue to pursue my activities in every way I desired, that I found full support from all concerned in this respect, and that I have not the slightest reason for any complaint." Freud signed, but then he added one simple sentence: *Ich kann die Gestapo jedermann auf das beste empfehlen.* "I can most highly recommend the Gestapo to everyone."

There's brilliance, as well as a remarkable daring, in Freud's send-off to the Nazis. He offered them a statement with a latent and a manifest content, with a double meaning. And double meanings (and triple meanings and proliferating, complex meanings of all sorts) were precisely what Nazis were allergic to, what they had, in effect, constructed their world to shut out. To the Nazis, there always had to be one: one people, one nation, one leader, and one meaning, the truth. The Gestapo must have been most flattered by the old Professor's compliment.

Hitler, meanwhile, was thinking of Czechoslovakia, that small, abominable nation thrust like a fist into German territory. And the führer was continuing to reap the adulation of the Germans, and now too of the Austrian people. What he brought them, from the perspective of Freud's thinking at least, was an elixir like no other: he brought unity. People were divided in themselves; nations were split: the leader pulled all the achingly disparate parts together and dispensed a feeling of oneness. He healed the fragmented psyche—provided one did not wish to think for oneself, make one's own ethical judgments or interpret things in one's fashion—and he healed the broken polis, so long as one was not a Jew, a Gypsy, or a Christian who took too seriously the teachings of Jesus Christ.

While Freud can affirm, though not without a touch of irony, such mild intoxicants as love and art, he is nonetheless supremely suspicious of any doctrine or activity that promises to unify the psyche—or the nation or the people—and to do so for the long term. After alcoholic intoxication comes the hangover; after aesthetic contemplation, boredom; after the intoxications of romantic love, marriage. Love, art, and liquor are temporary ways of transcending the pain of being: they have limits built into them. But belief in the leader or in the one true God can continue on for a lifetime and sometimes then for generations.

Freud's implicit ethos in the face of the temptation that fascism and fundamentalism offer—the temptation of oneness—is counterintuitive. He believes that the inner tensions we experience within the psyche are by and large necessary tensions. This is so not because the tensions are enjoyable in themselves—they are not—but because the alternatives are so much worse. It's true that when internal dissonance becomes too strong, the result is likely to be neurosis. When the drives are too potently controlled—Freud's term for this is "repression"—they will express themselves in indirect, painful ways. But complete unbinding of the inner tensions is worse: that leads the way to public and private chaos.

For Freud, a healthy psyche is not always a psyche that feels good. The tension between the agencies within is manifest as an anxiety that is very difficult for the individual to explain or to remedy. One never feels exactly right in part because, virtually all the time, one is indulging a certain powerful agency and neglecting the others. One is, perhaps, striving for success and, accordingly, placating the over-I. But at the same time one is outraging the it, which cries for pleasure, and overwhelming the I, which cannot, no matter how hard the over-I pushes, live up to its demands for achievement and success. Because a good deal of the psyche's business goes on unconsciously, and because the demands of the various agencies change over time, it is difficult—perhaps it is nearly impossible—to follow Socrates' dictum and, with confidence, to know oneself. For Freud, the self is prone to oppose itself and often in ways that are simply incomprehensible to the individual. In one of the saddest sentences Freud ever wrote, he observes how someone suffering under an irrational sense of guilt becomes sick, but without knowing the source of his sickness. "As far as the patient is concerned," Freud writes, "this sense of guilt is dumb; it does not tell him he is guilty; he does not feel guilty, he feels ill."

But Freud also suggests that a measure of inner conflict is not the worst thing in the world: We need to learn to understand the conflict to whatever degree we can and perhaps modify it in certain ways. But overall we need to learn to see some inner tension as inevitable, and to live with it. Freud's view that we need to tolerate and even at times cultivate conflict is part of what makes his thought as radical as it is. Almost all other religious and spiritual traditions prior to Freud have held up inner peace as an ideal. Christianity celebrates peace above all things and tells its adherents to avoid war by forgiving their enemy and by turning the other cheek; Buddhism affirms the tranquility that meditation and detachment from desire can bring; the name Islam denotes peace; Judaism endorses the calm that attends on fulfilling the covenant with the Lord. There is room for turbulence in all these faiths to be sure: the Muslim enters spiritual struggle, jihad; the believing Christian wars against his tendency to sin. But ultimately the goal is to achieve inner union through the development of the spirit.

Jung once remarked that the objective of the yogi is to use breathing and postures, the asanas, to bring himself into a state of calm in which no material from the unconscious can penetrate the conscious mind. Such an activity is representative of a good deal of religious practice in both the West and the East. Prayer, fasting, meditation, penance, confession, chanting, song—all these activities can quell inner turbulence. But Freud affirms not inner peace but inner conflict. No part of the psyche must be suppressed in the interest of any other; the wages for such suppression are too dear. Any part of the self denied expression is bound to erupt—or at least to assert itself—in ways that will be harmful for the individual. "The mind," as Emerson says, "goes antagonizing on."

Just as a healthy psyche is not always a serene psyche, so Freud implies that a healthy body politic is not always a tranquil one. A healthy political society is one that allows for a good deal of ongoing tension. When the people surrender their will to the leader, as the Germans and, rather shockingly, the Austrians did to Hitler, the result is a certain sort of peace of mind. One wakes up with a sense of purpose: all the energies stream in the same direction; the world is a much clearer and simpler place. "The masses," Hitler wrote, "love a commander more than a petitioner and feel inwardly more satisfied by a doctrine, tolerating no other beside itself, than by the granting of liberalistic freedom with which, as a rule, they can do little, and are prone to feel that they have been abandoned." To be sure, living in a relatively liberal democracy, with its proliferation of ideas, interpretations, and values can be dizzying. There's a great deal of argument, controversy, difference. But in that difference, annoying and perplexing as it may be, lies the community's well-being. Freud suggests that if we are willing to live with inner tension, political as well as personal, we need never be overwhelmed by tyranny or fall into the anarchy that complete surrender to the unconscious brings.

Freud feared the United States of America as much as he did because to him it represented something like the dangerous inverse of Nazi Germany. Germany was insanely authoritarian. But America was dangerous because it always threatened to be dominated from below, by the appetites. (In his perception of democracy Freud resembles Plato, who in *The Republic* associates the rule of the people with the unqualified rule of the desiring, or appetitive, part of the soul.) Aggressive democracy, to Freud, meant discrediting all leaders, no matter how sane or useful, and allowing the majority to dominate completely. Freud knew how difficult it was to sublimate the drives—to turn erotic and aggressive energies to the interest of civilization. Most people wanted satisfactions that were crude and immediate. They would not wait, as the truly civilized man or woman does, to have their efforts repaid. A society that merrily disregards all leaders, the insane and the benevolent alike, is going to devolve into chaos—and this is what Freud expected to happen at any moment in America. The only thing that saved America, as Freud saw it, was that its people burned off most of their potentially destructive energy in the quest for wealth. But when that quest was comprehensively thwarted—as the Depression of 1929 threatened to do—then Americans could easily and readily turn to anarchy. When Freud thought of relatively free and enlightened nations, he thought of France and, above all others, of England, the country he revered from his young manhood on, and to which he was now, at last, making his way.

John Keats reflects in a letter on Adam's dream: "He awoke and found it truth," the poet says. The dream that the first man dreamed was of a beautiful lover and helpmate: he dreamed of Eve and woke up to find her there beside him. Freud had dreamed a dream as well: it was a dream of a world dominated by a primal man, a cruel half-mad figure of ultimate potency, worshipped by virtually all. What the primal man wants he takes; his whims, hateful as they may be, quickly translate into edicts and then into facts. Freud dreamed that dream and, like an accursed Adam, woke up and found it true. The world he had lived and thrived in was indeed dominated by such a man. And this happened not when Freud was twenty-five or fifty, when he might have had plentiful resources to fight back, but when he was in his eighties and very sick.

Yet while Hitler and his minions dominated the streets of Vienna, Freud labored for an hour a day on his Moses book, a book that he hoped would stand as part of his twenty-year analysis of the kind of debased authority that Hitler represented. If Freud's ethic might be called an ethic of civilized strife, then during his last days in Vienna he lived up to it in many ways. It was not easy for an old man to stand up to the Nazis, to strive with them. Nor was it easy to continue working away on his book, which, Freud often admitted, he wrote against multiple inner resistances.

But Freud was also willing to play a little bit. He could relax enough to sit with Anna and to translate, not a major work of literature, a tragedy by Sophocles or by Shakespeare, but a book about a dog. "Does Topsy realize that she is being translated?" Freud asked the princess. Well, Topsy was. During the perilous three months in Vienna, Freud, though old and ill, was in many ways at his height. He did his work, he cared for his family, and as well as he could, he sustained his spirits. He never lost his wits; nor did he—"I have never gotten so much for a single visit"; "I can most highly recommend the Gestapo to everyone"—ever lose his wit.

Yet there is more to the story. In his great elegy for Freud, W. H. Auden saw how "the autocratic pose / The paternal strictness he distrusted, still / Clung to his utterance and features." Surely it did, and in Vienna during the last days, as it was through almost all of Freud's adult life, there was an element of that patriarchal character clearly perceptible. Even at his best, there is something stiff and overly commanding about Freud. He is stubborn, hyperconvinced of his own opinion, deaf to other views. Persuading Freud to try to leave Vienna and save his life and the life of his family was a major endeavor.

Emerson, in what was, presumably, a hyperbolic moment, counsels that we should pretend that the other people around us are real. Who knows? he asks himself. Maybe they are. Freud's behavior toward others can sometimes suggest that he nourished pronounced doubts about their actuality too. He was capable of comparing the prospect of Anna's moving away and abandoning him and Martha with his having to give up his cigars. Freud's treatment of his other disciples is a complex subject, but one could never mistake him for a humane and humorous, much less a loving, mentor. He sometimes appears to believe that his disciples were created for the exclusive purpose of developing his work and enhancing his reputation. Their vocation in life was to think Freudian thoughts that Freud hadn't the time or occasion to think, then to listen to the master praise them for being loyal, even as he subtly disparaged them for being unoriginal.

The fact is, of course, that in the middle of his career, Freud arrived at a strong view about the kind of authority that commands obedience: masterful, patriarchal authority. At various times in his life and work, Freud was willing to imitate exactly such authority: his temperament leaned more than a little that way to begin with, and he saw how effective it could be to play the primal father's role. Freud, in short, was tempted by the kind of power that he spent a major phase of his career demystifying. Freud, one might say, was a patriarch who worked with incomparable skill to deconstruct patriarchy. He wrote and lived to put an end to the kind of authority that he himself quite often embodied and exploited.

II

London

Early on the morning of Monday, June 6, 1938, Sigmund Freud stepped down from a train at Victoria Station in London. The train had pulled in to a far corner of Victoria so that Freud could avoid the crowd that was gathered to greet him. His escape had been reported in the British newspapers and there was great public enthusiasm about his arrival. Though the weather was mild, Freud wore a densely woven three-piece suit, a heavy topcoat, a fedora, and thick black shoes. He was frail from his illness and still weary from the trip, so he made his way down from the train with considerable difficulty. His expression was uncertain, at times even slightly disoriented. A chance observer, seeing Freud on his arrival in England, might have thought of some lines by the great Irish poet William Butler Yeats, who, in June of 1938, was also nearing his end: "An aged man is but a paltry thing," Yeats said, "a tattered coat upon a stick." Surely on that day in June, Freud looked paltry enough, a sad, diminished ghost of his former self.

As Freud stepped off the train, he might well have thought that his trials were over. But here in England, Freud would find a new set of adversaries, different but not entirely unrelated to those he left behind in Vienna. Freud, who had often been ignored and derided in his home city, would, in England, become an admired figure. And surely public acclaim was something that Freud had wanted all his life. Yet in order to live up to his own aspirations as a writer and thinker—and as an individual—Freud would have to contend against his newfound celebrity. He would have to fight against his own urge to become—Yeats once again—"a smiling public man."

Then there was the matter of death: Freud had come to England, he said, so as "to die in freedom." He was aware that the cancer of the jaw that had been with him since 1923 was going to kill him, and relatively soon. But how was he to die? The fact that the illness was gradual and protracted gave him some choice in the matter. Freud understood that his way of dying was bound to be of consequence, and not just to himself and to those close to him. Freud had invented psychoanalysis, but he also embodied it. People looked to him as an exponent of a set of provocative, controversial ideas, but they also saw him as an exemplary figure, one who, in some ways at least, attempted to live by the findings that he offered the world. Socrates, Cicero, and Montaigne all had said that to philosophize is to learn how to die. Freud's death would inevitably be a commentary on the philosophy of life that psychoanalysis offered.

Perhaps more than anything else now, Freud wanted his work to last. He wanted his thoughts to be part of the thought of the civilized future—even perhaps to dominate that future. Over the past twenty years, Freud had reflected continually on how authority establishes and perpetuates itself, and much of what he had concluded was disturbing. He knew, or thought he knew, that the world longed for father-gods, the more severe, inscrutable, and potent, the better. To pass out of life in the guise of such a figure might help to ensure Freud's future authority. But would dying as a "great man" not undermine what Freud had written about the need for liberation from all oppressive patriarchs?

Getting off the train that Monday morning, though, Freud was simply relieved to be in London, happy to be alive. If his dream life was any indication, he was looking to the future with some hope. The night before, as he crossed over from France on the ferryboat to Dover, Freud dreamed that he was landing not at Dover but at Pevensey. When he told his son about the dream, he was forced to explain that Pevensey was where William the Conqueror had landed when he invaded England in 1066.

As tired as he was, Freud insisted that he wanted to see something of his new home. So Ernest Jones drove him north, toward his new residence, through the center of London. As they made their way, Freud showed Martha the sights: Buckingham Palace and the Houses of Parliament, Piccadilly Circus, Regent Street, and all the other places, which he had read so often about and also recalled from his time in England. As he passed the palace, Freud perhaps reflected on the near-perfect political balance that England had achieved. Here was a monarchy to absorb the people's need for commanding, parental figures, father- and mother-gods. But the monarchy was largely ceremonial; the kings and queens had little power to deploy. Meanwhile, England was governed by its most able men, none of whom the crowd could ever elevate to absolute heights, for the beloved rulers were already in place.

On an average day, Freud would have seen as many as a half million people on their way to work in what was now the largest city in the world. By 1939, London's population would be 8.2 million. But today was Whit Monday, the day later known as Late Spring Bank Holiday, and most people had the day off. Freud, coming into London, saw a heavy flow of cars heading out of the city and off in the direction of the seashore. That morning, the beaches were filling with young girls displaying the latest fashion: silk or knitted Snow White hoods, inspired by the recently released Disney movie. On the day that Freud arrived, the film was playing continuously from eleven to eleven at the New Gallery. In London, over 61,000 people would use the holiday to visit the zoo at Regent's Park, while an annual parade of 574 cart horses took place nearby. Elsewhere in the park, Mozart's *Così fan tutte*, an opera which Freud quite liked, would play at an open-air theater, though mostly to empty seats.

Looking out the window of the automobile as Jones drove him to his new home, Freud saw a London that on this holiday Monday seemed relaxed and confident. Yet in Parliament the week before, all the discussion had been about war, and in particular, about what effect high-intensity aerial bombardment would have on the city. Members asked what London would do if the telephone system failed. They wanted to know what safeguards were in effect for the water supply and the gas and electric systems.

Surely the political event that most preoccupied Freud that day was the annexation of Austria, with the rubbing parties and break-ins and the horrors on the street. The recent occurrence that most transfixed Londoners was not the Austrian conquest—thought that was disturbing enough—but the bombing of Guernica. A Basque town in the north of Spain, Guernica had been attacked by German planes in April of 1937. The Germans, allied with Franco and the Spanish fascists, were using Spain to train their soldiers and to try out their new weapons, and at Guernica that weaponry succeeded beyond all expectations. The attack occurred on a market day, with everyone out in the streets, and resulted in a horrible slaughter of men, and of women and children as well. An "experimental horror," Churchill called the Guernica bombing. Picasso's painting of the attack—with people and animals emanating their inaudible, ear-splitting screams—over time became an emblem for the brutalities of a new kind of warfare in which the armies did little to avoid civilian populations, and in fact often sought them out for slaughter.

In the spring of 1938, experts were telling the British population that a hundred thousand tons of bombs would fall on London during the first fourteen days of a war with Germany. Every ton of bombs, they calculated, would result in fifty casualties, so the prospects were terrifying. Bertrand Russell, probably England's most prominent public intellectual at the time, wrote that "London . . . will be one vast raving bedlam, the hospitals will be stormed, traffic will cease, the homeless will shriek for help, the city will be a pandemonium." In fact, the total of bombs dropped on the city never reached a hundred thousand tons, and the casualties would prove to be much less than the experts predicted, though they would be grievous enough. When Freud arrived in London, the British, as pre-occupied as they might have seemed with Snow White and beach holiday-going and the animals at the Regent's Park zoo, were in a state of fear, expecting that London could soon become Guernica on a grand scale, at least if Neville Chamberlain couldn't somehow arrange to placate Hitler. In June of 1938, Freud came to a London obsessed by peace and the appearance of peace and terrified by the prospect of war.

Freud was also arriving in a London that was unusually warm in its attitude toward the Jews. As a general rule, the British at the time had only a minimal interest in what went on in other nations—a post–World War I isolationism was potently intact. But that began to change when word of the way that the Germans were treating the Jews began to spread outside Germany and Austria. Up until this point, British culture in the twentieth century was mildly, but rather consistently, anti-Semitic. Jews were barred from golf and social clubs and the great public schools had strict quotas for Jewish admission. But Germany's Nuremberg Laws, with their restrictions on Jewish travel, marriage, and professional life, revolted the British and spread sympathy everywhere in the nation for the Jewish plight. As the historian A. J. P. Taylor puts it: "It was the [German] reversion to barbarism almost as much as the barbarism itself which made Nazi Germany peculiarly hateful, and some English people were no doubt the more annoyed at having to repudiate the anti-semitism which they had secretly cherished." Robert Graves and Alan Hodge put things more pungently. British fascists, they say, under the leadership of Sir Oswald Mosley, "tried to exploit anti-Semitic feeling in the East End, but with the surprising effect, rather, of making heroes of 'the kikes.'"

After taking in the London sights, Freud and his party stopped at 39 Elsworthy Road, the house that Ernst Freud had rented for his father and mother and Anna while the family looked for what would, in Freud's case, be a final home. Freud called 39 Elsworthy Road "a charming little house. My room," he said, "looks out onto a verandah which overlooks our own garden framed with flower beds and gives onto a large tree-studded park. Naturally it is only a temporary measure for three months. Ernst still has to find the definite solution which needs to fulfill all sorts of conditions which are seldom realized here. It is difficult for us to live vertically instead of horizontally." Gone was Berggasse 19, where the Freud family had lived its horizontal life; now, in a house with stairs, Freud would have to be carried from upstairs down to the main part of the house. Still, Freud found the new house appealing. The *Daily Herald*, which took a keen interest in Freud's arrival, described Freud's new residence as "a quiet, spacious modern house with a vivid green front door . . . The flower garden," the paper added, "is now ablaze with color."

Freud was soon out walking in the garden, which abutted Primrose Hill, with Regent's Park in the background. Confined inside his apartment during the Nazi takeover, Freud, who was in his way a nature lover, had become starved for light and air. The first time that he walked through the small garden at the Elsworthy Road house, he threw back his head, thrust out his arms and said, "I am almost tempted to cry out, 'Heil Hitler.'"

Yet Freud's feelings were actually more complex. On the day he got to London, he sat down and wrote a letter to his friend Max Eitingon, in which he revealed something of his inner state. "The emotional climate of these days is hard to grasp," Freud said, "almost indescribable. The feeling of triumph on being liberated is too strongly mixed with sorrow, for in spite of everything I still greatly loved the prison from which I have been released. The enchantment of the new surroundings (which make one want to shout 'Heil Hitler') is blended with discontent caused by little peculiarities of the strange environment; the happy anticipations of a new life are dampened by the question: how long will a fatigued heart be able to accomplish any work?"

And yet, almost despite himself, Freud began to feel at home in England. He had first come to the country in 1875, at the age of nineteen, to visit relatives in Manchester. Two years before the visit, Freud was already developing into a committed Anglophile: to his friend, Eduard Silberstein, he wrote: "I am reading English poems, writing English letters, declaiming English verse, listening to English descriptions, and thirsting after English views." Freud was delighted by what he found in Manchester and even thought of emigrating to England. When he returned home, Freud wrote again to Silberstein, saying, "I would rather live there than here, in spite of fog and rain, drunkenness and conservatism. Many peculiarities of the English character and country which other continentals would find intolerable fit in very well with my nature." From then on, Freud venerated England and English culture; he even named one of his sons Oliver, after Oliver Cromwell, the leader of the Puritan revolution. Surely there was now still a chance that what Freud had said sixty years ago was true and that England was something like his spiritual home.

The initial greetings Freud received when he returned to England now in 1938 might have convinced him of as much. Two days after his arrival, Freud, who was never easy to surprise, was genuinely taken aback by what he encountered. "Here there is enough to write about," he said, "most of it pleasant, some very pleasant. The reception in Victoria Station and then in the newspapers of the first few days was most kind, indeed enthusiastic. We are buried in flowers. Interesting letters come: only three collectors of autographs, a painter who wants to make a portrait when I have rested, etc." There was also a four-page telegram signed by "citizens of all faiths and professions," from Cleveland, Ohio, USA, inviting Freud to come to the heartland of America and make his home there. "We shall have to answer," Freud said, "that we have already unpacked."

What struck Freud the most were the many letters from strangers who were simply writing to say how happy they were that Freud and his family had arrived safely and peacefully in England. "Really," Freud added, "as if our concerns were theirs as well." Valuable antiquities came to Freud as gifts from people he had never met, but who knew that his adored collection was still in Austria. Taxi drivers were aware of the Freuds' whereabouts and whisked Anna home; the bank manager said, "I know all about you." Letters with the address "Sigmund Freud/London" came to the door. Said Freud, "England is a blessed, a happy land, inhabited by kindly hospitable people; that at least is the impression of the first weeks." The experience was stunning to Freud, who was finally tasting the public rewards of his long labors, finally feeling the recognition that his achievement and innovation deserved. "For the first time and late in life," he declared, "I have experienced what fame means."

Was Freud not famous in Vienna? From early in his career, Freud had been the doctor that singularly open-minded members of the Viennese middle class went to see when all the respectable options failed them. He was known for his peculiar techniques—hypnotism (though only for a while); the analysis of dreams; free association; a willingness to take the parapraxes, slips of the tongue and the pen, seriously. He was understood to be eccentric, brilliant, and perhaps a little dangerous. The unrelenting Karl Kraus sustained a constant attack on Freud and his doctrines: "Psychoanalysis," he sneered, "is the disease of which it purports to be the cure." That meant, among other things, that Freud's insistence on the determining power of childhood, trauma, and the past could become an obsession for a given individual, who, having encountered Freud's theories, would begin to think of nothing else. How to cure such an obsession? Well, only Sigmund Freud could begin to do that. In the early phase of his career, Freud had been infamous among many in Vienna; later he had been notorious. But even as his renown expanded across the world, Freud never tasted the day-to-day pleasures of fame, at least until he arrived in England.

Here in England he was recognized in the street (on the odd occasion he went outside); he was praised in the newspapers; he was the object of warm solicitude on the part of people he had never met (including, from afar, the leading citizens of Cleveland, Ohio). So this is what it felt like to be famous! This was what Goethe enjoyed and, closer to the present, what Freud's friend Einstein had the chance to savor every day. Freud, clearly, was taken by surprise, not only by his ascension to fame and goodwill, but also by how much he liked it.

Yet on some level, Freud probably felt that what he was experiencing was a form of "intoxication." After all, he was the one who had no use for alcohol, no use for religion, no use, during the great part of his life, for romantic love—the over-estimation of the object, as he liked to call it. Freud endorsed the life of spiritual sobriety and of inner and outer struggle. The psyche was a divided entity: to allow that division to be quelled for a protracted period was a formula for delusion and maybe disaster. He had spent his entire life in conflict with what he thought of as the "social superego." He'd always said the painful, nonpolitic thing: he had announced to the world that children are sexually hypercharged; he had insisted that we were inhabited by a strange impersonal force that determined our destinies in ways that most of us can barely understand; he had told people—maybe this was the most insulting thing of all—that they did not know why their own jokes were funny. All his life he had struggled against the external forces of social disapproval, which, his theory of the superego insisted, had an internal bearing as well. The over-I is, among other things, a precipitate of social strictures, an internalization of the fre-quently unwritten laws the collective will works to impose. We are society: society lives within us and is made strong by our own vital energies. So he who would struggle against society must struggle against a part of himself. The person willing to contend against the social norm must, accordingly, be ready to feel what amount to self-inflicted wounds.

Freud savored opposition: he had said that he always needed a foe to strive against as well as a staunch ally to support him. He had said that being a Jew, with the long history of persecution to look back on, was excellent preparation for doing his intellectual work in the world. "Nor is it perhaps entirely a matter of chance that the first advocate of psychoanalysis was a Jew," he said. "To profess belief in this new theory called for a certain degree of readiness to accept a situation of solitary opposition—a situation with which no one is more familiar than a Jew." But savor struggle as he might—not for nothing was Freud an admirer of Milton's Satan, the arch-rebel—struggle with the social norm was always going to be a source of anxiety. Almost as much as he loved opposition, Freud loved success, recognition, and all the secure trappings of bourgeois life.

Freud presumably understood that most of the people casually praising him here in England had not read a complete volume of his and that if they had, and could understand it, their reactions would range from incredulity to outrage. Maybe he was getting mildly inebriated, and maybe more than that, from what he—no democrat, no egalitarian—would have recognized as an especially cheap vintage, the praise of the newspaper-reading public. Freud, late in life, now faced a dilemma: Should he continue to be benignly gracious, enjoy his standing, and go gently? Or should he be Freud, the exuberant troublemaker, down to the end?

Freud had on his desk at 39 Elsworthy Road the third chapter of his Moses book, the chapter that would be by far the most incendiary. When it was completed—if it was—and bound together with the first two chapters, the book would create, if not a firestorm (there was too much happening on the larger stage of the world for that), then at the very least real controversy and surely some antipathy too. When Freud had been working on the book in Vienna, he understood that its publication would cause him problems: it was, he wrote, "bound to be something fundamentally new and shattering to the uninitiated. Concern for these uninitiated compels me to keep the completed essay secret."

Even in England the Moses book would more than likely bring an end to the acceptance and affection that Freud was enjoying. (Perhaps the only time in his life when he had encountered a comparable feeling of acceptance was in 1909, when he came to America and experienced what he called the "incredible daydream." But Freud had only contempt for the United States; for England, the country that now welcomed him, he felt something like adulation: in this love affair the affection flowed both ways.) Freud, sick as he was, old as he was, a refugee, with all the vulnerabilities of the newcomer in an adopted country, had to decide if he would dare to go forward. "I don't anticipate a friendly reception from the scientific critics," Freud said. "Jewry will be very offended." The two chapters of the Moses book that Freud had already published were in German and in a rather obscure journal, *Imago*. Yet there were already people who had read them and had their worried intimations about the third. Soon they began to bring pressure on Freud.

It is worth noting that happiness—if that is what Freud was experiencing in London—was something that Freudian thinking has very little commerce with. When it comes to describing human beings at their best, Freud has little to say. He can touch on genius when he describes failed or failing erotic love, accounts for jealousy, or maps the subtle dynamics of self-subversion. He can explain why one person is a miser, another is a hypochondriac, a third an inveterate ingrate. He can describe the dynamics of tyranny in striking ways. When adults act like dismaying children, Freud, better perhaps than anyone, illuminates the scene.

But of course if Freud is right, the human capacity for regression is always present. The hunger for Hitler, or someone like him, never really goes away. The urge to be cruel, be destructive, be brutal, is perpetually there. By describing people at their worst, one is nonetheless getting close to something like their essence. Some people have seen Freud as a reductionist; perhaps it is better to see him as someone with brilliant insights into human beings when they are at their most reduced.

In Freud's descriptions of humanity at its worst, he barely takes into account history, or economics, or the specific qualities of a given culture. He has no interest in thinking about how various external pressures—the loss of a horrible war, an unfair treaty, alternating periods of inflation and depression—could help bring on the tyranny he describes in *Group Psychology*. Freud is not at all interested in pondering the relations between perceived cultural chaos and the onset of the kind of fundamentalist religion he describes in *Future of an Illusion*.

Freud once remarked that the objective of psychoanalysis was to transform hysterical misery into common, everyday unhappiness. In saying so, he exhibited not only his personal temperament, but also his thinking's bandwidth. Freud is a superb student of misery and unhappiness, <u>but about what makes life worth living, he has surprisingly little to say.</u> Freud cannot contribute much to understanding what makes a happy marriage or a flourishing family life. <u>He cannot tell where genuinely consequential art comes from: he can offer a superb analysis of Hamlet the character, but not of *Hamlet* the play.</u> Hamlet the character he can treat like a patient of his, though a singularly complex one; <u>the play itself, in its freshness and power, passes beyond his terms of analysis.</u> Similarly, he cannot explain how an individual moves past narcissism or the will to personal power, and lives for the good of others or for the good of humanity as a whole.

<u>This is true because for Freud all human behavior is defined by its origins in childhood.</u> The childhood past (like the primitive past, as Freud sees it) is <u>inevitably tormented;</u> Freud's child always wants what he cannot have and has what he does not want. To Freud, the present is fundamentally a repetition of what has come before: in fact there is, strictly speaking, <u>no pure present, no "now,"</u> in the thought of Sigmund Freud.

On the matter of unhappiness, Freud's work suggests that we might reverse Tolstoy's famous observation. From the Freudian perspective, it is all the unhappy families that are more or less alike. They repeat and repeat the old patterns of frustrated desire and mysterious aggression. In them the dynamics of the Oedipal complex are in full and constant play: the past is all and the present virtually nonexistent. The Dutch psychoanalyst, J. H. van den Berg evokes this limit to Freud's thinking when he observes that "the theory of repression . . . is closely related to the thesis that there is a sense in everything, which in turn implies that everything is past and there is nothing new." Freud's thought cannot encompass something new, something not directly and definingly related to the repressed past. He could never really explain how people broke the mold—how they did unpredictable, productive things. Freud, one might say, had no theory that could begin to explain how someone as original and bold as Sigmund Freud ever existed.

Perhaps one of the reasons Freud distrusted democracy so much is that if he had admitted its promise, he would also have had to admit that human beings could develop a fresh, effective way of governing themselves, which swerved away from the old familial patterns of domination (father over all). Freud intended to write a paper on the dynamics of sublimation—that is, on the way that instinctual energies stop sustaining old patterns and move on to invest the creation of fresh achievements in commerce, art, and science—but he never managed to do it. Freud can account for our behavior but not our acts, our sorrow but not our happiness.

Freud in London now, in 1938, feeling better than he had in a long time, was facing a perplexing condition. Struggle and strife he was abundantly accustomed to; he knew all the dynamics (and the pleasures) of conflict. And he believed that he knew all the vicissitudes of intoxication as well. But was this feeling of pleasure at arriving in a free nation perhaps something else: might it be that strange, elusive thing called happiness?

\*   \*   \*

On Friday, June 10, Freud went off to visit his chow, Lün, who had been taken from Dover, where the Freud party landed, off to a quarantine kennel at Ladbroke Grove. The trip garnered some media attention: "Nothing could have kept the great scientist away from his dog friend," Michael Molnar quotes an Australian sports newspaper, the *Referee*, as saying. The paper went on to cite the kennel's director, who averred, " 'I have never seen such happiness and understanding in an animal's eyes. . . . [Freud] played with her, talked to her, using all sorts of little terms of endearment, for fully an hour. And, though the journey is long for a man of his years, he said that he was resolute about coming to see Lün as often as he can.' " Here and elsewhere around him in his new home, Freud could find a new image for himself, a not-an-entirely-disagreeable one: that of the mellow, sweet-natured magus, benignly savoring ripe old age.

The next day, Freud received a visit from Abraham Shalom Yahuda, a Jewish Bible scholar who also lived on Elsworthy Road. Yahuda is the first visitor to the new house in England whose arrival Freud notes in his diary, though he does misspell the scholar's name as *Jahuda*, a sign perhaps of Freud's overall feelings about the visit. Yahuda came to meet his distinguished neighbor, to welcome him to England and to pay due respects, but he had another purpose as well. He wanted to entreat Freud not to publish the Moses book. The Jews, Yahuda said, were already facing enough tribulations in the world, which was of course something that Freud, the refugee from Hitler's Austria, knew as well as anyone. Why should Freud want to add to the Jews' many woes by publishing what was bound to be an inflammatory—perhaps even an anti-Semitic—book? Yahuda, it seems, was aware that Freud was going to go so far as to question Moses's identity as a Jew.

Yahuda was not the only one who begged Freud to drop the Moses project. The same month, Freud wrote to Arnold Zweig about receiving a letter "from a young American Jew imploring me not to deprive our poor unhappy people of the only consolation remaining to them in their misery." Then Freud asked, a bit too ingenuously, "Is it really credible that my dry essay, even were it to reach him, should disturb the belief of a single believer conditioned by heredity and upbringing?" On June 21, Freud, so far undaunted by opposition, internal or external, went back to work on the Moses book, trying to mold the refractory third essay into shape.

Freud had already written forcefully against religion in the 1927 volume *Future of an Illusion.* There he describes Western faith as nostalgically and oppressively patriarchal. Human beings long for the father, he says; more precisely, they long for the childhood father's return. At one time, Freud says, almost all of us lived in total security, or at least in the illusion of total security. For in early life, the father offers the child what seems to be complete protection and also a clear, unassailable sense of right and wrong. As people grow, they inevitably lose faith in their individual parents, who reveal themselves as flawed, inadequate, lacking in judgment, and anything but omnipotent. They are not the perfect beings that children, early on, take them to be. Yet as Freud insists throughout his work—the idea is at the core of his thinking—people will never voluntarily leave what they have once felt to be a fully satisfying emotional situation. The id, once it has committed itself to a given object or idea and found that commitment to be fulfilling, resists letting go with all its might. A patriot loves his country to the death, right or wrong; a woman continues to adore the cheating husband who once gave her joy; the father never stops mourning his departed child. When reality deprives us of something we love, our first impulse, and often our last, is to reconstitute it through fantasy. There are few more satisfying situations, Freud says, than the feeling that we are protected and watched over by an all-loving superior being, who knows with certainty the distinction between right and wrong, true and false. When our judgment shows that no such figure actually exists, the psyche rebels and re-creates a Supreme Being in conformity with its wishes. This occurs in religion and also, of course, in politics. So the father of merely mortal nature is reconfigured and reborn as the immortal sky god and as the omnipotent leader.

Freud asserts that human beings combat their feelings of helplessness in a hostile world by concocting a collective supreme fiction: "When the growing individual finds that he is destined to remain a child for ever, that he can never do without protection against strange superior powers, he lends those powers the features belonging to the figure of his father; he creates for himself the gods whom he dreads, whom he seeks to propitiate, and whom he nevertheless entrusts with his own protection. Thus his longing for a father is a motive identical with his need for protection against the consequences of his human weakness."

Like the dictator, the patriarchal god is an answer to the crisis of the superego. The superego, at its worst, is unconscious, overly demanding, and cruel, often to the point of sadism. It punishes us, Freud insists in *Civilization and Its Discontents*, not only for the transgressions we commit, but also for those that we merely conceive of committing: it disciplines not only the act, but also the desire. The external superego, the patriarchal sky god, can be cruel and demanding as well, but he has also left mankind his commandments. Through his scriptures and his prophecy, people understand what placates him, or perhaps even what wins his favor. Like the dictator, the sky god introduces clarity into situations that are disturbingly over-complicated. Now we know what is just and what is not; now we know how to conduct ourselves so as to assure prosperity on this earth and salvation in the next. "Thus," says Freud in *Future of an Illusion*, "the benevolent rule of a divine Providence allays our fear of the dangers of life; the establishment of a moral world-order ensures the fulfillment of the demands of justice, which have so often remained unfulfilled in human civilization; and the prolongation of human existence in a future life provides the local and temporal framework in which these wish-fulfillments shall take place." Human beings, Freud suggests, wish perhaps more than anything else to find the Truth, the one right way to live in the world, and then to organize their lives around it. One of Freud's major hypotheses in the last phase of his work is that people would usually rather have Truth through union with what is greater than themselves than have pleasure that they can enjoy for its own sake, moment to moment and day to day. It often feels better to have absolute meaning in life than it does to have stimulation, variety, complexity—a world rich and marvelous but not entirely explicable. The cost of a relatively open-ended existence can be fierce anxiety—anxiety most people are desperate to discharge as expeditiously as possible. Recall Hitler's telling lines: "The masses love a commander more than a petitioner and feel inwardly more satisfied by a doctrine, tolerating no other beside itself, than by the granting of liberalistic freedom with which, as a rule, they can do little, and are prone to feel that they have been abandoned."

Freud suggests that the qualities that culture has associated with women—love, nurture, care—are not ultimately the qualities that human beings want to spend their lives pursuing and possessing. What we seem to desire most, men and women both, is to get ourselves into stabilizing contact with power and authority. We want to find those things, subordinate ourselves to them, and to do so we will, if necessary, forego love and all the other intimate human satisfactions. In his late writings, Freud stops thinking so much about the Oedipal desire of the mother, which he comes to feel that individuals may be able to surmount in time, and begins thinking more about the human hunger for patriarchs, about the need for kings.

When Freud published *Future of an Illusion* in 1927, many Anglo-European intellectuals were declaring that religion was gradually withering away. Even in the mid-nineteenth century, writers like Matthew Arnold were worried about the world that would come into being when humanity had done the seemingly inevitable and ended its commitment to transcendental faith. The world might then become a place where, in the well-known line, "ignorant armies clash by night." Arnold and others like him expended considerable intellectual effort trying to figure out what to do when the day came and faith was fully extinguished. This is something that even Nietzsche—who was not terribly prone to handwringing— worries about, perhaps most famously in his passage on the death of God in *The Gay Science.* " 'How shall we comfort ourselves, the murderers of all murderers?' " asks Nietzsche's madman, who in this case is probably close to being identical with Nietzsche himself. " 'What was holiest and mightiest of all that the world has yet owned has bled to death under our knives: who will wipe this blood off us? What water is there for us to clean ourselves? What festivals of atonement, what sacred games shall we have to invent? Is not the greatness of this deed too great for us?' " Then comes the ultimate Nietzschean question: " 'Must we ourselves not become gods simply to appear worthy of it?' " Karl Marx, Thomas Carlyle, Jeremy Bentham, John Stuart Mill, Ernest Renan, Charles Darwin, John Ruskin, Alfred Lord Tennyson—each in his way registered a sense that in his generation or the next, religion would die away.

Though there is a superficial optimism in *Future of an Illusion* about the birth of a comprehensive atheism, the main thrust of Freud's thinking about religion and the addiction to the patriarch brings no such hope. To Freud, the essence of Western religion—and he would surely include Islam in the indictment as well—is fundamentalism. People yearn to believe in a monolithic, all-seeing and all-knowing deity who controls life on earth and throughout the cosmos. Fundamentalism is at the heart of religion because it represents the most direct and intense recapitulation of the early state of things where the father and his powers were all. (The novelist Salman Rushdie avers that people have "a God-shaped hole" within them and Freud would surely agree.) All father religions, Freud indicates, have fundamentalism at their core, so that the believer, however nuanced or humane his belief may appear, can always be pulled as if by gravitational force back to unquestioning commitment to the father and his unerring word.

Accordingly, Freud does not go out of his way in *Future of an Illusion* to commend the less overtly patriarchal faiths. Fundamentalism is like tyranny—and like love and liquor—an intoxicant, and the only way to overcome fundamentalism is to cut off faith completely. Freud's answer to authoritarian religion is not personal religious experience, outside of institutional structures, which William James commends in *Varieties of Religious Experience*, nor is it that vague amalgam that, since Freud's time, has come to be called spirituality. Freud's recommendation is complete withdrawal from the drug, and that withdrawal takes the form of a militant atheism. Belief in no god is Freud's answer to what he takes to be the infantilizing force of faith. And once god is gone, the individual will do well to beware of god substitutes, which come in myriad forms, from leaders to social causes to patriotic dogmas to fervent commitments to this ruling idea or that. Sometimes, of course, atheists are among the most overbearingly religious people in the world, for they have displaced their will to believe onto some other absolute—or, they have made their atheism itself into something like an evangelical faith.

Because human beings need leaders to organize their collective lives, Freud believes that they should seek out humane, relatively un-self-interested people who have done something to conquer their own narcissism and their will to power. Always, though, there will be a risk of tyranny, for that is, after all, what human beings most want. The American diplomat and writer George Kennan seems to feel that he is offering a bracing truth when he says that, "The fact of the matter is that there is a little bit of the totalitarian buried somewhere, way down deep, in each and every one of us." Were Freud to hear this, he would probably laugh aloud. To Freud, Sylvia Plath is closer to the truth: "Every woman adores a Fascist," she famously declared in "Daddy": from Freud's perspective, every man does too.

For his conviction about the allure of the patriarch, Freud was not without evidence, nor has evidence been lacking for it in the years after his death. Hitler and Mussolini may have fallen, but there were also Stalin and Mao and Franco, and all the dictators large and small who have lorded it over often-worshipful masses in Africa and Asia, Latin America and Eastern Europe. Force has helped establish and consolidate these leaders, it's true, but often the adulation of the tyrannized for their tyrants has been of no little consequence either. Nor has religion become more comprehensively enlightened over time. In the twenty-first century a stranglingly intolerant version of faith is abroad not only throughout the Islamic world, but in the United States of America. Fundamentalist faiths have a number of identifying dimensions: belief in the absolute and unambiguous truth of this or that scripture; a sense of embattled righteousness; rule by males and a concomitant repression of women; pursuit of holy struggle and perhaps, in time, of holy war; a sense of pervasive crisis in the world; a demand for unquestioning obedience. But most saliently, for Freud, there is the presence of the patriarchal god, looking down on his worshippers, issuing his harsh but luminous commands, and blessing his chosen ones above all others.

It is hard to escape the view that when people subordinate themselves to cruel dictatorships and tyrannical deities, they are satisfying needs that are, among other things, psychological, infantile. They are creating sound, solid identities for themselves, rather than exploring human possibility. Freud pointed to the twofold horror of what one might call the patriarchal complex, tyrannical governments and tyrannical religions, and began to explain why they will probably be with us forever. This is true despite the fact that such governments and religions are palpably contrary to collective interests, and even frequently to the interests of the dictators and hysterical preachers themselves. Their fate is often epitomized by Benito Mussolini, who ended amply perforated with bullets and strung up in the public square in Milan.

But Freud didn't merely intend to repeat himself in the Moses book: he had, he believed, something new to say. He wanted to understand the character of Moses, a figure he had admired through his life; he wanted to get to the bottom of what made the Jews the people that they were; he wanted to arrive at a psychoanalytical explanation for anti-Semitism. More than that, the book he was writing would be an indirect autobiography and a meditation on what psychoanalysis was and what it might become. But Freud had been working on the book now for at least four years and had declared it finished more than once, only to return to it for more development. The Moses book, he wrote to Ernest Jones, "plagues me like a 'ghost not laid.' I wonder if I shall still manage to pull together this third part, despite all the external and internal difficulties. For the time being, I cannot believe it. But *quien sabe?*"

On June 23, two days after taking up work on the Moses book again, Freud got a taste of what was perhaps the most flattering elixir that England could dispense. Three secretaries of the Royal Society, Sir Albert Seward, Professor A. V. Hill, and Griffith Davies, came to visit Freud at home to ask him to sign the society's charter book. In general, only the king, an honorary member of the society, actually had the book brought to him to sign; all others had to make their way to the society for it. But Freud, because he was unwell and could not readily travel to Burlington House, had the book brought to him. (Two weeks before, Freud had managed to go out and journey to see his dog, Lün, at the quarantine kennel, but the Royal Society couldn't seem to elicit the same commitment from Freud as his beloved chow.) Freud signed his name beneath that of Isaac Newton, and also of Charles Darwin, one of the figures Freud most admired and whose work he saw as a prelude to his own. For years he had been signing only his last name to letters and documents: Freud. But in England, signing with the last name only was the prerogative of a lord, so Freud, for what may have been the first time in forty years, was compelled to sign his whole name.

Surely the Royal Society honor was official public testimony that Sigmund Freud was what he had always, at least in some part of his spirit, aspired to be and feared he was not, a scientist. In fact, Freud was never entirely sure how to describe his work. His most passionate, overt hope was that psychoanalysis was in fact scientific. He had started out as an empirical researcher, after all, working on, among other things, the structure of the medulla oblongata, the hindmost section of the brain, which he once described as a "very beautiful object." As speculative as his work became—in time he would offer theories of the compulsion to repeat, the Death Drive, and the titanic strife between what he called Eros and Thanatos—Freud nonetheless held on to the hope that, in time, biological data would arise to confirm all his hypotheses.

At other times, Freud took a different view: he said that the poets were there before him; they were the first true students of the unconscious. The difference between Freud's knowledge and the poets' was simply that the poets had proceeded by intuition, whereas Freud managed to build a systematic account. Freud referred to his theory of the drives, which he was constantly reformulating, as "our mythology." He called himself a "conquistador" because of his swashbuckling intellectual ambitions; and he confessed that he always aspired to be a philosophe, a thinker in the mode of Voltaire, who took up all of the major questions, from the cosmic to the intensely private, and did so with freewheeling and spontaneous, if also highly cultivated, intelligence.

Yet Freud understood that a scientific identity, especially in the first half of the twentieth century, when the prestige of science was compounding, would give him a larger share of cultural authority. It would mean that more people would listen to him and take him seriously. Freud feared, and rightly, that psychoanalysis was perpetually in danger of being dismissed as the palmistry or phrenology of its day. To be known as a scientist would help to solidify the new standing that Freud had achieved on his arrival in London. Signing the Royal Society book made Freud look more like what he had always wanted, or half wanted, to be: a man of science, who opened up the secrets of life.

And yet, Freud knew that the new book was not going to be science. It would speculate, supported by thin enough evidence, that Moses was not a Jew but an Egyptian; that monotheism was an Egyptian innovation, brought to the Jews by Moses; and that the Jews eventually murdered Moses for his pains. To publish such a book would surely be to undermine the gift that the magi of the Royal Society had brought to Freud, inclusion in the coterie of serious and estimable men, men of science. Why not do the expedient thing? Why not simply let society tell you who and what you are, especially when its verdict flatters long-maintained wishes—for success, for status, and of course, in a certain sense, for love—that have been frustrated for a long time?

Perhaps it would have been best if Freud were willing to think of his writing as something like "wisdom literature." After Freud's death and before it, many critics of his work have demonstrated that it does not stand up to the strict requirements of science: the findings he offers are not quantifiable, not repeatable, not falsifiable. These critics have actually done Freud a service. They have released him from a standard that he cannot meet and helped to redefine his work in ways that will in time allow its true value to emerge. Freud may have covered his office with pictures of the scientists, or aspirants to science, whom he most admired, men like Charcot and Helmholtz. But his real intellectual predecessors were, most directly, Schopenhauer and Nietzsche, philosophers who were both speculative and practical. (Freud once said that he had not read much of Nietzsche, virtually all of whose books he nonetheless owned, because he was afraid that in Nietzsche's work he would find too many of the truths of psychoanalysis anticipated.) Freud provides a way of looking at experience that—like Samuel Johnson's way, or Montaigne's or Emerson's—can be proved or disproved not by scientific standards, but by individuals deploying his ideas and honestly chronicling the gains and losses that follow. No one has ever lost sleep wondering if Montaigne is a scientist, nor should anyone do so about Freud. Philip Rieff and, later, Adam Phillips have led the way in understanding Freud as a possible guide to life, a post-religious thinker whose concepts have a practical use, or as William James would say, a cash value, if they have any value at all.

But Freud never took this path, never identified himself with Nietzsche and Schopenhauer: Freud thought that the only way he could genuinely succeed was as a scientist. He had been preoccupied with the matter of success on the grand scale from early in his life. Freud frequently recalled that when he was a child, a Gypsy told his mother that he would accomplish great things and that his mother had readily believed it. She liked to call her son "my golden Siggy" and gave him every chance to advance himself in the world. He had his own room in a small, very crowded house and all were compelled to keep quiet while he did his work; his sister Anna recalls having to stop her piano playing so that Freud could concentrate. Freud's father loved and admired his son, but his mother believed in him with an incandescent faith. Later in life, Freud would say that the most important condition for a man's success in life was the unqualified love and confidence of his mother, and this he enjoyed.

In *The Interpretation of Dreams*, Freud recalls a particular incident that he forever after associated with his desire to succeed. "When I was seven or eight years old," he says, "there is [a] domestic scene which I can remember very clearly. One evening before going to sleep I disregarded the rules which modesty lays down and obeyed the calls of nature in my parents' bedroom while they were present. In the course of his reprimand, my father let fall the words, 'The boy will come to nothing.'" Freud says that this must have been a "frightful blow," because when in later life he thought of the scene, he always began to enumerate his achievements and successes, as if to say to his father: "You see, I have come to something." Forever after, Freud would associate urinating in public or involuntarily losing control of one's bladder with strong ambition. "Look at me!" the perpetrator wants to say. Though what he's done is hardly commendable, he still wants attention so badly that he'll suffer embarrassment to get it. Perhaps later he'll find more apt ways to draw the crowd's gaze, but for now this is what's in his repertoire.

Freud was no longer a child and no longer needed to soak himself in front of others to get the attention he wanted. He had earned what he desired so much from childhood through hard work and daring. Freud remarked once that getting rich doesn't make people happy because happiness only comes from the fulfillment of childhood wishes. It may be that no three-year-old wishes for a strong and amply diversified portfolio, but surely a young child can hunger after fame. Now the Royal Society testified to Sigmund Freud's standing. It must have been tempting to imagine how he could stand back, forget about the Moses project for a while, and enjoy what he had earned.

But Freud had been intrigued by Moses for quite some time. In 1914, the year that Freud's work underwent a major change, and his fascination with the issue of authority began to crystallize, Freud published his anonymous article about Michelangelo's statue of the prophet. Freud had seen it in the church of Saint Peter in Chains in Rome and become transfixed. "I stood in the church in front of the statue," he wrote, "studying it, measuring it, and drawing it." (Freud was a surprisingly good draftsman.) The brief essay, which came out in *Imago*, was, according to Freud, an attempt to figure out why the statue had the allure for him that it did. Freud says that when he cannot explain how a work of art achieves its effect, he cannot obtain any real pleasure from it. "Some rationalistic, or perhaps analytic, turn of mind in me rebels against being moved by a thing without knowing why I am thus affected and what it is that affects me."

The sculpture depicts the prophet clasping tightly on to the Ten Commandments, which he has just brought down from Mount Sinai. Freud is curious about what Moses is actually doing with the tablets of the law. Conventional interpretation has it that he is about to hurl them down at the Israelites who are dancing around the golden calf. But Freud believes that Michelangelo had something much different in mind. For, Freud says, the prophet, as he's depicted, has not given in to anything like full-fledged anger. He isn't about to visit holy wrath on the wayward people. Rather, Michelangelo's Moses is a divided being: he is angry, yes, but he is also in the process of containing the emotion. "In his first transport of fury," Freud says, "Moses desired to act, to spring up and take revenge and forget the Tables; but he has overcome the temptation and he will now remain seated and still, in his frozen wrath and in his pain mingled with contempt. Nor will he throw away the Tables so that they will break on the stones." Freud's Moses has contained his anger, kept his passion in check.

Freud believes that the sculptor swerved away from the biblical text to assert that Moses, enraged though he was about the Israelites' transgression, nonetheless manages to control himself. He is, to use Freud's idiom, sublimating his anger rather than giving in to it, and it is, presumably, from his ability to sublimate that he gains his authority as a leader. Michelangelo, Freud says, "has added something new and more than human to the figure of Moses; so that the giant frame with its tremendous physical power becomes only a concrete expression of the highest mental achievement that is possible in a man, that of struggling successfully against an inward passion for the sake of a cause to which he has devoted himself."

The authority Moses achieves in his self-division is unconventional, from the perspective of Freud's later work, in that, in general, authority comes from appearing to be completely at one with oneself. The leader knows at all times what he thinks about all things, and he is always right. His presence is constantly, as Freud says in *Group Psychology*, masterful and self-assured. But in Moses, Freud believes that he is confronting someone who is certainly a leader but who nonetheless is able to dramatize his self-division. Moses—or at least Moses as Freud believes the sculptor sees him—is manifestly candid about the state of his interior life. Presumably his standing as a leader comes from that honesty. He is able to reflect the authentic state of his followers' psyches, for they too (like all of us) are prone to be divided, yet they nonetheless accept him as an authority.

It's possible that Freud is suggesting that this power of dramatic sublimation is characteristically Jewish. And he may also be suggesting that he himself, by virtue of his capacity to discern the feat of sublimation that Moses enacts, may embody this presumably rare power—and so be able to lead humanely. "Moses," Freud will say at the very end of his life, "is flesh of sublimation," and in this enigmatic remark he concentrates much of what makes the prophet so fascinating to him.

In London now, Freud continues to work. Quite sick, not fully rested from his journey, he sits in his unfamiliar study on Elsworthy Road and speculates about Moses. His beloved collection is still in Vienna under the control of the Nazis and might never return. On his desk he has a few terra-cottas given to him by the princess when he stopped in Paris on the way to England; in the midst of them is posed his treasured figure of Athena, the warrior intellect. He has few books at his disposal because his library remains under Gestapo control. Lün, who usually sits by him while he writes, purring gruffly and diffusing her doggy smell, which to Freud is more than agreeable, is still quarantined at the kennel. He is officially forbidden cigars, but it's hard to imagine that he doesn't enjoy one from time to time, since they are, after all, the food of thought. Against no little resistance, Sigmund Freud keeps going.

In mid-July, Freud received a visit from a longtime admirer, the Spanish surrealist painter Salvador Dalí. Dalí—handsome, loquacious, self-promoting—had for many years wanted to meet Freud, whom he thought of as one of the major influences on his paintings and on the surrealist movement. In his autobiography, *The Secret Life of Salvador Dalí,* Dalí recalls his early attempts to meet with the great man. "My three voyages to Vienna," he says, "were exactly like three drops of water which lacked the reflections to make them glitter. On each of these voyages I did exactly the same things: in the morning I went to see the Vermeer in the Czernin Collection, and in the afternoon I did *not* go to visit Freud because I invariably learned that he was out of town for reasons of health." Dalí recalls instead spending his afternoons walking haphazardly through the streets of Vienna, eating chocolate tarts, which, he claims, possessed a bitterness accentuated by the meeting that never took place. "In the evening," he recalls, "I held long and exhaustive imaginary conversations with Freud; he came home with me once and stayed all night clinging to the curtains of my room in the Hotel Sacher."

A few years after his last failed attempt to see Freud, Dalí was sitting in a restaurant in France, eating a dish of snails and talking with his companions about Marie Bonaparte's recently published book on Edgar Allan Poe. All of a sudden, Dalí says, he saw a picture of none other than Sigmund Freud on the cover of a newspaper and learned that Freud had escaped from Austria and just arrived in Paris. "We had not yet recovered from this news," Dalí says, "when I uttered a loud cry. I had just that instant discovered the morphological secret of Freud! Freud's cranium is a snail! His brain is in the form of a spiral—to be extracted with a needle!"

On July 19, a little more than a month after Freud got to London, Dalí, in company with Freud's friend Stefan Zweig, made his way to Elsworthy Road, where he finally had the chance to meet the Professor. As he approached the house, the artist encountered something arresting. "I saw a bicycle leaning against the wall, and on the saddle, attached by a string, was a red rubber hot-water bottle which looked full of water, and on the back of the hot-water bottle walked a snail!"

Dalí had high expectations for the meeting, though it's not entirely clear what those expectations were. Perhaps Dalí aspired to be anointed as Freud's first authentic visual disciple, or maybe—Dalí was nothing if not confident—Freud's coeval. Just as Freud had described the unconscious in detail, so perhaps Dalí—with his paintings of melting clocks and inner deserts and gaudily misshapen human forms—aspired to render that unconscious, to make its productions visible. Perhaps Freud would bless his work and tell him that he had gotten things exactly right. If Dalí did have such expectations, he did not know much about the character of Sigmund Freud.

For the entire time they sat in Freud's study, Freud hardly said a word. ("We devoured each other with our eyes," Dalí asserted.) Freud had just suffered another attack of temporary deafness brought on by an infection, but in all probability, Dalí knew nothing of this. To Dalí, Freud was simply a great stone face. At one point in the visit, a frustrated Dalí tried to draw Freud's interest to his article on the subject of paranoia. "I explained that it was not a surrealist diversion, but was really an ambitiously scientific article, and I repeated the title, pointing to it at the same time with my finger. Before his imperturbable indifference, my voice became involuntarily sharper and more insistent. Then, continuing to stare at me with a fixity in which his whole being seemed to converge, Freud exclaimed, addressing Stefan Zweig, 'I have never seen a more complete example of a Spaniard. What a fanatic!' "

But there was worse. The subject of surrealism came up and Freud informed Dalí, "In classic paintings I look for the sub-conscious—in a surrealist painting for the conscious." This, presumably, was Freud's way of saying that Dalí's apparently spontaneous dreamscapes were overly intellectual, schematic, mere illustrations of ideas—and Sigmund Freud's ideas at that. The effect was not lost on the painter. "This was the pronouncement," says Dalí, "of a death sentence on surrealism."

Freud's relationship to artists and to art was always, to say the least, fraught. In the essay he called "Creative Writers and Day-

Dreaming," he demeaned literary art as wishful fantasy. It allowed people to immerse themselves in pleasing delusions that were akin to their own daydreams, but more graphically presented and more fully elaborated. Through literary fantasy, the wimp becomes the gunfighter; the stay-at-home transforms himself into the world voyager. Freud's archetypal reader is not unlike the one Philip Larkin describes in his "Study of Reading Habits": he deals out justice to villains twice his size; as to women, he "clubbed" them with sex, and broke them up "like meringues." "The creative writer," Freud says in the essay, "does the same as the child at play. He creates a world of phantasy which he takes very seriously—that is, which he invests with large amounts of emotion—while separating it sharply from reality." There is, Freud argues, only one consequential differences between fantasy and creative writing and that is form. "The writer," says Freud, "softens the character of his egoistic daydream by altering and disguising it, and he bribes us by the purely formal—that is, aesthetic—yield of pleasure which he offers us in the presentation of his phantasies." Art, from this point of view, is guilt-free fantasia, egoistic dreaming that the reader can savor because of the apparent distancing that form provides. Form makes daydreaming palatable to the over-I, or so says Freud in his best known essay on the matter.

But at other moments, Freud is willing to confess that the artists are the ones who can achieve stunning insight, and do so in a flash without the hard labor that the prosaic investigator, the psychoanalyst, must invest. Even then, what the poet knows, he knows in a nonsystematic, unself-conscious way: he cannot organize and make coherently available what it is he feels. If Freud was putting on a too-somber face in front of Dalí, he might have been expressing his own anxieties about the work he was preparing to bring into the world. Freud was compelled now to see himself at least from time to time as something of an artist. One of the early working titles for the Moses book had been "Moses, a Historical Novel."

Dalí and the Royal Society, art and science—those were the borders between which Freud's work unfolded. He would love to be a scientist, so as to assume science's abundant cultural authority; but he never wanted to be constrained by the limits of empirical thinking. (Here, as elsewhere, Freud was as rebellious as he was conventional.) Freud wanted to speculate; he wanted free play for his mind. Art, too, drew Freud: he adored literature and sculpture, and wasn't immune to painting. (For music, he did not care all that much.) But art, however great, could never command the level of respect, and more important, of belief, that Freud thought psychoanalysis deserved. Part of what makes Freud's work so rich is that he was unwilling to commit himself to either side of the art/science divide. He let his urge to be imaginative and his urge to get it all absolutely right challenge, confound, and interanimate each other. This made Freud's mental life quite strong and complex, but it didn't make things terribly easy for the likes of Salvador Dalí. To be fair, though, if Freud and the visiting members of the Royal Society had gotten down to a discussion of the scientific bases of the Oedipal complex, matters would not have unfolded so smoothly either.

\*    \*    \*

On one front at least, Freud had considerable reason to be satisfied. Anna had proved herself to him by the way she acted in the last days in Vienna. She had not only stood up bravely to the Gestapo; she had managed almost all the family's affairs, dealing frequently with highly placed German and Austrian Nazis. As the Freuds' liaison to Ernest Jones and the princess, Anna showed herself to be both prudent and tough. Freud, who'd long pondered the matter of his successor, left Austria sure that Anna was the right choice. Now in England, she was continuing to prove her father's judgment to have been good.

Late in July, Anna, having gone through the difficult work of procuring an alien's travel visa, went to the Fifteenth International Psychoanalytical Congress in Paris and represented Freud admirably. Standing in for her father, as she would when he was gone, Anna read a segment from the final chapter of the Moses book. And she also stood up against the Americans on the matter of lay analysis.

The Americans aspired to make psychoanalysis a part of the medical establishment: only medical doctors, they argued, should be licensed to practice Freud's therapy. Though he was himself trained as a physician, Freud did not concur. What mattered most to him was that therapists be intelligent, cultivated, and self-aware, undergo a training analysis, and be willing to submit themselves from time to time to being analyzed again, if only briefly, by a supervisor. "It is unjust and inexpedient," Freud says in *The Question of Lay Analysis,* "to try to compel a person who wants to set someone else free from the torment of a phobia or an obsession to take the roundabout road of the medical curriculum." Freud hoped that humanists would carry forward his legacy, not scientists, and the desire reveals an important dimension of his thinking. Though Freud desperately wanted respectability for psychoanalysis, he also wanted it to work, and he believed that medical training, while desirable, wasn't a crucial ingredient for creating a successful therapist. On the matter of lay analysis, Freud was, rather surprisingly, willing to put aside his hopes for institutional success and to go with more pragmatic, intuitive views. Here as elsewhere, when it came time for Freud to choose between conformity and innovation, the results were unpredictable.

On July 17 he was able to declare in his journal that the Moses book was finished. Of course, he had proclaimed as much before. But even if it was now true, questions remained. Given all the pressure against him, it was no certainty that he would go ahead and publish the book. And if he did, it was surely an open question whether he would have it translated into English and expose his new hosts directly to his thinking. But these concerns did not seem to hold Freud back, at least for the present. He was so exhilarated that he went to work on another manuscript. This would eventually become *An Outline of Psycho-analysis*, and in it Freud would hold forth on the most central and the most controversial matters of psychoanalytical doctrine. Nowhere near as speculative and adventurous as *Moses and Monotheism*, the new work was in many ways Freud's attempt to impose orthodoxy after he was gone. (Even as he was at his most adventurous, as he was with the Moses book, Freud could always find reasons to be prudent.) Whatever the new book's contents, Freud was very pleased simply to be writing again. Creation was crucial to Freud's sense of what existence was about: when he did not write, he did not feel alive.

Freud took pleasure in visits like the one he received from Salvador Dalí, and he took a good deal more pleasure from Anna's growing confidence and capability. Yet many things continued to disturb him during the days at Elsworthy Road, while his son Ernst looked for a new home for him and Martha. Freud had left four sisters in Austria, and he was worried about them. In early August, he got news that the money he left them was now at their disposal, which did something to salve his concerns, but surely not enough. Marie Bonaparte was making efforts to help them and they had other friends besides. Yet under the circumstances, Freud knew that no one could possibly accomplish enough. Princess Bonaparte was doing what she could not only for the Freud family, but for Jews generally. She even proposed purchasing a section of southern California to be used as a Jewish homeland—and was willing to contribute richly to the cause.

Freud's health continued to deteriorate. Late in August, Max Schur saw that Freud had developed a new lesion behind the area of the last operation, "more ominous because harder to reach." Schur asked Freud's surgeon, Hans Pichler, to come to London and to consider performing surgery. Pichler left Austria and arrived in London on September 7 to have a look at his famous patient.

The cancer, which Freud sometimes called "my old friend," had been with him since 1923, when he found what he first thought was a benign growth on his jaw and palate. Freud had encountered swelling in that region of his mouth as far back as 1917, but it had all but disappeared when he began smoking a particularly fine brand of cigars and so he had barely mentioned it. The growth Freud found in 1923 was too troubling to say nothing about, or to try to cure by upgrading. In April of that year, Freud's internist, Felix Deutsch came to examine Freud. "Be prepared," Freud told him, "to see something that you won't like." Deutsch didn't like it: he recognized the lesion immediately as cancerous. But he neglected to tell Freud as much, wanting to protect him from the shocking news; rather he assured his patient that the growth was benign.

Freud sought out a surgeon, Marcus Hajek, in whom he seemed to have little confidence, to have the growth excised. During the operation things went amiss—which, given Hajek's general level of skill, was all too likely—and Freud soon ended up in a small recovery room, bleeding heavily, his only companion there a rather kindly, though mentally impaired, dwarf. Freud pulled the rope on the bell to summon help, but the bell didn't work. The dwarf, seeing Freud's distress, ran off down the corridor and got help for Freud, who otherwise might well have bled to death.

Strangely enough, in 1924, Franz Kafka, perhaps Europe's greatest living writer, also came under Hajek's care. Kafka was suffering from the tuberculosis that would soon kill him, but Hajek seems to have done little or nothing for his gifted patient. When Max Brod, Kafka's close friend and editor, tried to get

Kafka more considerate treatment, Hajek "energetically explained that he could not look upon Kafka as anyone else but the patient in room number so-and-so."

Though Freud said that Hajek's procedure had greatly improved his health, all during that summer of 1923 he continued to suffer from pain in his jaw. Freud spent the summer months in Bad Gastein and then in Lavarone, Italy, on what was supposed to be a vacation. But the pain was so intense that he had to summon Felix Deutsch again, who examined his mouth, and saw that the growth was still active and that Freud would need another procedure. On September 26, Freud wrote to Ernest Jones to say that "it has now been decided that I have to undergo a new operation, a partial resection of the upper jaw as the growth reappeared on this ground. It is promised I will be able to start work 4–5 weeks later, but you know what it all means."

This time, though, Freud found himself a superior oral surgeon, Hans Pichler, who performed the operation in two stages, on October 4 and 12. Schur describes the operations this way: "On October 4, 1923 . . . the external carotid artery was ligated and an extensive dissection of the submaxillary and jugular glands was performed to prevent a spread of the cancer. Fortunately, the enlarged glands revealed no malignancy. Only on October 12 . . . did Pichler perform the radical surgery, consisting of a resection of a major part of the right maxilla, a considerable part of the mandible, the right soft palate, and the buccal (cheek) and lingual (tongue) mucous membranes." In other words, Pichler cut out a large quotient of Freud's right upper jaw and the right side of the roof of his mouth. All this was done under local anesthetic. A few weeks later, Pichler took a biopsy, found more malignant tissue, and went to work again. Then, finally, after four operations, the cancer seemed to be gone. What was left was to fit Freud with a prosthesis that would enable him to talk, to eat, and of course to smoke.

"Then," says Ernest Jones, "began sixteen years of discomfort, distress and pain." The prosthesis, "the monster," was a huge denturelike device designed to close off the mouth from the nasal cavity. It needed to come out at frequent intervals for cleaning, but removal was no easy matter, nor was reinsertion. Freud couldn't open his mouth very far, so it could sometimes take as much as half an hour to get the prosthesis back in. In doing this, Freud had one helper and one only, and that was Anna. Anna and her father made a pact that they would always deal with "the monster," and with every other thing pertaining to Freud's health, with complete detachment, as though they were a pair of surgeons working on a case together. And this they did. But "the monster" created many hardships. For Freud to eat and to talk, it needed to fit snugly. But that caused irritation and no little pain. Sores broke out on the inside of Freud's mouth. But when he took the prosthesis out to give his aching mouth a rest, the tissue that surrounded it shrunk and sometimes made reinsertion impossible. Then "the monster" had to be modified.

The prosthesis distorted Freud's speech, making it both nasal and thick. Arthur Koestler, who visited Freud in London, recalls him speaking with his lips stretched very tight and the corners of his mouth pushed out, "rather in the manner of children imitating the speech of their toothless elders in cruel mockery."

Eating also became very difficult and Freud almost never did so with others around him. The damage done to Freud's eustachian tubes by the cancer and by the operations impaired his hearing, until he became completely deaf on the right side. This was the side he had used to listen to his patients as they lay down, so he had to install himself on the other end of the couch and listen to them with his left ear.

What Freud would not do was to give up smoking. The cigars irritated his mouth, or what was left of it, so over the following years, Freud required more than twenty-five procedures to remove various nonmalignant growths. "Thus in 1926," Max Schur says, "there began an endless cycle of leukoplakia, proliferation, precancerous lesions. Each of them had to be treated surgically, by excision, electrocoagulation, or a combination of both." For all these years, Freud constantly suffered pain, sometimes mild, sometimes moderate, sometimes more. His response to that pain was to take some aspirin, to smoke another cigar, and to keep working. After virtually every procedure, Freud jumped back to life: in a day or two he was seeing patients and at his desk again.

Now, in London, in 1938, Schur and Pichler encountered what they took to be another flare-up of the cancer—which would make it the first actual malignancy in fifteen years—and Pichler operated. Freud took a general anesthetic called Evipan, an equivalent, Schur says, of sodium pentathol, and continued with nitrous oxide through a nasal catheter. Pichler was compelled to split Freud's lip and carry the incision up along his nose to get full access to the new lesion. The surgeon used a needle to excise the tumor on the cheek, and found the tissue that he removed was very hard, more like scar tissue than he had expected. When Pichler was sure that he had taken out everything that could be toxic, he inserted the prosthesis and packed the wound cavity with gauze. That night Freud was already up and reading. As it turned out, the tissue that Pichler removed was precancerous, making Exner, one of Freud's British specialists, and Schur wonder if the whole procedure had been necessary at all.

Necessary or not, the operation was brutal, and despite Freud's apparent good health on the night of September 8, recovery was slow and hard. A month later, Freud wrote that he was still not able to work, to sleep well, or to speak as he would like. Nor could he, he confessed, smoke, at least not with any ease. He told Marie Bonaparte that "this operation was the worst since 1923 and has taken a great deal out of me. I am dreadfully tired, and feel weak when I move. I have actually started work with three patients, but it isn't easy. The after-effects are supposed to be over in six weeks, and I am only at the end of the fourth." As miserable as Freud felt physically, he might have taken some pleasure from the fact that he was still an esteemed figure in England: a score of newspapers carried stories about his operation.

Four days after Freud's operation, Adolf Hitler delivered a fierce denunciation of the Czechs at a party rally in Nuremberg. The terms of abuse were not unlike those that he had used to make way for the Austrian invasion. The German minority in

Czechoslovakia was being roundly persecuted, their rights violated at every turn. Hitler was demanding that the Czechs cede the Sudetenland, where most of the nation's Germans lived. England and France both had strong interests in the Czech situation: France was bound by treaty to declare war if Germany attacked. And now Hitler was testing, as he had in Austria, to find out if the Western powers would rise against him. Some members of the German General Staff were distraught, fearful that Hitler was going to ruin them all, but the führer claimed that he knew the leaders of the Western democracies better than they knew themselves.

Neville Chamberlain, the British prime minister, decided that the best course was to negotiate with Hitler, and so on September 15 he flew to the airfield in Munich. When the Czechs heard the news, they were overwhelmed: they had declared martial law; they had put down agitation by the Germans in the Sudeten; they were ready to stand up against the Nazis. But now, one of their two most potent allies was going off to entreat Hitler on his own territory. The first thing that Chamberlain heard when he landed in Germany was a radio broadcast demanding the immediate annexation of the Sudeten areas to the Reich. Then, much as Schuschnigg had done six months before, Chamberlain went off to meet Hitler at Berchtesgaden. Chamberlain sat and listened to Hitler tell him how modest his designs were. Said Chamberlain after the conference, "In spite of the hardness and ruthlessness I thought I saw in his face, I got the impression that here was a man who could be relied upon when he had given his word."

Soon after, Hitler spoke in Berlin and announced that the Czechs would have to clear out of the Sudetenland by September 26, at which point the land would become a part of Greater Germany. "This is the last territorial claim I have to make in Europe!" Hitler declared.

A conference in Munich at the close of the month involved the nations that Churchill called the Big Four—England, France, Germany, and Italy. But the Czechs themselves had no representation. The Czech diplomats stood outside the door and waited as their powerful friends, the two democracies, did what they were willing to do to defend Czechoslovakia against the fascists. When the meeting among the four ended, the Czechs learned that Hitler would have his way completely. All of the Sudetenland was to be given over to the Germans, with the territory to be evacuated within five days, beginning on October 1. A few days before the Munich Accord, Chamberlain said, "How horrible, fantastic, incredible it is that we should be digging trenches and trying on gas masks here because of a quarrel in a far away country between people of whom we know nothing."

Chamberlain returned to England and cheering crowds, who lined the road on his way back from the airport. Londoners wept in gratitude and relief: their city was not going to be a second Guernica. Chamberlain waved the treaty terms from the window at Downing Street and claimed that he had secured "peace with honor." Then came the line that would become famous: "I believe it is peace for our time."

In his journal on September 30, 1938, Freud scrawled the word "Peace." A few days later, he wrote to Marie Bonaparte,

"Everything here is rather strange, difficult and often bewildering, but all the same it is the only country that we can live in, France being impossible on account of the language. During the days when war seemed imminent the behavior on all sides was exemplary, and it is wonderful to see how now that the intoxication of peace has subsided, people as well as parliament are coming back to their senses and facing the painful truth. We too of course are thankful for the bit of peace, but we cannot take any pleasure in it."

The Munich Accord probably saved Adolf Hitler's life. Many of his senior officers were sure that Germany was not prepared for an all-out war with England and France. A group of them were so distressed that they put together a plot to arrest Hitler and the other leading Nazis and to take over the government themselves. But seeing Hitler's great success at Munich, the plotters backed off and the plan came to nothing. At last convinced that Hitler was the man he said he was, the army fell in behind him. The German population became yet more enraptured with the savior, who seemed able to perform miracles.

Carl Jung, breathless when he contemplated the führer, said, "I saw pictures taken of him in the Czechoslovakian crisis; there was in his eyes the look of a seer. . . . Hitler is the mirror of every German's unconscious. . . . He is the loudspeaker which magnifies the inaudible whispers of the German soul until they can be heard by the German's unconscious ear." Then comes Jung's pronouncement: "Hitler's power is not political; it is *magic*."

\* \* \*

On September 27, Freud moved into the house that would always be associated with his memory, 20 Maresfield Gardens in London. "Far too beautiful for us," Freud said of his new address, and it was indeed a lovely house, especially after Ernst finished fitting it out for his mother and father. The price for the house was steep, sixty-five hundred pounds. Freud secured a loan for four thousand from Barclays Bank and soon began worrying about how he would manage to pay it off. One of the reasons—but far from the only one—that Freud was eager to sell an American edition of the Moses book was to help pay down his considerable mortgage.

The house had eight bedrooms, three bathrooms, and two garages. There were gardens at the front and in back, as well as a lawn for playing tennis. (A brochure produced five years before Freud moved in mentions that a few of the rooms had space for a billiard table—not Sigmund Freud's game, alas.) It was a brick house, and though built in 1920, it looked older. The architect, Albert Hastilow, designed it in a revivalist style and Ernst Freud described it as neo-Georgian. The house was sedate and comfortable, and it offered modern appurtenances including gas, electric lights and power, a telephone, constant hot water, and a system of partial—Freud would soon find it far too partial—heating.

Freud called the new house "incomparably better" than Berggasse 19 and declared that he was going "from poverty to white bread" in a stroke. Ernst, he observed, had been busy ruining the house in order to restore it. Freud's son worked to install a lift so that Freud, who was too frail still to manage the stairs, could be transported from one floor to another. But

Ernst's major innovation was to have the wall knocked out between two rooms downstairs, so as to give Freud a large area that would serve as both study and consulting room. This was a sun-brightened space, unlike Freud's darker precincts at Berggasse 19, and here Freud would be able to sit at his desk, brood, talk, answer his correspondence, and make notations in his diary as the light poured in.

But there was still the matter of Freud's furniture: his books, his antiquities, his paintings, and his carpets, all the things that in Vienna had made Freud's sanctum what it was. Freud, skeptical about all human endeavors, with the possible exception of those that he undertook himself, was not at all sure that the Nazis would release his property. He had paid all the taxes and duties, unjust as they were, and yet, as he observed, the Nazi gangsters were not a predictable lot. When Freud heard that his things were actually packed, he simply said, "There's many a slip between cup and lip."

At the end of the first week of August, Freud's shipment had arrived and now, moving into Maresfield Gardens, he could begin to restore his old life. Here was his library, or at least the balance of it. (Before he left Vienna, he had been compelled to part with about eight hundred volumes, which eventually turned up in New York City.) Here was the famous couch, a gift from an early patient, a Mrs. Benvenisti, who presented him with it in 1891. And, most warming to Freud surely, here was his collection of antiquities, fully intact. For the past few months, he had been forced to subsist on his terra-cottas; on the gifts that people, sometimes strangers who knew all about his love for these works, kindly sent his way; and of course on the statue of Athena that Marie Bonaparte had smuggled out of Vienna for him.

Now Freud had his picture of the great physician Charcot, one of his first inspirations, to hang over the couch. He had his rendering of the Roman forum, by Luigi Kasimir, which would recall to Freud his intense, abiding interest in archaeology and his conviction that the mind was structured like a grand archaeological site, with city on top of ruined city, memory atop memory. Now Freud had his rather bland bust of that anonymous Roman citizen, which, for whatever reason, he gave pride of place to, posing it on a column of its own. He had his photographs of the erotic trinity, the two of Marie Bonaparte, and one each of Lou Andreas-Salomé and of Yvette Guilbert, who would actually come and visit Freud at Maresfield Gardens when she was in London in 1939 for her three performances at Wigmore Hall.

Freud not only had his desk, but the anthropomorphically shaped chair designed to make Freud comfortable, or as comfortable as possible, when he twisted his body up to read. Now Freud had access to the portraits of some of the men he thought of as his masters: Hermann Helmholtz, the arch-materialist; Ernst Brücke; and Ernst von Fleischl-Marxou. In the middle of it all sat Freud, like a monarch whose kingdom had, late in his life, been restored to him.

\*　　\*　　\*

Yet from his new, light-drenched study, Freud was forced to contemplate events that were anything but lovely. On November 7, a seventeen-year-old Polish Jew named Herschel Grynszpan, who had grown up in Germany, learned that his parents had been deported from Germany to Poland. Grynszpan, living in Paris at the time, got himself a revolver, walked into the German embassy, and shot the first official he met. Ernst vom Rath, third secretary of the German embassy, was badly wounded. Goebbels exploited the event for all it was worth. The Nazi newspapers described the shooting as an attack launched by something called "world Jewry" against the integrity of the Reich. The papers promised "the heaviest consequences" for German Jews.

Late in the afternoon of November 9, Hitler learned that Ernst vom Rath was dead and almost immediately issued orders to Goebbels for a full-scale attack on all Jews living in the Reich. Hitler also informed Goebbels that the death of the Nazi diplomat would be the excuse for seizing available Jewish assets and for exiling the Jews from as many aspects of German life as possible. Quickly the orders went out to set about burning synagogues and destroying Jewish homes. One typical set of instructions ran this way: "A Jew has fired a shot. A German diplomat is dead. In Friedrichstadt, Kiel, Lubeck and elsewhere there are completely superfluous meeting houses. These people still have shops amongst us too. Both are superfluous. There must be no looting. There must be no manhandling. Foreign Jews must not be touched. The action must be carried out in civilian clothing and be concluded by 5 a.m."

Many of the storm troopers who received such orders were still in their beer halls, celebrating the fifteenth anniversary of Hitler's attempted putsch of 1923. They were in no condition to be told not to manhandle anyone and not to loot. Almost immediately, the brownshirts hit the streets, carrying clubs and knives and swinging cans of gasoline. Soon nearly every synagogue in Germany was burning. By the end of the night almost a thousand were destroyed. The Germans also went from Jewish shop to Jewish shop, smashing the windows, and leaving the sidewalks inches deep in broken glass. Thus the evening acquired its name, Kristallnacht, the Night of the Broken Glass. Of the nine thousand Jewish-owned shops in Germany, the Nazis destroyed seventy-five hundred that night. In some places, storm troopers went to Jewish cemeteries and smashed the gravestones. In Esslington, brownshirts forced their way into the Jewish orphanage, broke the furniture, and destroyed the books while the children watched, in tears.

In Saarbrücken the Jews were compelled to dance outside their synagogue, and to sing religious songs; then the Nazis drenched them with water and left them standing in the frozen air. In Essen, storm troopers set the beards of Jewish men on fire. In Meppen, Jewish men were forced to kiss the ground in front of SA headquarters, and while they did, brownshirts kicked them and walked over them. In many cities and towns Jews had to wear placards proclaiming that they were the murderers of vom Rath. By the time it was over, between one and two thousand Jews were dead, three hundred had, or would soon, commit suicide, and thirty thousand had been arrested and taken off to Dachau, Buchenwald, and Sachsenhausen. Summarizing the events of Kristallnacht in the *Racial Observer*, Goebbels said, "The German people are an anti-semitic people. They take no pleasure or delight in allowing themselves to be provoked as a nation by the parasitic Jewish race."

In Vienna, where the same violent protocols were observed that night, the Nazis got their hands on Freud. Arthur Freud was a professor, fifty-six years old at the time; he was a journalist in Vienna and held a passport from Czechoslovakia. In the morning, he walked out to a Jewish community center, hoping to get more information on the events of the day, and believing that his foreign passport would protect him. At the center, Professor Freud encountered a detachment of Nazis who politely let him pass. But once inside, he met another one and they attacked. The commanding officer grabbed him by the shirt and demanded to know who and what he was. When the professor gave his name, there came a cry of triumph: "Now they have him!" And for a while the Nazis did in fact believe that they had apprehended Sigmund Freud.

Finally, the troopers released Arthur Freud, who went home that night and had his apartment searched by two more Nazi thugs, pretending that they were looking for weapons. What they did find were some works by Sigmund Freud's Viennese nemesis, Karl Kraus, who had died in 1936. One of the Nazis commanded Freud to burn them because, he insisted, "that one was the biggest Jewish filthy fellow." Though Sigmund Freud probably never learned anything about the fate of his namesake on Kristallnacht, he was well aware of events. "Pogroms in Germany," he wrote in his diary.

After Kristallnacht, Jews throughout Germany and what had been Austria fled in great numbers. But they did not always have an easy time of it. An ocean liner called the *Saint Louis* left Hamburg with about a thousand German Jews onboard, all of whom had permission to enter the United States—not immediately, but in either 1940 or 1941. The ship docked in Cuba, where the refugees hoped that they could stay until they became eligible to enter the States, but Cuba would not allow them to come ashore. Nor would Argentina, Brazil, Chile, Colombia, Panama, Paraguay, or Uruguay take a single one of the Jews. Soon the ship was passing back and forth along the Florida coastline as the American government debated whether to offer refuge or not. The answer was no; and with that, the *Saint Louis* could do nothing but turn around and make its way back to Europe. The boat docked in Antwerp and the refugees went off to various nearby countries, including France, Belgium, and Holland, all of which were soon overrun by the Nazis, who visited on many of the passengers from the *Saint Louis* the predictable fate.

But not every nation—or every person—turned away from the survivors of Kristallnacht. "Many of those in Britain," Martin Gilbert says, "who took in Jewish children after Kristallnacht hardly had the resources to do so, but wanted to help, and willingly accepted the hardships involved. In Archway, North London"—not far from Freud—"Miss Harder, who ran a sweet and tobacconist shop, and lived in a two bedroom flat, took in two sisters who reached London from Prague on June 2. Six months after taking them in, she died of tuberculosis. But during the short time she looked after them, she took them on holiday, on the Isle of Wight, at her own expense, and tried—in vain—to get their mother out of Czechoslovakia."

Freud responded to the events of early November 1938 in part by publishing a letter on anti-Semitism in *Time and Tide*. "I came to Vienna as a child of four years," he wrote, "from a small town in Moravia. After seventy-eight years of assiduous work I had to leave my home, saw the scientific society I had founded dissolved, our institutions destroyed, our printing press ("Ver-lag") taken over by the invaders, the books I had published confiscated or reduced to pulp, my children expelled from their professions." All was true and all grievous enough. But then Freud adds something surprising: "Don't you think," he asks the editors, "you ought to reserve the columns of your special number for the utterances of non-Jewish people, less personally involved than myself?" What Freud hoped for, it's clear, was for others—for gentiles—to speak out against Nazi barbarity, rather than leaving that task to the Jews, who could be seen simply as protecting their own interests. What the Nazis were doing was bad enough to anger any sane and civil person, so why should the Jews have to be in the forefront of protest?

The brief letter to *Time and Tide* echoes a piece that Freud published two weeks before Kristallnacht: his "Comment on Anti-Semitism." There, Freud says that he is drawing from an essay by another writer, though Freud cannot remember precisely who it is. The unremembered writer, whom the reader presumes to be a gentile, does the work of defending the Jews and in their behalf says some rather flattering things. "The Jews are not worse than we are; they have somewhat other characteristics and somewhat other faults, but on the whole we have no right to look down on them. In some respects, indeed, they are our superiors. They do not need so much alcohol as we do in order to make life tolerable; crimes of brutality, murder, robbery, and sexual violence are great rarities among them; they have always set a high value on intellectual achievement and interests; their family life is more intimate; they take better care of the poor; charity is a sacred duty to them."

The writer whose voice and thoughts Freud is borrowing is Mark Twain and the essay is called "Concerning the Jews," which Twain published in *Harper's Magazine*. Some of the things that Twain goes on to say in his so-called defense of the Jews are a little less palatable than the lines that Freud remembers and adapts. The Jew, Twain says, "has a reputation for various small forms of cheating and for practicing oppressive usury, and for burning himself out to get the insurance, and for arranging cunning contracts which leave him an exit but lock the other man in, and for smart evasions which find him safe and comfortable just within the strict letter of the law, when court and jury know very well that he has violated the spirit of it."

Yet even had he recalled this passage, Freud might have been forgiving, for he dearly loved Twain's work and even went to see him perform in Vienna once, where Twain told a story about stealing a watermelon that Freud remembered for a long time and eventually used to illustrate a point in *Civilization and Its Discontents*. Twain, in fact, spent a few years in Vienna when he was at the height of his fame (hotels offered reduced rates to have him on hand) and Freud was a relative unknown. Had the two ever met—there is no evidence that they did—they could have taken up a mutual favorite subject: both strongly doubted that William Shakespeare had written the magnificent works with which the world credited him.

The defenses of the Jews that Freud made in his letter to *Time and Tide* and in the short essay where he borrowed from Twain are not, strictly speaking, Freudian pieces of writing. They are civic and thoughtful. They don't investigate the strange passions that give rise to racial hatred; they don't attempt to shock the reader with new insights. Be decent, they say—and little more. They are the work of a public man addressing public issues in a clear-minded, humane way. Freud's deeper, more arresting ideas on the hatred Jews could generate was at the center of his new work, the book on Moses.

Over time, Freud was becoming something of a monument in Maresfield Gardens. Everyone with literary or cultural aspirations in London, it seemed, needed an audience with him. Ernest Jones and Anna did what they could to shield him from the pressure of his new fame, but they did not always succeed: Freud was too important, too esteemed—and maybe even loved.

A hundred or so years before, another figure had ensconced himself in a dwelling not so far from 20 Maresfield Gardens. In the latter part of his career, Samuel Taylor Coleridge became the sage of Highgate. His great poems—"The Rime of the Ancient Mariner," "Kubla Khan," "Christabel," and the rest—were well behind him. He lived with the kindly physician James

Gilman, who managed Coleridge's opium supply (or tried) and helped the greatest literary talent of the age—according to many; sometimes even according to Coleridge himself—to impose a measure of regularity on what had been a rather dissolute life. Coleridge at Highgate became part of the grand tour. Young men like Ralph Waldo Emerson and Thomas Carlyle presented themselves for an audience with the magus. Some time well after noon, Coleridge trundled into the parlor and began holding forth on anything from the linguistic theories of Horne Tooke to the strange and probably inexplicable vagaries of his digestion—opium having a peculiar effect on the belly and the bowels.

By this time, Coleridge had become an intellectual pillar of the existing order. He wrote on behalf of the established church and the ruling state. His work became a cornerstone of conservative political and social theory. If he never quite renounced his earlier scandalous, sometimes terrifying, poetry—the influence of which in time traveled everywhere, from Poe to the multiplex cinema—he had left all that far behind. Now STC, as he preferred to be called, wrote little verse. In his premature old age, the sage of Highgate turned away from what was most rich and strange in himself and became an ever-talkative, ever-blander public man.

The question now was whether the sage of Maresfield Gardens would wither into respectability the way that Coleridge did. Like Coleridge, Freud received a great number of visitors: Arnold Zweig came, stayed a fortnight, and left with an apology to Freud for tiring him out; H. G. Wells, who tried unsuccessfully to get British citizenship for Freud and was one of the few who dared call Freud by his surname, also turned up; and naturally, the princess came: she visited nearly ten times and her presence was each time greatly treasured by Freud. There had been Dalí with his fears about the death of surrealism; Yahuda had come with his anxieties about the Moses book. Though prone now to deafness, Freud gave all his visitors a measure of rather serene attention. He was far from having the strength to deliver Coleridgean monologues, not that he had ever had such an inclination very often. He spoke his mind in compressed sentences, exhibited courtly, old-world manners, and did his best to keep his guests occupied.

One of the more intriguing visits to Freud was from Leonard and Virginia Woolf. Virginia was arguably the preeminent British novelist of the time; her husband, Leonard, was a journalist, a political theorist, and the director of the Hogarth Press, which had been publishing Freud's books in English translation and would soon sponsor James Strachey's grand Standard Edition. Leonard was gaunt, hyperintellectual, pipe-smoking; Virginia still beautiful, high-strung, and—to both herself and others—sometimes almost unbearably perceptive. On Saturday, January 28, 1939, they went to have tea with Freud at 20 Maresfield Gardens. "Nearly all famous men are disappointing or bores, or both," Leonard recalls in his memoir. "Freud was neither; he had an aura, not of fame, but of greatness. . . . It was not an easy interview. He was extraordinarily courteous in a formal, old-fashioned way—for instance, almost ceremoniously he presented Virginia with a flower." The flower was a narcissus, a strange enough gift, given Freud's ideas about the female proclivity for narcissism and Woolf's repudiation of such thoughts—to her, men were by far the greater practitioners of self-love. "There was something about him," Leonard continues, "as of a half-extinct volcano, something somber, suppressed, reserved. He gave me the feeling which only very few people whom I have met gave me, a feeling of great gentleness, but behind the gentleness, great strength."

They sat down for tea in Freud's consulting room, which seemed to Leonard "almost a museum," and they talked, naturally, about Hitler. Virginia expressed a sense of guilt, saying that if the Allies had not won the war of 1914, there might have been no Nazis and no Hitler. Virginia's idea was a form of the notion, which has not disappeared, that it was the mistreatment of Germany at Versailles, by France in particular, that had led to the current crises. Freud disagreed. Hitler and the Nazis would still have come and they would have been yet worse if the Germans had won the war.

Leonard, who was not always the most tactful of men, went on to tell Freud a story. He described a recent court case in which a man was convicted of stealing a number of books from Foyle's, including a volume of Freud's. The magistrate who heard the case fined the man, but he expressed another wish for the thief's punishment. According to Leonard, the magistrate wanted to sentence the man to the reading of all of Freud's work.

Freud was amused, or so Leonard claims, and self-deprecatory about his own achievements. "My books have made me infamous," Freud said, "not famous." Yet what perhaps allowed Freud to say as much was how famous he had now become, at least in London. One exception to the consensus about Freud's greatness seems to have been Virginia Woolf, whose account of the afternoon is rather different from Leonard's. She recalled Freud as "a screwed up shrunk very old man: with a monkeys light eyes, paralyzed spasmodic movements, inarticulate: but alert." Later she added that "all refugees are like gulls with their beaks out for possible crumbs." Anna Freud was developing a book, Martin hoped to place a novel—and they made the error of asking Virginia for advice.

Perhaps before they left, Leonard and Virginia Woolf told Freud the story of Mitz the marmoset, for it was surely one that Freud would have relished. In 1935, the Woolfs went off on a driving tour of Western Europe in Leonard's Lanchester 18 car, which had a Tickford roof that retracted to leave the vehicle completely open. With them, they took Mitz, Leonard's pet marmoset, who often sat perched on his master's shoulder. One day, in Germany, the Woolfs found themselves driving into a crowd. The road was lined with Nazis in uniform and school-children carrying swastika flags. The people were drawn up very closely on both sides awaiting the arrival of some high Nazi official, and Leonard had to drive quite slowly through them. Leonard, who was a Jew, was naturally worried about what was going to happen next.

"We were closely penned in," he said, "by what . . . seemed to be an unending procession of enthusiastic Nazis. But we soon found that there was no need for us to worry. It was a very warm day and I was driving with the car open; on my shoulder sat Mitz. I had to drive at about fifteen miles an hour. When they saw Mitz the crowd shrieked with delight. Mile after mile I drove between the two lines of corybantic Germans, and the whole way they shouted 'Heil Hitler! Heil Hitler!' to Mitz and gave her (and secondarily Virginia and me) the Hitler salute with outstretched arm."

Surely the most surprising figure to pass through Freud's London life was Doctor Anton Sauerwald, the Nazi commissioner who handled Freud's case in Vienna, and who turned up in London early in October of 1938. His name is inscribed in Freud's diary, which is what Freud usually did after receiving a visitor, and yet there seems to be no other evidence of a meeting between Freud and his former oppressor turned advocate. Max Schur attests to the fact that Sauerwald did go and visit Freud's brother, Alexander.

By now, it was clear to the Freud family that Sauerwald had saved Freud from serious trouble by holding back information about his finances and particularly his overseas bank accounts from the Nazis. Alexander asked him about this directly. "The Führer," Sauerwald replied, "who of course knows best, realizes that the fatherland is in a state of siege. The Jews, due to their internationalist leanings and their tendency toward individualistic behavior, cannot form a reliable element of the population. Thus they have to be eliminated. This might be deplored, but the end justifies the means. This does not mean, however, that an individual should not be permitted to alleviate individual hardship in selected cases."

Max Schur came to suspect that Sauerwald was in England as a spy. But given Freud's current standing, it is possible that at least one reason for Sauerwald's trip was to pay homage to the great and good man who had deeply moved his Nazi heart. By his own later account, Sauerwald came to London by Freud's invitation to discuss various financial matters. Sauerwald went on to claim that during the visit, Freud asked him to arrange for Pichler, the surgeon, to come and to examine him as soon as was reasonably possible. Sauerwald said that he did as much, even going so far as to roll the expense of the visit into "moving expenses" and thus save Freud an extra payment.

In his postwar trial for war crimes, Sauerwald gave himself credit for attempting to save the books in stock at the Verlag by an agreement with Marie Bonaparte, which alas fell through at the last moment. Nonetheless, he said, he did manage to get the books out of Vienna and distributed to numerous universities all through Europe. He also said that he convinced the director of the Austrian National Library, Paul Heigl, to have the library store boxes of books that contained nearly all the volumes that the Verlag had issued. After the war, when Anton Sauerwald went on trial, Anna Freud and Marie Bonaparte wrote letters in his behalf, describing his services to the Freud family and entreating the court for mercy, which in fact was granted.

It is not all clear how much of what Sauerwald recounts about his trip to London is to be believed. Perhaps he did admire Freud; perhaps he did take an interest in psychoanalysis, but the bomb maker who so efficiently investigated his own explosions seems to have had one salient talent in life: the ability to play both sides of the game. Nothing that the commissioner ever did should escape the assumption that some form of duplicity was involved.

*   *   *

Amid all the adulation that Freud received in London, there was one discordant sound. Freud received endless advice—sometimes it was closer to warning—not to publish the Moses book. Charles Singer, a distinguished historian of science, pleaded with Freud, through his son Ernst, to suppress the manuscript. To Singer, Freud wrote, "I have spent my whole life standing up for what I have considered to be the scientific truth, even when it was uncomfortable and unpleasant for my fellow men. I cannot end up with an act of disavowal. Your letter contains the assurance which testifies to your superior intelligence, that everything I write is bound to cause misunderstanding—and—may I add—indignation. Well, we Jews have been reproached for growing cowardly in the course of centuries. (Once upon a time we were a valiant nation.) In this transformation I had no share. So I must risk it."

Finally for Freud, the time of ease and acceptance—of intoxication—ended, and all warnings assimilated but none obeyed, he sent *Moses and Monotheism* out into the world. On Thursday, February 2, 1939, Allert de Lange, in Amsterdam, printed the book in German. A month or so later, Freud received two copies from Holland; one he kept, the other he gave to Princess Bonaparte.

What Freud wanted most now was to see his volume come out in English and exactly as he had conceived it. He chided Ernest Jones and his wife, Katherine, for being too slow and slack with the translation. (Jones may have been many things, but he was never slack.) And Freud also pressed Leonard Woolf to make sure the book would come out in English exactly as Freud wished. When Woolf wrote to

Freud and asked him if the Hogarth Press might change the book's title and call it simply "Moses," because the longer word, "monotheism," would scare off readers, Freud, "nice man" that he was, shot back that there would be no such change. He even wrote ahead to his American publisher, Knopf, to say that the title of his book would be *Moses and Monotheism*, and that was that. On May 19 Freud had the satisfaction of seeing his long-pondered, already much-criticized work in the language of his new country. The deed was done: as Peter Gay says, Freud "had conceived his *Moses and Monotheism* in defiance, written it in defiance, published it in defiance."

The most immediately scandalous parts of *Moses and Monotheism* were Freud's reflections on the identity of Moses. "To deprive a people of the man whom they take pride in," says Freud on the book's opening page, "is not a thing to be gladly or carelessly undertaken, least of all by someone who is himself one of them." To prove the point that Moses was an Egyptian and not a Jew—if in fact he did prove it or come close—Freud drew on a couple of possibilities. The name Moses, he asserted, was not a Jewish one, as scholarship had long understood, but Egyptian. Then too, Freud said, the biblical story of Moses's origins does not make psychoanalytical sense. In that most common of fantasies, which Freud called the "family romance," the child believes that though he may live with a humble family, his true parents are well-to-do aristocrats, perhaps even a king and a queen, from whom he was separated early in life. The biblical story about Moses being rescued by an Egyptian princess reverses the usual direction of the family romance: in it the child goes not from wealth to poverty, but from poverty to wealth. This fact provokes Freud's analytic interest. "In every instance which it has been possible to test," he says, "the first family, the one from which the child was exposed, was the invented one, and the second one, in which he was received and grew up, was the real one." In the Moses story, the first family is the poor family of Jews, the second family is Egyptian. So, Freud declares Moses must have started out as an upper-class Egyptian and somehow been taken up and adopted by impoverished Jews.

Then there is the matter of the origins of monotheism. Drawing on his anthropological and archaeological researches, Freud speculates that monotheism was not a Jewish, but rather an Egyptian invention. It was Amenhotep IV, not Moses or any other Jew, who converted to the monotheistic cult of Aton and began to spread the command to worship one god. Amenhotep, according to Freud, changed his name to Ikhnaton and attempted to impose his severe religion on the Egyptian polytheists. Moses was originally one of Ikhnaton's closest associates, but Ikhnaton died young, the Egyptians refused monotheism, and Moses turned instead to the Jews, who had been in Egypt for a few generations. He led the Jews out of Egypt, defying the pharaoh, and in the desert gave them laws, introduced them to circumcision, which had been an Egyptian custom, and persuaded them to worship Aton.

The Jews eventually repudiated Moses and Aton: the worship of one god was too cold and abstract for them. Angry because of all he has asked them to relinquish, they killed Moses and then lapsed back into their old forms of polytheism. Yet the memory of Moses and his religion persisted. The Jews felt remorse for what they had done, and that remorse exalted Moses's memory—what Freud calls a "reaction formation" took place. Slowly, a Midianite tribal god lost his violent qualities until he was nearly identical to the old Mosaic god, Aton, and so became, accordingly, the precursor for Yahweh. The repressed returned—in the form of monotheism—and the slain Moses came to be Judaism's great man.

One would be hard put to argue that these ideas are among Freud's most astute or grounded. Freud was letting his mind roam; he was speculating, guessing. And this is where many of Freud's perceptions come from, his best and worst alike. Freud got ideas in part because he was so open to them. He wrote them down for better and worse, and he let the bad take him to the good, and sometimes the good to the bad. The reader of Freud often has to do some work: in Freud's richest, strangest volumes, the reader occasionally has to play the part of ego to Freud's creative id, and sift matters out, see what might be true, what not. Early in his career as a consequential writer—which means in the middle of his life—Freud quoted Schiller on the philosophy of composition. Open it all up, the poet says. Let it run. Only once you've allowed the unconscious to express itself should you bring your judgment into play. Or as Saul Bellow, in his way an heir of Schiller's romanticism, puts it, "Everybody knows there is no finesse or accuracy of suppression; if you hold down one thing you hold down the adjoining."

Moses was not a Jew but an Egyptian; the Egyptian's were the first to disseminate the idea of there being one god and one only; the Chosen People murdered their greatest prophet. These are, perhaps, the kinds of perceptions Freud allowed in so as not to hold down the adjoining ones. And in fact in its deeper precincts, *Moses and Monotheism* is one of Freud's most illuminating books. Yet the public headed immediately for what was most vulnerable and least valuable about the work.

The reviews and early responses to the Moses book were generally about as furious and uncomprehending as Freud anticipated. Martin Buber, the formidable Jewish theologian, would sneer at the book as "regrettable" and "groundless." To Abraham Yahuda, the thoughtful neighbor on Elsworthy Road, who enjoined Freud not to publish at all, the book could have been the work of a Christian fanatic out to malign the Jews. Peter Gay quotes one Father McNabb, who, in London's *Catholic Herald,* wondered how long "free, generous England" would continue to extend a welcome to the author of so scandalous a work. Freud, the pious father claimed, was a champion not only of atheism (as he surely was), but also of incest. The reviewer for the *New York Times* closed by observing that Freud's "flimsy theories, which in part involve an interweaving of those he admits borrowing from others, are not the type of 'knowledge' that is worth the misunderstanding and the ill will that it is more than likely to breed at this time." An anonymous letter from the United States observed that it was regrettable that the German gangsters had not put Freud in a concentration camp, which was surely where he belonged. A writer in Palestine called Freud an "*Am Haaretz*," a bumptious know-nothing.

Freud's response was characteristic enough. He reveled in the book's strong sales figures—by June of 1939 it had sold 1,800 copies in its German edition—and he took the criticism in his stride. Now eighty-three years old, so sick that he had trouble walking and in constant pain, he still had the stuff for a fight.

Surely the sense of safety and contentment that Freud acquired when he first came to London and was greeted with flowers and gifts was now diminished. What Freud would have called the social superego stood in a much more complex and fraught relation to him. Any sense of inner unity and calm that Freud experienced during the halcyon early days in free, liberal England was now compromised. Freud was once again the person who caused trouble. He was the one who caught the middle-class asleep and stirred it up. Once again, Freud was the author of *The Interpretation of Dreams* and *Three Essays on the Theory of Sexuality*, books that caused upset in readers and brought conflict to Freud. Once again he could claim to be, as he told the Woolfs, not famous but infamous. The publication of the Moses book must have made Freud anxious, as conflict does, and it must have infused him with some energy, for conflict does that too. And by returning Freud to his early days of mental fight, as Blake would call it, the publication of *Moses and Monotheism* probably did something else too. It probably made Freud feel, for however brief a span of time, as though he was again young. "An aged man is but a paltry thing, / A tattered coat upon a stick." So far true enough, perhaps. But Yeats adds something more: "An aged man is but a paltry thing, / A tattered coat upon a stick, unless / Soul clap its hands and sing, and louder sing / For every tatter in its mortal dress."

"Quite a worthy exit," Freud himself said of the Moses book in a letter to Hanns Sachs, which was true enough.

At a certain point, pain became Sigmund Freud's element; it was a constant factor in his life, like the air he was breathing. After the operation that Pichler performed in September of 1938, Freud suffered constantly from pain in his jaw and related complications. Winter came on, and the weather was cold; the house at Maresfield Gardens, elegantly appointed as it may have been, was drafty, and this of course increased Freud's discomfort. At the end of January, Freud complained of an acute ache in his jaw. It turned out that a chip of bone, left in after Pichler's operation in September, was causing irritation. Schur removed it, but in the process he encountered more swelling in the back of Freud's mouth. This time, it looked to Schur like a malignancy.

The next month, Freud wrote to Max Eitingon to say that he had developed "a strong antipathy" toward his supposed savior, Doctor Pichler. Freud was referring overtly to the months of bone ache he had suffered, but perhaps indirectly to his exasperation with Pichler for prolonging a life that was more and more arduous. Yet as a rule, Freud would still not take any medication stronger than aspirin. Though he was writing little, if at all, for publication, Freud continued to read plentifully, to compose letters, to receive guests, and to conduct therapy; for these things, he needed his mind to be clear.

Late in February of 1939, Freud had X-rays taken of the right side of his face and head, the cancerous side. They were presided over by Doctor Lacassagne, whom the princess brought from Paris expressly for the purpose. It was Lacassagne who, a few years before, helped to save Princess Bonaparte's dog, Topsy. The X-ray that Lacassagne took depicts Freud's skull in a soft, luminous white against a shaded background. There, toward the rear of his jaw, is a large, irregular hole—it looks like the site of a bomb blast—where once there had been teeth, gums, and bone. The X-ray makes the jaw look like what it was, a gaping hole of pain. Some tissue was taken as well and the biopsy revealed what Freud expected, more malignancy, more cancer. And now there could be no further surgery—assuming Freud would have consented to suffer through yet another operation—because the cancer was much too close to Freud's eye socket and perhaps even too close to his brain. After the X-rays, Freud wrote to his younger friend Arnold Zweig, "I have had some unpleasant weeks, not just being ill and in pain, but also complete indecision about the next steps to be taken. Operation and radium treatment (Paris) were finally abandoned and an external application of Roentgen ray was decided on; this is due to start tomorrow. (There is now no further doubt that I have a new recurrence of my dear old cancer with which I have been sharing my existence for sixteen years. At that time naturally no one could predict which of us would prove the stronger.)"

The X-ray regimen was brutal: Freud lost the beard from the right side of his face; he got headaches, became dizzy; he bled from the right side of his mouth. Yet nonetheless, Freud continued to see his patients. Finzi, another one of Freud's physicians, would eventually write, that "He absolutely refuses to let us give him any pain relieving medicament of any sort except aspirin." What Freud really needed, the physician said, was psychoanalytic treatment to make him a little saner and so induce him to take some stronger drugs. But of this, Finzi admitted, there was not much hope. Freud detested the X-ray treatment, but observed that it was better than the other salient alternative, which was cutting off his head.

On May 6, 1939, Freud celebrated his eighty-third birthday. He sat for a while in the garden and received birthday greetings from family and friends, which were, as per the Freud family tradition, tied around the necks of the household dogs and sent Freud's way. But Freud could only bear company for so long. He tottered briefly around the garden exchanging greetings, but was soon back inside his study again and trying, insofar as the pain would allow, to get some rest.

Adolf Hitler, Freud's antagonist, had recently observed a birthday himself, albeit under much different circumstances. On April 20, 1939, two weeks before Freud tremblingly opened his birthday messages, Hitler celebrated his fiftieth birthday with an enormous parade. All three branches of the military turned out, as well as the Waffen SS. By the führer's orders, all the latest German armaments were on display: there were tanks, antiaircraft guns, and searchlights. Overhead, air force fighter planes and bombers roared. Back in his retreat, there was a special birthday gift for Hitler. For more than a year, workmen had been laboring away on an elevator that would take the führer from the bottom of the Kehlstein to the mountain's top, so that he could survey his domains. For Hitler's birthday the work was completed. The door to the elevator was plated with gold and inside there were padded seats, carpets, and sophisticated safety devices. But Hitler only went to the mountaintop three times; the air, he complained, was too rare for him there: he could hardly breathe.

After a while, Freud took up residence in the downstairs consulting room and library. He tried to read and to write letters, surrounded by his books and his antiquities; he slept there on the couch, which so many patients had used before him; he looked off into the spacious garden he had come very quickly to love. Anna was his constant nurse and companion (Martha was now in the background; Aunt Minna was too sick to attend well even to herself); Schur lavished all the care he could muster onto his lone, distinguished patient.

When, following Marie Bonaparte's recommendation, Freud took Max Schur on as his doctor in 1929, Freud made Schur promise that he would always be completely honest about Freud's medical condition, however severe it might become. There was another matter too: "Promise me," Freud said, "when the time comes, you won't let them torment me unnecessarily." Schur agreed and the two men shook hands.

In April, Schur took a brief trip to the United States. Planning to emigrate there eventually (one can imagine Freud's verdict on this idea), he took his family over to get them settled as he began the process of acquiring an American medical license. When Schur came back in July, Freud had lost a good deal of weight and he seemed relatively apathetic, at least by his usual standard of intellectual vigor. "I also had the definite impression," Schur said, "that a new carcinomatous ulceration had developed behind and slightly upward of the old lesion, in the direction of the base of the orbita. The bone was extremely tender, and there was a fetid odor."

In one of his most profound essays, "Mourning and Melancholia," Freud suggests that loss is so common and pervasive in life that we may be in the process of mourning almost all the time. If that is so, then Freud's mourning in the last weeks of his life must have been particularly intense, for he was losing a great deal and very rapidly.

One of Freud's first losses was his psychoanalytical practice. This time Freud must have understood that the loss was permanent and not temporary, as it had been when he ceased to see patients in Vienna. On the first day of August, Freud took the step of disbanding what had been a fifty-three-year endeavor. He had worked with Dora and the Rat Man and the Wolf Man and Little Hans, but he had also consulted with hundreds of others, including all of the first-generation of analysts, down to his daughter Anna. (Simply to be a first-generation analyst meant that one had been analyzed by Freud: there was no other central authority.) Freud had begun his career as a medical doctor and often thought of himself foremost as a healer—though to be sure he was many other things. Bringing to bear what remained a formidable intelligence, he now created synopses of each of his current cases for Anna, so that the patients could continue their therapeutic work.

With one case in particular, late in his life, Freud had reportedly become aggravated. When the patient did not make progress after weeks and weeks, Freud cried out in frustration, "You do not think that it is worth your while to love an old man." In the final phase of therapeutic practice—the mode of healing that Freud finally settled upon after trying a number of others—love was, in fact, at the heart of everything. Having made use of hypnotism and free association and dream inter-pretation, Freud now put himself, the physician, at the center of the drama. Freud became an analyst of what he called "the transference."

Over time, Freud came to the conclusion that his patients were falling in love with him. But he also recognized that they were doing so for reasons that transcended his own charms, such as those might be. For a neurotic individual, Freud asserted (and for almost everyone else, he at times suggested), a new figure who arrives on the scene promising enlightenment, a cure, the truth, love, will activate a spectrum of childhood emotions. The patient will transfer feelings once directed to the mother and the father, and later to other figures of authority, onto the person of the doctor. From this transference of feeling, the analyst can learn the dynamics of the patient's erotic life. All the failures and sorrows that have been part of his past relations with objects of desire and of authority will in time be manifest in what Freud thought of as "the theater of the transference." The patient will repeat his old prototypes, with the physician as the object. Freud observes that in therapy "the patient does not *remember* anything of what he has forgotten and repressed, but *acts* it out. He reproduces it not as a memory but as an action; he *repeats* it, without, of course, knowing that he is repeating it."

But finally, because the analyst does not reciprocate, but instead *analyzes* the offering of love from a detached, disciplined position, he can help the patient to see his old frustrating patterns. The patient will be able to apprehend, for instance, how all of his relations with figures of power in his life, no matter how distinct and singular they appear to him to be, are actually repetitions of old prototypes. Perhaps he has always embraced authorities fervently, and then, at a certain point, turned against them with bitter ingratitude. Perhaps all his erotic relations have ended in a certain sort of revulsion and what appears to be an inexplicable loss of sexual interest on his part. In therapy, the consistent patterns of frustration come to the fore, and with the therapist's assistance, they become visible. They become something that the patient comprehends. And with this gain in awareness, there can be change in behavior. By putting self-aware ego where repetitious id had been, the patient acquires some measure of experiential freedom. At the core of Freud's humanism, measured as it generally is, there lies the belief that if a person can describe his inner life with some accuracy—apply words where before there has only been silence and compulsion—then he can be just a little bit freer, and maybe (dare one say it?) a little bit happier than he has been in the past.

"The transference," Freud says, "creates an intermediate region between illness and real life through which the transition from the one to the other is made. The new condition has taken over all the features of the illness; but it represents an artificial illness which is at every point accessible to our intervention." For the cure to begin, though, the patient had to capitulate in the transference; he had to succumb to the allure of the physician.

So from about the midpoint of his career as a therapist, Freud had, day by day, hour by hour, been the object of the most passionate feelings from his patients, both male and female. He had been fiercely and often eloquently desired. But of course, with Eros being the ambivalent force that it is, Freud had been detested too. Within the confines of his magus's lair, amid the carpets and the statues and the overflow of scholarly books, Freud had lived a life of supreme erotic intensity. He had been courted, teased, insulted, worshipped, adored—and, the morning's sessions done, he had repaired to the front of Berggasse 19 for his noon meal, followed by his walk, his purchase of a book or newspaper, his beard trim. Then back again in the afternoon to the labors of Eros. Freud had led the life of a chaste Don Juan—and much like Byron's Don Juan, he had in fact been much more often pursued than pursuing.

But something else is noteworthy about the dynamics of transference analysis as Freud developed it. At the height of the transference, Freud may have been manifest to a given patient as the most magisterial figure of authority imaginable, the ultimate subject who is supposed to know, in Jacques Lacan's useful phrase. But Freud's objective was not to maintain this position. No, the aim of therapy was to demystify absolute authority, which meant, most immediately, to demystify Freud. The patient who is able, at last, to become self-aware about his hunger for unassailable truth and complete love takes up a new relation to all objects of desire and authority in his life, past and future. And he also takes up a new attitude to the analyst, to Freud. By the end of therapy, the patient who has passed through the vale of the transference is able to see Freud the therapist as another suffering, striving mortal, not unlike himself. He might be aware of Freud's high intelligence and his remarkable originality, but because of the analysis, the patient would no longer see Freud as anything like a mortal god.

The ritual of psychoanalytical therapy has at its central objective the deconstruction of all figures of absolute authority, Sigmund Freud included. However frequently Freud, in writing, in his personal life, or in his career as an institution builder, may have seemed devoted to setting himself on the primal father's throne, day to day there was a whole other dimension to Freud's work. What Freud did almost every morning and afternoon was to allow people to cultivate an inflated image of who and what he was, and then guide them in the process of dismantling that image. Over and over again, Freud showed his patients how to draw the gigantic figures in their own past down to size, and they learned this in no other way than by learning to draw Freud himself in more modest, human contours. Freud the sometimes patriarch didn't just develop theories about the destructive effects of patriarchy; he developed a form of teaching that gave people the chance to undo oppressive authority.

Shortly after Max Schur returned from New York, Freud had an attack of "cardiac asthma," and Schur rescued Freud, who by this point did not entirely care to be rescued. Freud now, as it were, forgave Schur for abandoning him, forgave his trip to America, and the old unequal friendship of the great man to his trusted retainer, Lear to Kent, was restored. "During August," Schur recalls, "everything went down hill rapidly. There could be no doubt about an extended recurrence with ulceration. The discoloration of the cheek became more and more marked, indicating the development of a skin necrosis." The odor that came from Freud, Schur says, got worse and worse and was soon impossible to control. It was the stench of Freud's jawbone, rotting away from the cancer. In time, the skin over Freud's cheek became gangrenous. A hole formed, creating what Schur called "open communication between the oral cavity and the outside." The odor became stronger, and flies gathered, so Freud's bed in the study needed to be covered by netting to keep them away. Freud's study, as Schur says, became his sick bay, and he could do nothing but lie there, looking out into his garden.

But the great problem was with Lün, Freud's chow, who had been released from quarantine. The dog had always adored her master. Freud had petted her, walked her, and frequently, too, talked with her: she sometimes seemed to him the sanest presence in his life. But now she cowered on the far side of the sick room because of the smell of decomposition coming from her master.

Freud said that dogs lived fully and even at times joyously because they did not suffer the fundamental human curse of ambivalence. Dogs did not love and hate the same object. They fawned on their masters and snapped at their enemies. They were, to Freud of course, what human beings could never be: creatures who attained a blameless purity of feeling. Freud did not wish to consider the palpable truth that, like humans, dogs are creatures of nature that have undergone domestication and so both love and hate the restrictive world where they find themselves. Freud's idealizations—his intox-ications—were few, though he did, it is true, once remark that the only pure love that could exist in the world was the love between a mother and her son: strange news coming from the theorist of the Oedipal complex. But on the matter of dogs, Freud was consistently starry-eyed. He could imagine pure love flowing from his dogs to him—and maybe sometimes from himself back to them. Now this pleasure too was gone. Freud's life was becoming, what he called it in a letter to Princess Bonaparte, "a small island of pain floating on an ocean of indifference."

At the end of the first week of August, the week when Freud surrendered his practice, he also saw the last of the princess—he lost her too. Freud had, in a certain sense, saved the princess's life years ago. It was not that her analysis with him was so successful; at best it had been partially complete. (Though as Freud was never tired of observing, to ask for too much in these endeavors can be foolhardy: in therapy the better is often the enemy of the good.) No, what mattered was that Freud had discerned the princess's energy and good-heartedness, and had seen her intellectual promise as well. He helped her to become an analyst, and he encouraged her to begin writing psycho-analytic studies, which she did with no little success. (Despite Freud's much-publicized skepticism about women's intellectual powers, he could be a potent supporter of women who wanted to develop their minds.) What Freud helped to save the princess from was a life of high-society intrigues, futile love affairs, tourism, and relentless self-absorption.

Then, later in life, Princess Bonaparte helped to save Freud. All the qualities that she developed in her long friendship with him and her association with his strange art—her vitality, confidence, intelligence, bravery—came to bear during the struggle to get Freud out of Vienna. An unusual fairy tale played itself out there: the beautiful rich princess, not the questing knight, arrived to rescue the aged monarch and conduct him out of the Wasteland to a greener, more fertile place. And now the princess was leaving and Freud surely understood that the odds were he would not see her again. For someone as pugnacious as Freud could be—as willing to take offense, as ready to quarrel—he had an extraordinary power to make and to keep friends. People were fond of him. They liked his candor, the vigor of his mind; they liked his humor, which, though it grew darker as time passed, never quite disappeared. Freud had many admirers and disciples and many friends too, but he probably never had a better friend than Marie Bonaparte, who now departed, but who, for the rest of her life—she died in

1962—would be a fierce proponent of the Professor and his cause.

Much of Freud's family was lost to him too. Every day he certainly spent at least some time thinking about his four sisters, for whom he and the princess had been unable to secure visas. They stayed back in Austria, well funded, and with the princess doing all that she could to protect them. Originally there had been five of them in Vienna: Anna, Adolphine, Mitzi, Pauli, and Rosa. Anna, the oldest of the girls, married a brother of Freud's wife, a man named Eli Bernays. She died in New York City on March 11, 1955, at ninety-seven years old.

Adolphine, or Dolfi as she was called, was the only one who never married; she spent most of her life taking care of Freud's mother, Amalia. People thought of her as, in Martin Freud's words, a "rather silly old maid." But Martin tells a story about walking one day in Vienna with his aunt and passing an ordinary-looking middle-class man. Martin did not hear him say anything, but when he had passed, Dolfi exclaimed, "Did you hear what that man said? He called me a dirty stinking Jewess and said it was time we were all killed." At the time, Martin recalls, many of his friends were gentiles—lawyers, doctors, professors. "It seems strange," he says, "that while none of us . . . had any idea of the tragedy which would destroy the children of the Jewish race, a lovable but rather silly old maid foresaw . . . that future."

Dolfi was starved to death in the Jewish ghetto at Theresienstadt; she died on September 29, 1942. The other three sisters were transported from Vienna to Theresienstadt and from there to the concentration camp at Treblinka. They died, murdered by the Nazis, in 1942.

During that September, Freud also lost something along with the rest of the world: that was peace. Three weeks after Freud disbanded his practice, Russia, which Winston Churchill had called "a riddle wrapped in a mystery inside an enigma," became considerably less mystifying. Russia came to terms with Germany and signed a mutual nonaggression pact. Hitler had been declaring communism a mortal enemy from long before the day he came to power in 1933; and Stalin felt little better about Nazism. Yet shortly after the signing, Stalin proposed a toast to the former street rat: "I know how much the German nation loves its Führer," Stalin intoned, "I should therefore like to drink his health."

Hitler ordered that photographs be taken of Stalin at the signing, partly because the führer was curious to know whether Stalin's earlobes were "ingrown and Jewish," as he feared, or "separate and Aryan." The pictures quelled Hitler's anxiety: one shot in particular, a profile, affirmed that Stalin's earlobes were indeed of the non-Jewish variety. Stalin's smoking did, however, concern the führer: in every photograph of Stalin reviewing the treaty and signing it, a cigarette dangled from his mouth. "The signing of the pact is a solemn act that one does not approach with a cigarette in one's lips," Hitler, the lifelong antismoking evangelist, said. (He offered a gold watch to any member of his inner circle who quit tobacco.) Hitler told the photographer to paint out Stalin's cigarettes before releasing the pictures to the press.

Churchill claimed that it was an open question whether Hitler or Stalin loathed the nonaggression pact more. The intrinsic opposition of the two systems was, Churchill believed, unalterable. But Freud's work points to a different interpretation. The distinct economic dispensations, and the diverse iconographies and liturgies of Russian Communism and German Nazism make less difference than one might imagine. These were both governments of the patriarch, appealing to the same perverse and all-too-human desire. The fact that Hitler and Stalin would eventually go to war suggests that under the sun there can only be one genuine man-god; this is so because the contenders for the prize wish it to be and because humanity, alas, often seconds their wish.

The way was open now for Hitler's next move. On September 1, a day when Freud lay in his study, doing what he could to control the pain in his jaw, Nazi troops burst across the border into Poland. The Poles fought back ferociously; sometimes to the last soldier. When the Nazi Panzer divisions came on, Polish cavalrymen charged them with lances set, to predictable effect. Soon the nation would be overrun by the Germans. Hitler took himself up very near to the front to be close to the soldiers: "Front line troops must be assured that the officers share their privations," he said. Every day he was out among the army, riding in his open-topped car when the weather permitted, flourishing his oxhide whip. He took a particular interest in all aspects of the fighting men's lives, particularly their diets. When Hitler's staff suggested that he might go and meet the first trainload of wounded German soldiers, Hitler said that he could not: the sight of their suffering would be too much for him to bear.

Not much later it occured to Hitler that it would be a good idea to eliminate all Polish people from the earth's face and, with the help of many other Germans, he would set to work. But now Hitler simply savored his amazing victory. On the day of the invasion, Britain had sent Hitler yet another of its ultimatums, which he duly ignored. Two days later, both France and England declared war and the conflagration began. The last words that Freud wrote in his journal, a week before the Polish onslaught, were "war panic." Whatever hopes Freud might have had for a tranquil solution to the world's crises were now also lost. When Schur asked Freud if he thought that this would be the last of all wars, Freud answered simply, "My last war."

To Freud's way of thinking, there would probably never be an end to war. He believed that human beings carried a potent charge of aggressive energy and that in the deployment of this energy they generally had only a pair of choices. They could allow their aggressive libido to stay bottled up within, un-discharged. That energy, Freud believed, would frequently become the property of the superego, which would use it to punish the individual, perpetually enhancing his sense of guilt. But there was a salient way out of this dilemma. The individual could aim the force outside, turning it against the world at large. The more passionately he did so, the more fully he would purge himself of inner tensions. Violence opens the blocked spirit, Freud said. But it also creates horrible destruction. Human history, from the Freudian point of view, moves between anxious periods when culture inhibits the destructive drive and periods when the drive can turn outward, in murder, rape, and conquest.

The alternative that Freud offered was for human beings to initiate themselves into the arts of sublimation. It was possible, Freud believed, to convert instinctual energy into energy for science, commerce, and artistic creation. But it was not at all clear how many people would ever be able to manage such a conversion. Freud thought that most people not only lack the capacity to rechannel their instincts, but also lack the ability in art or intellectual pursuits that would make such rechanneling pay off. During Freud's lifetime the world had propelled itself into two world wars, two great upsurges of destruction. This was so for many reasons, Freud suggests in his essay "Why War?" but most saliently because for the great majority of people, it is simply too hard to live with the anxiety and with the relatively attenuated satisfactions that peace can bring. Peace is not only tedious; it causes ongoing suffering, because during peacetime, even the human beings most adept at sublimation deny their fundamental nature. Freud did not believe that much of any civilization could give the majority of its citizens the same measure of satisfaction that acting on instinct could give, and so the chances for an end to war were virtually nonexistent.

In his later work, Freud speaks of something called the Death Drive, by which he means the drive of an organism—human or animal, complex or one-celled—to seek its own destruction. And yet, Freud insists, the organism seeks such destruction exclusively "after its own fashion." The Death Drive, Freud indicates in "Why War?" is the direct result of too much acquiescence to the demands of civilization; it is the result of the steady augmenting of tensions and a corresponding inability to find sufficiently intense pleasure or rewarding work in peaceful civilization. As Freud observes in *Civilization and Its Discontents*, "An artist's joy in creating, in giving his phantasies body, or a scientist's in solving problems or discovering truths, has a special quality. . . . At present we can only say figuratively that such satisfactions seem 'finer and higher.' But their intensity is mild compared with that derived from the sating of crude and primary instinctual impulses; it does not convulse our physical being. And the weak point of this method is that it is not applicable generally: it is accessible to only a few people." In general, to read a book or to write one is no substitute for burning down a library—or at least to doing so in the interest of one noble cause or another.

Arrayed against death is the power that Freud called Eros, which is the force that draws human beings together in large, civilized, and civilizing groups. Yet as Freud understood, humanity can turn collectively against Eros, turn collectively against love's pleasures, and affirm death exclusively. "Long live death!" the Spanish fascists used to chant; Freud would have had no trouble understanding why.

It is odd, but one of the final losses, and in a sense the loss that Freud found to be least bearable, was a very simple one. At a certain point late in his illness, Freud became too weak to read. Freud said once that he invented psychoanalysis because it had no literature—that is, psychoanalysis had no official body of scholarly texts that one had to master to enter the field. What that meant was that Freud could read as he liked. And this he did, constantly. Freud read a small library's worth of archaeology; he read extensively in anthropology for *Totem and Taboo*; he read Twain and Heine, Goethe and Schiller; he read Shakespeare in English, drawing one idea after another from the plays; he read Milton's *Paradise Lost*, calling it one of his favorite books. He liked Kipling, Zola, Anatole France, and Macaulay. He might have found time to read a scientific treatise or two and perhaps, despite his protests, a work of non-psychoanalytical psychology as well. Freud read because he wanted to know about every significant kind of human behavior, collective and individual, past and present; he wanted to experience every kind of art that had moved people.

The last book Freud was able to read is a variation on the Faust myth, Balzac's *La peau de chagrin* (*The wild ass's skin*). In it, the protagonist, Raphael de Valentin, acquires a wild donkey's skin that he can use to grant all of his wishes. But in Balzac's cosmos, as in Freud's, there are no consequential pleasures that go unpaid for: nothing is got for nothing. Each time Raphael makes a wish, the skin shrinks. When the skin dissolves completely, he is given to know, his life will end. Raphael starts out by wishing for the kinds of things that his creator was known to pine after, and that Freud himself believed motivated most passionate, worldly men: fame, wealth, and the love of beautiful women. Near the opening of the book, there is a drunken, debauched orgy scene of the sort that only Balzac can write. Raphael gets everything that he's been hoping for there and later, but the price is exorbitant. With every granted wish, not only does the wild ass's skin diminish, but Raphael loses more of his vigor until, in time, he becomes a waning, withered medical curiosity, poked at, prodded, and condescended to by a troupe of the most distinguished physicians in Paris. What makes it the more plangent—in Balzac anything plangent must be made more so—is that Raphael has finally found true love, in the glowing form of Pauline, once his impoverished neighbor in the rooming house her mother owns, and later a stupendously rich but still innocent girl.

How could Freud have borne such a book? In it, Raphael enjoys all the worldly pleasures, from sensual indulgence to intellectual creation. (In his lonely room before he gets rich, he composes what sounds like a Schopenhauerian book on the subject of the will.) Raphael lives in Balzac's charged world, where everything is preternaturally heightened: the kitchen maids have regal beauty, the stable boys are geniuses in the making, the silver at dinner shines like the moon, and the mud on the road is a foot deep and reeks of the graveyard. In reading the novel, Freud surely did not see his own life pass before his eyes: the strange mixture of adventure and quiet, daring and restraint, combined to feed Freud's singular genius is not readily to be found in Balzac's fiction. But Freud did see *a* life pass before him, and a vitally intense one at that. How, reading this volume, could Freud at least not sometimes have pined for some remission from his illness? How could he not have begged life for a second chance?

Then there is the manner of Raphael's dying. As he makes more wishes, often against his conscious intentions—the book chronicles what Freud would have seen as the war between the hungry id and the often-baffled ego—the magic skin shrinks and Raphael's health declines. He ends up in a sanitarium, where the other patients despise him, and gradually, horribly, he wastes away. "This was the proper book for me to read," Freud told Max Schur when he had finished with it. "It deals with shrinking and starvation." Freud, as Schur remarked, could look on Raphael's panic in the end, as he too shrunk to nothingness, and resolve to do better. He could resolve to die with quiet dignity, rather than to succumb to terror. Whatever inner use he made of the book, after he finished it, there was to be no more reading: Freud had to face what he was going to face without the consolation of books, sacred or profane.

On September 19, Ernest Jones, Freud's most loyal retainer, came to the house at Maresfield Gardens to see Freud and, Jones believed, to say good-bye. When Jones arrived, Freud was unconscious, lying on the couch, beneath the mosquito netting. "I . . . called him by name as he dozed," Jones recalled. "He opened his eyes, recognized me and waved his hand, then dropped it with a highly expressive gesture." To Jones that gesture conveyed "a wealth of meaning: greetings, farewell, resignation. It said as plainly as possible, 'The rest is silence.'"

On September 21, Max Schur sat at Freud's bedside, looking at the wasted old man, with his decaying, foul-smelling jaw. It must have been difficult for Schur to believe that here before him was perhaps the most potent and influential intellect of his century, the man who had probably done more than any other to change the way people in the West thought about who and what they were. Now Freud simply looked cadaverous: he was pale and brittle and weighed next to nothing. But Freud still had some strength of will in him. He took his doctor's hand and said, "My dear Schur, you certainly remember our first talk. You promised me then not to forsake me when the time comes. Now it is nothing but torture and makes no sense anymore."

Schur let Freud know that he had not forgotten the promise he made. "Ich danke Ihnen," Freud said. "I thank you." He told Schur to "talk it over with Anna, and if she thinks it's right, make an end of it." Schur spoke to Anna and Anna sorrowfully concurred with her father's wish.

That same day, Schur gave Freud an injection of three centigrams of morphine, a dose much stronger than he would have used if the objective had only been to relieve pain. Schur was now assisting in a suicide. He gave Freud another injection that day, then a third on September 22. Freud lapsed into a coma, but he held on to life. Midnight came and on Saturday, September 23, Sigmund Freud was still alive.

That day was Yom Kippur, the Jewish Day of Atonement, and in the morning many Jews in London would be making their way to synagogue, continuing the ritual of prayer and fasting begun the night before, entreating the God whom Sigmund Freud had done all he could to do away with for forgiveness. All through London now, there were sandbags in place, in preparation for the air raids, which would begin soon and at horrible cost. Red pillar boxes had been marked with yellow detector tape to test for poison gas and people carried gas masks with them as they did their daily business. All through the city, statues were being removed or enclosed in brick for protection. British war planes flew over London, frightening dogs and cats with their eerie drone. Overhead floated barrage balloons, enormous airships supposedly strong enough to destroy any aircraft that collided with them. In the London parks, there were no more deck chairs for concert-goers, for fear that the chairs would block access to the recently dug trenches. (Rumors were spreading that the trenches were to be used as burial sites after the inevitable slaughter the air raids would cause.) Soon the great statue of Eros would be gone from Piccadilly Circus to protect it from bombs. Eros's antagonist in Freud's mythology, the force he simply called Death, was ready to ascend.

At three in the morning on Saturday, September 23, 1939, Sigmund Freud died from cancer and from Schur's morphine overdoses.

Many years before, Freud had divulged a wish about the way that he hoped to die. He wanted, he said, never to have to live without his mental capacities intact. He feared nothing so much as a stroke, paralysis not only of the body, but more disturbingly, of the mind. Freud declared that he wanted to "die in harness." Writing to his friend Oskar Pfister, he put it this way: "With all the resignation before destiny that suits an honest man, I have one wholly secret entreaty: only no invalidism, no paralysis of one's powers through bodily mis-

ery. Let us die in harness, as King Macbeth says." Freud
wanted to go down doing his work, with his sword—his
intellect—still flashing.

And Freud did that, or very nearly so. The weeks leading up
to his major decline in August were trying for him because,
though he could read and think with some clarity, he did not
have the strength to write. Perhaps for a while he thought that
the power to write—to put his imprint on the world—might
return. But when he saw that it would not, he knew he had to
make an end of it. Freud, the longtime atheist, never called out
on God; he never asked celestial forgiveness; he never recanted
his lack of faith: he was a stubbornly secular man to the end.
When he was sick and dying, he stuck to his arduously created
views and values, affirming what he had in other, better days.
Freud was true to himself through to the end.

Freud particularly relished a story that goes something like
this: An atheist, who has sold insurance for a living, lies on his
deathbed. There comes to visit him in his hour of need a
minister determined to save the poor man's soul. The minister
spends two hours, then three sitting with the man, grappling
with Satan, or whatever force it is that stands between salvation
and the wayward salesman. When the minister finally leaves the
sickroom, all the man's friends crowd around. Is he saved? Is his
soul pure? No, no, the minister has to admit, all his entreaties
failed. But the minister is happy to announce that he's now the
owner of a new insurance policy acquired at a splendid dis-
count.

What touched Freud in the tale, no doubt, was that salesman's cheerful defiance; he possessed an admirable share of

what Emerson liked to call "good-humored inflexibility." As to Freud, he was more than capable of such inflexibility until the end of his life, as his determination to publish the Moses book dramatized well enough. When the social superego smiled on Freud in London, he nodded in gratitude, but worked on in his own way, and finally gave the world *Moses and Monotheism*, when what it wanted from him was something far more conforming and tame. In Vienna, he had, in the words of the Puritan poem he so much admired, fallen "on evil days . . . / In darkness and with dangers compassed round." Yet the old man stayed firm and brave; he even had the equanimity to produce a flourish of wit from time to time.

Freud died without religious or metaphysical consolation. For the past two thousand years, the great majority of people in the West have died with hope for an afterlife intact. Freud left the world as a believer in one thing only—in the future promise human beings might have to know themselves a little more (which sometimes meant simply knowing how ignorant they could be about themselves) and because of such knowledge to live better than they would have. Freud left the world with a certain composure, for he had done his work. He had reached that point aptly described by Nietzsche: "The most fortunate author," he says, "is one who is able to say as an old man that all he had of life-giving, invigorating, uplifting, enlightening thoughts and feelings still lives on in his writings, and that he himself is only the gray ash, while the fire has been rescued and carried forth everywhere."

An institution, Emerson says, is the lengthened shadow of a single individual, and of no institution and no individual could this be truer than of psychoanalysis and of its founder, Freud. By dying as he did, Freud increased the length and breadth of the authoritative shadow that he would cast forward into time. He died in a way that would enhance his reputation as a leader, that would engender people's loyalty over the years, that would move them in the way that kings' and potentates' passing can do, move them with the majestic sense that here was a man who was more than a man. This was someone worth believing in with fervor and worth following into the future. Freud wanted to create belief and adherence down through the time, and—though it is not entirely tasteful to say as much—he arranged his death in such a way as to help him to do exactly that.

Pondering the death of Sigmund Freud, one thinks of the lines Auden wrote about him in the great elegy, about how "the autocratic pose, / The paternal strictness he distrusted, still / Clung to his utterance and features." Auden's lines apply to all of Freud's career, but have an especial bearing on the hour of his death. There was, perhaps, something too decorous, too stoic, too managed about it, at least when one considers the kinds of things that Freud, overall, stood for. Freud had his agreement with the younger retainer, Schur, a man who admired and even adored Freud; he had Anna to do his bidding; he had his reconstructed study, which he'd loaded with his books and treasures, like a pharaoh surrounding himself with his possessions for transport into the next world; he had his memorable farewell utterance: "Now it is nothing but torture and makes no sense anymore."

Consider, by contrast, some other parting words. Oscar

Wilde, mortally ill in a Paris flophouse, announced, "I am in a duel to death with this wallpaper. One of us has to go." Goethe cried out, enigmatically, movingly, "More light!" John Maynard Keynes, looking back on a life that was not without its pleasures, said, "I wish that I had drunk more champagne." Standing on the scaffold, about to die, Sir Walter Raleigh proclaimed, "This is a sharp medicine, but a sure remedy for all evils." Picasso petitioned all and sundry to drink to him. P. T. Barnum, American to the last, as Freud would see it, inquired into that day's circus receipts from Madison Square Garden. At his own end, Freud was sober and correct: "Now it is nothing but torture."

Freud had spent the past twenty fertile years deconstructing the human need to submit to figures of absolute authority. No one knew more about the subtle intricacies of power than did he. Yet the "autocratic pose" did indeed cling to him. It is not surprising that it did. Freud believed that he had unlocked the secret of power: he saw why people reduced themselves to quivering submission before a certain kind of greatness. And all through his life, he was tempted to take on the great man's role. When he did, the world was more likely to listen, more likely to believe. Freud was a speculative genius, but also an institution builder, and for the institution called psychoanalysis to last, Freud occasionally felt impelled to trade on some of the tactics of domination that psychoanalysis existed to undermine. With his death, Freud contributed to an image of himself and of his work that is at some variance with the best of what psychoanalysis teaches. As Adam Phillips suggests in a brilliant essay on Freud's last days, Freud died as an authority, writ large, yet he wrote and often lived as someone who asked humanity to turn away from all large-scale coercive powers. Freud's death concentrates the ultimate riddle of Sigmund Freud: he was the great cultural patriarch, who stood for nothing so much as for the dismantling of patriarchy.

If one looks at the Moses book a little more patiently than its first reviewers were in a position to do, another dimension of Freud comes to the fore, one that enriches and complicates the image of the authoritative Sigmund Freud. *Moses and Monotheism* may take off from the fierce critique of religion, monotheism in particular, that goes back to *Future of an Illusion*. But the book, despite the denunciations from the pious it received, is better disposed toward faith, and toward Judaism in particular, than any of Freud's prior work. To Freud, the essence of Judaism, whether it originated with the Jews or the Egyptians, lies in its adherents' ability to believe in an invisible god. The Jew is the one who can invest himself in what is not present, for God exists in the mind of the Jew and there alone. This salient fact distinguishes Judaism from the desert faiths it developed near and competed with. No matter who may have conceived of monotheism first, the Jews were the ones who were able to sustain it. Surely the Jews always threatened to slide back into idol worship, as they did when they danced around the golden calf while Moses was on Sinai receiving the Laws. For the Jews, like everyone else, deeply desired *to see* divinity.

The pleasures of sight, Freud insists, are intense, nearly instinctive pleasures. Human beings revel in appearance: they delight in the many-toned glories of the world. To renounce the visible in the interest of the unseen is an enormously difficult human task. An intense satisfaction is then replaced by a satisfaction that is less vital, less intense, but more valuable in the long run. "Among the precepts of the Mosaic religion," Freud says, "there is one that is of greater importance than appears to begin with. This is the prohibition against making an image of God—the compulsion to worship a God whom one cannot see. . . . If this prohibition were accepted, it must have a profound effect. For it meant that a sensory perception was given second place to what may be called an abstract idea—a triumph of intellectuality over sensuality or, strictly speaking, an instinctual renunciation, with all its necessary psychological consequences."

When Salvador Dalí came to visit, Freud remarked to him rather enigmatically that "Moses is flesh of sublimation." What he meant, it seems, is that Moses was the man who had fully absorbed the imperative to accept the abstract god. He had surrendered more direct, more instinctual satisfactions for the civilized and civilizing satisfactions of believing in a sole, unseen deity. Yet sublimation hurts. It means subordinating one aspect of the psyche, the id, to others, the ego and superego. But the id does not easily remain in a subordinate position. Sublimation creates inner tension, creates pain. Moses presumably suffered from the effort of continuing to believe in an invisible god when so many other tantalizing religious illusions were available. Similarly, Moses suffered when (at least in Freud's interpretation) he compelled himself to sublimate his anger at the reveling Jews who betrayed Yahweh while Moses was on the mountain. Moses was someone capable of more inner tension, more inner conflict than others: he could want and not want something at the same time, feel both desire and its antithesis, and live in that state for prolonged periods. Freud suggests that the ability to sustain such tension tuned to a high degree is what makes someone a hero of civilization. The great swordsman Achilles or one of his many, many descendents can allow all his energies to move in one direction, toward glory. But sword law is not civilization. Ambivalence that has been fully assimilated, that has infused the flesh as well as the mind and spirit, is what civilization is about for Freud, and in this regard Moses was heroic, and heroic in a new way.

In *Moses and Monotheism*, Freud argues that taking God into the mind enriches the individual immeasurably. The ability to internalize an invisible god vastly enhances people's capacity for abstraction. If they can worship what is not there, they can also reflect on what is not there, or on what is presented to them in symbolic, not immediate, terms. So the mental labor of monotheism prepares the Jews to distinguish themselves in mathematics, in law, in science, and in literary art—in all the activities, in other words, that involve making an abstract model of experience, in words or numbers or lines, and working with the abstraction to achieve control over nature or to bring humane order to life.

Freud calls this internalizing process an "advance in intellectuality," and it makes its practitioners not only more adept at certain activities, but also rather proud. The ability to renounce a deep satisfaction always results in pain for the individual, but because the over-I approves of that pain and the renunciation that causes it, the individual is likely to develop an exalted sense of himself. He becomes proud about what he has achieved through sublimation and he looks down on those who cannot effect the same feat. "Moses," Freud says, "conveyed to the Jews an exalted sense of being a chosen people. The dematerialization of God brought a fresh and valuable contribution to their secret treasure." The hero of sublimation is anxious, yes, but his anxiety comes in the service of higher ideals; if he is a martyr, he is a martyr to civilization, and that is something to be proud of.

So according to Freud, Judaism has made a grand contribution to collective life. But that contribution is not enough: Judaism is still a form of monotheism, and accordingly, an infantilizing system of belief. Freud's implication is that humanity needs to take another step on the road of inwardness and abstraction. For belief in the invisible God might prepare the ground not only for science and literature and law, but also for belief in that internal, unseen structure that Freud calls the psyche. Someone who can contemplate an invisible God, Freud suggests, is in a much better position to take seriously the invisible, but perhaps determining, dynamics of the inner world. To live well, to begin to know himself, the modern individual, with his divided psyche, must live with abstraction. This Judaism, with its commitment to one unseen God, opens the way for doing. But it is psychoanalysis that truly makes such introspection possible, offering the terms—ego and id and superego and all the rest—that allow individuals to begin to know their mysterious inner lives.

This gift of inwardness, Freud suggests, is a gift of Judaism, and not of Christianity. Christianity began by taking a cultural step backward in the direction of pagan idolatry. Christianity diluted Judaism's insistence on the invisible—and so compromised its intellectual bequest—by resurrecting the whole panoply of pagan gods. The old idols came back as the Christian saints; the old temples returned as Catholic churches full of color, pomp, scent, and sound. Christianity, despite Protestant urges to fight idolatry, was still, to Freud, essentially a throwback to the old religions. (The Protestants, however severe, still believed in a God who had walked the earth.) Judaic abstraction led to the true development of the mind. In Freud's revised way of thinking, God is still a figure to displace, but belief in him is a necessary stage on the way to far better belief.

Fascism, Freud would have noticed, is emphatically eye-intense. Fascism gives pageantry, color, light, and noise to people who suffer from the kind of privation that Judaism brought to the world and that influenced Protestantism, especially puritanical Protestantism, as well as Islam. Freud speculates, questionably but shrewdly, that one of the causes of anti-Semitism might be Christian rage at the instinctual satisfactions that the Jews have taken away. The Jews effected the great renunciation. The Jews were the ones who would not believe that the gods walked the earth and could be seen among mankind. Humanity wants those old gods back, wants the pagan grandeur, and in fascist pageantry, humanity gets something of the miracle and mystery and authority that it craves. There is no social ceremony more antithetical to Judaic and psychoanalytic inwardness than the mass rally, where the torches flare, the searchlights play against the sky, the banners float and snap in the wind, and the leader reveals the truth behind all appearances.

*Moses and Monotheism* suggests a genealogy of culture that runs from paganism to the Jewish faith, as exemplified by Moses, then on to the highly secular faith that is psychoanalysis. In this genealogy, Freud becomes a second Moses, leading his small band out into the wilderness, beset and troubled, but confident that in the long run the Western world will adapt to the ethos of psychoanalysis, much as it has to the belief in one invisible god. All through his life, Freud resisted the idea that psychoanalysis could be what its detractors liked to say it was, a Jewish science. But at the end of his career, he implicitly joined his way of thought to the Jewish tradition, and joined his own sense of self to his image of the paragon of Judaism, Moses.

The identification with Moses has another, perhaps more consequential dimension to Freud. For by brooding on Moses, Freud comes to see what kind of hero he himself aspires to be. In Moses, Freud sees a new kind of authority. Up until this point, Freud's reflections on authority have ended up at the same place. Authority is inevitably male, narcissistic, overbearing, self-interested, arbitrary, and, quite often, tyrannical. Yet in Moses, Freud often (though not always) sees something different. Moses can project all the patriarchal qualities, true. But Moses is distinct from other sorts of leaders in that he is a hero of sublimation: he is a divided being who achieves his authority not by being self-willed and appetitive, but by intelligently rechanneling his impulses and teaching others to do the same. He renounces the pagan gods; he gives laws that rest on prohibition; when the Jews rebel, Freud argues in his early essay on the prophet, Moses succeeds in restraining himself from raging against them. Freud's Moses, unlike the archetypal leader, lives with inner conflict and anxiety, and he does so in the interest of civilization. What Moses surely suggests to Freud—and should suggest to us—is that it may be possible to be an authority, to have an influence, without being a conventional patriarch.

The fascist leader, who embodies the general will, sees what he wants and takes it; desires this or that, and moves when the time is right. He has no internal conflicts, at least as the world apprehends it: he wants what he wants. The hero of civilization, on the other hand, knows how to restrain his immediate desire in the interest of something better. He knows how to live with the anxiety that conflicting and unresolved wishes bring and he takes this anxiety as a condition of life, rather than as something for which he needs to find a personal or cultural remedy. Perhaps he is never terribly happy, but his self-aware restraint is appealing to others—it gives them new powers in science and art and government; it makes them proud of themselves, because they have been able to perform a piece of instinctual renunciation. Unlike the fascist leader, Freud's leader is capable of signifying his self-division: he can be ironic; he's not averse to making a joke. (Both ironic speech and joking, Freud indicates, show awareness that there is more than one simple reality to take into account, one truth: they testify to there being contending forces at play in the world, contending interpretations of experience.) And too, the civilized leader's example of restraint and circumspection stops people from devouring one another, which on a certain level is what they most wish to do.

Freud saw that the human relation to authority would always be ambivalent: it would involve both love and hate. We adore the primal father for his capacity to provide unity, purpose, assurance, and truth. But in time we can come to detest him too. For we see that his pure truth is too simple to be effective, that his unity is too painful to sustain, and that he suspends too many human freedoms. Then we turn against him furiously. Freud can at times look like a dictator of the cultural realm; so it is to be expected that his reputation will go through the oddest and most apparently inexplicable turns and twists. Now he is up, now he is down, for reasons that are rather unreasonable. But of course Freud is different from other patriarchs in politics and culture in that he is constantly teaching us how much we need to debunk patriarchy and giving us the conceptual tools to do so. (Hitler, after all, did not come on with a program to end all Hitlers.) The fact that Freud is both patriarch and anti-patriarch makes his cultural presence all the more difficult to assimilate and causes many strange perturbations in the way the world conceives of him. Those perturbations genuinely matter when they divide us from what is best in Freud's thinking.

Freud, one might say, triggered a large-scale transference in the mind of the West. That is, people have aimed at him all the hopes and hatreds that have in the past infused their relations to authority. Accordingly, Freud inspires what he would call "an artificial illness," in which the regressive dynamics of authority are made visible and susceptible to analysis. All of the best that

Freud offers—his ideas about dreams and jokes and the structure of the psyche, his suggestion that there is more to know and less to judge than we had imagined possible—all of this legacy at times disappears. In its place, we have Freud the cocaine user, Freud the misogynist, Freud the ersatz scientist. Perhaps this phase will pass and Freud will become a mortal god, a cultural patriarch, again; but really that is very little better.

The West can, and perhaps in time it will, use analysis to stop repeating its strange relation to Freud (which he of course in many ways brought on himself) and finally work it through. The objective of such analysis isn't to dismiss or debunk Freud, but to be able to read his work with irony, humor, detachment, and due openness when what he has to say proves to be illuminating—as it so often is.

In his later period, Sigmund Freud predicted two shocking phenomena of the twentieth and twenty-first centuries. The first was the rise of tyranny. The revolutions of the eighteenth and nineteenth centuries, in the United States, in France, all through Latin America, and elsewhere, persuaded many people that an age of democratic liberalism had begun. Monarchy and aristocracy seemed to be waning everywhere. Walt Whitman was in many ways representative when he prophesied the rise of the common man, the widening of the franchise, the freeing of slaves, majority rule. But it turned out that people did not always want freedom or equality; they found democracy ineffectual, unglamorous, and disorienting. It fomented confusion inside the self and out. Human beings dreamed of order, and lo there stepped forward all the figures of destiny glad to offer purpose, resolution, and Truth. If this tendency began in the twentieth century with Lenin, Franco, Mussolini, and Hitler, then continued on through Stalin and Mao, it surely has not come to an end. It sometimes appears that in the twentieth century and the twenty-first, human beings have been engaged in counterevolution. They have turned back to more primitive states of mind and of government. Freud offers some strong hypotheses about why this should be so: he begins to account for humanity's revolt against its own better interests.

Freud's work also predicts the new birth of the fundamentalist urge. Religion in the twentieth and twenty-first centuries did not become more private, more provisional, more nuanced—at least not for many. And it did not disappear— far from it. Rather, the centuries have seen the rise of ferociously patriarchal religions, not only in Islam, but in the Christian world as well. The most powerful and most technologically advanced nation in the twenty-first century has a sizable constituency who wish for little so much as religious rule by the state, theocracy.

From the Freudian perspective, authoritarian religion and authoritarian politics are two sides of one debased coin. They feed off each other, borrow techniques, modes of persuasion, and iconography. They traffic in the same sorts of miracle, mystery, and authority. And they are the most plausible form of human destiny: they are where humanity will go without potent efforts of resistance. Freud's work suggests that no one should ever think that fascism and fundamentalism are gone and done with. There is no such thing as an eternal triumph over them. Because they are so integral to what it is to be human, no one should even think that humanity has defeated them once and for all. This was the error of the liberal nineteenth century.

Freud also warns against thinking that the fascist and the fundamentalist are radically other. Book after book, essay after essay, has come into the world trying to show what set the German Nazis apart from everyone else. It was their political past, their culture, their military tradition; it was the debased Treaty of Versailles; it was the Depression of 1929. The same scholarly ritual is visited on Japan and, to a lesser extent, on Italy. We seem desperate to know how different these peoples are from ourselves. Freud indicates that such thinking is delusory: we are all fascists, we are all fundamentalists, at least potentially. Through authoritarianism we attain assurance and happiness—though of a certain sort. It is only constant critical labor that keeps the worst political and religious possibilities from becoming fact.

Freud also suggests that fascism and fundamentalism, because of their amazing powers of attraction, will always constitute an emergency. When a powerful or rich nation turns to either, something must be done, and the more quickly, the better. One of the reasons that France and England may have been slow to act prior to the Second World War was that their statesmen did not understand the joy—no less a word should attach to it—that fascism offers people. Inner strife dissolves and the people become powerful and strong. They have never felt so good before and they will not readily give that feeling up. Others see their joy and are drawn to it. Such people make determined and potent foes.

When religious fundamentalism crosses national borders and aligns itself with authoritarian politics, nations that aspire to democracy must deal with an enormous threat. Democracy's foes, then, are exultant with purpose and full of hunger for battle. Their doubts are gone. Democracy's struggle is all the more difficult because its proponents must resist becoming as unified, monolithic, and unquestioning as their foes. They must restrain themselves from becoming fundamentalists who fight for human freedom.

One of the ways that some people attempt to resolve the crisis of authority is to believe in nothing at all—or to pretend to. If one does not invest in any authority, if one is skeptical of everything, then surely one will not succumb to the over-I at its worst. This way of life, which sometimes goes under the name of postmodernism, denies the human hunger for belief entirely. As such, it starves the individual of what he desperately needs— authority in some form—and leaves him all the more open to being appropriated by this or that coercing system when the bad times come, as they will.

To Freud, the self-aware person is continually in the process of deconstructing various god replacements and returning once again to a more skeptical and ironic middle ground. The sane, or relatively sane, self is constantly being duped by this Truth or that (the hunger is very strong; that's simply the way we are) and then coming back to himself and finding more reasonable authorities. He's perpetually consulting his experience, sifting data, questing amid the knowledge of the past and the day-to-day life of the present to find out what is good in the way of belief. He'll ultimately surrender neither to the belief in nothing, nor to the belief in the great One. His life is one of constant self-criticism, and even then he's perpetually surprised at how often he falls for another idol or decides, however wittingly, to give it up and to believe he believes in nothing. But his is also a life of discovery and pleasure at the unexpected, if provisional, truths and fresh possibilities that the world throws his way. He feels, on balance, more than fortunate to be alive. Such people can be quite formidable when they're pushed to the wall. (Fundamentalists and fascists should be warned.) They are accustomed to thinking for themselves and to doing what the moment requires. They are practical and resourceful and they do not always need to wait for orders from on high. They don't freeze up when their leaders disappear or die. They don't need their fathers to be with them all the time.

# Acknowledgments

Anyone writing about Freud's life has not one, but two remarkable biographies to acknowledge: Ernest Jones's humane, generous three-volume treatment, *The Life and Work of Sigmund Freud*, and Peter Gay's astonishingly comprehensive and thoughtful *Freud: A Life for Our Time*. A writer treating the last phase of Freud's life has yet a third figure to thank, Michael Molnar, whose editing of *The Diary of Sigmund Freud* is distinguished for its wide range of learning and knowledge of Freud's thought. The secondary literature on Freud is of high quality and I have profited from all of the books listed in the bibliography and more. Still, for the purpose of the current study, two authors stand out. One is the late Philip Rieff, whose *Freud: The Mind of the Moralist* is a model of ethical engagement; the other is Adam Phillips, who in more than a dozen volumes has described and analyzed Freud's thinking—and brought it forward in multiple ways.

This book also profited from generous institutional backing. The John Simon Guggenheim Foundation supported the project, as did the Daniels family and the National Endowment for the Humanities, sponsors of a Distinguished Teaching Professorship at the University of Virginia. (Thanks to Raymond Nelson for working to create the professorship and to Marva Barnett for guiding its deployment.) My deans,

Edward Ayers and Karen Ryan, gave crucial help in speeding this book along, as did the ever-generous chair of the English department, Gordon Braden. To all three, I am extremely grateful. Thanks to my other department chairs as well, Michael Levenson, Jahan Ramazani, and Alison Booth, and to all of my colleagues in the University of Virginia English department. I am grateful also to the University's President, John Casteen, whose conferral of a University Professorship was a great honor and encouragement.

Gillian Blake again gave me the benefit of her brilliant editing, making the book better in a dozen ways. I'm most fortunate to have her as ally and adviser. This is the fourth book of mine that Chris Calhoun has represented. He was involved at every stage, as analyst, negotiator, supporter, and friend—and for all of this I am again grateful. Michael Pollan read this book in draft, as he has all of my books, and made it much better with sharp editorial comments. Yet more important was the gift of his ongoing friendship: his generous encouragement was crucial to my getting the book done. His example as an author who brings challenging ideas to a general audience, and who writes with constant respect for his reader, served as an inspiration throughout. I am grateful, too, to Nick Meyer, not only for helpful comments, but for being exemplary in his effort always to reach the highest possible standard in writing. I also thank Richard Rorty; the benefits of having him as a colleague, a coteacher, friend, and critic have been beyond expression: no writer has given me more by way of example than he has.

For help on matters of history, thanks to Erik Midelfort, Maya Jasanoff, and Alon Confino. For research help, I am indebted to John Havard, Katie Matson, Peter Teigland, Sara Hoover, and Ryan Condell. For exemplary work in the last phase, thanks to Mike O'Connor, Cheryll Lewis, and Ben Adams.

Thanks, too, to my former teachers, D. R. Lenson (sax-man extraordinaire), Doug Meyers (who did a turn as Frank Lears), Alan Cheuse (who understood this project from the beginning), and (from the days of my dissertation on Freud) four marvelous and singular instructors, J. Hillis Miller, Harold Bloom, Geoffrey Hartman, and Leslie Brisman.

Thanks to Alex Star, gifted, generous editor, who gave me a chance to begin developing some of the ideas in this book for the *New York Times* and to Paul H. Fry, whose invitation to speak on Freud helped push the project out of some dense springtime mud. The Philoctetes Society in New York kindly offered me the opportunity to contribute to discussions on Freud as did the sponsors of the conference on Freud's Jewish World, and for those opportunities I am grateful.

My wife Liz showed me how and why this was a consequential project, even when I doubted it, and supported me with her vast generosity throughout the process. She also read the manuscript astutely and made fine suggestions. Matthew, my older son, infused some of his high spirits and zest for living into the writing. My brother, Philip, and my mother, Eileen, took a generous interest in the development of this work, for which I warmly thank them. To Willie, my fellow maker and perpetual inspiration, this book is dedicated.

All errors and slips (Freudian though they may appear) are mine.

# Notes

## Vienna

For the narrative of Freud's life in Vienna, this section draws particularly on Peter Gay's *Freud: A Life for Our Time*, Ernest Jones's *The Life and Work of Sigmund Freud*, and Michael Molnar's annotations to *The Diary of Sigmund Freud*. For information on Hitler, the chapter makes use of John Toland's *Adolf Hitler* and Ian Kershaw's *Hitler*, as well as of August Kubizek's contemporary account. For the historical events in Germany and in Austria during the late 1930s, the chapter frequently looks to Richard J. Evans's excellent volume *The Third Reich in Power*, as well as eyewitness accounts by William L. Shirer and G. E. R. Gedye.

7   "some incredible daydream": S. Freud, *An Autobiographical Study, Standard Edition*, vol. 20, p. 52. (Henceforth cited as *SE*.)

10   "burning my books": Jones, vol. 3, p. 182.

12   "than any other German": Schuschnigg account, p. 15. For Schuschnigg's version of the meeting, see pp. 3–27.

16   "needed it most": E. Freud, ed., *Letters*, p. 8. (Henceforth cited as *Letters*.)

17   "a homosexual competition": S. Freud, *Civilization and Its Discontents, SE*, vol. 21, p. 90.

20   "Foolish Body decays": Erdman and Bloom, p. 783.

21   "and its ideology": Gedye account, p. 242.

21   "into audible words": Gedye, p. 243.

21   "come into consideration": cited in Molnar, p. 228.

24   "vengeance on the Romans": S. Freud, *The Interpretation of Dreams*, *SE*, vol. 4, p. 197.

25   "afresh with both": S. Freud, *Interpretation of Dreams*, *SE*, vol. 5, p. 483.

25   "in the opposition": *Letters*, p. 367.

26   "not altogether unjust": Jones, vol 1, p. 348.

27   "hour has struck": Clare account, pp. 173–4.

27   "clear and open manner": cited in Toland, p. 466.

28   "the pro-German population": Toland, p. 468.

29   "he was hanged": Churchill, pp. 243–4.

30   "prepared to do": Paskauskas, ed., p. 419.

33   than Sigmund Freud: Gay, p. 454.

34   "God save Austria": Shirer account, p. 99.

35   "Hang Schuschnigg": Gedye account, p. 295.

35   "never, whatever happens": cited in Evans, 651.

36   "both your houses": *Letters*, p. 420.

36   "fall on me": E. Freud, ed., *Letters of Freud and Zweig*, p. 133.

37   "to Rome, like you": Paskauskas, ed., p. 757.

38   "get them so fast": Shirer account, p. 103.

41   "became commonplace everywhere": Gay, p. 590.

42   "holy is profaned": Marx and Engels, p. 223.

44   "estranged from barbarism": McGuire and Hull, eds., p. 194.

45   "the medium of revelation": DeLillo, p. 72.

46   "I am here": Huss, pp. 19–20.

47   "the German Reich": Brook-Shepherd account, p. 201.

47   "Jews killing themselves": Shirer account, p. 110.

48   " 'and start scrubbing' ": Danimann account in Schmidt, ed., pp. 44–5.

48   "weeps all night long": Shirer account, p. 110.

48   " 'Jewish looking fellow' ": Shirer account, p. 109.

51  "in bright daylight": Zweig, p. 405.

53  "I can blame them": Koestler, p. 499.

54  "reinforcement from others": S. Freud, *Group Psychology and the Analysis of the Ego, SE*, vol. 18, p. 123.

54  "check on narcissism": ibid., p. 124.

56  guide his performances: Toland, p. 232.

59  "body marched off": M. Freud, p. 210.

61  "to give up smoking": Pfeiffer, ed., p. 113.

62  "for her later life": *Letters*, p. 440.

71  contained, sublimated anger: S. Freud, "The Moses of Michelangelo," *SE*, vol. 13, pp. 211–38.

72  "for a single visit": Jones, vol. 3, p. 219.

72  "to leave Vienna": cited in Clark, p. 505.

74  "what I mean": Paskauskas, ed., p. 61.

74  "done with life": Jones, vol. 3, p. 219.

77  "I were ruined": cited in Bertin, p. 156. For material on Freud and the princess, see Bertin, pp. 155-7.

78  "upon American opinion": cited by Clark, p. 506.

80  "a shopping expedition": M. Freud, p. 212.

84  "the Hero of Culture": Jones, vol. 3, p. 180.

86  "by personal experience": Ibid., p. 221.

87  " 'unkind to the Jews' ": Ibid., p. 222.

87  "Amazing March": cited by Molnar, p. 232.

88  "beings also": Friedrich, p. 385.

90  "of my imagination": *Letters*, p. 424.

90  "to the present day": ibid., p. 439.

91  "in my story": H.D., p. 162.

91  "she understood everything": cited in Molnar, p. 214.

92  "this production, too": *Letters*, p. 434.

92  " 'Unites us both' ": *Letters*, p. 434.

93  "little golden head' ": Bonaparte, p. 123.

93  "written the *Iliad*": ibid.

93  "is being translated": *Letters*, p. 437.

96   "your children, Kubizek": Kubizek, p. 280. For an account of the meeting, see Kubizek, pp. 278–281.

96   "joy could say": cited in Weyr, p. 73.

97   "its deepest humiliation": Weyr account, p. 74.

97   "hour of my life": Toland, p. 483.

99   "retreat from danger": S. Freud, *The Ego and the Id*, SE, vol. 19, p. 56.

101   "form of action": S. Freud, *Group Psychology*, SE, vol. 18, p. 117.

102   "and fantastic hopes": Bullock, p. 219.

104   "the unconscious mind": cited by Molnar, p. 233–4.

106   "I no longer": *Letters*, p. 442.

106   "sorry for you": cited by Gay, p. 170.

108   "stuff of work": Gay, p. 384.

110   "see no sign": cited by Toland, p. 488.

112   "a kind of longing": cited by Gay, p. 612.

113   "all-controlling factor": Paskauskas, ed., p. 763.

113   "die in freedom": *Letters*, p. 443.

116   "to the Gestapo": M. Freud, p. 216.

121   "Anna brought along": *Letters*, p. 445.

122   "the Gestapo to everyone": Gay, p. 628.

124   "he feels ill": S. Freud, *Ego and the Id*, SE, vol. 19, p. 49–50.

126   "have been abandoned": Hitler, p. 42.

# London

For the story of Freud's life in London, the book again draws on Gay, Jones, and Molnar, and also on Max Schur's *Freud: Living and Dying*. For historical background, the section makes use of Peter F. Clarke's *Hope and Glory* and Piers Brendon's *The Dark Valley*, as well as contemporary accounts by Winston Churchill and A. J. P. Taylor. For events on the continent, Evans's *Third Reich in Power* is again the most prominent source.

137   "be a pandemonium": cited by Porter, p. 338.

138   "had secretly cherished": Taylor, p. 419.

138   "heroes of 'the kikes'": Graves and Hodge, p. 439.

140   "accomplish any work": *Letters*, p. 446.

140   "after English views": cited by Gay, p. 31.

140   "with my nature": cited by Davies et al., p. 9–10.

141   "the first weeks": *Letters*, p. 447.

141   "what fame means": ibid., p. 448.

144   "than a Jew": S. Freud, "The Resistances to Psycho-analysis," *SE*, vol. 19, p. 222.

145   "the completed essay secret": *Letters*, p. 422.

145   "be very offended": ibid., p. 440.

148   "there is nothing new": Van den Berg, p. 176.

149   "as he can": cited by Molnar, p. 240.

150   "heredity and upbringing": Jones, vol. 3, p. 234.

151   "his human weakness": S. Freud, *The Future of an Illusion, SE*, vol. 21 p. 24.

152   "shall take place": ibid., p. 30.

153   "have been abandoned": Hitler, p. 42.

154   "worthy of it": Nietzsche, *Gay Science*, p. 181.

158   "But *quien sabe*": Paskauskas, ed., p. 763.

162   "'come to something'": S. Freud, *Interpretation of Dreams, SE*, vol. 4, p. 216.

163   "that affects me": S. Freud, "The Moses of Michelangelo," *SE*, vol. 13, p. 211.

164   "on the stones": ibid., p. 229–230.

165   "has devoted himself": ibid., p. 233.

167   "the Hotel Sacher": Dalí, p. 23. For Dalí's meeting with Freud, see pp. 23–5.

168   "sentence on surrealism": ibid., p. 397.

169   "sharply from reality": S. Freud, "Creative Writers and Day-Dreaming," *SE*, vol. 9, p. 144.

169   "of his phantasies": ibid., p. 153.

172 "the medical curriculum": *The Question of Lay Analysis*, *SE*, vol. 20, p. 247.

173 "harder to reach": Schur, p. 508.

175 "number so-and-so": Brod, p. 204.

175 "what it all means": Paskauskas, ed., pp. 527–8.

175 "and lingual (tongue) mucous membranes": Schur, pp. 362–5.

176 "distress and pain": Jones, vol. 3, p. 95.

176 "in cruel mockery": Koestler, p. 498.

177 "combination of both": Schur, p. 364.

178 "of the fourth": *Letters*, p. 451.

179 "given his word": Toland, p. 502.

180 "we know nothing": Churchill, p. 283.

181 "pleasure in it": *Letters*, p. 452.

181 "it is *magic*": McGuire, ed., p. 117–8.

183 "cup and lip": cited by Molnar, p. 247.

187 "parasitic Jewish race": for an account of Kristallnacht, see Evans, pp. 590–592.

187 "Jewish filthy fellow": Gilbert, p. 55.

189 "out of Czechoslovakia": ibid., p. 216.

189 "involved than myself": S. Freud, "Anti-Semitism in England," *SE*, vol. 23, p. 301.

190 "duty to them": S. Freud, "Comment on Anti-Semitism," *SE*, vol. 23, p. 292.

190 "spirit of it": Twain, p. 358.

194 "gentleness, great strength": Woolf, pp. 168–9.

195 "for possible crumbs": Bell, ed., p. 202.

196 "with outstretched arm": Woolf, p. 191.

196 "in selected cases": Schur, p. 499. For more on Sauerwald, see Murray G. Hall, "The Fate of the Internationaler Psychoanalytischer Verlag," in Timms and Segal, eds.

198 "must risk it": *Letters*, p. 453–4.

199 "published it in defiance": Gay, p. 648.

199 "one of them": S. Freud, *Moses and Monotheism*, *SE*, vol. 23, p. 7.

200   "the real one": ibid., p. 15.

203   For the reviews of *Moses and Monotheism,* see Gay, pp. 645–8.

206   "prove the stronger": E. Freud, *Letters of Freud and Zweig,* p. 178.

206   "sort except aspirin": cited in Schur, p. 525.

208   "a fetid odor": ibid.

210   "is repeating it": S. Freud, "Remembering, Repeating and Working Through," *SE,* vol. 12, p. 150.

211   "to our intervention": ibid., p. 154.

213   "and the outside": Schur, p. 526 and 527.

216   "foresaw . . . that future": M. Freud, p. 16.

217   "inside an enigma": Churchill, p. 403.

221   "a few people": S. Freud, *Civilization and Its Discontents, SE,* vol. 21, pp. 79–80.

224   " 'rest is silence' ": Jones, vol. 3, p. 246.

225   " 'I thank you' ": Schur, p. 529.

227   "King Macbeth says": E. Freud and Meng, ed., *Psychoanalysis and Faith,* p. 35.

228   "carried forth everywhere": Nietzsche, *Human, All too Human,* p. 125.

230   Phillips's essay appears in *Darwin's Worms,* pp. 67–111.

232   "necessary psychological consequences": S. Freud, *Moses and Monotheism, SE,* vol. 23, pp. 112–13.

234   "their secret treasure": ibid., p. 115.

# Selected Bibliography

Arendt, Hannah. *The Origins of Totalitarianism.* New York: Schocken Books, 1948.

Balzac, Honoré de. *The Wild Ass's Skin.* Translated by Herbert J. Hunt. New York: Penguin Books, 1977.

Behling, Katja. *Martha Freud: A Biography.* Translated by R. D. V. Glasgow. Cambridge, England, and Malden, MA: Polity Press, 2005.

Bell, Anne Olivier, ed. *The Diary of Virginia Woolf.* Vol. 5, 1936–1941. San Diego, New York, and London: Harcourt Brace & Company, 1984.

Berman, Paul. *Terror and Liberalism.* New York: W. W. Norton, 2003.

Bertin Célia. *Marie Bonaparte: A Life.* New Haven: Yale University Press, 1982.

Blom, Philipp. *To Have and to Hold: An Intimate History of Collectors and Collecting.* Woodstock and New York: Overlook Press, 2003.

Bonaparte, Marie. *Topsy: The Story of a Golden-Haired Chow.* New Brunswick, NJ: Transaction, 1994.

Bowie, Malcolm. *Lacan.* Cambridge, MA: Harvard University Press, 1991.

Brabant, Eva, Ernst Falzeder, and Patrizia Giampieri-Deutsch, eds. *The Correspondence of Sigmund Freud and Sándor Ferenczi,* Vol. 1, 1908–1914. Translated by Peter Hoffer. Cambridge, MA: Belknap Press of Harvard University Press, 1993.

Breger, Louis. *Sigmund Freud: Darkness in the Midst of Vision.* New York: John Wiley and Sons, 2000.

Brendon, Piers. *The Dark Valley: A Panorama of the 1930s.* New York: Alfred A. Knopf, 2000.

Brod, Max. *Franz Kaflka: A Biography.* New York: Schocken Books, 1947.

Brome, Vincent. *Ernest Jones: A Biography.* New York: W. W. Norton, 1983.

Brook-Shepherd, Gordon. *Anschluss: The Rape of Austria.* Westport, CT: Greenwood Press, 1976.

Bullock, Alan. *Hitler and Stalin: Parallel Lives.* New York: Random House, 1991.

Churchill, Winston S. *The Gathering Storm.* Vol. 1, *The Second World War.* Boston: Houghton Mifflin, 1948.

Clare, George. *Last Waltz in Vienna: The Rise and Destruction of a Family, 1842–1942.* New York: Holt, Rinehart and Winston, 1980.

Clark, Ronald W. *Freud, the Man and His Cause.* London: Jonathan Cape and Weidenfeld and Nichols, 1980.

Clarke, Peter F. *Hope and Glory: Britain 1900–1990.* London: Penguin Press, 1996.

Cocks, Geoffry. *Psychotherapy in the Third Reich: The Göring Institute,* 2nd ed. New Brunswick, NJ, and London: Transaction, 1997.

Dalí, Salvador. *The Secret Life of Salvador Dalí.* Translated by Haakon M. Chevalier. London: Vision Press, 1948.

Davies, Erica, J. Keith Davies, Michael Molnar, Susan O'Cleary, Ivan Ward. *20 Maresfield Gardens: A Guide to the Freud Museum.* London: Freud Museum, 1998.

DeLillo, Don. *White Noise.* New York: Viking, 1985.

H.D. [Doolittle, Hilda]. *Tribute to Freud.* New York: Pantheon, 1956.

Edmundson, Mark. *Towards Reading Freud: Self-Creation in Milton, Wordsworth, Emerson, and Sigmund Freud.* Princeton, NJ: Princeton University Press, 1990.

Engelman, Edmund. *Berggasse 19: Sigmund Freud's Home and Offices, Vienna 1938.* Chicago and London: University of Chicago Press, 1976.

Erdman, David V., and Harold Bloom, eds. *The Complete Poetry and Prose of William Blake.* New York: Random House, 1988.

Evans, Richard J. *The Third Reich in Power, 1933–1939.* New York: Penguin Press, 2005.

Fine, Reuben. *A History of Psychoanalysis.* New York: Columbia University Press, 1979.

Freud, Ernst L. *Letters of Sigmund Freud.* Translated by Tania and James Stern. New York: Basic Books, 1960.

Freud, Ernst L., ed. *The Letters of Sigmund Freud and Arnold Zweig.* Translated by Elaine and William D. Robson-Scott. New York: Harcourt, Brace & World, 1970.

Freud, Ernst L., Lucie Freud, and Ilse Grubrich-Simitis, eds. *Sigmund Freud: His Life in Pictures and Words.* Translated by Christine Trollope. New York: Harcourt Brace Jovanovich, 1978.

Freud Ernst L., and Heinrich Meng. *Psychoanalysis and Faith: The Letters of Sigmund Freud and Oskar Pfister,* translated by Eric Mosbacher. London: Hogarth Press, 1963.

Freud, Martin. *Sigmund Freud: Man and Father.* New York and London: Jason Aronson, 1983.

Friedrich, Otto. *Before the Deluge: A Portrait of Berlin in the 1920s.* New York: HarperCollins, 1972.

Gamwell, Lynn, and Richard Wells, eds. *Sigmund Freud and Art: His Personal Collection of Antiquities.* London: Freud Museum, 1989.

Gay, Peter. *Freud: A Life for Our Time.* New York: W. W. Norton, 1971.

Gedye, G. E. R. *Fallen Bastions: The Central European Tragedy.* London: Victor Gollancz, 1939.

Gilbert, Martin. *Kristallnacht: Prelude to Destruction.* London: Harper Press, 2006.

Goggin, James E., and Eileen Brockman Goggin. *Death of a "Jewish Science": Psychoanalysis in the Third Reich.* West Lafayette, IN: Purdue University Press, 2001.

Graves, Robert, and Alan Hodge. *The Long Week-End: A Social History of Great Britain, 1918–1939.* New York: Norton, 1940.

Hall, Murray G. "The Fate of the Internationaler Psychoanalytischer Verlag." In *Freud in Exile, Psychoanalysis and Its Vicissitudes.* Edited by Edward Timms and Naomi Segal. New Haven, CT: Yale University Press, 1988.

Hamann, Brigitte. *Hitler's Vienna: A Dictator's Apprenticeship.* Translated by Thomas Thornton. New York: Oxford University Press, 1999.

Hitler, Adolf. *Mein Kampf.* Translated by Ralph Manheim. Boston: Houghton Mifflin, 1943.

Huss, Pierre. *Heil and Farewell.* London: Jenkins, 1943.

Janik, Allan, and Stephen Toulmin. *Wittgenstein's Vienna.* New York: Simon and Schuster, 1973.

Jones, Ernest. *The Life and Work of Sigmund Freud.* 3 vols. New York: Basic Books, 1957.

Jung, Carl G. *Memories, Dreams, Reflections.* New York: Pantheon, 1963.

Keegan, John. *The First World War.* New York: Random House, 1998.

Kershaw, Ian. *Hitler: 1936–1945 Nemesis.* New York: W. W. Norton, 2000.

—————. *Making Friends with Hitler: Lord Londonderry, the Nazis and the Road to World War II.* New York: Penguin Press, 2004.

Koestler, Arthur. *The Invisible Writing: The Second Volume of an Autobiography: 1932–1940.* London: Hutchinson & Company, 1954.

Kubizek, August. *The Young Hitler I Knew.* Translated by E. V. Anderson. Westport, CT: Greenwood Press, 1954.

Mann, Thomas. *Freud, Goethe, Wagner.* New York: Alfred A. Knopf, 1937.

Marx, Karl, and Friedrich Engels. *The Communist Manifesto.* New York: Penguin, 1967.

Masson, Jeffrey, M., ed. and trans. *The Complete Letters of Sigmund Freud to Wilhelm Fliess, 1887–1904.* Cambridge, MA: Belknap Press of Harvard University Press, 1985.

McGuire, William, ed. *The Freud / Jung Letters: The Correspondence Between Sigmund Freud and C. G. Jung.* Translated by Ralph Manheim and R. F. C. Hull. Princeton, NJ: Princeton University Press, 1974.

McGuire, William, and R. F. C. Hull, eds. *C.G. Jung Speaking.* Princeton, NJ: Princeton University Press, 1977.

Miller, Jonathan, ed. *Freud: The Man, His World, His Influence.* Boston and Toronto: Little, Brown & Company, 1972.

Molnar, Michael, ed. and trans. *The Diary of Sigmund Freud, 1929–1939: A Record of the Final Decade.* New York: Charles Scribner's Sons, 1992.

Nietzsche, Freidrich. *The Gay Science.* Translated by Walter Kaufmann. New York: Vintage Books, 1974.

————. *Human, All Too Human: A Book for Free Spirits.* Translated by Marion Faber with Stephen Lehmann. Lincoln: University of Nebraska Press, 1986.

Paskauskas, R. Andrew, ed. *The Complete Correspondence of Sigmund Freud and Ernest Jones, 1908–1939.* Cambridge, MA: Harvard University Press, 1993.

Payne, Robert. *The Life and Death of Adolf Hitler.* New York and Washington, DC: Praeger Publishers, 1973.

Pfeiffer, Ernst, ed. *Sigmund Freud and Lou Andreas-Salomé: Letters.* Translated by William D. Robson-Scott and Elaine Robson-Scott. New York: W. W. Norton, 1985.

Phillips, Adam. *Darwin's Worms.* London: Faber and Faber, 1999.

————. *Equals.* New York: Basic Books, 2002.

————. *Terrors and Experts.* London: Faber and Faber, 1995.

Porter, Roy. *London: A Social History.* Cambridge, MA: Harvard University Press, 1994.

Rickels, Laurence A. *Nazi Psychoanalysis Vol. 1, Only Psychoanalysis Won the War.* Minneapolis and London: University of Minnesota Press, 2002.

Rieff, Philip. *Freud: The Mind of the Moralist.* Chicago: University of Chicago Press, 1959.

Roazen, Paul. *Edoardo Weiss: The House that Freud Built.* New Brunswick, NJ, and London: Transaction, 2005.

————. *Freud and His Followers.* New York: Alfred A. Knopf, 1975.

Romm, Sharon. *The Unwelcome Intruder: Freud's Struggle with Cancer.* New York: Praeger, 1983.

Rosenbaum, Ron. *Explaining Hitler: The Search for the Origins of Evil.* New York: Random House, 1998.

Rosenzweig, Saul. *The Historic Expedition to America: Freud, Jung and Hall the King-Maker.* St. Louis: Rana House, 1994.

Said, Edward W. *Freud and the Non-European.* London and New York: Verso, 2003.

Schmidt, Elfrede. *1938 . . . and the Consequences.* Translated by Peter L. Lyth. Riverside, CA: Ariadne Press, 1992.

Schorske, Carl E. *Fin-De-Siècle Vienna: Politics and Culture.* New York: Random House, 1981.

Schur, Max. *Freud: Living and Dying.* New York: International Universities Press, 1972.

Schuschnigg, Kurt von. *Austrian Requiem.* Translated by Franz von Hildebrand. New York: G. P. Putnam Sons, 1946.

Shirer, William L. *Berlin Diary: The Journal of a Foreign Correspondent, 1934–1941.* New York: Alfred A. Knopf, 1941.

Smith, Dennis Mack. *Mussolini: A Biography.* New York: Alfred A. Knopf, 1982.

Sontag, Susan. *Under the Sign of Saturn.* New York: Farrar, Straus, Giroux, 1980.

Steiner, George. *The Portage to San Cristobal of A.H.* New York: Simon and Schuster, 1981.

Strachey, James, et al., eds. *The Standard Edition of the Complete Psychological Works of Sigmund Freud,* 24 vols. London: Hogarth Press, 1953–1974.

Taylor, A. J. P. *English History, 1914–1945.* Oxford: Clarendon Press, 1965.

Toland, John. *Adolf Hitler.* 2 vols. Garden City, NY: Doubleday, 1976.

Trevor-Roper, Hugh. *The Last Days of Hitler.* Chicago: University of Chicago Press, 1971.

Twain, Mark. *Collected Tales, Sketches, Speeches and Essays, 1891–1910.* New York: Library of America, 1992.

Unwerth, Matthew von. *Freud's Requiem: Mourning, Memory, and the Invisible History of a Summer Walk.* New York: Riverhead Books, 2005.

Van den Berg, Jan Hendrich. *The Changing Nature of Man: Introduction to a Historical Psychology.* Translated by H. F. Croes. New York, Delta, 1961.

Weyr, Thomas. *The Setting of the Pearl: Vienna Under Hitler.* Oxford: Oxford University Press, 2005.

Woolf, Leonard. *Downhill All the Way: An Autobiography of the Years 1919–1939.* London: Hogarth Press, 1967.

Wright, William E., ed. *Austria, 1938–1988: Anschluss and Fifty Years.* Riverside, CA: Ariadne Press, 1995.

Yerushalmi, Yosef Hayim. *Freud's Moses: Judaism Terminable and Interminable.* New Haven, CT, and London: Yale University Press, 1991.

Young-Bruehl, Elisabeth. *Anna Freud: A Biography.* New York: Summit, 1988.

Zaretsky, Eli. *Secrets of the Soul: A Social and Cultural History of Psychoanalysis.* New York: Random House, 2004.

Zweig, Stefan. *The World of Yesterday.* Lincoln: University of Nebraska Press, 1943.

# Index

## A Note on the Author

Mark Edmundson teaches at the University of Virginia, where he holds the rank of University Professor. A prizewinning scholar, he has published a number of works of literary and cultural criticism, including *Literature Against Philosophy, Plato to Derrida, Teacher: The One Who Made the Difference,* and *Why Read?* He has also written for such publications as *Raritan,* the *New Republic,* the *New York Times Magazine,* the *Nation,* and *Harper's,* where he is a contributing editor.

A Note on the Type

The text of this book is set Adobe Garamond. It is one of several versions of Garamond based on the designs of Claude Garamond. It is thought that Garamond based his font on Bembo, cut in 1495 by Francesco Griffo in collaboration with the Italian printer Aldus Manutius. Garamond types were first used in books printed in Paris around 1532. Many of the present-day versions of this type are based on the *Typi Academiae* of Jean Jannon cut in Sedan in 1615.

Claude Garamond was born in Paris in 1480. He learned how to cut type from his father and by the age of fifteen he was able to fashion steel punches the size of a pica with great precision. At the age of sixty he was commissioned by King Francis I to design a Greek alphabet, for this he was given the honorable title of royal type founder. He died in 1561.